The Tourism Area Life Cycle, Vol. 2

ASPECTS OF TOURISM
Series Editors: Professor Chris Cooper, *University of Queensland, Australia*
Dr C. Michael Hall, *University of Otago, Dunedin, New Zealand*
Dr Dallen Timothy, *Arizona State University, Tempe, USA*

Aspects of Tourism is an innovative, multifaceted series which will comprise
authoritative reference handbooks on global tourism regions, research volumes, texts
and monographs. It is designed to provide readers with the latest thinking on tourism
world-wide and in so doing will push back the frontiers of tourism knowledge. The
series will also introduce a new generation of international tourism authors, writing
on leading edge topics. The volumes will be readable and user-friendly, providing
accessible sources for further research. The list will be underpinned by an annual
authoritative tourism research volume. Books in the series will be commissioned that
probe the relationship between tourism and cognate subject areas such as strategy,
development, retailing, sport and environmental studies. The publisher and series
editors welcome proposals from writers with projects on these topics.

Other Books in the Series
Sport Tourism: Interrelationships, Impact and Issues
  Brent Ritchie and Daryl Adair (eds)
Tourism, Mobility and Second Homes
  C. Michael Hall and Dieter Müller
Strategic Management for Tourism Communities: Bridging the Gaps
  Peter E. Murphy and Ann E. Murphy
Oceania: A Tourism Handbook
  Chris Cooper and C. Michael Hall (eds)
Tourism Marketing: A Collaborative Approach
  Alan Fyall and Brian Garrod
Music and Tourism: On the Road Again
  Chris Gibson and John Connell
Tourism Development: Issues for a Vulnerable Industry
  Julio Aramberri and Richard Butler (eds)
Nature-based Tourism in Peripheral Areas: Development or Disaster?
  C. Michael Hall and Stephen Boyd (eds)
Tourism, Recreation and Climate Change
  C. Michael Hall and James Higham (eds)
Shopping Tourism, Retailing and Leisure
  Dallen J. Timothy
Wildlife Tourism
  David Newsome, Ross Dowling and Susan Moore
Film-Induced Tourism
  Sue Beeton
Rural Tourism and Sustainable Business
  Derek Hall, Irene Kirkpatrick and Morag Mitchell (eds)
The Tourism Area Life Cycle, Vol. 1: Applications and Modifications
  Richard W. Butler (ed.)

For more details of these or any other of our publications, please contact:
Channel View Publications, Frankfurt Lodge, Clevedon Hall,
Victoria Road, Clevedon, BS21 7HH, England
http://www.channelviewpublications.com

ASPECTS OF TOURISM 29
Series Editors: Chris Cooper (*University of Queensland, Australia*),
C. Michael Hall (*University of Otago, New Zealand*)
and Dallen Timothy (*Arizona State University, USA*)

The Tourism Area Life Cycle, Vol. 2
Conceptual and Theoretical Issues

Edited by
Richard W. Butler

CHANNEL VIEW PUBLICATIONS
Clevedon • Buffalo • Toronto

Library of Congress Cataloging in Publication Data
The Tourism Area Life Cycle: Conceptual and Theoretical Issues
Edited by Richard W. Butler.
Aspects of Tourism: 29
Includes bibliographical references and index.
1. Tourism–Economic aspects. 2. Economic development. I. Butler, Richard. II. Series.
G155.A1T5898283 2005
338.4'791–dc22   2005015059

British Library Cataloguing in Publication Data
A catalogue entry for this book is available from the British Library.

ISBN 1-84541-029-7 (hbk)
ISBN 1-84541-028-9 (pbk)
ISBN 1-84541-030-0 (electronic)

Channel View Publications
An imprint of Multilingual Matters Ltd

UK: Frankfurt Lodge, Clevedon Hall, Victoria Road, Clevedon BS21 7HH.
USA: 2250 Military Road, Tonawanda, NY 14150, USA.
Canada: 5201 Dufferin Street, North York, Ontario, Canada M3H 5T8.

Typeset by Datapage Ltd.
Printed and bound in Great Britain by the Cromwell Press.

DEDICATION

To my wife, Margaret, and my children, Caroline, Richard and Ántonia, who have lived with 'the cycle' and its demands and been there with support and encouragement over the last three decades, and:

IN MEMORIAM

To my father, Sgt. Pilot Richard Butler, RAF (VR), 106 Squadron, whom I never had the privilege of knowing, and the more than 55,000 men of Bomber Command, who like him, were killed in action in the Second World War.

'When you go home, tell them of us, and say:
For your tomorrows we gave our today'

Contents

Acknowledgements

There are many acknowledgements that have to be made for the publication of any book, but in the case of edited works there are inevitably more needed than for a single authored work. In the first place I must thank most sincerely the authors whose writings appear in this and the accompanying volume. They have done most of the academic work in terms of their contributions, and it is a truism to say the books would not have appeared without their efforts. Of all the people I approached, some old friends, some former students (and hopefully still friends), some recent acquaintances and some known only to me by their writings, only one did not reply, and only one was finally unable to contribute a chapter. Some responded early (5.00 a.m. in one case), others performed more like myself, cutting it rather fine. Virtually all wrote exactly what was asked of them, sometimes at rather short notice, all took my comments and suggestions in good spirit and some have even yet to take me up on the offer of a beer. Perhaps above all, I wish to thank them for finding the TALC of interest and using it in the first place.

Second of course, there are those involved in the publication of the books. At the University of Surrey, my long-suffering secretary Margaret Williamson and at various times, Malcolm Thompson, for assistance with Word and word processing, and Paul Fuller and John Briggs for rescuing various items from faulty laptops and illegible files on more than one occasion. At Channel View publications, first and foremost, Mike Grover, for his support, particularly as this project grew from one book of 80,000 words and 15 chapters to one book of about 20 chapters, and then to two books of nearly 40 chapters and over 200,000 words in total, and to his family team, whose efforts I appreciate greatly.

Third, there is the general support team. Conceptually in its creation the TALC owes a great deal to Jim Brougham, the nearest person to a Renaissance man I have ever come across in person. Many good arguments, parties, football matches and above all, incomparable folk singing (on his side) contributed greatly if tangentially at times, to the final product. He was one of many former students at the University of Western Ontario, including Brian Keogh, Peter Keller, James Strapp, Colin Harris, Dave Weaver, Winston Husbands, Dave Telfer, Stephen Boyd, Tom Hinch and Bryan Smale, all of whom helped develop, test and refine the model in various ways. There are also many more graduate and undergraduate students, unfortunately too many to list, at Western and at the University of Surrey who have used the model and also helped in its development. Peter Murphy (once English, then Canadian and now Australian) should be acknowledged (or blamed) particularly for TALC seeing the light of day in terms of publication, first by nagging me to produce a paper for the Canadian Association of Geographers' meeting in Vancouver, and then by persuading the Association to publish the first ever special edition of *The Canadian Geographer* (24 (1), 1980) (which he edited), one devoted to papers on tourism and recreation.

Since 1980 in particular, many colleagues have assisted greatly, either by using the model (including all those featured in these volumes), or by just being there to talk, and to share ideas and good times. Some legitimately might feel their research should be included (or may be relieved it is not!), Gareth Shaw and Allan Williams in the UK in particular, but I do have one representative from the south west at least included, who was influenced by their work. Klaus Meyer-Arendt, Paul Wilkinson, Ngaire Douglas and Gerda Priestly especially are also owed apologies for apparently being ignored, but only by noninclusion of papers I can assure them. There are also a vast number of other writers who have used the TALC, most, if not all, included in Lagiewski's bibliography, and an even larger number of students at universities around the world who have probably driven their supervisors mad by using the model. (Arriving at an Australian university on sabbatical in 1992 I was greeted at coffee by a staff member there, with the comment, 'So you're the bugger that wrote that, I've just had to mark 20 reports using it!') Finally there is the family support team, to whom these books are dedicated, who have been hoping to heaven 'it' is finished soon and doing their best to make sure it is. They have eventually won and I am very grateful, not only for their support and encouragement, but for the ideas, suggestions (mostly) and willingness to lose sandpits, rooms and furniture buried under TALC-related material for far too long.

More formally and finally, I should also like to thank the Canadian Association of Geographers, not only for publishing the article in *The Canadian Geographer* in the first place, but also for giving me permission to reproduce the original article (Chapter 1, this volume). I trust this book will relieve some pressure on their office at McGill University by reducing the number of requests for copies!

Contributors

Names and e-mail addresses of Contributors to TALC Books.

Book 1

Richard 'Rick' M. Lagiewski, Rochester Institute of Technology
Rick.Lagiewski@rit.edu

K. Michael Haywood, retired, at time of writing University of Guelph
Michael.Haywood@sympatico.ca

Gary Hovinen, retired at time of writing
ghovinen@yahoo.com

Jan O. Lundgren, McGill University
jan.lundgren@mcgill.ca

Jigang Bao, Sun Yat Sen University
eesbjg@zsu.edu.cn

Chaozi Zhang, Sun Yat Sen University
No e-mail, use Bao (above)

Stephen Boyd, currently University of Ulster (Coleraine Campus)
sw.boyd@ulster.ac.uk

Antonio Paolo Russo, Erasmus University
russo@few.eur.nl

Jane Malcolm-Davies, at time of writing University of Surrey
jane@jmdandco.com

David B. Weaver, University of South Carolina
dweaver@gwm.sc.edu

Charles S. Johnston, Auckland Institute of Technology
charles.johnston@aut.ac.nz

Jerry D. Johnson, Montana State University
jdj@montana.edu

David J. Snepenger, Montana State University
dsnep@montana.ed also dsnepenger@earthlink.com

Bonnie Martin
bmartin@mail.wcu.edu

Juanita Marois, University of Alberta
Juanita-marois@aol.com

Tom Hinch, University of Alberta
thinch@ualberta.ca

Sanda Corak, Institute of Tourism, University of Zagreb
sanda.corak@iztzg.hr

Charles Stansfield, retired from Rowan College, New Jersey
ruthig@rowan.edu

Bill Faulkner, deceased at time of writing, Griffith University

Carmen Tideswell, Auckland Institute of Technology
carmen.tideswell@aut.ac.nz

Brian Wheeller, at time of writing NHTV Breda, Netherlands
wheellerbrian@yahoo.com

Book 2

Tim Coles, University of Exeter
T.E.Coles@exeter.ac.uk

Andreas Papatheodorou, at time of writing University of Surrey, now
University of Aegean
academia@trioptron.org

C. Michael Hall, University of Otago
cmhall@business.otago.ac.nz

Rosslyn Russell, Royal Melbourne Institute of Technology
rosslyn.russell@rmit.edu.au

Sabine Weisenegger, University of Muenchen
weizenegger@bwl.uni-muenchen.de

Stephen Wanhill, at time of writing Bournemouth University, now University of Limerick
Stephen@Wanhill.force9.co.uk

Sven Lundtorp, as Wanhill (above)

Neil Ravenscroft, University of Brighton
neil@ravenscroft.fsnet.co.uk

Ion Hadjihambi, KPMG Services (Pty) Ltd.
ion.hadjihambi@kpmg.co.za

Chris Cooper, University of Queensland
c.cooper@mailbox.uq.edu.au

Sheela Agarwal, University of Plymouth
S.Agarwal@plymouth.ac.uk

Mara Manente, CISET, University of Venice
mtourism@unive.it

Harald Pechlaner, Catholic University of Eichstatt-Ingoldstadt, Bavaria
Harald.Pechlaner@ku-eichstaett.de

Ted Berry, Lower Kuskokwin School District, Alaska
Tedberry_aus@yahoo.com

Introduction

C. MICHAEL HALL

It is an indication of the significance of a concept that it starts to attract
not only articles but entire books as to its nature. And, as the reader will
find in going through the various chapters in the two volumes of this
book, the Tourism Area Life Cycle (TALC) is one of the most cited and
contentious areas of tourism knowledge (the original article, published in
The Canadian Geographer, is to be found in volume 1). Indeed, the TALC is
arguably one of the most significant contributions to studies of tourism
development because of the way it provides a focal point for discussion
of what leads to destination change, how destinations and their markets
change and, even, what is a destination. Moreover, the two volumes
highlight the manner in which theory informs the development and
generation of tourism knowledge, the importance of understanding the
intellectual history of tourism ideas, and the disciplinary dimensions of
tourism studies.

The TALC also has a wider significance beyond a focus on tourism
destination development because it challenges the notion of tourism
studies having a simplistic theoretical base. As Meethan (2001: 2)
commented, 'for all the evident expansion of journals, books and
conferences specifically devoted to tourism, at a general analytical level
it remains under-theorized, eclectic and disparate.' Similarly, Franklin
and Crang (2001: 5) observed:

> The first trouble with tourism studies, and paradoxically also one of
> its sources of interest, is that its research object, 'tourism,' has grown
> very dramatically and quickly and that the tourism research
> community is relatively new. Indeed at times it has been unclear
> which was growing more rapidly – tourism or tourism research. Part
> of this trouble is that tourist studies has simply tried to track and
> record this staggering expansion, producing an enormous record of
> instances, case studies and variations. One reason for this is that
> tourist studies has been dominated by policy led and industry
> sponsored work so the analysis tends to internalize industry led
> priorities and perspectives... Part of this trouble is also that this
> effort has been made by people whose disciplinary origins do not

include the tools necessary to analyze and theorize the complex cultural and social processes that have unfolded.

Yet the TALC actually remains a clear indicator of the importance of theory in tourism research and from people with a wide range of disciplinary origins. As Oppermann (1998: 180) noted: 'Butler's model is a brilliant example of how scientific progress could and should work. ... [having] been scrutinized in many different contexts with modifications suggested to fit specific situations and circumstances.' In fact these volumes extend the analysis of a significant concept even further by also providing a basis for an examination of the prehistory of the TALC and its origins in a manner that depends on our understanding of its contemporary application. Immediately, one of the things that then strike you in reading the various chapters in this volume is that substantive theoretical research in tourism studies, and in the geography of tourism in particular, has a lineage that dates to the 1920s and 1930s, with significant insights into the destination development process already being drawn by the 1950s and 1960s (Butler, this volume; Hall & Page, 2005).

Just as importantly, the discussions on the TALC indicate the importance of understanding the diffusion of ideas, not only within disciplines but also between disciplines. For example, a key point of debate in relation to the TALC is the relative importance of marketing and geographical/spatial ideas regarding life cycles, with several chapters in this volume arguing that the spatial dimensions of the TALC have not been sufficiently appreciated in the majority of writing on the TALC (Coles, this volume; Hall, this volume). Indeed, both Coles and Hall also emphasise that an understanding of the TALC also needs to appreciate the wider debates that have occurred within geography as to the significance of model building and the philosophy of knowledge (Johnston, 1991). Such discussions have immense practical significance for the student of tourism. It means we should be asking how is tourism knowledge developed, what is its relevance, to whom is it relevant, in what situation does and doesn't it apply, and why is there competition between ideas? In fact, for many students one of the greatest values of the two volumes, and this one in particular, is the extent to which you can trace the intellectual history of an idea. Unfortunately, the nature of technology and research means that increasingly many students just rely on works they can download or find on the world wide web. Yet, as both volumes demonstrate, there are a number of early studies that are not readily available for download and require either browsing through the library to access or even accessing on interlibrary loan. In addition, the second volume becomes especially valuable as authors of some of the earlier, predownload days, applications of the TALC in specific locations have been able to revisit their earlier work and reflect on it. Again, this is something else that is, unfortunately, relatively rare in tourism, yet provides tremendous insights into the research process and the generation of tourism knowledge.

One of the other important dimensions of the TALC is that it was first published in a geography journal and not tourism. As noted above, and in a number of chapters in both volumes, the geographical and spatial dimensions of the TALC are important for understanding its intellectual history as well as issues surrounding the scale at which it applies. However, the fact that it was published in *The Canadian Geographer* also emphasises the blurred and shifting boundaries of tourism studies and of the traditional academic disciplines such as geography, sociology, economics and psychology as they relate to tourism studies. Although, it must also be noted that there has been a vast growth in the number of tourism journals since the TALC was published. By 1980 there were 13 refereed English-language (full or part) academic journals on tourism and cognate subjects; by 2003 Hall *et al*. (2004) had recorded 75, with the figure likely to be an underestimate. Nevertheless, the publication of the article in *The Canadian Geographer* and its first application by Gary Hovinen (1981) also in the same journal, was soon picked up in the *Annals of Tourism Research* and *Tourism Management* by Geoff Wall (1982a,b), a fellow Ontario tourism and recreation geographer and a person who had had the opportunity to personally discuss the implications of the TALC concept with Butler for a number of years. The importance of Wall's articles, and a second article by Hovinen (1982) which was published in *Annals of Tourism Research*, on the incorporation of Butler's (1980) ideas on TALC into the tourism literature, cannot be overestimated, as they immediately lay the foundations for the contested theoretical terrain that is the TALC. Arguably without the early focus on the TALC by Wall and Hovinen in tourism journals the incorporation of TALC into the tourism body of knowledge would have been significantly delayed and the nature of the debate may have been substantially different. Significantly, the vast majority of publications on the TALC have appeared in tourism journals and publications not in geography publications, unless they specifically relate to tourism and recreation geographies. This is not to say that TALC does not have implications to wider geographic debate, far from it; given the concern of the geographer on place, changing notions of place and competition between places, there is much in the debate on TALC that should be of interest. Indeed, it is telling to note the chapters in this volume that seek to connect TALC with wider geographies of space and place.

This second volume pays particular attention to the theoretical debate that surrounds the TALC. Ideally, it should be read in conjunction with the original article and the account of the various applications of the

TALC in the first volume, particularly as much of the conceptual contestation that exists in this volume has been substantially impacted by empirical research. It is divided into five main sections. The first examines some of the conceptual origins of the TALC (although also see the first section in the other volume which includes some of Butler's own insights) with a discussion of epistemological and ontological dimensions of TALC by Johnston as well as an examination of the extent to which the TALC has become legitimised as a theory of tourism development and change by Haywood. Indeed, Haywood's comments as to the extent to which life cycle ideas have not been incorporated into the tourism industry's development discussions, at least in the Canadian context, may also provide significant insights into issues surrounding the diffusion of ideas, not least between the academy and industry.

The second section draws together some of the geographical and spatial analyses of the TALC. Coles and Hall both relate the TALC to broader concepts of spatial analysis and the intellectual history of ideas, more than has been the case in many other discussions of the TALC, while Papatheodorou also draws upon the concepts of competition between location in space as a way of highlighting the extent to which destinations should not be seen in isolation.

The third section provides a wider array of conceptualisation of TALC in relationship to entrepreneurship theory and Chaos Theory (Russell), the relationship between TALC and concepts of change with respect to protected natural areas (Weiznegger), the implications of Lamarckian theory (Ravenscroft & Hadjihambi) and time path analysis. All of these chapters indicate the importance of TALC with respect to analogue theory (Hall, this volume), while it is also interesting to note the parallels between some of the spatial considerations in Coles and Hall and the time-path analysis by Lundtorp and Wanhill. Indeed, these chapters are also noteworthy in their attempt to provide a mathematical basis for TALC (also see Butler, the origins of TALC, other volume).

The fourth section investigates a particular stage of TALC, by examining the issue of the renewal stage and the rejuvenation of destinations, an issue of contemporary importance to many destinations in Europe and North America. Cooper discusses the anatomy of the rejuvenation stage while Agarwal examines the restructuring of coastal resorts with particular reference to the UK situation. Baum also poses a fundamental question as to whether it is possible for a place to exit tourism, and therefore TALC, or otherwise reinvent itself. Issues of renewal and reinvention are also the subject of the final section that examines the extent to which TALC is predictive and features contributions from Manente and Pechlaner, and Berry. Finally, the volume concludes with a chapter by Butler on the future of the TALC in which he highlights issues surrounding its key elements of dynamism, process, carrying capacity, management, spatial analysis, triggers, as well as its potential continued relevance.

Given the undoubted interest in these two volumes and the ongoing utilisation of the life cycle by students of tourism, there is little likelihood that the relevance of TALC to contemporary tourism will decline in the near future. We are therefore in these two volumes witnessing something of the life cycle of the life cycle. We have reached a stage of maturity in which there is the opportunity for a collective look back as to the trajectory of the TALC concept and the publications and debate it has spawned. It is also highly likely that the collection of work in these two volumes will only serve to further encourage continued discussion and debate for a new generation of studies and conceptualisations of TALC that will provide the basis for ongoing rejuvenation of studies of destinations and that will also be a lasting legacy of Richard Butler's contributions to the study of tourism.

Part 1

The Conceptual Context and Evolution of the TALC

RICHARD BUTLER

Prologue

The opportunity to revisit one's own work is never easy, for one tends to see in it that which one wishes to see or imagines is explicit, while to others such insights may remain at best obscurely implicit, if present at all. In this introduction it is clearly neither appropriate nor possible to consider all of the applications, modifications undertaken and suggested, and criticisms of the original paper (Butler, 1980). Others have done such reviews, and Prosser (1995) in particular has written much of what this author would have been tempted to say. As well, Legiewski in his chapter (other volume), examined in considerable detail a good number of the earlier applications and evaluations of the TALC, concluding with a detailed table of the majority of the published applications of the model, thus it would be pointless to repeat or précis these earlier works. The purpose of this introduction, therefore, is to set the scene for the chapters that follow, which individually perform specific roles of criticism, reconceptualisation, theoretical modification and presentation of alternative variations on the original model. This short chapter represents a more personal discussion of the role and place of the model in tourism research, rather than a full review of its use. There are many additional references to those not specifically cited here or elsewhere in this volume that reflect the variety of ways and frequency with which the model has been utilised, particularly by students. Almost inevitably, by the time this volume is in press, it is likely that other variations and applications will have appeared, hopefully building on and improving the basic model. The next section reviews the literature on tourism (and recreation and leisure) that was particularly influential in providing the conceptual base for the TALC.

Introduction

The specific origins of the TALC have been discussed in the first chapter in the accompanying volume, in which I trace the links between the early versions of the TALC, and the literature on tourist flows and resort development that existed at that time. I noted in that chapter, and repeat here, that the 1960s were not a period of great conceptual development in tourism research, primarily because there was very little tourism research being done in the academic realm. Much of the research that was being done was of a descriptive nature and in many cases, primarily single case studies not related to models or theories. Criticism along these lines was still being made in the 1970s (Mitchell, 1979) and 1980s (Smith, 1982) with considerable relevance, and to a lesser extent is still valid today (Hall & Page, 1999). Part of the reason may relate to the fact that tourism is often not considered a proper academic discipline, a position which I support, although others would disagree. It has meant that tourism research, where it has utilised concepts and theories, has generally taken them from other disciplines, such as anthropology, economics, geography, management and sociology. (*The Annals of Tourism Research* has twice published special issues dealing with distinct disciplinary approaches to tourism, which while useful, have perhaps served to perpetuate the fragmentation that exists within tourism.)

The 1960s did see some significant developments in the academic literature on tourism and recreation. To present day readers it is perhaps important to point out that in this time period much of the relevant research for tourism was being done under the headings of recreation and leisure, particularly in the USA. At the time of writing the original article and its predecessors I was at the University of Western Ontario in Canada, and fortunate by being there, to have access to the North American research being published in these areas. Much of this research was published in the form of government reports, specially commissioned studies, and not in conventional academic publications such as journals (in the 1960s there were no academic tourism journals in English and none of the current major recreation or leisure journals either). Of considerable relevance to tourism and in particular TALC development were three elements. One is a very small group of publications, including one particular book, *The Economics of Outdoor Recreation* by Marion Clawson and Jack Knetsch (1966), which built on the ideas expressed by Clawson in his earlier report for the Resources for the Future Foundation, *The Crisis in Outdoor Recreation* (1959). This latter review was perhaps the first publication to recognise and enunciate the pressures that were beginning to build in North America (and, although not stated, in Europe also) on recreation, tourism and leisure facilities as demand built up from the economic and population boom of the post-war 1950s. Clawson and Knetsch's book was a superb exposition of then contemporary theories, concepts and approaches to research in outdoor recreation, and remained relevant for some two decades, not least because of the quality of the writing and clarity of explanation. It was particularly significant because it introduced to outdoor recreation concepts such as the recreation experience (with its five components of anticipation, journey to site, on-site experience, journey from site and recollection), which has been much utilised and modified since then. Two other volumes from that period were of specific relevance to tourism in terms of highlighting some of the issues existing and unfolding with respect to pressures on destinations. One was *Man and Nature in the National Parks* by Darling and Eichorn (1967), which presented results of a study of the US National Parks system, and revealed clearly the management problems being experienced as a result of rapid growth of tourism and recreation travel in the USA. Finally, although not directly related to tourism or recreation, was Ian McHarg's (1967) *Design with Nature*, an articulate expression of why mankind should accommodate nature rather than the other way around, and a precursor of techniques such as Geographic Information Systems in terms of the use of overlays for land use and resource planning.

The second element was the publication at the end of the late 1950s, over a series of years, of the 27 volumes of the Outdoor Recreation Resources Review Commission (ORRRC, 1962). This represented a breakthrough in recreation research, and while not all volumes are of equal high standard, overall, this set of publications represented a real benchmark in terms of 'modern' research into outdoor recreation. (An excellent comprehensive review of the ORRRC reports is contained in Wolfe's article *Perspectives on Outdoor Recreation*, 1964.) These reports were in many ways the key reference works for researchers in outdoor recreation, tourism and leisure for at least a decade, and their scale and comprehensive nature have never been matched in any country before or since.

Finally, there was also an ongoing series of reports on research being conducted by the US Forest Service, research which is ongoing and still available. Among the many excellent (and generally free) publications in this series were two in particular that received wide citation among other researchers in the 1960s. This research, and these two publications in particular, reflected the realisation among public sector agencies that, as Clawson (1959) had argued, the pressures on outdoor recreation (and tourism) resources were increasing rapidly, and that these pressures brought with them the potential for very considerable negative impacts on both the environments being visited and the quality of the visitor experience in these sites. One of these studies was by J. Alan Wagar, *The Carrying Capacity of Wildlands for Recreation* (1964), which was the first study to draw out the links between motivations to participate in outdoor recreation (and by implication, tourism) and crowding or carrying capacity. The second was by R.C. Lucas (1964), *The Recreational Carrying Capacity of the Quetico-Superior Area*, and in this study for the first time a researcher demonstrated how carrying capacity levels could be produced for a specific area.

These two studies started an ongoing research relationship between carrying capacity and related management issues for wilderness areas in the USA which continues today, and has produced innumerable other valuable reports such as *The Limits of Acceptable Change* (Stankey & Cole, 1985) and *The Recreational Opportunity Spectrum* (Clarke & Stankey, 1979). The research on carrying capacity led directly to the importance placed upon this concept in the development of the TALC, and is similarly reflected in subsequent research reviewing the relationship between tourist destination development and carrying capacity (Getz, 1983; Martin & Uysal, 1990). The idea that the overuse of resources would ultimately lead to both environmental deterioration in the quality of the resources involved and thus diminished visitor satisfaction, and ulti- mately reduced visitation is both logical and, in the 1960s and 1970s, fairly obvious on the ground in an increasing number of places.

The 1970s were a time of greater conceptual development in tourism. Many of the models and concepts put forward in that decade are still quoted in the literature today, including the work of Cohen (1979), Doxey (1975) and Plog (1973), although much of this appears with hindsight to have been based on 'seat of the pants' intuition and personal experience. At a time when there was little research on tourism, such a state of affairs was neither unusual nor unreasonable. It is, perhaps, a tribute to the insight of these individuals that their ideas continue to be debated, tested and used in the current literature. Despite these pioneering efforts, and those discussed elsewhere (Butler, other volume), there was still continuing criticism in the tourism academy about the relative absence of conceptualisation and theoretical development. Smith (1982) empha- sised this point in his inimically titled paper *Reflections on Geographical Research in Recreation – Hey Buddy Can you S'Paradigm?*

The research noted above, particularly the work of Clawson, and also that of Wolfe (1951, 1962, 1964, 1966) suggested that the pressures on recreation areas were likely to be felt on tourist destinations also, and that just as outdoor recreation sites were having to change to meet the increasing and changing demand, so too would tourist destinations have to reflect market shifts in preference and taste, and changes in mobility and accessibility. One thing which seemed apparent in the late 1960s and 1970s was the failure of many destinations and those involved with the planning and development of tourism to recognise that the offerings of the pre-World War II era would not be capable of meeting the needs and desires of the post-war generations. It did not seem a blinding revelation to this writer that there were a number of general similarities between what was offered at a tourist destination and what is offered by producers of any other product made available to the market. Once this idea was accepted, it seemed equally obvious that what happened to other products was likely to happen, in its own form, to tourist products, i.e. destinations. The most widely known model appeared to be that of the Product Life Cycle (PLC), and intuitively this seemed to fit the tourism destination scenario. This served to provide a rationale and a conceptual base from which to challenge the then current wisdom. This can perhaps be summed up as 'once a tourist destination, always a tourist destination', with little need to accommodate the changes taking place in the external world (or in more current idiom, 'having built it, (even 50 years before), they will always come').

The TALC, as it finally appeared in 1980, was certainly a product of its own times and its creator's training and interests. As several of the authors in this volume discuss (Agarwal, Coles, Hall, Johnston and Papatheodorou), it has very clear geographical antecedents and links to theories and models commonly used in geography. As I note in the introductory chapter in the other volume, in the first attempts at developing the TALC, one of the key ideas related to the location of destinations and the process of new destinations being established in other locations as the older resorts lost their initial attractivity and competitiveness. Perhaps ironically, given the current predominance of tourism in universities being located in management schools, the business literature associated with the PLC (see Coles, this volume) was never discussed in either the very first version of the model (Brougham & Butler, 1972) nor the original article. In essence the basic PLC idea was appropriated for what was essentially a geographical article, and to my now embarrassment (as a staff member in a School of Management), none of the relevant business literature was ever cited. In many respects it is others who have focused on the comparison with the well established PLC in business, along with the relevant criticisms (for example, Haywood, 1986, this volume). I am particularly grateful to Coles (this volume) for discussing much of this literature and its relevance to the TALC and thus helping correct a rather large omission in my literature review.

While obviously feeling that the model had validity and was worthy of application, this author did not anticipate either the scale or positive nature of the reaction to the model over the past two decades. The first reaction to the model was positive but raised some valid criticisms (Wall, 1982, this volume), and the second review article was even more specific in its identification of shortcomings and problems (Haywood, 1986, this volume). Interestingly enough, however, the first application of the model came only one year after publication (Hovinen, 1981), and since then the number of papers using the model has been very considerable (Legiewski, other volume). The examples used have ranged from single resorts (e.g. Weaver, 1990) to multiple groups of islands (e.g. Choy, 1992), in a wide range of physical, social and economic contexts. Not surprisingly, practical and theoretical issues have been identified, and the chapters in this volume focus on the latter set of problems (the other volume of this pair of publications contains chapters providing examples of applications and modifications of the cycle in a wide range of settings and at different scales).

The frequency of use and the range of applications analysed in the literature would tend to support the view that the TALC has validity in terms of being a descriptive model, with applicability in a wide variety of spatial, temporal, cultural and economic situations. It provides a conceptual hook for case studies of specific locations, and given the propensity for case studies from an industry and business perspective in tourism and the desire to undertake specific field work examples in research, the TALC would appear to still provide a valuable methodology and a stimulus for continued conceptual development in tourism research. Because the TALC is a generalised and essentially simplistic model, it is inevitable that it would not fit perfectly, or in some cases even closely, every specific situation to which it has been applied. The question best asked perhaps, is whether, in its original form, it successfully described and explained the process of tourist destination evolution. Whether it really does represent a paradigm in tourism research on destination development is a judgement better left to others, but after almost two decades of use the model may just cause Smith (1982) to question his earlier opinion.

Chapter 1
The Ontological Foundation of the TALC

SAMUEL JOHNSTON

Introduction

Martin Oppermann (1998: 179) wrote, in response to a paper by Agarwal (1997): 'I am sure that almost everything that can be said about the advantages and disadvantages of Butler's model has indeed been said already.' Yet on the next page he was to note:

> Butler's model is a brilliant example of how scientific progress could and should work. In fact, it is probably the only model in tourism that has been scrutinized in many different contexts with modifications suggested to fit specific situations and circumstances. (Oppermann, 1998: 180)

This is certainly true. Since 1980 there have been dozens of published works utilising the TALC model. Most of these focus on basic research but, in addition, the model is now included in text books (Boniface & Cooper, 1987) and defined in glossaries (Middleton & Hawkins, 1998). In one case study, Burns and Murphy (1998) noted that tourism operators at a mature destination in Australia had used knowledge of the model to determine they would be in trouble if they didn't plan ahead. These examples show that, a score of years after publication, Butler's message is truly 'out there'. Within the contemporary research community, however, there is little consensus about the model's usefulness. The depth and breadth of criticism is now extensive. Further, Pearce's (1993) complaint that there has been no solid comparative work done continues to be valid.

Because of this situation, the objective of this paper is to raise and examine ontological and epistemological issues, as an attempt to shore up the theory underlying the model and, hopefully, facilitate future comparative research. The organising method for the paper was a modified form of 'grounded theory'. This is an inductive approach to research developed by Glaser and Strauss (1967). These authors asserted the major goal of inductive research was to generate theory, not verify it. This was considered particularly useful in new contexts, for which theory had not been established. The extant body of work on the destination life cycle model seemed to represent such a situation. Here, ontology will be discussed first, then epistemology. Points from TALC literature will be introduced when relevant, as illustrations. Because the focus is on ontological and epistemological underpinnings, the chapter attempts to be something more than a literature review, but is also less than a fully described grounded theory of destination development. The final section of the paper is synthetic and suggests a formula for integration in case study research.

Ontological Considerations

As a word, 'ontology' is generally defined abstractly as relating to the 'nature of being' (Webster, 1983). In this paper the word is used to define a set of basic concepts that underpin the understanding of the reality Butler's model attempts to describe. This is not an idle exercise, for it relates to the basic question: 'How can a tourist destination – a *place* – have a life cycle?' Haywood (1992) and Agarwal (1997) have wondered aloud whether the concept of the 'resort cycle itself' has validity. Choy (1992: 2), in his study of Pacific Island destinations, cited Hart, Casserly and Lawless to show that there were cases in which the product life cycle did not apply. It is therefore crucial to settle the issue of whether the model is based merely on a metaphor, or whether it has a firmer ontological foundation.

Structuration theory

Giddens' (1984) theory of structurationism provides the necessary underpinning to answer the question. As well as providing an ontological basis for concepts such as 'structure' and 'agency', Giddens established that there were 'institutions' of social behaviour which were real in an ontological sense. He defined 'institutions' as the sets of practices of individuals that encompass 'the more enduring features of social life' (p. 24) and are 'deeply embedded in time and space' (p. 13). Based on these definitional elements, tourism can clearly be interpreted as an excellent example of an institution. Writers such as MacCannell (1976: 49) and Urry (1990: 9) have in fact referred to the institutional nature of tourism. Cohen's (1972: 169) section on 'The Institutionalised Forms of Tourism: The Organized and the Individual Mass Tourist' is perhaps the most developed treatment. In contemporary tourism, there are at least four sets of practices that are 'institutional' in nature: the practices of tourists themselves; the practices of the tourist industry; the promotional efforts from which evolve a standardised image of the destination; and the practices of the community in relation to the presence of tourists.

Besides defining recognisable sets of behaviour as institutions, Giddens asserted these did not occur randomly but were situated in time and space at *locales*. A locale was not of any fixed size, it could be even an area within a room, or it could be something larger. The importance of the concept is Giddens' assertion that place makes a difference to behaviour. Conceptually, then, tourism at a destination can be considered as locale-based institutional behaviour. By itself this is atemporal. But Giddens also asserted institutions had life cycles; he referred to this as their *longue durée*. Within such a life cycle the institutionalised behaviour was passed (and evolved) from generation-to-generation and could last several hundred years or more. A destination can therefore be said to have a life cycle on the basis that, as a locale, it is in the process of completing its *longue durée* with respect to the institution of tourism. This in turn allows the assertion that *all* destinations can be interpreted to have begun a life cycle once minimum definitions of institutionalisation have been met. Ontologically there are no exceptions, whether or not the model is capable of predicting aspects of the life cycle of a particular area, or whether in its generalised form it fits a specific destination very well. The question – when does life begin? – is as tricky here as it is with human life. A general answer, applicable to many situations, would be that a destination's tourism life cycle has begun when *any* aspect of tourism has become institutionalised. A more specific answer, based on research done in Kona (Johnston, other volume), is that the involvement stage of the cycle began when institutionalised features of the tourism industry were constructed at the locale.

A conceptual expansion may be made at this point. When tourism is considered as an institution, it is apparent that it will be just one of many to dominate a locale over the course of its history. Such an idea is familiar in the discipline of geography, as expressed through Whittlesey's (1929) concept of a locational 'sequent occupance', consisting of several eras. Over the course of the longer sequent occupance, tourism will be just one of many institutional eras. There will likely have been pretourism eras, and post-tourism eras will follow after the institutional 'death' of tourism (Baum, this volume). Butler did not discuss this broader picture in any detail, though Young (1983) has theorised a pretourism era with two stages.

Relying solely on Giddens has limitations, for he did not theorise the nature of the institutional *longue durée* beyond defining it. Yet as will be seen, other life cycle models break down the whole of the cycle into meaningful stages and substages. Butler (1980) focused on identifying stages; so has all subsequent case research. Therefore, the stages of the life cycle become an important component in the concepts of institution and longue durée. This is an aspect that Giddens failed to examine and inspiration must be sought elsewhere.

'Basic process' theory

The stages of the *longue durée* relate to the process which the institution of tourism undergoes while progressing through its life cycle. The word 'process' can be used to refer generally to a 'progressive course' but this often includes 'a number of steps' (Webster, 1983). The word also has ontological significance when used in research about social life. Glaser (1978: 98) has noted that the concept of process is 'a way of grouping together two sequencing parts of a phenomenon'. That is, a process can be ontologically defined when there are two or more temporally distinct parts to a phenomenon and these occur directionally, from one to the next. An 'institutional process', then, may be defined as one in which the *longue durée* can be broken into stages and substages occurring directionally.

Glaser (1978: 97– 100) has also noted that certain processes are 'basic social processes' because they are 'fundamental patterns in the organization of social behavior as it occurs over time.' Basic social processes were considered to have three properties: 'stages', 'variability' and 'pervasiveness'. With respect to stages, he asserted they are relatively unique in form/condition and consequences. They have 'breaking points' that can be discerned on the basis of a sequence that has general time limits. Stages are in fact 'theoretical units' and the point of identifying them is to be able to show that variations exist in the pattern of behaviour being studied, and to account for these variations. The length of time for each stage is not fixed, but is a function of the conditions that create the changes leading to the next stage. These conditions might occur quickly, in which case there would be a 'critical juncture' or more slowly, as a 'blurry transition'. It is unlikely that they will occur identically in different case situations. Basic social processes are thus variable in the sense that no two entities ever go through a specific process in exactly the same manner. The final point is that social processes were considered *basic* because they were pervasive. They occur again and again because of the 'patterned, systematic uniformity flows of social life'.

From this description it would not seem unduly assertive to claim that Butler's destination life cycle model focuses on what could be called a 'basic geographical process'. The model captures the general sequence – the set of stages – through which destinations go as they evolve from isolated areas, to developed resort towns, to fully urbanised towns (or abandoned derelict landscapes). The concepts of 'pleasure periphery' (Turner & Ash, 1975) and 'periphery frontier' (Zurick, 1992) show that the pervasiveness of tourist destination development is increasing worldwide. Lastly, life cycles will be destination specific, as Cooper (1992: 149) has asserted. The existence of this variability, however, cannot be used to disprove the general accuracy of the theory upon which the model is based. Rather, it can be argued that the reverse situation exists – the theory and model become validated as reasonably accurate portrayals of a basic geographical process whenever a researcher is able to utilise them. Because the theory and model are inductive, all subsequent variation discovered in case studies should therefore be interpreted in such a way as to broaden the general theory of destination development.

Epistemological Considerations

Trusted (1981: 23) has defined 'epistemology' as 'the theory or science of the methods or grounds of knowledge'. Tribe (1997) has recently written a discussion of how epistemological questions can be applied to tourism studies. He noted that pertinent concerns include the use of concepts and boundaries, and the character, validity and reliability of claims of knowledge about tourism. Focusing on aspects such as these would seem useful in removing what he regarded as the excessive 'indiscipline of tourism' (the title of his article), and get at the 'how do you know?' considerations. Pollock (1986) has shown these are crucial to epistemology. The next part of the paper discusses such epistemological concerns.

Beyond having an operational definition, it is necessary to identify a set of epistemological elements that could be used to shore up the theory in the existing corpus of literature. A variation of the 'constant comparative method' (Glaser & Strauss, 1967) was used to do this. Specifically, literature on four other types of process research was read and compared to see what elements were held in common and therefore might be transferable to the study of a tourism process. The literature was chosen simply on the basis of familiarity; the processes identified were: the human life cycle, the product life cycle, port development and ecosuccession models. The reading was not exhaustive, yet the exercise in comparison was successful, in that seven epistemologically oriented elements were found to be (mostly) held in common. These are: the entity undergoing the process; its internal characteristics; its users; stages as conceptual units; the mechanisms that cause stage changes; the macro-structural conditions under which the process occurs; the typical sequence and the variability of stages. The comparative details are provided in Figure 1.1. The next section of the paper will elaborate on each element and also discuss it in relation to salient points found in the destination area literature.

Type of Process → Epistemological Element ↓	Human Life Cycle	Product Life Cycle	Port Development	Ecosuccession
Unit-Entity	Individual lives	A specific product	A coastal port	A patch of vegetation
Internal characteristics	Biological Cultural Psychological	Product type and modification Marketing and costs Parts and servicing Trade-ins, etc.	Port physiography Built environment of port facilities + nearby urban areas Linkages to inland cities	Vital attributes of key component species
Users	None	Consumers	Shippers	None
Stages	Infancy Childhood Adolescence Adulthood Old age	Introduction Development Maturity Decline	Primitive era Marginal quay expansion Marginal quay elaboration Dock elaboration Simple lateral quayage Specialized quayage	Varies with types of plants: simplest version = grasses, shrubs, trees
Mechanisms of stage change	Generally "blurry transitions"	Competition	Change in ship design	Based on properties of plant species
Typical sequence and variation in stages	Precociousness Premature aging	Product non-acceptance Mass marketing Innovation	None	"Pathways" Facilitation Tolerance Inhibition
Macro-structural conditions	Family Community Society	Economic system, Levels of technology and communication Organizational capability	Trade conditions	Climate Latitude Altitude

Figure 1.1 Epistemological elements found in the literature on several types of process research
Sources: Bird, 1963; Noble and Slayter, 1981; Onkvisit and Shaw, 1989; Rink and Swan, 1979; Spirer, 1981

The entity undergoing the process

In any process research there is always some type of 'entity' that represents the 'unit' of analysis. In the human life cycle, that entity is an individual human being. A human being of course has a discrete scale, his or her physical body. This is not always the case. With product life cycles, the boundary can be inexact and sometimes an imposition of arbitrary definitions is required. As an example, Rink and Swan (1979: 225–227) have noted that for tobacco, there existed three levels of product aggregation. The 'class' was composed of all tobacco products. The major 'forms' they comprised were pipes, cigars and cigarettes. 'Brands' were the subdivisions of each. Butler's (1980) discussions of the typical features of each stage were general and lend themselves to analysis at many types and scales of destination areas. Subsequent theoretical development has not shown much epistemological concern over boundaries. In terms of Rink and Swan's (1979) discussion of tobacco products, we might say that different classes, forms and brands of destinations have all been compared against a single model. Transferring these ideas, the epistemological issue becomes one of bounding tourist destinations so that they can be compared. Three points require examination: the nature of the destination entity; the type of destination; and the spatial scale.

By the late 1990s, confusion seems to have arisen over the nature of the entity being studied. Butler adapted the product life cycle model to *destinations* going through a particular life cycle. Other writers have chosen to focus on some component of the tourism product at the destination rather than the destination itself. Haywood (1998), for example, noted that different products within a destination will display their own patterns of evolution. Based on the discussion of institutional behaviour above, this is undeniably true. Thus both the destination and sectors contained within could be legitimate objects of study. However, the capability of studying the life cycle of, say, the attractions sector, does not neutralise the validity of studying the life cycle of the destination itself.

Perusal of case studies in the literature shows that several 'types' of destinations have been examined. Getz (1992) has studied the cities of Niagara Falls (Ontario and New York state), which are built near the waterfall, an environmental attraction. Hovinen (1981, other volume) looked at Lancaster County, Pennsylvania, where the cultural practices of a religious minority were the main draw. (See Weizenegger this volume for a discussion on the validity of identifying protected areas as destinations, editor's note). These are destinations at which tourists have very different types of experiences and at which the institutional development has been very different. In an inductive approach to theory generation, each of these types of destinations might require its own subtheory, with a corresponding model, because the resource base providing the foundation for institutional behaviour is different.

Research has also been conducted at a variety of spatial scales. At one extreme, di Benedetto and Bojanic (1993) (and Bao & Zhang, other volume) have studied the life cycle of a theme park, Cypress Gardens, while at the other extreme McElroy *et al.* (1993) compared the island regions of the entire Caribbean Sea with those of the Pacific Ocean. With this range of variation, it would seem epistemologically important to determine, or at least narrow down, the legitimate spatial boundaries that the model can handle without requiring extensive modification.

Ontological points made above permit this. Examination of the case literature indicates that many studies have now been done on resort towns, i.e. at the urban scale. Smith (1992: 304) has in fact asserted that beach resort evolution represents a form of urbanisation. In terms of the existing theory, tourism as an institution develops when tourists arrive at a particular destination site, to experience some feature of it, and when businesspeople respond to their presence by developing a tourist industry. Together, the attraction and the commercial area constitute a locale. Thus the spatial scale for which the TALC model is most appropriate, in its present form, would seem to be a resort town that has an environmental or cultural resource as its basis of attraction, plus a recreational business district (or the potential for one to be built). Studies of destinations at scales much larger or smaller than this may require modification to the model because the institutional nature of tourism development would likely be different.

Numerous studies have been done on destination areas much larger than a resort-city scale. At large spatial scales, a difference that must be taken into account is the existence of multiple destinations. When there is more than one, the concern becomes that different types of destinations, and destinations that have individually developed during different time periods (see Formica & Uysal 1996), are all being aggregated into a single life cycle. When multiple site development occurs, what is going on at individual areas must not be glossed over without examination. Such glossing may miss important variations that are occurring at each locale. Digance (1997), and Priestley and Mundet (1998) have done studies that analysed such situations of multiple site development within a larger region.

Characteristics of the resort

Any sort of entity undergoing a process has internal characteristics that are what in fact changes. It is the state of these at any given point in time that provides an indication of what stage the entity is in. Agarwal

(1997: 65) has noted that there has been more attention of late in examining the internal dynamics of resort development. This section attempts to underpin which characteristics to consider.

Research on ecosystems and ports was found to have particular relevance to the study of resorts. First, ecosystem patches contain 'key component species' that have 'vital attributes' (Noble & Slayter, 1981: 313). In any successional patch some species dominate physically; plants of that species took up most of the area of the patch. Their presence was in fact what determined the stage in the succession. Second, Bird's (1963) study of ports indicated that the state of docking facilities was critical. These were just one feature of the port, along with the condition of the shoreline, suprastructural facilities (e.g. warehouses) and structures representing control (e.g. the customs house). Yet it was the docking facilities that were the crucial feature and stage interpretation was based on their level of development.

Butler defined quite a number of internal characteristics that might be considered important. Subsequent case researchers have expanded on these and studied a bewilderingly wide variety. Figure 1.2 aggregates some of them into a smaller group. The left column identifies three main characteristics that seemed particularly important at destinations.

The first characteristic is the 'base resource' that provides the major experience/s which tourists visit the destination to have. This is the

CHARACTERISTIC UNDERGOING CHANGE	SUB-TYPE	SUBSTANTIVE EXAMPLE
BASE RESOURCES	Environmental	Beaches, ski mountains, spa
	Cultural	Ethnic group
SERVICE RESOURCES	Tier 1*	Accommodation, food, souvenirs
		New resource creation: - Casino
	Tier 2 & 3	Doctors
	Post-hoc Tier 4 services	Housing
GOVERNMENT	Post-hoc services	Post Office, police/jail
	Infrastructure	Public works projects - Beach modification - Transportation
	Structuring documents	Development plans Legislation at large

Figure 1.2 Important internal characteristics of tourist destination areas
*Tier 1 shops serve tourists almost exclusively; tier 2 shops serve both tourists and locals; tier 3 indirectly serves the tourist industry; tier 4 serves locals only (see Smith, 1988)

attraction resource that provides the basis for the institutional development. These resources are commonly environmental or cultural.

The second characteristic is the set of 'services' that develops at the
resort. Using a typology developed by Smith (1988), these have been
divided into 'tiers'. Tier 1 services – those established specifically for and
used mainly by tourists – represent the 'key component species' in an
ecosystem. More specifically, accommodation facilities at the destination
contain what might be considered the 'vital attribute' – rooms (or beds).
The number of rooms that becomes available is roughly analogous to the
increasing dominance of the key component species in a patch. Some
writers have now asserted that a graph of numbers of accommodation
units could be used to interpret the stage changes (e.g. Foster & Murphy,
1991), or have utilised accommodation change in some way as a means to
understanding stage change (e.g. Haywood, 1998; Juelg, 1993; Young,
1983). Graphing annual change in accommodation units seems a
particularly effective way of showing the extent to which tourism has
come to institutionally dominate the destination area.

Government is the third major internal characteristic of the resort.
Several types of services are shown in Figure 1.2. These are broken into
subtypes on the basis of whether they produce tangible changes to the
resort, as happens when public works projects are completed, or whether
they are documentary in nature (e.g. regional development plans),
constraining some types of activity but enabling others. These activities
by government are extremely important in the long-term development of
a resort. Priestley and Mundet (1998: 89), for example, discussed the 'role
of planning, and of its absence' in three Catalan resorts.

Tourists: The users of the resort

Neither the human life nor the ecosystem has a 'user' as such. Two
processes – products and ports – did have them. For ports, the users are
the shippers who own the vessels and/or control the flow of cargo. For
products, users are obviously the consumers who buy them. There are at
least two ways that users can be further analysed, on the basis of their
quantity or by the different types into which they can be segmented.

With respect to product quantity, the S-curve of unit sales was initially
considered to be the proper conceptualisation of change over the life
span of the product. However, Rink and Swan (1979) later showed this to
be only one possibility, and that there were at least 11 other curves that
had been described. Regarding type, Onkvisit and Shaw (1989: 69–71)
discussed the sequence in which the users appeared. They segmented
users according to 'adopter categories'; the product would be initially be
purchased by 'early adopters' but towards the end of its life span people
identified as 'laggards' would be the main purchasers.

Tourists are the users of resorts and thus the considerations just mentioned are applicable. Butler himself brought features of both quantity and type into his discussion. He adopted intact the idea of the S-curve of tourist volume, adding that it was asymptotic in relation to carrying capacity. He also mentioned works by Christaller (1963) and Plog (1972). Both of these researchers identified types of tourists and asserted they would visit in a sequential way as the resort evolved.

Researchers of destination area life cycles have typically taken their cue from Butler and attempted to show how stages have emerged on the basis of tourist volume. This has led to the same realisation that occurred with products (noted by Haywood, 1986, this volume) – there is wide variation in the curve that occurs over the course of the resort's life cycle.

The type of tourist and sequence of visitation have also been discussed by a number of researchers. George Washington once visited Barbados and was subsequently identified as an 'explorer tourist' by France (1988). Owners of second homes and cottages at the resort, who are sometimes retirees, have been included as tourists by Strapp (1988) and Foster and Murphy (1991). Juelg (1993: 23) has analysed a destination area on the basis of visitation by 'excursionists'. It is evident from these examples that the types of people under examination transcend the usual definition of 'tourist'.

This becomes important in the context of the longer sequent occupance of the resort. There are 'pretourism' and 'post-tourism' eras and during these the majority of people visiting cannot properly be called 'tourists'. George Washington may or may not have been behaving in ways that were consistent with the institutional behaviour of tourists of the time. 'Snow birds', however, who live at the resort for half the year might be said to represent a transitional type of visitor, i.e. they are not quite tourists. Juelg's (1993) analysis of a destination visited mainly by excursionists also emphasises the importance of 'bounding' tourists. Excursionists have been categorically differentiated from tourists since the 1960s. This is clearly important when tourism as an institution is considered. A destination visited mainly by excursionists, who do not require accommodation facilities, will likely go through an institutional *longue durée* that is very different from one for which accommodation is required.

Two points emerge from these considerations. First, the volume of tourists over time will always vary at different destinations. No two will ever have exactly the same curve, and the S-curve represents but an interesting starting point for theory generation. Second, the institution of tourism at the locale requires visitors to behave like tourists. When the people at the destination behave in some other way, say, as 'home owners', it may be more theoretically appropriate to interpret that the locale has passed out of its tourism era into a new one.

Recognition of stages in the life cycle

Stages are perhaps the key feature in the destination area model. As mentioned above, Glaser (1978) has noted that to be a basic social process there must be at least two distinguishable stages. Critics of research using Butler's model have focused on this epistemological component, wondering about what a stage is and how the years in which it exists get defined. Oppermann's (1998: 180) comment was typical; he noted that writers are 'never quite revealing why those years were chosen and based on which criteria.' It is fundamental, then, that a model that focuses on stage development should have a means of recognising stages.

For some processes (human life, ecosystems) it is the internal characteristics that change over time. Each stage in the process must be distinguishable in terms of these. Being distinguishable means it is recognisable. Childhood should look like childhood; a patch in its maturity stage should have climax species dominating. Thus the pertinent question becomes: what exists in the destination's development that can be recognised, to provide a visible indicator of the stage the resort is in?

The literature on 'resort morphology' indicates that there is in fact a way to at least begin to recognise the stage a resort is in merely on the basis of what the tourism industry development looks like. Wong (1986) has developed a beach resort typology for Malaysia, while Meyer-Arendt *et al*. (1992) have done something similar for the Dominican Republic. Each work pinpointed the scale of buildings (and indirectly the level of capital required to build them) as the key feature of recognition. A synthesis of these two articles enabled the following sequence of 'forms' to be established: 'local', 'domestic', 'international.' A concept borrowed from ecosystem research – 'overtopping' – provides a way to distinguish each. When the resort displays the 'local' form, small buildings one or two stories high will be on the landscape. As the amount of capital for construction increases, buildings will get larger and taller. High-rise hotels along and back of the beach indicate the resort has reached the 'international' form. The 'enclave' form was also specified by these writers; this was quite different in appearance. An enclave was generally constructed somewhat outside the urban resort and typically spread horizontally rather than vertically. Enclaves were considered a variation of the 'international' form on the basis that they required huge amounts of capital to build.

Field research in Kona (Johnston, other volume) indicated that a more complicated form also exists for resorts. In Kona, urban development had begun initially in Kailua town. Just as it seemed as though the 'international' form would become dominant in the town, a large landowner began to construct an enclave several miles down the coast, at Keauhou. For about a decade, the two 'resorts' functioned independently. However, in the late-1970s a condominium construction boom 'linked' them functionally, meaning they were again perceived as one place – Kona. Such a 'linked' form has been noted elsewhere in the literature. Weaver (1986) put forth the concept of 'heliocentrism' to describe this lateral spread of development. Priestley and Mundet (1998: 89) have also used the term 'linked' to discuss the 'formation of ribbon urban development' along the Catalan coast of northern Spain.

One other aspect of the appearance of the resort can also be discussed. It is apparent that each stage will look different not only in terms of the features that can be seen, but also in terms of the type and level of activity that is going on. These changes create an 'ambience' typical at each stage. In the early stages (exploration and involvement) resorts generally have a 'sleepy' appearance. As the development stage begins in earnest a construction 'boom' occurs. Priestley and Mundet (1998: 100) have noted that for Sitges, Spain, after 1950, 'there was a gradual increase in the number of hotels, accelerating into a boom.' Creating a scenario, we can expect to see cranes on the skyline, streets are torn up for infrastructural improvements; the resort is clearly growing fast. One way of visualising that 'consolidation' has occurred is that this boom ends; the resort looks 'finished'. The large hotels are open, pedestrians again have access to sidewalks, trees in planters shade the pedestrians as they walk from shop to shop; the shops themselves display familiar signs as retail chains replace the previous generation of individually owned businesses. For a time, the resort appears stable and prosperous from the spending of midcentric tourists. Eventually, when the stagnation phase is manifest, 'seediness' becomes visible. The appearance of businesses begins to look run-down, empty shop fronts appear, the carpets of the hotels look worn. Da Conceiçáo Gonçalves and Roque Águas (1997: 19) have commented that visible features of stagnation include 'places going out of fashion and the divorce of the resort's image from the environment, especially in matters related to urbanisation and planning.' Ultimately, if the resort continues to decline, this gets worse, but if rejuvenation occurs then new construction, recreating the chaos of the original development stage, may be seen in the resort.

The scale of development that has occurred (producing the specific morphology) and the ambience accompanying this together provide visual cues to the stage in which the case researcher finds the resort. In-and-of-themselves, these are not perfectly adequate ways of ascertaining either the current stage or the sequence through which the resort has passed. However, as a first approximation, these features do provide a means of recognition (see Berry, this volume), something that critics have asserted has been lacking in destination area research.

Mechanisms of stage change

If the destination life cycle represents a basic geographical process, then at least one stage change must occur. Butler (1980) specified five changes in his model. We have just seen that change in the morphology of the tourism industry represents one of the main components of the process. The resort is thus 'dynamic' (e.g. Bianchi, 1994: 186; Laws, 1995: 8) and there are 'turning points' (e.g. Cooper, 1992: 149; Priestley & Mundet, 1998: 96) in the life cycle.

Turning points can be said to be mechanistic in the sense that they *cause* stage changes. Glaser (1978: 99–100) asserted there are two typical types occurring in basic social processes. The first is the 'critical juncture' – an important point in development, the resolution of which pushes the process along. Such a juncture is clearly mechanistic. On the other hand, there are 'blurry transitions', slow changes in a particular characteristic. No single change in the characteristic causes the stage change, however they cumulatively do so over time. Together, these two types of mechanisms can be used to add rigour to analysis of destinations.

When examining other types of processes, it became apparent that mechanisms, whether critical or blurry, occur as events. That is, something happens, the event occurs, and the entity undergoing the process moves into a new stage. Comparison of events in processes indicated they could be abstractly grouped into three classes: 'additions', 'alterations' or 'cessations'. A new type of docking facility built at ports was an addition to the old set of facilities. Product improvement is a form of product alteration. People die when their hearts cease to beat. Research on Kona further indicated that a conceptual distinction can be made between critical 'events' and 'junctures'. The former consist of events that force an interpretation that the stage has changed. For example, in 1949 a new airport enabled (caused) the development of a local-scale morphology, by reducing isolation. A critical juncture, however, represents an issue which, once resolved, may or may not mechanistically cause a stage change.

Butler (1980) did not specify mechanisms of change, rather, he described the state of the internal characteristics in each stage. Several examples of 'critical' events, however, have been noted in the destination area literature. These are nearly always additions. For example, one feature that has been noted (e.g. Douglas, 1997; Russell & Faulkner, 1998; Young, 1983) is the construction, early in the resort's development, of a hotel that is built at higher-than-local standards, and draws a new sort of tourist to the destination. Such a facility might be termed a 'pioneer hotel', and its opening represents a critical event because it catalyses tourism development at the destination. Other additions in the internal characteristics include an airport (da Conceição Gonçalves & Roque

Águas, 1997), 'street works' (LePelley & Laws, 1998) and the design of a strategic plan (Priestley & Mundet, 1998). (Editor's note: the opening of the first casino in Atlantic City (Stansfield, other volume) could be seen as another such critical event, marking the beginning of the rejuvenation stage of that resort.)

While additions might occur more towards the beginning of development at the destination, alterations and cessations occur more in the middle and later stages. Butler (1980) noted for example that local facilities are replaced by those from outside. An alteration has thus occurred when the nationally owned convenience store replaces the corner grocery. Cessations occur when facilities, representing institutional functions, go out of business or reopen as something else not connected to tourism. The conversion of hotels to permanent accommodation, mentioned by Butler, is an obvious example.

The series of important events that produce stage changes can be listed in a table. Da Conceiçáo Gonçalves and Roque Águas (1997: 20) have constructed one along these lines. Such a table can pinpoint when a destination was in the 'core' years of a particular stage or substage, as opposed to when it was in transition to a new one. The table complements the graph of accommodation units as an essential heuristic device for showing interpretations of stage changes.

Macrostructural conditions

Destinations do not exist in isolation from the rest of the world and thus they are not immune from the impacts of what might be termed 'macrostructural conditions'. These are roughly synonymous with 'external events' that have been discussed in the destination area literature (Agarwal, 1994; Haywood, 1986). Macrostructural conditions are important ontologically because they function as structures, meaning they constrain or enable development from outside — the role of climate in ecosuccession, for example. When macrostructural conditions are stable, the resort can progress through its stage sequence within the normal range of variation. Such stability would thus seem to be an enabling factor. Radical change in macrostructural conditions could be either enabling or constraining however, because, depending on the nature of change, the life cycle could be either prolonged or shortened. With respect to the latter, the role of macrostructural conditions is quite important. Major change can often end life cycles. A new innovation can wipe out a product, as cassette disks did to records.

The macrostructural conditions that have been mentioned in the destination area literature have generally been quite important to the particular places they affected. War has been cited as a macrostructural condition in several destinations (e.g. Douglas, 1997; Ioannides, 1992;

Patoskie & Ikeda, 1993; also see Corak, other volume). Meyer-Arendt (1985) discussed the devastating impacts of a hurricane on Grand Isle, Louisiana. While it was certainly a constraint to development in the short term, the hurricane also enabled Grand Isle to make a fresh start. Transportation innovations can create macrostructural change, such as when the railroad improves accessibility (Russell & Faulkner, 1998). When there is change in more than one macrostructural condition simultaneously, there is clearly the potential for the combined impact to create a critical juncture. Priestley and Mundet (1998: 96), for example, noted the following set happened in and to Catalonia during the course of a single season: a strong Spanish currency, a blockage of access to the Spanish coast by French truck drivers, poor weather and a steep increase in accommodation prices through speculation over demand during the 1992 Olympic Games in Barcelona.

A final point about macrostructural conditions emerges from the nexus of the life cycle of the destination with the life cycle of the institution of tourism itself. Several aspects of this are notable. Tourism, a global phenomena, manifests itself at locales. As destinations develop they tend to lose the local quality that made them attractive in the first place, and become generic. As an example, the differences in 'international' form, discussed above as high-rise hotels or enclaves, are more likely related to trends initiated by the global tourism industry than to conditions specific to a particular destination resort. One obvious implication is that the international form of the beach resort during the 1960s and 70s may in fact have seen its day and will no longer figure significantly in the development of resorts in the future. Da Conceição Gonçalves and Roque Águas (1997) commented on another factor of international tourism: how the development of the institution of 'tour operator' enabled improvements in the ability of tourists to make their own travel arrangements, and this was in turn crucial for the Algarve reaching the development stage. Oppermann (1995) discussed the 'travel life cycle' of tourists themselves. The implication is that a destination that appeals to one generation will stagnate as this group ages. Haywood (1998) noted that business and real estate cycles also affect the life cycles of destinations. Expansions and recessions in generating countries have repercussions felt at the resorts at which tourists spend their disposable income.

Typical stage sequence and variability

The last epistemological issue to be considered relates to the typical sequence of stage occurrence and variation from it. This issue has been contentious in the literature and it is clear that the institution of tourism plays out in different ways at different locales.

For basic social processes, Glaser (1978) showed there was no inevitability that stages would always come in exactly the same order, or that they would always take the same amount of time. But he also asserted that a typical order must be discernible in order for the phenomenon to be a distinctive process. In some other processes, however, there can be more than one sequence of stages that is 'typical'. In ecosystems (Noble & Slayter, 1981: 312–313), different plant species have different adaptation strategies. Based on these, they described three typical 'pathways' for stage changes in patches. Some plant species modified their environment in such a way that the offspring of other species could out-compete their own. This is the 'facilitation' pathway, also known as 'relay floristics'. Other plant species did just the opposite, they modified the environment is such a way that only plants that typically grew much later in the sequence could replace them. This is the 'inhibition' pathway and represents an example of how stages can be skipped. Lastly, there was also a 'tolerance' pathway, in which species that grew faster tolerated the presence of slower growing ones. The latter, however, eventually came to dominate.

For resorts, Butler (1980) described a sequence in which each new stage grew out of the previous one more-or-less naturally. Such a progression is the obvious equivalent of the 'facilitational' pathway; perhaps it could be referred to as 'relay touristics'. Butler's description includes a complete set of stages, from the birth to the death of the institution of tourism at the locale, and this set has been shown to be capable of describing destinations that have existed since the dawn of tourism as an institution. On this basis, Butler's set of stages could be considered to represent the 'classical' sequence and the set represents an idealised picture of resort development up to the time of publication. It is idealised, however, for Butler himself cited Cohen's (1979) work on 'organic' versus 'induced' development, which allows for variation from the classical sequence.

Butler's classical sequence has withstood the test of time, and intense scrutiny, quite well. Yet, based on factors discussed above, some suggestions made by later researchers would improve the graph of the model. At the beginning of the life cycle, for example, Young (1983) added two 'pretourism' stages; this fits well with the idea that tourism is only one era in a broader sequent occupance.

Other research has tended to focus on the latter stages in the destinations life cycle. Strapp (1988) and Foster and Murphy (1991) have both noted that, when cottage owners and retirees entered the picture, the resorts tended to stabilise. Getz (1992) noted something similar had occurred at Niagara Falls; in over 200 years neither the Canadian nor American towns on opposite sides of the waterfall had ever really stagnated. He suggested that a 'maturity' stage be recognised.

This seems consistent with the concept of the *longue durée*: as long as the resource underlying the destination's attractiveness remains intact and important, the institution of tourism can last for centuries. Butler's 'consolidation' stage thus really represents but the first phase of 'maturity'. It may be followed by 'stability', without 'stagnation' as Getz (1992) has suggested.

Recently, case research has focused on what has been called the 'poststagnation' stage (Agarwal, 1994, 1997, this volume). This is a state that resembles Butler's rejuvenation, in that planners steer a course that attempts to avoid the rocks of 'decline' by attempting to influence the pattern of additions, alterations and cessations. Juelg (1993: 20) notes that this can occur when there is 'substitution' of an old product by a new one. Overall, such research endorses the state of things that Butler graphically described. In between his rejuvenation and decline path-ways, Butler drew three additional curves to indicate variation would likely occur at this point in time even in the classical model. Agarwal's poststagnation stage would seem to have been best captured by the line segment below rejuvenation, which indicates the resort has had limited success and tourist visitation numbers have begun to increase again.

The poststagnation phase could thus be seen as a part of the maturity stage during which the resort adds some new features and is able to lure people back in slightly greater numbers. Poststagnation could possibly be differentiated from a more-or-less complete rejuvenation on the basis of morphology. Strictly speaking, when rejuvenation occurs, there is sufficient change in the morphology (and ambience) to make the resort seem like a brand new place. Further, the institutional basis of tourism is likely to change dramatically. When Atlantic City rejuvenated, the construction of casinos created the new look, and the behaviour of tourists visiting changed dramatically (Stansfield, other volume). Argu-ably, Atlantic City was no longer a 'seaside' resort because of this change in institutionalised behaviour. In essence, then, a 'rejuvenation' stage represents a second occurrence of 'development' that creates a new identity for the resort.

This point segues toward a different aspect of variation in the typical sequence, stage directionality. In a typical life cycle, the direction is from birth to death. The possibility of a return to youth is discouragingly dim. However, when a graph of tourist arrival numbers dips dramatically then rises, it can look as though stage reversal has occurred. This is something of a false indicator. When it is recalled that the life cycle model represents progression in the institutional development of tourism, particularly those aspects relating to the morphological form (and most particularly numbers of accommodation units) that has been built, then true stage reversal would seem more problematic, though not impossible. To successfully go backwards in stage, a resort with an 'international' morphology would have to somehow revert to a 'domestic' or 'local' form, for example. Unless drastic action is taken by the community, or a macrostructural event such as a war occurs, it would be difficult for a destination to effectively recreate an earlier stage. Success at the poststagnation phase of development might, on the other hand, lead to a second occurrence of the stability phase, within the longer maturity stage.

Synthesis

A synthesis of these ontological and epistemological points is now in order. The first section will discuss features of a 'revised' model. The second will elaborate on a suggested 'formula' for utilising these theoretical shorings in future research.

Butler's (1980) classical sequence of stages has been redrawn in Figure 1.3. The title of the figure indicates, first of all, that the revised model is intended to theorise development at a locale akin to a single destination, such as a resort town. It is not necessarily intended to portray institutional development at very large spatial scales, where multisite tourism development has occurred. It is also not necessarily intended to model stages occurring at small scales, such as a theme park, or at destinations visited by excursionists or others who fall outside of the generally accepted definitions of 'tourist'. It is anticipated that future

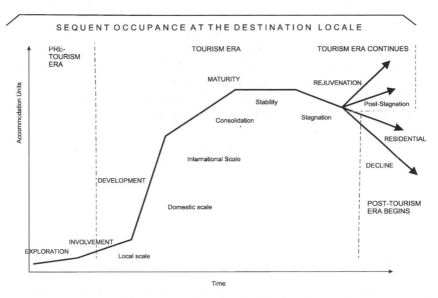

Figure 1.3 A revised version of Butler's (1980) 'classical' sequence of stage for a resort town

research will show that several variations of the model will exist, in addition to this 'classical' pattern.

Within the figure, tourism is shown to be just one of at least three eras in the longer sequent occupance. The pretourism era is theorised to extend past the exploration stage into involvement, on the basis that whatever institution developed earlier will continue to dominate up to that time. The beginning of a tourism era does not necessarily coincide with a tourism stage change because a critical juncture occurring in the institution that was dominating previously may be responsible for the latter's decline. Such a juncture can happen at any time and is not necessarily related to tourism development. The tourism era itself will 'classically' carry on through the maturity stage, which may also include a poststagnation phase. Clearly, if rejuvenation occurs this will extend the tourism era. The post-tourism era begins when a new institution begins to dominate at the locale. This may occur in the residential stage, during which time former tourists become residents (perhaps only seasonally). Such a change may be a blurry transition and the exact year it occurs may be hard to pinpoint. The post-tourism era may of course also begin some time during the decline stage.

The y-axis variable represents the number of accommodation units available at the destination, rather than the number of tourist arrivals. This replacement is made on the basis that the number of rooms in hotels, motels, condominiums, etc. is less likely to fluctuate. The S-curve of development has been replaced by line segments showing the typical rate of increase for specific stages. The slope of any particular segment is not meant to be taken literally as shown. It is meant to show a relative relationship of 'speeding up' or 'slowing down' of accommodation availability with respect to an earlier or later stage. The breaking up of the line into specific segments symbolically represents the occurrence of mechanisms – critical events or blurry transitions – that are interpreted as indicators of stage change (Berry, this volume). The time line, which shows the length of time each stage will exist, is completely arbitrary.

The different forms of resort morphology are located along the graph, as phases (substages) of development. Their precise location along the graph can be expected to vary somewhat. For example, it is obviously possible that, given the right circumstances, a much larger 'local' morphology may be constructed during a development stage. The 'linked' form has not been shown on the basis that it can occur whenever two or more spatially separated tourism regions become integrated into one larger destination. The maturity stage has been expanded to include phases of consolidation, stability, stagnation and poststagnation. Rejuvenation is here considered a separate stage on the basis that new resource development will significantly change the institutionalised nature of the destination.

In the previous section of the paper, the seven epistemological elements were not prioritised. It is suggested that all are important and that each should be incorporated into the analysis of any particular destination. This could likely be done in many ways. To date, all case studies have utilised 'stage sequence' as the organising principle. The discussion begins at exploration and ends at whichever stage the research indicates the destination has attained in the present. A chronological presentation of this nature has the linearity of time as its strength and may continue to be the most efficient way to illuminate the *longue durée* of tourism.

A variation of this type of presentation can be suggested, on the basis that two analyses can inform case research. First of all, a 'boundary analysis' – which tackles the problems 'what is the region?' and 'what type of region is it?' – should be done to eliminate or at least minimise issues of spatial fetishism and multisite development. This permits 'comparing apples with apples', and will facilitate comparative research.

The second issue concerns the stage sequence. To get at this completely, two analyses need to be done as part of the research. First, there must be an 'analysis of mechanisms', which identifies and justifies the critical events and blurry transitions that will be used to interpret that one stage or phase has succeeded another in the sequence. The heuristic devices – a table of specific mechanisms and a graph of accommodation units – work together here to produce a more complete picture. Photos of the destination at different time periods would complete the triangulation.

The second analysis involves obtaining a complete understanding of the institutional development of tourism at the destination. This can be called a 'pathway analysis' and incorporates the remaining elements (internal characteristics, resort morphology, users, macrostructural conditions) so as to bring out aspects of facilitation, tolerance or inhibition (or some different pathway type) that have occurred.

These analyses were done for research on Kona, Hawai'i Island, and are presented in the other volume. The structure is of course an experiment in style and only time will tell if it is acceptable. Its strength, however, is that researchers are forced to explicitly consider spatial and temporal boundaries, as well as the factors that have impinged upon them. This method also enables a certain amount of projection into the future, by establishing the internal and external conditions that are affecting the institution of tourism in the immediate present.

Conclusion

This paper has attempted to shore up Butler's (1980) original work, not prove it wrong. As can be seen, Figure 1.3 above is not that different from Butler's 'classic' model. As models, neither will capture the totality of the life cycle variation that occurs at destinations. Rather, they represent but one of many possible patterns of development. Instant resorts will graph differently because they begin in the development stage. Destinations that become residential may enter the post-tourism era sooner. Transport innovations that enable excursionists to dominate alter the *longue durée* in a different way. The challenge is to identify further patterns that represent fairly pervasive ways that resorts develop. The three just mentioned are hardly likely to be the only ones found.

This paper has also intended to show that relying solely on a graphical model is no longer adequate to study a pervasive process. To fully understand the *longue durée* of the institutional development of tourism, it is necessary to expand research to explicitly incorporate study of mechanisms and pathways. This is the best way to get at the 'how' questions asked by epistemology. Answering these questions will hopefully drive destination area life cycle analysis in the future. The use of examples from the destination life cycle literature has attempted to show the width of the gaps in theory that exist in many places. So, to come full circle, it is perhaps best to end by saying that we have not yet learned everything about this topic. Rather, we have hardly begun to learn what there is to know.

Chapter 2

Legitimising the TALC as a Theory of Development and Change

K. MICHAEL HAYWOOD

Introduction

The notion that tourism areas or destinations pass through a life cycle suggests that they are living entities. Indeed tourism researchers, over the past two decades, have dedicated tremendous effort in profiling and documenting the life stages and vitality of tourist areas and attractions around the world. Armed with economic, environmental and socio-cultural impact performance data, their evidence suggests that in their formative years tourism areas provide tremendous promise. During the aging process, however, they become unhealthy and unproductive, and proceed eventually to premature demise. Articulated in a strategic way, destinations pass through periods of expansion, but, along the way and over time, ruin their resource base, undermine their competitive advantages, and subvert their value creation activities. Long-term sustainability is compromised. Attempts to improve the quality of life of the host community, to provide high quality visitor experiences, and to maintain a vibrant and supportive environment, become increasingly difficult to achieve and maintain (WTO, 1993).

While it is presumptuous to declare that destinations die or disappear altogether, the life-to-death framework of the Tourism Area Life Cycle (TALC) model has garnered 'qualified' empirical acceptance. The model has been described as simple, comprehensible, sufficiently intuitive and is purported to have descriptive as well as prescriptive power. Within the industry, however, the TALC concept is virtually ignored; it rarely receives mention at mainstream industry conferences; and is used infrequently as a planning and management tool. For example, in gathering data for the report, 'Research Issues Facing the Canadian Tourism Industry' (CTC, 1997), the author actually commented that life cycle concerns had not received a single mention from respondents. Is this a function of ignorance, disinterest or disbelief; or is the industry simply following Alfred North Whitehead's admonishment: 'Seek simplicity and distrust it'? Whatever the reason, life cycle researchers cannot afford to ignore practitioners' suspicions about and dismissals of the life cycle. Greater awareness as to their thinking, language and behaviour with respect to development and change within tourism areas and tourism organisations is required. For example, if the industry is predisposed to mastering the tasks of the present while struggling with the difficulties associated with pre-empting the future, can the life cycle be used as a tool for learning in a complex world? How can the TALC model be used to demonstrate relevance to practitioners? Can it reflect a more dynamic systems view of the industry in relation to society and the environment – each of which creates its own survival and improvement mechanisms?

Lack of acceptance and pragmatic usefulness within the industry implies that TALC may need to be reconceptualised. Operational ambiguity must be overcome. For example, if destinations are to avoid the pitfalls associated with growth and development, the stages of, and states within, the life cycle need to be better understood, anticipated and managed. This means that the major underlying causes and conditions of various stages, and the accompanying transitions, need to be appreciated (Haywood, 1986). Because stages imply entrenched behaviours, these must be identified. And, if behaviours represent root cause of movement to another stage, attention should be focused on how they can be altered. Transitions to new and hopefully preferred states can be painful, so the knowledge provided through life cycle analysis must be insightful and meaningful.

In unravelling the mysteries of TALC, this chapter discusses tourism as a 'living industry' and the implications of this concept. Seeing tourism areas as living entities, composed of formal and informal organisations and a network of relationships, implies that they create their own processes – they change only if people are willing and able to change them. Life cycles, however, represent only one model for learning about and appreciating the complexities of change. As such, other theories that broaden our understanding of development and change in tourism areas are explored in relationship with the life cycle. In embracing the dynamic qualities of tourism areas, some of the life cycle research explaining the evolution of tourism areas is then put into context.

Tourism as a Living System

The over-riding impression gained from reading critiques of tourism is that, as an industry, it has become a mechanistic system for making money; created by others; controlled by its operators; governed by relentless pursuit of management goals; and susceptible to becoming run down, unless it is rebuilt. Little wonder that some people have developed a strong antipathy to tourism organisations – many of which are not seen as being responsive to the needs and goals of communities.

Nevertheless tourism areas or destinations must be seen for what they are – broadly based composites or clusters of people (hosts and visitors who are living systems) as well as organisations and governing bodies (also living systems), each striving to be viable. While little thought is ever given to the inevitability of decline – the self-fulfilling prophecy that the TALC predicts – there is a need to bring about changes in the way communities and organisations pursue their power and influence, and shape tourism areas. This requires a shift in thinking; hence the need for concepts and ideas that over-ride cynicism, and build hope, vitality and the ability to learn.

A tourism area as a living entity is such a notion. Consider the fact that tourism takes advantage of and operates within dynamic ecosystems that are essential sources of resources and services to the industry as well as society as a whole. On the environmental front, it has been commonly assumed that tourism businesses do not take responsibility for the natural resource base, and thereby take it for granted. Protection and conservation are often seen as peripheral activities or at worst major threats to the challenge of maximising corporate advantage in an increasingly competitive global marketplace. Environmental performance is often a matter of regulatory compliance (Crosbie & Knight, 1995; Paehlke & Torgerson, 1990), an activity that is often considered by many as adding nothing but economic cost, and legal and political complications to the corporate bottom line. This set of beliefs, however, is under siege. Destinations and tourism organisations recognise that environmental performance confers competitive advantage. Over the course of the past decade, a growing number of tourism associations and corporations have pioneered new policies and guidelines for integrating the environment into their overall strategies and for simultaneously improving their environmental, industry and business performance.

Broadened strategic self-interest in the environment is bringing about many conceptual breakthroughs. One of these is industrial ecology. It asks managers, policymakers and planners to treat environmental problems as design problems. Industrial ecology views firms, and industry supply chains, as living systems participating in the larger biological and physical systems of the earth's biosphere. The contention is that use of technological innovation, and product and process design, can ameliorate environmental problems. Indeed, a key to using design to reduce industry's environmental impacts is to learn from nature. Viewing businesses as living systems (Clippinger, 1999; de Geus, 1997) offers considerable value for tourism areas whose dependency on the sustainability of the natural environment is becoming better appreciated. Similarly, there appears to be value in using natural ecosystems as models for organisational and tourism sustainability, even for the determination of appropriate business policies and strategies (see Hall, this volume; Ravenscroft & Hadjihambi, this volume). For example, tourism areas and tourism organisations recognise that they must become more adept at overcoming loss of competitiveness due to lack of adaptation or out-performance by rivals (see Papatheodorou, this volume).

The applicability of industrial ecology to tourism can be approached in various ways, two of which seem relevant in this chapter. The first suggests that ecology provides a useful blueprint or template for designing destination and business strategies. The second is to think of lessons from ecology as providing constraints, or boundary conditions. How useful are these viewpoints to tourism? First of all, insights into ecology derive from thermodynamics, evolution, and plant and animal physiology and behaviour. The mode of analysis is complex systems analysis (Russell, this volume). While it is impossible here to even summarise what ecology teaches, we do know that natural systems are inherently unstable; that stability is sought through predator/prey interactions; that the driving force behind succession is catastrophe; and that ecological and evolutionary systems do not promote equality or justice. Existing tourism systems that appear to be modelled on such a nature-based, competitively driven system are all too common; and have been subjected to immense derision (Pattullo, 1996). While this version of nature as a blueprint for tourism areas touches a nerve, and is graphically portrayed by the TALC, it does not reveal the entire picture.

A more appropriate line of inquiry might be exploration of nature as a process, rather than nature as the product. Constraints are fundamental to this process. Constraints are the catalysts that begin the process of development of any ecosystem or any economy. In business, for example, constraints are the cost of doing business. They stimulate the adaptations that lead to evolution of the system. The process of evolution has allowed nature to use limited resources to generate a continuous evolution of matter into forms which overall have followed a progressive direction, even though significant back-tracking is often the norm. If tourism businesses and destinations are to become sustainable, the study of industrial ecology implores recognition of a wider range of constraints that impinge on tourism – social, cultural, ecological, environmental, economic, political, legal, technological and temporal. By recognising these boundary constraints, and adapting to them rationally and effectively, it is expected that sustainability is more likely to be realisable (Hawken *et al.*, 1999).

Constraints are also important because they stimulate feedback. Tourism organisations and destinations that identify their constraints and costs, and feed the information back as quickly and efficiently as possible, should be better able to adapt to the limits. Feedback in a business system or in an ecosystem stimulates a domino set of ecological principles that starts with adaptation. This in turn leads to specialisation where organisms become differentiated and perform particular activities. Specialisation then leads to diversification of an ecosystem as different organisms proliferate. Diversification leads to more complex ecosystems. The more complex ecosystems with more specialists move from competitive ecosystems toward more cooperative ecosystems because there are more organisms working in specialised functions as part of this larger whole. Cooperation between elements in ecosystems leads to synergy, which then leads to those magical combinations from which new qualities emerge.

In the tourism industry these adaptation processes, along with increased competition, have occurred with alarming speed in recent years, and will continue as the industry evolves. With boundary conditions changing so rapidly, however, it could be argued that the relevance of these ecological principles is becoming more critical. If social, cultural and environmental benefits are rare and inadvertent by-products of competitive market dynamics, application of industrial ecology has the potential to provide deliberate incorporation of environ-mental, social and cultural values into corporate management strategies and the design of tourism products and processes. Similarly, as more tourism organisations recognise that their boundary conditions are also about people they employ, communities in which they do business, relationships with these communities, as well as their social and sacred responsibilities in doing so, they will gain knowledge that should alert them to the unsustainability of current business models.

While the number of tourism areas and organisations attempting to develop comprehensive 'tourism ecology' models is unknown, there exists a distinctive challenge in helping industry leaders and managers develop a holistic world view, and in avoiding the inevitable 'policy resistance'. In other words, the difficulty in changing existing decision-making capabilities that are inherently static, narrow and reductionist, to capabilities that encourage learning about complexity, and thinking more systematically, must be addressed (Sterman, 2000). Translating 'tourism ecology' into executable tourism policies and strategies requires determination of distinct advantages, plus recognition that personal, interbusiness and destination management transformation, as well as structural and process changes, must be undertaken. While it can be argued that the competitive dynamic of the marketplace has always driven smart managers to search for ways to achieve efficiencies, dematerialise production processes and eliminate waste products, these goals are primarily self-serving. There needs to be resolve in dealing with and accepting responsibility for new, broader and more complex problem sets that are more socially, culturally and environmentally grounded. Self-interest will not disappear and will still be demonstrated;

however, as tourism areas and organisations recognise the need to extend their responsibilities to building community goodwill, creating business relationship value, and helping build distinctive competitive advantages, they are more likely to appreciate that the success of a tourism area depends on the ability to create and distribute wealth and value to all primary stakeholder groups (Jawahar & McLaughlin, 2001). If the obstacles to accomplishing this mandate are to be surmountable, new ways of thinking and behaving must be found.

Adding value to the tourism experience, by minimising environmental footprints and sociocultural dislocations, demands determination of interdependent environmental, social, profit and biodiversity priorities. Interdependency, however, necessitates a more systematic approach to tourism management – in effect the creation of networks where knowledge is shared, systems-thinking prevalent, and innovation activated. In other words, a paradigm shift towards the strategic renewal of entire tourism areas may be required. Such a renewal calls for the simultaneous harmonisation of continuity and change at community, as well as organisational levels. The process for making this happen, organisational learning, is fundamental to achieving sustainable competitive advantage and requires application of knowledge management techniques (Haywood, 2001). Learning takes time and is thought to move through four subprocesses – intuiting, interpreting, integrating and institutionalising. At the community level, cooperation among individuals, groups and organisations is required (Crossan *et al*., 1999). To make this happen, everyone in a tourism area needs to be alerted to the fact that the delivery of tourism experiences at the community level necessitates the cooperation of 'extended enterprises' (Raia, 1993) throughout the tourism value chain. This suggests that the ultimate source of both community and organisational wealth is determined through relationships with critical stakeholders, not simply transactions with visitors and suppliers. The critical challenge, therefore, is recognition of the mutual interests among the stakeholders, leading to the development of consistent and supportive policies, and strategies for dealing with them at different points in time.

Theories of Development and Change

Based on the premise that tourism is a 'living industry', taking place within living communities, it is evident that development of the industry (through stages of conception, creation, configuration, competition and conclusion) results in ongoing change of tourism areas. The industry and all the organisations within it are also changing. Organisational members reweave their webs of belief and habits of action in response to local circumstances and new experiences. Indeed managers and planners influence and intervene in a continuous stream of organisational actions. Their systematic stream of interactions and situated initiatives, however, seems at odds with the typical set of episodic events characterised by the TALC. Appreciation of the constancy, content, character, consistency and cause of change of tourism areas and organisations is strengthened when viewed from a variety of theoretical perspectives on the nature of change. The benefits are distinctly two fold. First of all, change becomes a more centralised object of study, thereby deepening understanding of the development of destinations or tourism organisations. Secondly, change, or more precisely, changing, is a management preoccupation that requires intensive appreciation of the process of transformation – the manifest adoption of ever-present and evolving states of being and behaviour, as well as the process of moving from one state to another. As the title of this chapter suggests, TALC studies cannot afford to marginalise questions of transformation; therefore, an appropriate objective of this chapter is to provide the rationale for moving this process closer to centre-stage.

In accomplishing this objective, consider that destinations throughout the world, as well as the majority of public and private, visitor-serving organisations, are constantly seeking to understand the conditions underlying tourism development, growth and competitive advantage. While the basic parameters are known and becoming better articulated (Ritchie & Crouch, 2000), a turbulent operating environment can render today's competitive advantage as tomorrow's albatross. If history and some TALC studies are to be a guide, current practices and business models that confer advantages for today's most successful destinations do so only because of particular factors at work, under particular conditions, at a particular time. Clearly these advantages, many of them thought to be unassailable, are proving to be transitory because the underlying factors change. For example, TALC research has shown that tourism activity can cause any part of the bundle of tangible and intangible resources attributed to a destination and the composite of organisations within it, to become overburdened, stressed and abused. If these resources are not protected and/or maintained, their deterioration is magnified.

Furthermore, the very existence of competitive advantage can set in motion creative innovations that, as competitive destinations strive to build market presence and predominance, cause the advantage to dissipate. Migration of value (Slyworthy, 1996) also occurs when visitor priorities change, or if there are failures in offering visitors what they want or expect (Butler, other volume). These and other developments and changes affect a destination's sustainability (Russo, other volume). Economic viability is threatened when the ability of tourism organisations to earn profits or decent returns on investment is curtailed or nullified – a risk that is enhanced due to the seasonal nature of tourism and the sensitivity of the travelling public to perceived safety and security concerns. If a negative situation persists, reinvestment may be abandoned, premature organisational exit from the industry may be hastened, and infrastructure improvements may have to be put on hold – life cycles become shortened.

Industry leaders, strategists, planners and managers, therefore, are anxious to attune themselves to the underlying developments and changes both within and outside their destination. They have cultivated their own understanding of the processes and progress of all the factors that underlie development, competitive advantage, sustainability and value creation over time. The predominant school of thought, which guides their thinking and decision making, can be characterised as a philosophical doctrine that argues that purpose or goal is the determining factor in guiding development and change; hence emphasis is placed on strategic processes (Flagestad & Hope, 2001; Ritchie & Crouch, 2000; Tse & Elwood, 1990). As a teleological theory, the aspiration and will of managers, developers, planners and investors are revered as the prime drivers of change. The associated tasks of crafting, implementation and achievement of vision, mission, goals, objectives and strategies, however, present complex challenges; their realisation is often thwarted. Nevertheless managers will often state that it is the setbacks and nagging sense of dissatisfaction with current results that energises movement towards goals and outcomes. In the constant pursuit of solutions to resolve problems and capitalise on opportunities, practitioners are constantly battling with processes of transformation. Perfection is sought through such activities as product and process innovation, benchmarking, total quality management, branding, business model reconfiguration and re-engineering.

An inherent aspect of these teleological approaches is the constraining of progress due to recognised limits on action. A destination's environment and resources determine what can be accomplished; hence Ritchie and Crouch's (2000) warning that 'competitiveness is illusory without sustainability'. Some of these constraints are embodied in prerequisites of institutions and prominent stakeholders. Influences in the external environment also exist; they frequently create instabilities that push destinations and tourism organisations toward new development paths. For example, it has been argued that the collective power of external forces in shaping the success, and the ultimate sustainability, of any tourist area is based on a wide variety of factors:

- rivalry among existing tourist areas;
- development and development of new tourist areas;
- substitutes for the tourism/travel experience;

- environmentalists and concerned publics who oppose tourism or tourism development;
- transportation companies, tour operators, travel intermediaries, lodging chains and suppliers – their bargaining power;
- tourists – their needs, wants, perceptions, expectations, price/value sensitivity and satisfaction with the tourism experience; and
- government, political and regulatory bodies and forces (Haywood, 1986).

Taking a cue from the prior section, these forces represent boundary or operating conditions that demand adaptation or innovative response. Goals can be reconstructed and enacted, even though specific trajectories are not anticipated. The typical approach is to articulate a set of possible paths that are subjected to norms of decision and action rationality to prescribe certain paths (Brunsson, 1982).

In the study of the sustainability of tourism areas, it seems unfortunate that attention has not been attuned to explaining how teleological theories account for change and development, despite the fact that the strategic management literature is rich in its appreciation for, and conceptualising of, these transitional processes. With well hyped promises for economic development, the need for a dynamic theory of the role of tourism organisations in economic development is vital. TALC studies point to the importance of a demand-side perspective, but attribution of development and change in accordance with the market-place has not been thoroughly explored. Even an understanding of economic development from the supply side is inadequately appreciated (Ionnides & Debbage, 1998; Prideaux, 2000), even though TALC studies do pay attention to how resources, particularly natural resources, are accessed and (over)used. Similarly, little is known about economic development both as an iterative process of creating and realising (and eventually losing) value through resource combinations and exchanges, and as an interactive process between tourism organisations and relevant institutions that may, or may not, be part of a particular tourism area.

As geographic regions that are subjected to colliding events and forces, tourism areas contain, as well as interact, in pluralistic worlds of stakeholders with differing values and agendas. These worlds compete as well as cooperate with each other in their individual struggles for survival; therefore there is a dialectic theory in play here. It suggests that stability and change are explained by reference to the balance of power between competing entities (Papatheodorou, this volume). Those struggles and accommodations that seek to maintain the status quo among opposing forces are said to seek coherence, and thereby produce stability. Change occurs, however, when competing forces, values or events gain sufficient power and momentum to confront and engage the status quo.

For example, the success of many remote destinations is virtually dependent on airlift. When it is cancelled, a destination is likely to mount a vigorous challenge. While there can be no reassurance that the dialectical conflict can produce a creative resolution, either side may mobilise sufficient power to replace the status quo. The destination may face a situation in which its tourism business model may have to be radically altered, and its competitive advantages compromised. Win–lose outcomes are not uncommon in the development of tourism, particularly during the more vulnerable periods of early development. Destination strategies, therefore, have to be carefully crafted during the life cycle in order to recognise the organisational interdependencies that exist at given points in time. The interactions and network effects that dominate tend to determine the sustainability of destinations. Growth and development of destinations is dependent on the careful nurturing of relationships with an extended number of stakeholders, who are increasingly being recognised as the ultimate sources of destination wealth and longevity (Post *et al.*, 2002).

It was previously suggested that development results in cumulative change in the structure and strategies of the tourism industry and the community at large. From an evolutionary point of view, it can be argued that these changes occur as a recurrent, cumulative and probabilistic progression of variation, selection and retention (Cooper, 1992; Hannan & Freeman, 1977). Variation, or the creation of new tourism organisations, would be explained as emerging in a random way – an 'emergent strategy' in teleological terms. Selection of tourism organisations would occur principally through competition for scarce resources – money, land, employees. Decision makers in the destination would be seen as playing a critical role in selecting those organisations that best fit the resource base and community. Retention, then, would be argued as involving forces that perpetuate and maintain certain tourism organisations and organisational practices. As such, evolutionary theory suggests that the motor driving development and change could be more or less prescribed, in that the actuarial probabilities of the changing demographic characteristics of, let's say, organisational populations in a destination, might be specified or anticipated. This is particularly true when it comes to determining the potential for new accommodation businesses (Haywood, 2003). Although prediction of whether a particular destination or organisation will survive or fail cannot be predicted, the overall population persists and evolves through time, according to specified organisational dynamics.

There are other evolutionary theories suggesting that destinations evolve in terms of how traits of behaviour are inherited (Ravenscroft & Hadjihambi, this volume), the rate of change and the unit of analysis. For example, it has been suggested that traits are acquired within a generation through learning and imitation (Burgelman, 1991). Consequently, it could be argued that as destinations embrace the knowledge economy and capitalise on creating competitive advantage through intellectual capital, they are likely to attempt to create change in continuous, gradual, Darwinian manners ('logical incrementalism' according to Quinn, 1982), but also at saltation rates, as explained in Gould's (1989) punctuated equilibrium theory. For instance, most destinations and organisations experience critical junctures (states of revolution) in which there is rapid or quantum transformation (activation or deactivation) of the industry; that is, there can be a massive improvement in infrastructure, addition of a major tourism attraction, crises or chaotic change in supply or logistic networks (Miller & Friessen, 1984), each of which are likely to lead to major alterations to a destination's inherent or essential characteristics (see Johnston, Russell, this volume).

While the preceding theories of development and change are not uncommon, the prevailing theory, and metaphor of choice, to depict and explain the development of destinations, from their inception to their demise, remains the TALC. In accordance with the principles of life cycles, change is expected to be imminent; that is, destinations move through a progression of change events in a unitary sequence of stages or phases. The life cycle theory posits that every destination has within it an underlying form, logic or programme that regulates this process of change. Thus in an early stage of development the form that is latent, premature and homogeneous becomes progressively more realised, mature and differentiated. External events and processes are expected to influence the way the destination expresses itself, but these are expected to be mediated by all the rules, logic and programmes (in the natural and material world) that govern development. Because each stage is more or less prefigured, there is a historic sequence of events, each of which is a precursor to, and sets the stage for, each succeeding stage. While TALC researchers might disagree on the number of stages (paradigm shifts) in the life of a tourist area, these stages are few and far between. The implication, both implicit and explicit, is that change is the exception, and stability is the norm. Consequently, the bulk of TALC research has been oriented toward providing synoptic accounts of 'exceptional' change in tourism areas. These accounts view change as an accomplished event whose key features, variations, causal antecedents and consequences, need to be explored and described. Such knowledge to date has been generated primarily by viewing change from the perspective of outsiders, whose common source of information may be statistical data bases, observation and/or perceptual studies of change. As such, TALC takes the form of a stage model in which the tourism area is shown to have distinct states at different points in time. In tourist lingo, snapshots of key dimensions are taken at different points in time (Greenwood & Hinings, 1996; Tushman & Romanelli, 1985).

The knowledge generated from most TALC research, indispensable as it is, suffers from limitations. Given its synoptic nature, it does not do justice to the open-ended microprocesses that underlay the trajectories described; it does not capture the distinguishing features of change, that is, its fluidity, pervasiveness, open-endedness and indivisibility. Intellectually, TALC studies portray change by transforming it into a succession of positions, but fail to capture the distinctiveness of the voyage from point A to point B (see Wheeller, other volume, for a discussion of this point in the context of Elvis Presley and ecolodges, editor's note). That is, the change that transpires during the journey is ignored. It is reduced to a series of static positions, and the distinguishing features of change are lost from view. The process of development and change, therefore, remains elusive. It is little wonder that industry leaders, managers and planners, who experience daily reality from within the industry, find little in TALC that helps them navigate through a sea of ever-changing tides, winds and operating conditions. Their kit bag of tools, indicators and performance measures, and hence their mindset, remains teleological, and is predominantly located in the strategic management camp.

If TALC researchers are interested in moving toward a deeper knowledge of configurations of the cycle and the true nature of change, the microprocesses of change and the interaction of the precipitating and enabling dynamics, in response to pressures to change needs, cannot be ignored (Greenwood & Hinings, 1996). There remain hundreds of unanswered questions in understanding the life cycles of tourism areas. What makes tourism organisations and destinations move from and change archetypes? How are new archetypes or business models uncovered and legitimised? By whom, and using what means? How is change actually accomplished? Leaders, managers and planners want to be assured that change programmes will work on any given occasion; they do not work themselves out. Change programmes work insofar as they are fine-tuned and adjusted by people in particular contexts. Change, therefore, is an on-going process; it is an ongoing improvisation (Orlikowski, 1996). TALC theorists and practitioners might be advised, therefore, to adjust their vocabulary and thought processes – from the concept of 'change' to the process of 'changing'.

Because the TALC is a concept or framework still in transition and evolution, the predominant teleological and dialectical, evolutionary and life cycle theories of development and change need not be considered as opposing views; each can provide consistent accounts of change processes in destinations and tourism organisations. If, over time, a destination moves from one state or stage of development to the next, then strategy making and conflict resolution become two of many processes for managing changing conditions and making transitions within, between or among states. In other words, transformation may have evolutionary, dialectical and teleological root causes. It is an inevitable and on-going consequence of every stage, in which there is time for both coherence and change. For example, the employment and use of strategy is rarely about change at all; it is about coherence and continuity – whether as a deliberate plan to establish patterns of behaviour, or as an emergent pattern by which such patterns get established. In other words, while the process of strategy making may set out to change the direction a destination is taking, the resulting strategies stabilise that direction. As a lifecycle theory, TALC, to some extent, reflects this reality. It implies the relative stability of strategy (vision, mission, goals, objectives, plans) within given states, interrupted by occasional and sometimes disruptive leaps to the next state.

Up to this point in time researchers have portrayed and examined the TALC as a particular, or ideal, type of development and change. While many tourism scholars use the life cycle (TALC) as a metaphor of change, there is evidence to suggest that TALC is, and could be, used more effectively to represent a composite of development and change theories. Considering the inherent inadequacies associated with the life cycle – indeed with all the change theories – it seems appropriate to ask where and when these theories might best be applied. The rationale is obvious. The context of development and change extends over space and time, so it is possible that various engines of change apply at any given time, and if combined could provide greater explanatory power. Development and change are also influenced by diverse organisations and people, both inside as well as outside the destination, each imparting their own momentum and level of urgency to the development process. In the scientific literature, precedents for these combinational or interaction theories are quite extensive. In the corporate world two examples come to mind. In explaining the evolution of technologies, Clark (1985) proposed the interplay of teleological and lifecycle engines of change nested within the overall life cycle progression from product to process. And, in what is now recognised as an extremely influential attempt to explain the organising process in dynamic fashion, Weick (1979) noted the interaction of life cycle, teleological and evolutionary engines.

The TALC has potential to become a nesting ground for alternate, though complementary, change theories. TALC has the appropriate intellectual heritage: its hitherto focus on the fragility and ruination of a tourism area's resource base suggests a life cycle of development–growth that sows its own seeds of its destruction. Secondly, as a localised industry, numerous tourism organisations, including their products and services, are also subjected to life cycles; these in turn affect the performance and sustainability of the destination. If TALC became a nest for other theories of development and change, however, there would be a necessity to work out the relationships among them. The macro and micro links would have to be specified, particularly during various stages in the development and growth of the tourism area. A confounding factor, to be reconciled, would be the sequence of change events. For example, life cycle and evolutionary theories incorporate *a priori*, prescribed sequences of events – the channelling of development in specific directions, while maintaining and incrementally adapting in stable and predictable ways. Teleological and dialectical theories, on the other hand, operate in a constructive manner – change that is unprecedented and novel, and often represents discontinuous and unpredictable departures from the past.

Similarly, when it comes to explaining patterns of relative stability and change, alterations in the relative balance between constructive and prescribed engines of change would have to be explained. For example, during the initial stages of development, destinations are typically comprised of small, entrepreneurial, start-up organisations, especially in an emerging industry. A constructive engine is at work as these organisations and the destination depend on entrepreneurial leaders, visionary strategies and rather simple structures. As the entrepreneurial-driven destination ages, grows and settles into maturity, informal structures give way to more formalised ones under so-called professional managers who depend on planning processes. Over time a more prescribed engine of change seems to come into play, and may suppress or dampen organisational variety and development, as the industry begins to act more rigidly and predictably.

Prescribed and constructive engines of change suggest that every stage of a destination's life cycle implies a mixture of entrenched and idiosyncratic behaviours and patterns of activity. Most of the time, however, a destination appears to remain in some stable form and can be described according to specific behaviours; it adopts a particular form of structure matched to a particular kind of context which causes it to engage in particular behaviours and activities that give rise to a particular set of strategies. In tourism enterprises the primary goal is to focus upon and master the present – attract visitors and satisfy them. In evaluating performance, lagging indicators tend to be sufficient to determine if the destination and tourism organisations are on track; however, periods of stability may be deceptive. They hide ongoing processes of transformation, and may be interrupted by chaotic or unanticipated patterns of change (Faulkner & Russell, 1997; Russell, this volume). The extent to which institutional routines evolve and change over the course of time may determine whether constructive engines of change can catch hold and dominate. As many destinations and tourism organisations are discovering, anticipatory tools and devices are required to succeed in the new task of pre-empting the future – leading, not lagging, indicators are required to guide the way (Berry, this volume). Strategy making in this situation becomes a reframing device in order to change behaviours, develop new competencies, and make the transition to new states.

The key to maintaining competitive advantage and value creation activities is to sustain stability or at least adaptable strategic change most of the time, but periodically to recognise the need for transformation and to manage disruptive processes without destroying the destination or organisation. Accordingly, if transforming processes are to work, managers and consultants who practice or prescribe transformation must thoroughly appreciate the details and nuances of change inherent throughout the successive stages of the life cycle. The prescriptive nature of TALCs, as self-fulfilling prophecies, would be an anathema.

Part 2

Spatial Relationships and the TALC

R.W. BUTLER

As was discussed in the other volume (see The Origins of the TALC), the conceptual development of the model owed much to this author's geographical interest and training. Geography is, in my opinion, the ideal discipline from which to study tourism. This is partly because tourism is by necessity a spatial subject, it involves, at the bare minimum, the movement of people from one location to another and back again, and secondly because geography is a synthesising discipline and tourism is very much a multidisciplinary subject. It involves people and their interaction with other people as well as with the nonhuman environment and the impacts of people upon the settings for tourism. Where people go when they are being tourists, what they find attractive about the locations visited, and how those locations are modified for and by tourism are all elements that are central to the TALC.

The earliest form of the TALC had a much greater spatial focus than the 1980 published version and in a sense speculated on the spatial implications of a destination having gone through its 'cycle' and reached the point of diminishing attractivity and market appeal, in other words, its decline as a tourist destination. The simplistic assumption was that entrepreneurs and investors would seek to develop new resorts close to the declining one, as the general setting and existing access infrastructure would be amenable to development. The regional attributes of climate, and natural and cultural heritage would presumably still attract tourists while a new 'greenfield' site would offer lower land costs and the opportunity to develop more modern facilities, thus making the new resort more attractive than its older competitor. At the microlevel one could anticipate the development of and subsequent changes in a destination's morphology, as suggested by Barratt (1958) and Stansfield and Rickert (1970), although these aspects were not discussed to any degree in the original model.

In its published form, the primary emphasis of the TALC was the pattern and process of development of a tourist destination, described in terms of stages of development. The theoretical origins of this process were the Product Life Cycle model, whose origins and contributions are discussed by Coles (this volume). His chapter provides a good introduction to several of the other chapters in this volume, in terms of offering alternative models and approaches – wheels instead of cycles – from the geography and business literature. He makes some interesting comparisons with the retail area in particular, which, he argues, have considerable validity in the context of the TALC and could provide useful analogies and models from which to study the development of tourist destinations.

In a similar vein, Papatheodorou reviews developments in marketing and the relationship between marketing forces and spatial patterns in the context of overall competitiveness of destinations. In many ways his discussion goes back to the original focus of the TALC in its earliest form, the effect of attractiveness on competition and the realignment and relocation of developments. His analysis of core–periphery relations in tourism and their interdependence harks back to Christaller (1963) in a contemporary setting, reflecting the influence of changes in technology, in transportation and in facilities on the development of destinations. His arguments also echo the process described by Lundgren (other volume) in particular in terms of the spread of metropolitan cores and their impacts upon the resort periphery.

Hall's chapter is firmly focused on the role of spatial interaction and he draws even more heavily upon Christaller and his theory of central places and upon the gravity model as an expression of the relationship between distance and interaction. Hall uses wave analogue theory from which to discuss the process of the development of tourist destinations and their dependence on transportation innovation and improvement, and also the significance of socioeconomic factors. The time–space convergence concept, which has been helpful in explaining the spread of tourism across the globe, has perhaps experienced its first reversal with the demise of Concorde, but for the less affluent segments of the travel market, the advent of the Airbus 380, with an expanded range, thus reducing the need for refuelling stops, will continue the process of convergence of origins and destinations, at least in time if not in real distance.

The links between origins and destinations remain of critical importance to the development of resorts, and it was because of the dramatic improvement in transportation as a result of the development of the railway network that the rapid expansion in size and in numbers of coastal resorts took place in the mid-19th century. The second wave of mass tourism a century or so later, to the shores of the Mediterranean, occurred because of the advent of cheap fast air transport. Whether there will be a third wave of equivalent proportion appears unlikely, but forecasters probably made the same comment before Thomas Cook began his train chartering business in the early 1800s and Freddie Laker introduced the idea of charter flights more than a century later. Mass tourism destinations are dependent on easy access by large numbers of people for their success. The relationship between access and development is both simple and complex; the success of the relationship is mutually dependent on the wellbeing of both elements. Mankind's success in transportation innovation has served to both open up new destinations and to aid in the demise of existing ones because of increasing competition. Such a situation is unlikely to change as geography still exerts a powerful influence on the patterns of tourism development.

Chapter 3

Enigma Variations? The TALC, Marketing Models and the Descendants of the Product Life Cycle

TIM COLES

> We come out of the dark and go into the dark again, and in between lie the experiences of our life.
>
> Thomas Mann, *The Magic Mountain* (1924)

Introduction: The TALC and the Grand Model-building Tradition

One of the features of the Tourism Area Life Cycle (TALC) model that is often overlooked is the context of its appearance and its intellectual setting. Most of us who have used the model in classes, in our reading, or in our research will immediately recognise that it appeared in *The Canadian Geographer* in 1980 (Butler, 1980). Many readers may be asking themselves at this point what is so significant about apparently anodyne bibliographical details? First, this enduring set of ideas was in fact published in a geographical, not a tourism-related journal by a practising geographer; and second, it appeared at a time of profound intellectual development and paradigmatic transition in the discipline of (human) geography.

As in all the major social sciences, geography's practitioners have been constantly questioning the methods, techniques, approaches and philo-sophical underpinnings to their research. The 1970s were no different and they were notable for intense skirmishes on the philosophical battleground between advocates of long established paradigms and the proponents of new, radical epistemologies (Johnston, 1991). Among the former were the supporters of logical positivism, an enduring approach associated with the Quantitative Revolution of the 1950s and 1960s. Support for the Quantitative Revolution centred on its aims to locate geography as a social science, and hence to search for models of spatial structure (Gregory, 1994). The desire to make the discipline scientifically relevant – and recognised as such – was, according to Gregory (1994: 350), reinforced by logical positivists' perpetual search for the two types of postulates they regarded as meaningful: empirical statements, the truth of which had to be established by verification; and analytical statements of logic and mathematics, which were judged to be true by definition. Model building was a key pursuit in this era and it offered geographers a medium to express their ideas. Put simply, a model is an abstracted, idealised and structured simplification of a complex reality. In their ground-breaking collection, Chorley and Haggett (1967) noted that model building depends on 'analogue theory'; that is, as selective representations and through the elimination of incidental detail, models allow the fundamental, relevant or interesting aspects of the real world to be revealed in a generalised form. Models were deployed by geographers in more complex exercises to reveal the full intricacies of idealised landscapes and to write a series of definitive, universal, scientific statements about their structure and composition. Often, as was the case with the TALC, models were lent from one discipline and adapted for use in another. In the case of the TALC, the Product Life Cycle (PLC) model, which had become a mainstay of marketing science (cf. Dean, 1950), was tailored for use in the geographical study of tourism (Butler, 1980: 6).

Model building and its logical positivist context, although dominant in the 1960s and 1970s, did not go unchallenged (Johnston, 1991). A number of critiques were advanced, not least the call for more structuralist modes of interpretation (cf. Cloke *et al.*, 1991; Johnston, 1991). In brief, structuralists argued that it was important to move beyond visible, quasi-mathematical, universal 'truths' and to explore the human being as an active subject with conscious designs and to expose the logic which binds those designs together. Logical positivism, in its willingness to let the 'facts' speak for themselves, reduced the role of the individual human being to one of a passive receiver of stimuli, which it dutifully processed, and used to determine its activity patterns in a predictable manner. In contrast, structuralists were suspicious of the notion that human agency in its unbounded form was the basis for explanation of activity. Rather, structures of various forms constrained and shaped the outcomes of human actions over space. In the 1970s and 1980s, the structuralist agenda was advanced by further theoretical engagement with the ideas of realism, political economy and Marxism (Gregory, 1994: 599).

Philosophical skirmishes have continued unabated in human geography to the present day. In the late 1980s and 1990s, geographers embraced the concepts associated with postmodernity and started to abandon the idea of grand, or meta-theories espoused by their predecessors (Cloke *et al.*, 1991). As a consequence of the greater degree of theoretical plurality and sophistication over the past quarter of a century, model building as an activity has been increasingly marginalised within human geography. This is in spite of its continued popularity in what has become known more recently as 'tourism studies' and other (inter-) disciplinary study areas in social and management sciences.

The purpose of this potted history of geography is to contend that the TALC was published at an important moment within geography; that is, towards the end of the classic model-building era, at the threshold of a phase when models became largely unfashionable. As Shaw and Williams (1994, 2002) note, in the early 1980s tourism research, especially in geography, started to embrace new conceptual agendas (see also Hall & Page, 1999). Inspired by the work of de Kadt (1979), by and large geographers started to build a more critical approach, which first of all addressed the political economy of tourism (Williams & Shaw, 2002; see especially Britton, 1991).

Set against this background, this chapter has two main purposes. The first is to explore the intellectual genealogy of the TALC, above all by tracing its origins and the nature of its adaptation of the PLC model. The PLC has been the focus of rigorous criticism and of adaptations in other subjects. Interdisciplinary retail studies is one such area to have widely used and modified the PLC to explore institutional and locational change. Usage in this manner, as will be revealed below, has distinct similarities with the conversion of the PLC into the TALC. However, a quite different approach has been taken to adapt the PLC to talk to retail debates. Predicated on an assessment of its limitations, tourism research has dogmatically focused on making the TALC operational for particular destinations and/or modifying it to meet the distinctive conditions in localities. Unlike the TALC experience and unencumbered by the theoretical inquisition apparent in geography, critiques of the PLC in retail studies precipitated alternative models to address the new concerns. Here, it is argued that the way in which the TALC has emerged, debate over the application and relevance of the TALC has progressed, and alternatives in retail studies have emerged – hitherto unrecognised within tourism studies – are all functions of their distinctive intellectual settings. In the case of the latter, the proposal of alternative models has, in turn, precipitated a further round of criticism which raises interesting research questions for tourism studies. Thus, the second aim of this chapter is to showcase some of these models, to explore their potential relevance to tourism research, and hence to advance reasons why they have not as yet made their way into tourism studies.

'Marketing Myopia': The Product Life Cycle in Retrospect

Butler (1980: 6) explicitly identifies the PLC as the inspiration for the TALC. As Davidson *et al.* (1976: 90) recognise, the emergence of the PLC in North American marketing thought can be traced back to the 1950s (Dean, 1950). For them, its beauty lies in its ability to inform product line discussions, particularly in the consumer packaged goods field. By recognising that change is inevitable within the market place, it offers marketing managers the opportunity to monitor the performance of their products and to make strategic business decisions based on the possible trajectories of sales.

The basics of the PLC are that it attempts to map sales (sometimes cumulative) against time over the duration of the product's marketing. Hypothetically at least, the PLC is argued to have a classical S-shape (Figure 3.1). A biological metaphor is adopted to explain how the product progresses over time through four distinctive stages: introduction, growth, maturity and decline. Put prosaically, each product is considered to have a distinctive lifespan, each is born (i.e. introduced), each progresses through its adolescent growth to adult maturity, each eventually stagnates and declines in the twilight of its years, and – in theory at least – each product should eventually die out. As Kotler (1976: 230) puts it, 'new products are launched by companies in the hope that they will enjoy a long sweet life of growing sales and profits. Some do, but along the way many more meet all kinds of problems that threaten to end the product's career prematurely.'

In terms of the detailed mechanics of the cycle, Baker (1991: 6) notes more fully that,

> at birth or first introduction to the market a new product initially makes slow progress as people have to be made aware of its existence

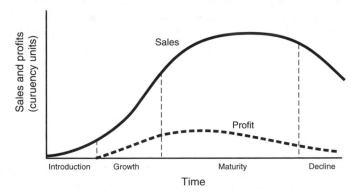

Figure 3.1 The PLC
Source: Abridged from Kotler (1976) and Baker (1991)

and only the bold and innovative seek to try it as a substitute for the established product which the new one is seeking to improve or displace.

The precise time taken for take-off will depend on the product itself, its qualities and their appeal (or not) to the first innovative consumers. In general early progress is tardy but,

> [A]s people take up the new product they will talk about it and make it more visible to non-users and reduce the perceived risk seen in any innovation. As a consequence, a … bandwagon effect will be initiated as consumers seek to obtain supplies … and producers recognizing the trend, switch over to making the new product in place of the old. The result is exponential growth.

While strong and continued growth is considered a virtue, inevitably all markets are finite entities and the rates of sales growth will begin to slow as the market becomes saturated. As Baker notes,

> Thereafter sales will settle down at a level which reflects new entrants to the market plus replacement/repeat purchases which constitutes the mature phase of the product life-cycle.

Profits peak in the maturity phase according to Kotler (1976: 231). In narratives of the PLC, the presence of competition is usually invoked at this stage as a precursor to a hypothesised potential decline; death, that is withdrawal from the market, is not normally considered (Baker, 1991; Kotler, 1976).

Consumers are assumed to be inherently lacking in loyalty to products and brands. In general, they are perceived to be motivated by self-interest and the desire to obtain the best deal possible. As such, they are quite willing to switch allegiances should they perceive a better deal elsewhere (Baker, 1991). Without action to maintain the product's appeal, quality and/or competitiveness, a gap in the market appears which other businesses may exploit. By taking advantage of complacency through the introduction of an appealing, alternative product, the competition erodes the extant business's sales, market share and ultimately profit in that product. Where action is taken to shore up the product, this frequently takes the form of increased marketing outlay in the maturity phase. Costs of this type erode the profitability of the product, but may preserve or indeed help reinvigorate sales. Somewhat inevitably, products may not be maintained indefinitely through marketing and a decline period (eventually) sets in. Sales continue in a downward drift and profits erode rapidly towards the zero point (Kotler, 1976: 231).

By invoking the metaphor of life, it is easy to be drawn into an unduly optimistic reading of the PLC as a business tool: namely, it exists to facilitate and to sustain the life of the product. One of the most frequent misuses of the model arises when businesses try to deploy the PLC as a specific predictive device (Baker, 1991). In fact, the PLC is better interpreted as a warning against complacency among marketing executives with established products and brands, or a guard against what Levitt (1960) terms 'marketing myopia'. In a stinging polemic of business practice, Levitt (1960: 47) believes the PLC embodies a 'self-deceiving cycle'. At the heart of his criticism is that shortsighted managements threaten their businesses and that there is no such thing as a growth industry. He contends that,

> the history of every dead and dying 'growth' industry shows a self-deceiving cycle of bountiful expansion and undetected decay. There are four conditions which usually guarantee this cycle:
>
> (1) The belief that growth is assured by an expanding and more affluent population.
> (2) The belief that there is no competitive substitute for the industry's major product.
> (3) Too much faith in mass production and in the advantages of rapidly declining unit costs as output rises.
> (4) Preoccupation with a product that lends itself to carefully controlled scientific experimentation, improvement and manufacturing cost reduction.

As Baker (1991: 5) notes, the second belief has never been true. However, it does point to the fact that, as a conceptualisation, the TLC implies competition and competitors in the wider market place, but these are never represented in the model explicitly (Papatheodouro, this volume). They are practically invisible, somewhere in the background of this introspective projection of the fortunes of a solitary product by a single business. By deploying a wealth of business history exemplars, Levitt contends that it is plain to see that the fortunes of many have been dictated by poor decision-making. After the struggles of introduction and stimulating growth, producers sit back and relax when they become established leaders in mature and profitable markets (Baker, 1991). They believe they know what the consumer wants. Instead of making consumer-oriented decisions, they make product-oriented decisions. The latter may be more convenient for the business, but less relevant to consumers and their needs. Hence, such imperfect operations open the business to threats from competitors who are more in tune with changes in consumer demand and capable of exploiting the associated niches. This leads Levitt (1960: 45) to conclude that '[i]n every case the reason growth is threatened, slowed or stopped is *not* because the market is saturated. It is because there has been a failure of management.'

(emphasis original). Charting the life of products leads him to believe that the future of the business is reliant on the quality of human organisation and leadership in a business, the vision and will to succeed, and by the recognition that producing goods and services is ultimately about buying customers.

The PLC is a straightforward model but much critical discourse surrounding it centres on its deterministic and reductionist nature, and whether such a simple concept is capable of dealing with the complexities of the 'real world' of commerce (Bennett & Cooper, 1984; Cox, 1967; Day, 1981; Dhalla & Yuspeh, 1976; Polli & Cook, 1969; Rink & Swan, 1979; Mercer, 1993). Given the definition of models proposed above, this may appear intrinsically oxymoronic. Nevertheless, to recall Mann's comments, we know that all living things are born and they die, but it is the complex pathways of life in between that are most difficult to rationalise, understand and explain. The same can be said of the PLC. All products are introduced and all products will (eventually) be withdrawn. What is less certain, critics would argue, is what happens in between.

Standard appraisals question the shape of the curve, the timing of change based on the particularities of individual marketing experiences and market conditions, and the identification of the boundaries between different stages (Baker, 1991; Cox, 1967; Dhalla & Yuspeh, 1976; Kotler, 1976; Table 3.1). More intricate rebuttals focus on the additional, implied features of the model that have to be grafted on to compensate for its inherent simplicity, and thus inability to deal with different types and sizes of business (see Kotler, 1976: 237–238). Others note variations in strategy, marketing approach and operational context which are hidden by the simple line to denote sales versus time (Dhalla & Yuspeh, 1976; Porter, 1980). Most vociferous among the critics of the PLC, Dhalla and Yuspeh (1976) extolled their readers to 'forget the product life cycle'. Thomas (1991: 288) summarises their emphatic confutation of the PLC as exposing its inherent weaknesses in two key areas, its conceptual and operational arguments. Finally, historical evidence questions the validity of the PLC. In an early commentary on the PLC, Cox (1967) describes six different PLC patterns. The most notable variant is that of the second cycle (or first recycle stage) in which sales oscillate once more. This is ascribed to a promotional push in the decline stage which rejuvenates sales (Kotler, 1976). Based on marketing evidence, Day (1981) identifies the timeless consumer product, the multiple function product, technological substitution processes and sequentially unfolding segments as foci that have fuelled doubts about the PLC. More recently, Mercer, (1993) reveals that a two-decade test of the UK's leading brands does not substantiate the more abstract PLC.

Table 3.1 Dhalla and Yuspeh's (1976) criticisms of the PLC

Conceptual arguments
• Products are not living things, hence the biological metaphor is entirely misleading.   • The PLC is the dependent variable, a function of the way the product is managed over time. It is not an independent variable as implied by the model.   • The PLC cannot be valid for product class, product form and brands.   • Fitting the PLC to empirical sales data is a sterile exercise in taxonomy.
Operational arguments
• The four phases or states in the life cycle are not clearly definable.   • It is impractical and impossible to identify precisely where a product is on the curve at any given moment in time.   • Thus, the concept is redundant as a planning tool.   • Evidence exists of businesses that have used the PLC for planning have made false and erroneous decisions based on a false confidence in the model and an incorrect interpretation of data. This has caused them to miss particular opportunities, abandon existing products and brands too early, and to pioneer new products when considerable potential still existed with their extant portfolio.

Source: Abridged from Thomas' summary (1991: 288)

The Progeny of the PLC: Space, Place and the 'Life Metaphor'

The TALC adapts the ideas of the PLC by assuming that particular spaces and their local characteristics, features and traits may be commodified as distinct place products to be bought and consumed by visitors and tourists of all types. According to Butler (1980: 6), the PLC has much to offer tourism through studies of destination evolution because precisely the same procedure is followed by place products as the PLC predicts so that,

> Visitors will come to an area in small numbers initially, restricted by lack of access, facilities, and local knowledge. As facilities are provided and awareness grows, visitor numbers will increase. With marketing, information dissemination, and further facility provision, the area's popularity will grow rapidly. Eventually, however, the rate of increase in visitor numbers will decline as levels of carrying capacity are reached. ... As the attractiveness of the area declines relative to other areas, because of overuse and the impacts of visitors, the actual number of visitors may also eventually decline.

For Agarwal (1997: 67), 'the [TALC] model provides a conceptual framework for understanding change within destinations'. As is the case with the PLC, the TALC is a poor forecasting tool, but very effective for planning and control purposes (Kotler, 1976). Similarly, at the time of its appearance it had a powerful message pertaining to self-deception, complacency and the inappropriateness of product-oriented delivery given the delicate position in which many destinations found themselves as the restructuring of society and economy was underway in the early 1980s.

Not surprisingly due to the close correlation between the PLC and TALC, many of the same criticisms have been made of the TALC as of the PLC. Other contributions in these two volumes describe in detail the difficulties associated with the TALC. However, suffice to say that there has been a strong body of work which has examined whether the TALC can in fact be made operational. Questions of its determinism, whether an area has to pass through all six phases, the shape of the curve, the differentiation between stages, the *exact* identification of the position at which a destination is located, the availability and application of empirical data, and the relevance of the number of visitors, not sales on the y-axis, all have a familiar feel when compared with discourse on the PLC (Choy, 1992; Cooper, 1990, 1992; Haywood, 1986; Shaw & Williams, 2002). Similar criticisms have been made of the conceptual aspects of the TALC. For instance, in view of the articulated nature of the tourism 'product' and its assembled components in the spatial container that is the destination (Hall & Page, 1999; Holloway, 1994), is it appropriate to consider trying to apply a single curve? Fundamentally, is the destination a single, coherent *product* that depends on the synergies among its constituent elements or is it a series of *products* in a loosely linked local configuration? Debbage (1990) notes the TALC focuses on the internal dynamics of specific resorts at the expense of external features such as the structure of the tourist industry, the market and competition from other resorts (Porter, 1980). Agarwal (1994, 1997, 2002) argues that the poststagnation phase of the curve is in need of reformulation. Instead of a discrete trajectory in poststagnation, regeneration, rejuvenation and restructuring are on-going processes that must be continually undertaken, and perhaps commence in a distinct 'reorientation phase' (Agarwal, 1994; Priestley & Mundet, 1998: 87). Reinvention of a single place product in this way contrasts with one of Baum's (1998) hypothesised trajectories beyond stagnation. He suggests that reinvention results in a series of S-shaped curves as a destination reinvents itself with a series of new products, each of which has its own life cycle (Baum, this volume).

What becomes clear from commentaries addressing the TALC is that, in spite of the difficulties and shortcomings associated with this descendant of the PLC, it has been, and continues to be, one of the most enduring and frequently deployed concepts within tourism studies (Haywood, this volume). As Agarwal (1997: 65) notes, this is 'despite the large volume of research reviewing the resort cycle, its validity, applicability and universality have yet to be successfully proven.' Furthermore, Prideaux (2000: 227) notes that there has only been some limited debate over whether any single model can explain tourism development (Bianchi, 1994; Choy, 1992; Prosser, 1995). To this end new forays into destination development modelling have been recently attempted to explain the unfolding temporal fortunes of tourism spaces (Prideaux, 2000; Weaver, 2000). However, over the last two decades the TALC has been breathtakingly dominant in our understanding of unfolding tourism place products of different types.

Why this should have been the case is an immensely difficult question. One answer is that in a self-fulfilling logic, the basic simplicity of the model as a representation has engineered its appeal to a great many readers and, as Weaver (2000: 217) implies, its contentiousness borne of its simplicity has inspired a great many commentators to devote their academic labours to its authentication, albeit without categoric acceptance or rejection. Notwithstanding the value of corroboration, it is curious that criticism has been highly introspective and sharply focused on the model itself rather than its relative merits versus possible alternatives. It is clear that tourism academics have been aware of the misgivings of the PLC in the marketing literature (cf. Hart et al., 1984 and Prideaux, 2000). As such, they must have been aware that marketing scientists have attempted to advance product theory and concept further. None the less, there have been precious few attempts to build on recent progress in marketing to further the tourism agenda.

Such tactics place tourism studies at odds with the approach taken in retail studies. There the PLC has been used as a means to explore the life cycle of retail organisations (or 'retail institutions' to use North American terminology) such as supermarkets, discount stores and department stores. Faithful to the PLC, Davidson et al. (1976: 90–91) identify a 'retail life cycle' (RLC) for each institution comprising the four very similar stages of 'early growth', 'accelerated development', 'maturity' and 'decline'. In this conceptualisation the retail institution becomes the proxy for the product and, like the products they represent, the institutions pass through an identifiable life cycle. Herein lies the similarity with the commodification of place in tourism. A retail organisation merchandises a number of products under one roof; that is, similar in concept at least to the resort, it bundles a number of items together in one contained, bounded space and it is this assembly that functions to attract (or not) customers. The product is actually the space and place, the territory occupied by the retail organisation as well as the meaning and importance attached to it by the consumer. Product as institution, just as destination as product, evolves and the internal characteristics of the product are refined to their final mature format (cf. Baum, 1998: 170). Just as the economic fortunes and physical manifestation of the destination reflect its popularity among visitors and tourists, the commercial destiny and its nature and form reflect its acceptance and usage by consumers. Further extensions of the retail life cycle and other similar models teased out their geographical connotations (Brown, 1987). As a retail organisation develops towards maturity, it changes its locational preferences to occupy prime sites to reflect its commercial omnipotence. As decline sets in and the retail organisation is challenged by a successor, spatial shift takes place. The prime site of the current retail organisation may not correspond with the locational preferences of the new thrusting competition leading to a diversion of trade and contributing to a loss of profitability. As Knowles and Curtis (1999) demonstrate, precisely such a scenario of spatial shifting has been played out in the geography of mass tourism consumption and production in post-War Europe.

Wheel or Cycle? Same Difference?

The retail life cycle is frequently invoked as an alternative to the 'wheel of retailing'. Originally devised by Malcolm McNair (1958), the 'wheel of retailing' postulates that a retail institution starts life as a cut-price, low-cost, narrow margin operation which subsequently 'trades up' (Figure 3.2). Improvements in display, more prestigious premises, increased advertising and the provision of credit, delivery and many other customer services all serve to drive up expenses, margins and prices. Eventually they mature as high-cost, conservative and 'top heavy' institutions with a sales policy based on quality goods and services rather than price appeal. This effectively creates a niche for the next low-cost innovator. And so the wheel turns, albeit that the 'predecessor' remains in the market, its fortunes waning as those of its 'successor' continually improve (Brown, 1988: 16; see also Russell's chapter on Chaos Theory and the TALC, this volume).

At face value there are certain basic similarities between the RLC and the wheel. Both are essentially deterministic models and rely on the self-deception of complacency. Both suggest that a particular organisational format will eventually run its course after passing through a distinct sequence of changes. They imply that early penetration into the market is slow; that how the concept is brought to the market will influence uptake and growth among the consumer base; and that profitability is strained towards the end of the cycle. Additional services are provided which assume an understanding (false as it transpires) of the market's needs

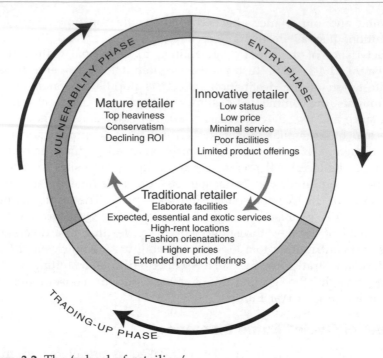

Figure 3.2 The 'wheel of retailing'
Source: Redrawn from Brown (1988: 17)

which open niches for the next wave of innovators (N.B. the wheel assumes consumers are price-sensitive primarily). Each identifies embeddedness and implies that an inability to respond to change effectively precipitates decline in both relative and ultimately absolute measures. Together they imply a spatial shift in the location of the principal consumption paradigm. However, there are also key differences. Price and its variation over time are central ideas of the wheel but feature less prominently in the RLC and PLC models. Similarly, at each stage of the wheel there is a different relationship between price- and non-price competitive measures. Last, and by no means least, the revolution of the wheel is highly dependent on the outcomes of entrepreneurial decisions. Without human agency, retail institutions would not emerge, individual businesses would not grow and decisions about the future would not have to be faced. Unlike the PLC, the RLC and the TALC, the entrepreneur is placed at the heart of the processes of innovation and change.

The wheel is not without critics. Davidson *et al.* (1976) argue that, like the life cycle, it is difficult to make the wheel operational. Like Hollander (1960, 1980), they also note that historical evidence points to several retail institutions which start their life on a high-cost basis. Within Europe some innovatory forms in their earliest stages adopted non-price competitive measures that are supposed to be characteristic of the maturation process (Coles, 1999a, 1999b). Hollander (1960) thus questioned the universality of the concept as well as the causes for trading up. Brown (1988: 19) identifies two strands: a secular view which sees trading up as a natural and enlightened response to growing consumer affluence and increased demand for a wide range of goods and services; and a competition-oriented view that interprets the process as a defensive mechanism whereby non-price measures are used as a means of creating differential advantage to ward off competition from other businesses in the sector. For all these criticisms, like the PLC and RLC before it, Brown (1998: 19, 30–31) contends that 'most commentators concur that McNair's hypothesis is valid' and 'one of the five most influential concepts in marketing thought'.

There are fragments of evidence of the wheel operating in existing work on resort evolution, although it is not recognised as such. Baum (1998) suggests that the reinvention of the resort marketing mix to reach new consumer groups may require the total abandonment of the traditional marketing paradigm in favour of an alternative. Some commentators would suggest that reinvention is best represented as an extension or even a second cycle on an extant line (Agarwal, 1997, this volume). This, though, implies the current product (i.e. place) is being reinvented, which may be disputed. In fact, inspired by criticism of the PLC rather than advocacy of the wheel, Baum (1998) notes a different set of place characteristics are being bundled together to produce an entirely new, discrete commodity and hence a subsequent sigmoidal curve should be added to the TALC model to denote the subsequent product. An alternative reading here would be that the wheel is revolving based on intradestination differentiation. An old, tired, unappealing and uncompetitive concept is being superseded (not annihilated) by a new, fresh product. This process is being driven by innovators who recognise the weaknesses in the preceding concepts as an opportunity to enter the market with new, more appealing and entirely different products (see Russell's chapter on Entrepreneurship, this volume). Furthermore, spatial shift may be in evidence as the settings for the components of the new product may not be the same as for the traditional paradigm.

From 'Wheels' to Dialectics and Hybrids: In Search of Other Long-lost Relatives

Alongside the less conspicuous retail accordion (cf. Hart, 1999), which postulates retail institutions oscillate between general–specific–general merchandising formats, the wheel and RLC form a group of ideas that contend that change takes place in an oscillatory pattern and is characterised by the recurrence of earlier patterns (see also Benson & Shaw, 1999). Intense debate within marketing science and retail studies has focused on two other distinctive categories of theories: the environmental and the conflictual (Brown, 1987, 1988; Markin & Duncan, 1981).

The former refer to the influence on organisational features of the operating milieu, while the latter propose that new retail institutions are in fact the outcome of interinstitutional competition. Both these categories and the respective ideas have their champions and detractors. Environmental theories are valued for their ability to incorporate changes in the economic, demographic, social, cultural and technological conditions that are reflected in the retail system and manifested in the evolution of the retail institution (Brown, 1987: 182). In contrast, conflict theories recognise that very few institutional innovations in retailing have been met without protest and dissention. Faced by such a challenge, retail institutions must respond or risk failure. Gist (1968) calls for a dialectical theory of retail evolution where an existing 'thesis' is challenged by an 'antithesis' so that a 'synthesis' emerges from the melding of the two. The synthesis becomes the thesis for the new round of negotiation and so the dialectic continues to resolve (Brown, 1987: 189–190). From this process of establishment and challenge, entirely new, hybrid forms of retail institution emerge.

Similarities exist in the assumptions of the theoretical strands. Indeed, attempts have been made to integrate the strands to produce new hybrid forms of theory. For instance, Brown (1988) explores the permutations and possibilities of integrating the various categories because none of the categories or the individual ideas are capable on their own of offering a complete explanation of retail institution change (cf. Prideaux, 2000 above). This sentiment is echoed by Evans et al. (1993), who argue that an open systems approach is a unifying perspective through which to view theories of retail change (cf. Roth & Klein, 1993).

Discussion: Why Hasn't Pandora's Box Been Opened Before?

Detailed testing of such retail marketing ideas in a tourism context is yet to take place (and this is not the context in which to start the process). Evidence can be located to underscore their relevance in advancing our understanding of destination trajectories over time. However, their value extends beyond assembling temporal and spatial chronicles of the destination. From an epistemological perspective, they suggest that retail studies have adopted a more progressive and thorough approach to modelling place and space as product. In fact, Brown (1988) argues that there has been a 'wheel of the wheel of retailing' as explanation of institution change started off with simple propositions (the wheel and RLC), became more intricate and detailed, and in turn this gave way once again to more simple representations as they became academic vogue.

Given the not insignificant level of debate over the modelling of retail evolution, it is curious that these ideas have not as yet been systematically explored in tourism research. Three main reasons immediately propose themselves. First, as discussed above, the highly contestable nature of the TALC model has lent itself heavily towards sustained discussion and analysis. Second is the changing nature of tourism studies. To parallel an expansion in interest in the 1990s, the research agenda has progressed to explore the panoply of issues associated with the late 20th-century restructuring of society, culture and economy; the new, alternative modes of tourism consumption these have precipitated; and the unfolding outcomes and impacts of change. In relative terms, resort management and destination evolution are not as conspicuous as they once were. The stagnation of British resorts in particular during the 1980s as a result of shifting social, cultural and economic conditions (environmental theory?) forced the TALC towards the forefront of the agenda (Williams & Shaw, 1998). Due to its implications for resort management, the TALC retained its relevance at a time when the model-based approach was being abandoned as a mode of enquiry for policy-oriented research especially in (human) geography. In the 1990s the sustainable tourism paradigm and its attendant intellectual baggage has dominated academic discourse in no small measure. While the TALC may have application in understanding some aspects of sustainable tourism management (Butler, this volume; Swarbrooke, 1999; WTO, 1998), for the investigation of many additional modes of consumption it has only marginal relevance. Equally, other models, were they to have been abridged from marketing science, would have had only limited resonance with the programme of the 1990s.

And finally, such alternatives have not been of a sufficiently high profile in marketing science and retail studies to force tourism research workers to take note of them. As this chapter has indicated, modelling organisational change became a major topic in retailing during the late 1980s and early 1980s. This was, however, a time when the TALC was courting strenuous debate within tourism over its applicability and intricacies, and hence an ideal moment when they could have been accessed by tourism discourse. However, this was also a time when the first signs of an epistemological change within retail studies manifested itself. Models of commercial space and place of this type are still frequently applied and taught in retail management programmes. Nevertheless, new modes of understanding were evolving, driven not least by further paradigm shift within retail geography. In keeping with the development of geography more widely, Wrigley and Lowe (1996) argued that a model-based approach was incongruous with the imperatives of the late 20th-century world. Simple supply-side explanations were inadequate. Rather, they proposed, and continue to advocate (Wrigley & Lowe, 2002), the abridgement of ideas from the so-called 'new economic' and 'new cultural' geographies of the late 1980s and 1990s into retail research. In short, these pursue more aggressively such themes as corporate culture and interests in the manufacture of major sites of consumption; the spatial switching of retail locations; the persistence of underperforming stores; the suboptimality of retail spaces and the reasons, often cultural, behind them; and the political economy of supply chains with their associated policy contexts and implications (Langston *et al.*, 1997, 1998; Wrigley, 1992, 1998; Wrigley & Lowe, 1996, 2002).

Perversely, the new agenda in retail studies does further warn of the limitations of models and hence their potential for adaptation in tourism research. However, the possible adoption of these newer ideas themselves should not go unnoticed. Why do small- and medium-sized enterprises stay in business when so many of them are so obviously suboptimal in performance? Lifestyle entrepreneurship may be one explanation (Ateljevic & Doorne, 2000); emotional and historic family ties may be another (Baum, 1998: 170). However, could it be because they have no exit strategy and/or that they are locked into the resort because of their sunk costs (Wrigley, 1992, 1998)? Do resorts in their current constellation exist not for positive reasons but as a consequence of highly embedded private capital that can't be released; that is, practically through a social tourism of production in which their marginal operation becomes a *de facto* ersatz for the welfare state? Exit has been discussed by Baum (1998, this volume). However, his interpretation views exit as part of a destination's exit portfolio, an element of a strategy recommended and facilitated in a top-down fashion by governors on local economy and society. Although this view has merit, the integration of these new critical approaches into tourism analysis would help develop a much fuller understanding of the embeddedness and endurance of sites of tourism 'consumption'. Top-down structural approaches may provide the first impetus towards wholesale change but ultimately it is individual businesses that will have to disengage with tourism to enable systemic exit to become a more realistic outcome.

Conclusion: Opening Pandora's Box?

For more than two decades since its first appearance the TALC model has been a highly conspicuous feature of tourism enquiry. It has been the subject of many an academic paper and a proliferation of theses, dissertations and course papers at doctoral, master's and undergraduate levels. As with all good models, it is a neat simplification of a complex reality. Published towards the end of the golden age of model building in human geography, it adroitly takes concepts from marketing science on the development and longevity of products and adapts them to the production, evolution and transformation of tourism space. As this chapter has demonstrated, if Butler's approach were to be repeated now, there are several models of product and institutional evolution and development from marketing science and retail studies that have as much, if not in some cases more, to offer the study of the unfolding temporal and local features of the tourism place commodity. For instance, as capable as the TALC may be, it lacks consideration of price in the changing life stages of the resort; it relegates the importance of individual human agency and entrepreneurship in resort change; it struggles to integrate external (environmental) influences on destination outcomes; and it flounders when trying to explain the presence of alternative types of tourist experience in the traditional mass tourist destination where a dialectic reading may offer greater insight. Moreover, in an almost Popperian sense, as models of institutional change have been rejected in new approaches to retail studies in the 1990s, there exists the possibility of capitalising on fresh, new perspectives on space, place and consumption to explore the trajectories of tourism destination development.

That Butler's approach hasn't been repeated may be a function of the model itself, the debate it has provoked, and wider disciplinary transformations. The latter raises two broader sets of concerns about tourism research. The first is that many of the grand and celebrated ideas in tourism (as well as recent, innovative ones) are frequently divorced from their temporal and disciplinary origins and contexts. In subjects such as geography and sociology, there have been repeated attempts to trace the intellectual antecedents of contemporary research. Current insight and modes of enquiry in all their complexity are understood to one degree or another to be a consequence of the rise, decline and/or persistence of particular philosophies, theories, concepts, practices, methods and approaches. Questions of how, why and where particular ideas originate offer insights not only into why they emerged, but also why other developments took place perhaps instead or in tandem. A forensic course is pivotal here. The TALC appeared at a transitional moment in (human) geography, when model building was becoming unfashionable, and when other issues and approaches were being advocated in its place. These same circumstances did not affect other disciplines. Alternatives were proposed to the PLC, but given the development of tourism studies more generally and geography more especially, these have not as yet made their way into tourism discourse. Thus, in order to understand the construction and setting of tourism knowledge, it is crucial to develop a deeper understanding of the outside 'genealogical' influences from other disciplines. Quite frequently the origins of tourism knowledge are little understood and/or taken for granted.

As a second concern, there is a worrying lack of integration and cross-fertilisation of ideas between tourism studies and retail studies. This is simply not just a parochial plea to consider alternative models and formulations to the TALC model. Given the diverse bloodlines cutting through its intellectual genealogy, it is somewhat unexpected that tourism has not drawn more heavily from retail studies. Ideas from the 'new economic geography' agenda have started to permeate their way into tourism more widely (cf. Ioannides & Debbage, 1998) and destination research in particular (Agarwal, 2002). In contrast, their adaptations via retail geography have been remarkable for their failure to enter tourism discourse. This shortcoming is compounded by the observation that the relationship between tourism, shopping and leisure is read – rightly or wrongly – as practically axiomatic (Coles, 2003). In spite of the multiple dimensions associated with tourism shopping events, there has been an unwillingness to explore them in favour of other more fashionable thematic 'priorities'. As demonstrated by the limited corpus on the topic, the relationship between tourism, shopping and leisure is far from straightforward (cf. Timothy & Butler, 1995), and it lacks a full treatment of retailing (Coles, 2003). Thus, there seems little doubt that in the future ideas from retail geography may help progress our understanding of tourism spaces and places.

Chapter 4
TALC and the Spatial Implications of Competition

ANDREAS PAPATHEODOROU

Introduction

The Tourism Area Life Cycle (TALC) theory is simple, plausible and yields interesting results; not unexpectedly, therefore, it has significantly influenced tourism research over the last 20 years. In fact, the TALC is the first serious analytical framework that combines features of demand such as consumer tastes, with elements of tourism supply like facilities and infrastructure. Moreover, by considering the economic, social and environmental dimensions of tourism within an explicitly dynamic context, the TALC may be regarded as a solid research vehicle for sustainable tourism development (Cooper, 1990).

Nonetheless, the TALC framework seems relatively insufficient to address issues of competition and competitiveness in tourism. More specifically, these notions should be understood in a dual interdependent context: at a macrolevel, there is rivalry among different destinations, whereas at a microlevel, tourist producers compete against each other to increase market share and profitability. In both scales, market players can either focus exclusively on price or alternatively engage in horizontal and vertical differentiation. The end configuration of tourist flows is essentially a result of the interaction of the above market strategies with different consumer preferences and constraints (Papatheodorou, 2001a). Consequently, by studying the evolutionary pattern of a single resort at an aggregate level, the TALC cannot deal with explicit systemic resort analysis and alternative market structures, conduct or performance in the tourism industries.

Moreover, and following the Schumpeterian tradition in industrial economics, competition should be seen as an evolutionary phenomenon where the characteristics of the successful tourist firms and destinations are endogenously determined by a perpetual battle for the survival of the fittest (Schumpeter, 1996). The TALC can easily tackle changes in the external environment (e.g. advancements in air transport technology resulted in increased popularity of the Mediterranean resorts from the 1960s onwards) or even endogenous developments in tourism demand (e.g. a positive word-of-mouth leads to a tourism boom until the resulting congestion and negative publicity renders a resort a victim of its own success). Nonetheless, the theory is not suitable as a base from which to study the dynamic perspectives of competition as it lacks the relevant analytical tools of industrial organisation.

It would be rather unfair, however, to criticise the TALC for these insufficiencies in retrospect. First, no theory can be fully comprehensive especially in the complex area of human geography: on the contrary, Butler's (1980) article in *The Canadian Geographer* was a very brave and successful attempt to establish tourism as a valid area of academic study. Second, the TALC is in fact a child of its era: in the 1970s, resort managers started perceiving the dangers from unsustainable growth and introduced the first controls on visitor inflows (Inskeep, 1994); furthermore, initial efforts were undertaken to attract the most profitable consumer segments. Market research and heavy advertising were regarded as the main tools of promotion analysis and the TALC offered the necessary framework for all these policies.

During the last 20 years of the 20th century, nonetheless, it was gradually realised that demand management was inadequate to cope with the accumulated problems. In terms of the general economic environment in the early 1980s, the emerging Thatcherism and Reaganomics focused on aggregate supply matters, believing that market deregulation and liberalisation would enhance flexibility and competition. Tourism policy was also characterised by a similar change of attitude (Hall, 2000). The airline industry was instantly deregulated in the USA in 1978 (Borenstein, 1992) and gradually liberalised in the European Union between 1988 and 1997 (Graham, 1998), whereas the General Agreement on Trade in Services facilitated the legal framework for transnational hotel corporations and tour operators by inducing the abandonment of national protectionist policies (WTO, 1995). Finally, at an administrative level, a number of countries at least in Europe (e.g. UK, Greece) have been restructuring their National Tourist Offices, empowering, at the same time, their regional authorities: not only are these expected to cater for destination promotion but also to offer special advice to tourist producers and set the conditions for successful partnerships.

Early results from market deregulation have been quite impressive; nowadays, however, the neoclassical euphoria is much more modest. This increasing scepticism stems from the inability of market mechanisms to operate efficiently in de facto noncompetitive environments (Papatheodorou, 2001b). Interestingly, this also seems to be the case with the evolution of the tourism sector, where issues of market power and territorial configuration should be explicitly addressed. This chapter aims therefore at extending the TALC from an industrial geography perspective to study a number of issues that have emerged since the original conceptualisation of the theory. A similar line of thought was originally followed by Debbage (1990) who applied the profit life cycle theory (Markusen, 1985) in the context of tourism. Unfortunately, however, this promising research area has yet remained underexplored: it is therefore important to move it forwards. On these grounds, the chapter discusses first the existing interdependence between market and spatial structures and then presents a model of tourism evolution both in the short and in the long run. It concludes by proposing a number of meaningful policy measures that may alleviate some of the emerging problems in tourism development.

Evolution in Market and Spatial Structures

Market structure

In principle, all industries associated with tourism have features close to the ideal of 'backyard capitalism' (Krugman, 1995). In fact, it is possible to set up an airline just by leasing a small aircraft and operating on a single route. Similarly, accommodation services can be offered by very small and low-cost establishments, while the initiation of tour operations requires nothing more than a computer, a telephone/fax and some knowledge of the promoted region. In reality, however, concentration and duality in horizontal and vertical dimensions prevail nowadays in the three above-mentioned sectors: global air carriers (e.g. Lufthansa) coexist with small regional airlines (e.g. European Air Express), large transnational hotel chains (e.g. Intercontinental) exist next to traditional family accommodation establishments (e.g. Takis Apartments) and powerful mass tour operators (e.g. TUI) share the tourism market with specialised independent travel firms (e.g. Explore Worldwide). These asymmetries in the market structure are an inherent feature of the evolutionary process in these industries. On these grounds, one should consider the self-reinforcing power of economies of scale and scope and effective market foreclosure, once the critical demand sustainability threshold of the respective operations has been surpassed.

More specifically, the various existing organisational routines in the production process come under severe pressure both in periods of booming demand and stagnation (Nelson & Winter, 1982). In the first case, adjustments are required for the seizure of profitability opportunities, whereas in the latter, restructuring is crucial for survival in an intensively competitive environment (see Agarwal, this volume). When the entrepreneurs are rational, forward-looking persons, the formation of appropriate demand expectations is sufficient to generate the necessary organisational changes (see Russell, this volume). In tourism, both cases have been observed in different periods; the exogenous increases in travel demand due to the significant world income growth up to the mid

1970s set the basis for industrial concentration, while the following years reinforced this trend because of the gradual intensification of rivalry and the need for price manipulations and differentiation within a global, mature market context.

In fact, the firms that participated successfully in this magnification process became associated with the standardised leisure and business tourist markets, where scale and network economies are of predominant importance. These enterprises operate in markets, where profits are more related to the achievement of substantial sales volume than to significant mark-up pricing. On the other hand, the companies that failed or abstained from this evolutionary process were found in a situation where the erection of entry barriers and the effective market foreclosure by the incumbents impeded head-to-head competition in the mainstream markets. Therefore, their survival as independent producers became identified with the provision of low-volume, high-margin tourism services where the production efficiency losses are compensated by ad hoc customisation and flexibility. In spite of their relative entrepreneurial success so far, some of these companies are likely to suffer in the future by the major consolidation practices in the contemporary neo-Fordist environment (Ioannides & Debbage, 1998). Consequently, they might be able to combine competitiveness and flexibility at a global level only by accepting the rules set by the big players, i.e. engaging in strategic alliances (e.g. Star Alliance) and consortia (e.g. Leading Hotels of the World).

Spatial structure

The prevailing industrial dualism is also expressed spatially through a number of practices which facilitate the emergence of a core–periphery pattern in tourism. Interestingly, these two terms of territorial classification are not used here according to their political economy meaning in regional theory (Freidmann & Alonso, 1974) and tourism geography (Christaller, 1963; Turner, 1976) that essentially refer to industrial cores and rural/tourist peripheries. In the present context, the notion of core is identified with popular sunlust and wanderlust destinations that emphasise the provision of tourist infrastructure and facilities within a densely built environment. These places are easily accessible by areas of major market potential due to a high frequency of services offered by large, deregulated airlines and their associate carriers. Similarly, in addition to the traditional hotel sector, core resorts host a significant number of imposing accommodation establishments, which are owned or managed by large hotel chains. In terms of the TALC, these are mature destinations likely to be found at their consolidation or stagnation stage.

This industrial pattern is further intensified by the presence of powerful tour operators who integrate vertically with airline and accommodation companies in order to sell these destinations more effectively in the origin markets. Moreover, the emergence of corporate transnationalisation in tourist resorts has transformed the industrial configuration from a competitive oligopoly to an oligopsonistic one. In particular, concentration in the tourist origin markets had limited final effects on the destinations until recently, unless the latter were dependent on a small number of tourism generating areas. The current trend towards chain affiliation and alliances at a global level, however, raises the probability of co-operation among producers and intermediaries of origin countries (regions) and augments substantially their bargaining power over the core destinations. In this context, the recent purchase of the Thomson Travel Group, one of the largest in Britain, by Preussag, the German leisure conglomerate (Harnischfeger, 2000), may have a significant impact on many Mediterranean destinations that rely particularly on the British and German origin markets.

Quite different from the above image is the concept of the tourist periphery, which is identified with a number of sunlust and wanderlust resorts that mostly promote the idiosyncratic elements of their natural and built environment. Accessibility from the origin areas may be much more difficult and expensive compared to the core. Air services, if any, are usually undertaken by small regional carriers, who may operate under a regulatory regime as local monopolies. Similarly, the accommodation infrastructure is often limited and characterised by monopolistically competitive small establishments that belong to local hoteliers. Moreover, tour operations (if any) are usually monopolised by specialised firms; in many cases, however, the visitors prefer to make their own travel arrangements. In terms of the TALC, these destinations are still in their early stages of development.

It seems, therefore, that the dearth of demand impedes the reaping of scale and scope economies and sustains organisational structures of a rather pre-Fordist, artisanal character, where economic rationality is mixed with personal relations between the producers and the consumers. In fact, though the markets of both the air services and tour operations may be characterised by monopolistic practices at a local level *ex post* (when the travel decision is already made), the dispersion of the numerous peripheral destinations in the global tourism context *ex ante* (before the decision) makes the actual industrial pattern converge towards monopolistic competition. In other words, the inability of the tourist producers to serve many destinations simultaneously or engage in affiliations of a wider territorial scale significantly reduces their market power.

Interaction of market and spatial forces

The emerging market/spatial dualism is also related to specific consumer tastes. In particular and following Plog's (1973) classification of visitors, the core resorts are visited by mid- and psychocentric tourists, whereas the peripheral destinations attract mostly the allocentrics. As the great majority of tourists fall within the first two categories, one may conclude that the existing spatial configuration is in fact the outcome of perpetual interaction between demand and supply: the psychocentrics visit the core resorts to enjoy the range of facilities that are offered by the large tourist conglomerates within a familiar and branded environment, while these corporations cluster in areas which attract the psychocentrics. In other words, consumer preferences and economies of scale and scope form together an explosive propulsive force of intertemporal agglomeration. Converse conclusions hold for the peripheral destinations, which attract allocentric tourists questing for the alternative and remote.

Interestingly enough, this framework is applicable to different levels of territorial scale. With respect to the European short-haul sunlust tourist product, for example, the Mediterranean region is the major pole of attraction, i.e. the core, whereas the rest of Europe plays a less important role. Moreover, this region is subsequently characterised by core and peripheries at a more micro scale; Spain and Greece constitute the heart of the Mediterranean British mass tourism movement, while other countries remain less important (Thomson Holidays, 1999). Similarly within Spain, prominent tourist areas such as the Balearics coexist with less developed ones; even within these islands, there is a provocatively asymmetric spatial pattern, e.g. between Majorca and Formentera. In other words, although tourism geography is definitely not a black and white picture, it seems that polarisation is apparent and reflects minor and major preference disparities among tourism consumers at all scales.

Admittedly, some of the previous discussion points have been previously raised by a number of researchers focusing on central place theory (Christaller, 1933; Lösch, 1940), the market potential idea (Harris, 1954), the cumulative causation argument (Pred, 1966) and, most recently, on the new economic geography (Krugman, 1995). However, most of these theories lack any strategic implications, assuming that producers and intermediaries are apathetic price-takers instead of price setters. On the other hand, this chapter aims at innovating by explicitly stressing the potential role of tourism agents in shaping the agglomeration pattern and affecting the direction of tourist flows to a significant extent. In this context, a conceptual framework of evolution is now presented, first for the short run and then for the long run.

Evolution of Tourist Resorts in the Short Run

The study of the short-run period may be perceived as the spatial equivalent of the macroeconomic business cycle analysis, i.e. it treats the stage of the urbanisation process as exogenously given and focuses on factors that affect tourist flows at a specific point in time. In particular, the present section regards both the core and peripheral tourist regions as predetermined territorial entities: in terms of the TALC we consider simultaneously resorts that are found at different stages of development. In this context, the spatial interaction among the origin regions is initially discussed; subsequently the focus shifts to flow exchanges of the core–core, periphery–periphery and core–periphery type. Figure 4.1 provides a useful benchmark.

Interaction among the origin regions

The upper elliptic shape in the figure represents the space of the origin regions. For reasons of exposition, only three tourist-generating areas are considered, namely O_1, O_2 and O_3; analytically, however, an infinite number of origins can be easily accommodated. It should be made clear that the interaction between the various origins does not refer to exchanges in tourism flows (because in that case these places would also be destinations), but in other domains explained in the subsequent discussion. The thickness of the two-directional dash arrows shows the

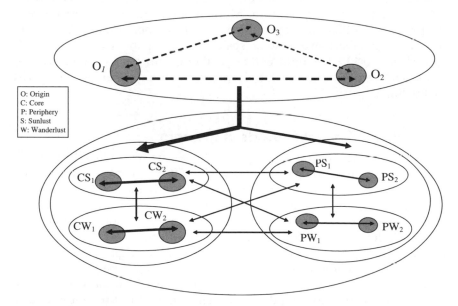

Figure 4.1 Tourist flows in the short run (based on Papatheodorou, 2004)

degree of interdependence among these spatial entities. In reality, the gravity relationship is occasionally asymmetric and involves heavier interaction one way compared to the other. For reasons of simplicity, nonetheless, it is assumed here that the interdependence is symmetric, i.e. the two-directional arrows are of the same thickness for a given pair of origin areas. This assumption does not affect the essence of the analysis.

Having the above in mind, interaction may be explained first in terms of cultural and trade exchanges that can result in homogenisation of consumer preferences; this seems to be the case between O_1 and O_3, and O_2 and O_3. More interestingly, however, inter-relation may be the outcome of corporate transnationalisation. In other words, the tourist firms can extend their operations in other regions or countries by establishing new subsidiaries and co-operating with existing companies. In this case, they are expected to treat the various tourist-generating regions as a single entity instead of separate units; the application of portfolio management practices may then significantly increase the interdependence among the previously isolated origin areas, irrespective of their effect on consumer preferences.

As an illustration of the above, consider a Finnish air carrier that cannot sustain charter flights to Corfu at reasonable prices due to the low level of the local Finnish demand. However, by co-operating with a mass market German tour operator the carrier can increase substantially its potential flight occupancy rates by using fifth freedom rights (Holloway, 1998) to take passengers from Munich en route to its final Greek destination. In this way, the linkage with another origin market and the subsequent achievement of scale (i.e. occupancy) and scope (i.e. spatial network) economies endow Finland with new sunlust destinations and redirect the tourist flows without any changes in tourist inclinations.

Interaction among the resorts of the core

The large ellipsis in the lower part of the figure represents the space of tourist destinations. Within this shape the left oval contains core resorts (C) whereas the right one is related to peripheral areas (P); further subclustering refers to sunlust (S) and wanderlust (W) tourist places. For reasons of exposition again, only two resorts are considered in each case. The thick, left section of the unidirectional broken arrow shows that the core is the main recipient of tourist flows from the origin regions. Within this area, the two-directional arrows express the spatial interaction among the various resorts. This interdependence is understood in the context of visitors choosing different destinations for different holidays; it does not refer to the case where tourists visit a place en route or while being on a holiday to another resort. Moreover and similarly to the space of the origin areas, a symmetric gravity relationship is assumed for a given pair of destinations.

In general, spatial interaction is much larger among leisure tourists than among business travellers, who usually engage in location-specific activities. More specifically, in spite of the existence of some brand name connotations (e.g. Majorca), the standardised and homogeneous character of the holiday product in core sunlust destinations, namely CS_1 and CS_2 in the figure, results in a high degree of substitutability. On the other hand, idiosyncratic features in core wanderlust areas, i.e. CW_1 and CW_2, are thought to reduce substitutability and the value of cross-price elasticities; however, the low level of repeat (over time) visitors entails that these places are also perceived as highly substitutable *ex ante* (e.g. before the travel decision) at least to the great majority of consumers. Finally, notable, albeit smaller, interaction exists between the core sunlust and wanderlust destinations; this may be attributed to their general popularity and variety of built environment. For example, the young British tourist who visits Paris mainly to see the Eiffel Tower could well be the same person who spends their summer holidays on the Costa Brava.

Due to the high degree of perceived substitutability among the core destinations, even slight changes in the prevailing conditions can trigger catastrophic diversions in the tourist flows leading perhaps to a range of poststagnation stages in the TALC. This is particularly important when one takes into consideration the power of the large tourist conglomerates in these areas. In other words, short-run fluctuations in tourist arrivals may be consistently explained by changes in the market practices of the major suppliers and intermediaries in the tourist circuit. In fact, the large tourist oligopolists may create temporary tensions with the local community and credibly threaten the various destinations with price and information manipulation in order to reap most of the benefits associated with tourism; on these grounds, for example, the tourist authorities of Cayman Islands had to finally rescind their objections to the idea of charter flights in the early 1990s, possibly under pressure by Airtours, the large British tour operator (Yale, 1995).

Interaction among the resorts of the periphery

The thinner, right section of the unidirectional broken arrow in Figure 4.1 represents the tourist flow from the origins to the periphery. Spatial interaction among these areas follows the same pattern as in core destinations; nevertheless, the relative thinness of the two-directional arrows reveals that the intensity of flow exchanges is much lower. In fact, in addition to the limited presence of tourists, substitutability among peripheral resorts is expected to be lower due to a substantial number of idiosyncratic characteristics, especially in wanderlust areas (PW_1 and PW_2). Having the above in mind, it may be concluded that the low level of cross-elasticities will probably preclude catastrophic diversions of tourist flows. On the same grounds, due to the limited market power of tourist producers, the exchange of visitors may be attributed to reasons that are more fundamental. For example, changes in relative prices are likely to be cost related, whereas bad reputation might be based on unfriendly local behaviour.

Interaction between core and periphery

As a final case, the flow exchange between the two spatial blocks is now considered. Not surprisingly, this is rather unsubstantial given the great disparity in built resources and attractions. Nevertheless, substitutability is expected to be relatively higher among regions that promote the same type of tourism. For example, the cross-price elasticity between core and peripheral wanderlust destinations is perceived as relatively significant by visitors mainly interested in sightseeing. Similarly, core and peripheral sunlust destinations may attract people who like to alternate cosmopolitanism with quietness. On the other hand, substitutability is likely to be much lower among areas that are associated with different tourism lifestyles. In fact, although there is a small group of people interested in visiting core wanderlust and periphery sunlust areas, it is rather unlikely that a significant number of potential tourists would be interested in visiting both core sunlust *and* peripheral wanderlust areas.

It seems, therefore, that most potential flow exchanges between the two spatial blocks may be explained in terms of idiosyncratic elements in consumer preferences. Though this statement is largely true, one should not underestimate, however, the importance of industrial organisation. In fact, some of these tourist diversions may be potentially justified by dramatic price changes that can compensate tourists for choosing a nonfavourable spatial configuration. In particular, a psychocentric would choose a peripheral destination, only if it were substantially cheaper than a core; an allocentric would take a symmetrically converse decision. The former case is consistent with very strong demand and/or tacit collusion of producers in the core market and fortified by the no-frills, competitive nature of the peripheral product. The second outcome may emerge in occasions of intense price wars in core destinations and is accentuated by the expensiveness of transportation to the periphery due to the loss of scale and scope economies.

Moreover, the gradual entry of large tourist conglomerates into peripheral markets through a number of vertical practices and affiliations suggests that the spatial impact of market structure may be something more than a purely theoretical possibility. In fact, it can be argued that in the long run the large tourist producers are potentially able to affect the urbanisation pattern and dictate the intertemporal territorial scale of tourist activities; nothing is static and core regions may become peripheries and vice versa leading to multidirectional changes in terms of the TALC. To this very interesting point, the focus now shifts.

Evolution of Tourist Resorts in the Long Run

The study of the long run may be understood as the spatial equivalent of macroeconomic growth analysis, i.e. it treats the stage of urbanisation process as endogenously determined within the urban system and focuses on factors that explain the emergence, consolidation or reversion of cores and peripheries. In this context, a number of alternative tourism agglomeration paths based on different initial conditions are first discussed; subsequently, the potential importance of industrial organisation in shaping long-run evolutionary patterns is stressed.

Locational advantages

It is not uncommon that a core–periphery spatial configuration emerges from an inherently asymmetric distribution of locational advantages. It may be argued, for example, that a number of resorts managed to become focal points in tourism due to their natural or wanderlust beauties and their proximity to areas of great market potential. In the same context, peripheral resorts are thought to remain underdeveloped because of poor resource endowment and insufficient accessibility. This aspect would be mainly supported by the proponents of the stasis approach in the regional economics literature (Arthur, 1994). According to this theory, spatial equilibrium is characterised by uniqueness and inevitability; in other words, disparities in locational advantages between core and periphery are always adequate to yield the same configuration irrespective of the actual historical and industrial initial conditions. Consequently, the existing spatial diversity is the optimal natural outcome of self-organisation in space.

Though this ergodic argument contains some interesting elements of truth, a number of caveats put its validity into question. In fact, multiple spatial equilibria cannot be precluded under different initial conditions. Moreover, even if spatial disparities may be explained by asymmetries in locational endowments, it is by no means inevitable that the actual agglomeration gap is the outcome of an optimisation process.

Historical dependence

According to the historical dependence approach, the observed spatial configuration is not unique and a different set of early events could have steered the locational pattern into a different outcome; settlement history is crucial and the urban system generates structure as it proceeds. This view is fundamentally dynamic and is associated with multiple, nonergodic equilibria (Arthur, 1994). In fact, a core–periphery outcome can emerge out of an initially symmetric spatial configuration; for reasons unrelated to rational choice and planning, an area may gain the required momentum to set the self-reinforcing agglomeration mechanisms in motion. Consider, for example, the case of a tourist entrepreneur who travels on vacation by car. Suddenly, a mechanical problem occurs in the middle of nowhere, obliging the vacationer to spend about two hours in the area waiting for road aid. In the meantime, (s)he observes the physical characteristics of the place, concluding that local tourist business activity could be profitable. In this sense, a new potential resort is discovered by the right person almost entirely by chance. Though this example admittedly borders on caricature, a number of destinations seem to have developed at least partly in this way.

Illustratively, Mykonos has no exceptional physical beauty compared to the other Cyclades Islands in Greece and especially to the volcanic island of Santorini. However, the concentration of spatial activities is provocatively asymmetric in favour of Mykonos; in fact, though the presence of ancient monuments in Dilos, a small island nearby, provides some initial locational advantage, the overwhelming majority of tourists to Mykonos do not visit these antiquities but prefer to enjoy the built environment, namely the cosmopolitan life in the white stony streets. This may not be attributed to a geographic shift of interest from the initial attractions in subsequent stages of tourism development, as from the very beginning the place had this joyful image of relaxation under the sun; it might be the case, therefore, that some members of Christaller's (1963) *jeunesse dorée* visited the area and initiated the whole agglomeration process. Similarly, tourism development in Amorgos, another island in the Cyclades, has been largely associated with the commercial success of *Grand Bleu*, the French movie that was shot there, while Acapulco in Mexico achieved international recognition after filming of the movie *Night of the Iguana*. All the above are alternative examples of the TALC exploration stage conditions.

Expectations

A core–periphery pattern may also emerge out of a symmetric initial spatial configuration in the presence of self-fulfilling expectations formed in a rational or speculative way. In the first case, publicised information about major tourist site development may inspire real estate activities even before the accomplishment of the actual plans; spatial pre-emption and rent seeking can be strong enough to generate construction activity and magnify the scale of urban entity. The case of Cancún in Mexico is a good example, where the current spatial development has already superseded the initial public planning. In fact, Cancún became an instant resort, due to the mass intrusion of transnational hotel corporations and large tour operators, following the encouragement of the State (Gordon & Goodall, 1992). If the government had favoured another destination for tourism development in the Yucatan Peninsula or elsewhere, the contemporaneous tourist spatial configuration in Mexico would have been completely different. After all, even if the choice of Cancún was evaluated using the right policy criteria, it is likely that some other candidate destinations could have been equally successful if they had received similar promotional effort.

Expectations can also be formed in a speculative way, giving rise to spatial 'rational bubbles' (Blanchard & Fischer, 1989). In a rather theoretical context, consider for example the establishment of a large chain hotel in a destination with no obvious locational advantages. The reputation of this corporation as a very successful hotelier, however, may induce other large tourist entrepreneurs to invest in the area following the logic that if this corporation invests, then there is definitely something behind the scenes. In this way, a whole new structure may emerge and even if it is discovered at some later stage that all that the hotel chain wanted from the very beginning was the exploitation of its reputation from the subsequent agglomeration, the bubble might not collapse (as it would, in the case of stock exchange markets), due to the presence of spatially sunk fundamentals, i.e. irreversible investment in infrastructure. In fact, appropriate marketing techniques may turn the new destination into a very profitable resort. In this sense, large agents' speculative expectations may have real and permanent effects on the existing spatial configuration.

Smooth optimal urbanisation patterns

These patterns can be easily identified with specific stages in the TALC. Spatial development in the case of locational advantages and/or historical accidents may commence with the emergence of a basic tourist infrastructure mostly dedicated to visitors who make their own travel arrangements (exploration and involvement in the TALC). Gradually, the area may establish its presence in the tourist market and if the incoming flow manages to surpass a specific threshold, then mass tourist activities become sustainable; air services and tour operations are introduced and modern large accommodation establishments are erected (development stage). From then on, accessibility and facilities are expected to increase in a self-reinforcing manner, inducing more people to visit the particular resort and casting agglomeration shadows in proximate tourist areas (consolidation stage in the TALC).

At some stage, however, development is expected to attain an optimal level due to the presence of spatial dis-economies of scale such as environmental degradation and high land rents (stagnation stage in the TALC). Consequently, the urban pattern in the area matures and further increases in tourist flows are accommodated by other regions. In this way, the periphery starts growing and gradually acquires the features of the core. Similarly, when the newly developed regions become satiated, agglomeration proceeds elsewhere (see Butler, other volume). As the number of potential destinations is practically very high, this wavy process of spatial diffusion is expected to continue indefinitely, augmenting the number of existing cores and emerging peripheries.

Abrupt sub-optimal urbanisation patterns

Growth may also be sharp from the very beginning irrespective of the initial conditions, as the large tourist conglomerates possess all necessary resources and information networks to transform a *terra incognita* into a popular instant resort, provided that the local potential is reasonably satisfactory: Butler (1980) himself recognised this possibility. In addition, the level and timing of spatial satiation do not depend only on the idiosyncratic characteristics of the various resorts but also on the agglomeration strategies of suppliers. Most importantly, however, there is nothing like an invisible hand that can ensure optimal urban development. In many cases, tourism diverts to new resorts only when irreversible environmental problems have degraded the existing areas, whereas on other occasions territorial growth ceases abruptly well before reaching its full capacity. Though these patterns may be explained by demand factors (such as consumer inertia and changing preferences) or even by exogenous shocks on the supply (such as natural disasters), it seems that industrial organisation theory may offer a convincing alternative justification.

In fact, many contemporary spoilt resorts found in the decline stage of the TALC were heavily dependent on sunlust mass tour operators in the past and/or characterised by co-ordination failure of the local small accommodation suppliers. Similarly, transnational hotel corporations that adopt a portfolio approach to their assets may find it optimal to pursue short-term business activities beyond the long-run sustainability level of a resort. Conversely, tour operators or hotel chains may suddenly realise or expect that other destinations are more advantageous for their activities and decide to quit a resort before its agglomeration maturity.

Even worse, abrupt abandonment may follow the bankruptcy of the most important developer, as happened in the late 1980s in Paradise Island, Bahamas (Debbage, 1990). It seems, therefore, that the point of maximum private profitability may deviate significantly from the one that optimises the public benefit. Moreover, co-ordination failure and territorial oligopsonies may have detrimental impacts on resort development especially in the poststagnation stage of the TALC. Consequently, the public authorities should not adopt a laissez-faire approach, but follow a number of appropriate sectoral policies as discussed in the concluding section.

Conclusions

This chapter aimed at complementing the TALC theory by nesting some of its existing extensions and critiques (e.g. Haywood, 1986) within a wider, internally consistent and explicitly systemic context (i.e. simultaneous treatment of different origins and resorts), whose spatial structure (i.e. core and periphery) is endogenously determined (i.e. result of the evolution in tourism markets). Interestingly, the present discussion has also very important policy implications as it suggests that the demand management policies of the TALC should be complemented by an integrated, supply-driven planning framework. This should aim at increasing the relative bargaining power of the core resorts against the international conglomerates of producers and intermediaries but it should also contribute towards the diminution of the regional gap between the tourist core and periphery. This is not meant to establish a protectionist regulatory regime, which is likely to create inefficiencies and rent seeking problems, but to ensure that competitive forces work properly within a sustainable natural and built environment.

From a more dynamic perspective, the tourist authorities should also implement active development portfolio strategies. On these grounds, policymakers may favour the growth of alternatives to the current air/ sea transport networks (e.g. motorways, high speed trains) where geographically and financially viable, in order to improve accessibility and challenge the bargaining power of existing carriers (Papatheodorou, 2001b). Similarly, the authorities may help the small independent hoteliers to achieve restructuring and efficiency by engaging voluntarily with large marketing or other hospitality consortia (Jones & Pizam, 1993). Moreover, policymakers may form partnerships with small tour operators, whose survival in the origin tourist market is usually related to their specialisation in a limited number of countries (regions) and/or specific types of tourism.

As a final remark, it should be understood that none of the above measures is meant to establish a climate of confrontation among the

various resorts or between destinations and the international conglomerates. This would be unwise, as tourism is, par excellence, a risk-averse
activity that depends heavily on the existence of a welcoming business
milieu. The proposed strategies aim at providing the platform upon
which the resorts can negotiate with the global corporations; only if the
process is held on equal terms, is mutual respect likely to develop.
Otherwise, a number of political problems and propagandistic tags will
emerge leading to conflicts and antagonist activities; given the gradual
maturity of the tourist market and the conquest of the last 'tourist
paradises', such an outcome would not only be detrimental for the
destinations but for the tourist conglomerates too. Competition among
destinations and tourist producers can be healthy and sustainable only if
it is considered within the context of their common future.

Chapter 5

Space–Time Accessibility and the TALC: The Role of Geographies of Spatial Interaction and Mobility in Contributing to an Improved Understanding of Tourism

C. MICHAEL HALL

Introduction

As this volume attests, the tourist area cycle of evolution (TALC) (Butler, 1980) has been one of the most influential and empirically investigated models in tourism studies (Johnston, 2001; Weaver, 2000). Arguably, it is one of the more substantial contributions of a geographer, and hence geography, to understanding tourism phenomenon (Hall & Page, 2001). Yet despite the wide range of critiques of TALC (e.g. Agarwal, 1994; Cooper, 1992; Cooper & Jackson, 1989; Debbage, 1990; Graber, 1997; Haywood, 1986; Oppermann, 1995; Priestley & Mundet, 1998; Russel & Faulkner, 1998; Wall, 1983), there is a surprising dearth of studies which note the inherently spatial characteristics of a tourism area and the implications which these may have for understanding the nature of TALC and therefore its explanatory power. As Johnston (2001) noted in his excellent review of Butler's tourism life cycle model and its associated literature, 'the basic question' in ontological considerations of the life cycle is 'How can a tourist destination – a *place* – have a life cycle?' (emphasis in the original). For the present chapter this question presents a point of departure that is fundamentally different from many other examinations of the tourism or destination or resort life cycle concept. The chapter argues that such tourist destinations should be primarily conceptualised as points in space that are subject to a range of factors which influence location and for which significant geographical theory already exists. Most fundamentally, the chapter argues that the TALC needs to be understood within the context of models and theories of spatial interaction, 'a broad term encompassing any movement over space that results from a human process. It includes journey-to-work, migration, information and commodity flows ...' (Haynes & Fotheringham, 1984: 9).

The chapter is divided into several sections. The chapter first discusses geographical influences on Butler's life cycle model particularly with respect to the work of Christaller (1963), Stansfield (1978) and, to a lesser extent, Wolfe (1952, 1964). This discussion is then used as a platform to identify a number of factors which serve as significant indicators of tourism location. These factors are then placed within the context of wave analogues in particular. The chapter concludes with a call for greater emphasis in tourism studies to be placed on utilising spatial interaction theory as a means of generating a better understanding of locational and environmental issues in tourism.

Geographical Influence on the Life Cycle Model

As noted above, in the various critiques which have been made of TALC, there is surprisingly little comment on the influence of geographers, and economic geographers in particular, on the TALC model. However, an observant reader of the original Butler (1980) article would note that the first three references which are cited in relation to 'the idea of a consistent process through which tourist areas evolve' (Butler, 1980: 5) are from geographers: Roy Wolfe (a Canadian geographer who contributed some of the earliest academic writings on second homes and their location), Walter Christaller (one of the most influential economic geographers of the 20th century who, coincidentally, also wrote travel guidebooks) (Preston, 1985) and Charles Stansfield (an American geographer with expertise in resort development and tourism). It is no mere coincidence that Butler cited these geographers at the start of the TALC article. Butler was himself trained as a geographer and has worked the majority of his academic career based in Departments of Geography but, just as importantly, the citing of these authors highlights the importance of the geographical dimension of space in understanding the cycle model (see also Butler, other volume, this volume).

Spatial interaction is the movement of people, commodities, capital and/or information over geographic space that result from a decision process. The term therefore encompasses such diverse forms of mobility as migration, commuting, shopping, recreation, leisure travel, commodity flows, capital flows, communication flows, transport passenger traffic and attendance at events (Haynes & Fotheringham, 1984). In each case, an individual trades off the benefit of the interaction with the costs that are necessary in overcoming the spatial separation between the individual and the possible destination. The pervasiveness of this type of trade-off in spatial behaviour which has made spatial interaction modelling an important subject in human geography and regional science though its utilisation in tourism studies has been relatively limited.

To Christaller (1963: 95) the 'spatial analysis of various economic occupations' could be undertaken in two ways, one in relation to the 'abstract idea of "pure" space; the other with the "real" area ... i.e. the landscape'. For Christaller (1963: 95), tourism lay at the intersection between these two approaches because of the extent to which 'tourism is drawn to the periphery of settlement distric[t]s'. Indeed, although Christaller is primarily recognised for his contribution to the development of central place theory, it is notable that in an article written in 1967 or 1968, but not widely available in English until after his death, he noted: 'I have tried to develop a polar counterpart to the theory of central places – a theory of "peripheral places". By this I mean, primarily resort areas, the areas of tourism and summer cottages' (Christaller, 1972: 610). Unfortunately, Christaller's polar counterpart was never fully developed, with his 1963 article being his best known contribution to tourism in Anglo-American tourism geography literature. However, this itself provides clues to the evolution of tourist areas to which both Christaller and Butler refer. (The second paragraph of Butler (1980) for example is a lengthy quote from Christaller (1963) in which Christaller outlines the development pattern of a resort area). In describing tourism, Christaller (1963: 95) distinguished between pleasure travel, which he saw as primarily oriented towards peripheral areas, and business and education travel, which were regarded as primarily an urban tourism function. According to Christaller (1963: 96),

> It is typical for places of tourism to be on the periphery. In this way, regions economically benefit from factors which cannot be utilized otherwise: high mountain chains, barren, rocky landscapes, heather, unproductive dunes ... it now happens that traffic no longer peters out near the periphery. Instead, during certain seasons peripheral places become destinations for traffic and commodity flows and become seasonal central points.

Two key elements exist in this quote and in the wider article – the importance of amenity landscapes in the attraction of pleasure tourists and the temporary flow of people between core regions and the tourism periphery. Christaller's notion of central places offers substantial clues to the nature of these flows. Christaller (1966) provided for the spatial arrangement of urban places as retail goods and service centres within a framework of nested hierarchies of settlements and market areas. He used the concepts of market range (the maximum distance a consumer would travel to purchase a good or service) and threshold (the minimum volume of business necessary for a firm to be economically viable) and noted that different retail functions had different ranges and thresholds for the goods and service they supplied. Figure 5.1 provides a model of idealised demand for central goods and services within the Christaller

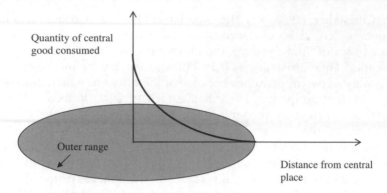

Figure 5.1 Idealised demand zones in the Christaller central place model

model. Given uniform transport costs, the demand for central goods and services falls with distance from the central place and the market range forms a circle. The centrality of an urban centre being therefore defined as the ratio between all the services provided there (for both its own region and visitors from the wider complementarity region that it serves) and the services needed just for its own residents (Haggett, 1975). Christaller's work was a major force in the development of the more mathematically and theoretically informed human geography of the 1960s (Johnston, 1991) and was extremely influential with respect to studies of shopping centres and journeys, city-size distributions and the function of central business districts (Berry, 1967; Dawson & Kirby, 1980; Preston, 1985). Christaller's theory of central places was not directly translated into the study of tourism. Nevertheless, issues of the spatial patterns of tourism-oriented settlements and corresponding concerns with changed transport functions, travel distance and distance-decay effects, which work on central place theory highlighted, has received some limited attention in the tourism literature (Krakover, 2002; Pearce, 1995).

Roy Wolfe's research on the location of cottaging activity and second homes which Butler also cites in his 1980 work on the life cycle was one such example of an interest in the role that distance played in tourism activity. Wolfe (1951, 1952, 1964, 1967, 1970) highlighted the extent to which the location of summer cottages needed to be understood in relation to the travel of cottagers from metropolitan regions with key considerations in terms of the location of cottages being the interaction between travel time/distance from first home and the nature of the landscape itself. In this sense cottage settlements should be understood as a specific interaction between an urban system (origin) and the adjoining rural hinterland (destination). Interestingly, Wolfe also noted, as Christaller did, the potential for tourism to change the character of amenity locations. In the 1950s Wolfe (1952: 62) characterised Wasaga Beach in terms of:

> Traffic jams are as satisfactory as any in Toronto itself. Cars and people fill all the streets. The tourist cabins are bursting and cars are parked in all the available space. The noise is tremendous as [children] shout to each other, car horns blow at them, motorboats roar on the river, and an aeroplane skins the rooftops. We are no longer in the country. We are back in the city again − or better, we are in the city away from the city.

Just as significantly for the purposes of the present discussion, Wolfe also noted the importance of changing patterns of accessibility as a factor in the changes which occurred in cottaging areas. Indeed, in discussing the shape of the curve of the tourist area cycle, Butler (1980) cited Wolfe's work on summer cottaging in Ontario as an example 'that each improvement in the accessibility to a recreation area results in signifi-cantly increased visitation and an expansion of the market area' (Butler, 1980: 11). In addition to Wolfe's work, Butler also cited the research of Stansfield (1972, 1978) as highlighting the importance of accessibility as a factor in influencing change in tourism destinations. Stanfield's (1978) discussion of Atlantic City and a cycle of resort change is particularly instructive with respect to transport and accessibility issues with Stansfield noting the influence of transport-related time/distance on the development of Atlantic City as a 'surf and sand' (1978: 242) destination:

> Connecting customers with the resort is the basis of all resort development; all recreation and tourism patterns take place within a time and space frame. Atlantic City's time-distance and cost-distance relative to Philadelphia were a successful blend of shortest straight line distance and the efficiency of the railroad. Just as the new economics and time-distance of the railroad era helped slow Cape May's growth as a resort, the railroad literally created Atlantic City and shaped its patronage base, its urban morphology and its history.

Unfortunately for Atlantic City, its dependence on the railroad meant that with the growth of automobile infrastructure and greater individual mobility through increased car ownership levels, the competitiveness of Atlantic City as a destination decreased. A morphology that had developed in relation to the point-to-point mobility of railroad users could not easily adapt to the demands of the car. As Stansfield (1978: 246) noted, 'The new highways that brought vacationers to Atlantic City also facilitated their going to other resorts, or their commuting into Atlantic City from less expensive locations. Highway improvements even increased the "day-trip" hinterland of the city.' Changing patterns of accessibility were therefore integral to Stansfield's understanding of resort cycles.

Stansfield's research, along with that of Wolfe and Christaller therefore highlights that changes in urban populations and transport technology, and consequent changes in transport geography, lead to changes in relative locational advantages and disadvantages for areas to attract tourists. How might such a situation be accounted for?

The Geography of Spatial Interaction

One of the most important geographical contributions to understanding issues of accessibility is in relation to the idea of distance decay (also sometimes referred to as inverse-distance relations or distant lapse rate). According to Tobler (1970), the first law of geography is that everything is related to everything else, but near things are more related than distant things. Distance decay therefore refers to the notion that the degree of spatial interaction (flows between regions, e.g. travellers) is inversely related to distance. The importance of a distance decay function has long been noted in studies of human mobility. For example, in 1885 Ravenstein reported that in the case of migrants there was a relationship between the distance and frequency of moves. The empirical regularity of this relationship became developed into demographic laws of spatial interaction which have been applied to a wide range of movements including not only human movements and the transport of goods but also the movement of ideas and concepts (e.g. Axhausen, 2001; Cole, 1989; Haggett, 1965; Stewart, 1947; Stewart & Warntz, 1958; Taylor, 1971; Zipf, 1949).

The curve in Figure 5.1 describes the distance decay effect between the quantity of central goods consumed and distance from the central place. However, different distance decay functions exist for different transport types. One of the simplest and most common ways of describing the curves that relate flows and distance is with the Pareto function of the form:

$$F = aD^{-b} \tag{1}$$

where F is the flow, D is the distance, and a and b are constants. Low b values indicate a curve with a gentle slope with flows extending over a wide area. High b values indicate a curve with a steep slope with flows confined to a limited area (Haggett, 1975). Behind the Pareto form of the distance-decay function is the gravitational concept which suggests that spatial interaction fails off inversely with the square of the distance

$$F = aD^{-2} \tag{2}$$

which can be rewritten as

$$F = a\frac{1}{D^2} \qquad (3)$$

This inverse square relationship is analogous to that used by physicists in estimating gravitational attraction. The inverse 'distance effect' is capable of a series of mathematical transformations which have usually been addressed as logarithmic functions (Taylor, 1971, 1975). However, constants tend to be different in different regions and in expressing different sets of spatial interactions. For example, Smith (1985), in one of the few studies of holiday travel patterns, noted that the distance exponent for a gravity model developed for each of the 16 US states in the study indicated significant state-by-state variations. Nevertheless, as Hay (1986: 186) noted, 'Despite its problems the gravity model is widely used in transport planning ... the great variety of forms means that an approximate fit can nearly always be made and the model then used to predict future flows.' In addition, to transport planning such gravitational affects and distant decay functions are also critical to models of retailing, real estate developments, business location and market potential. Empirical evidence for the gravity model in travel terms is provided in Table 5.1 which shows the distribution of trips by great

Table 5.1 Distribution of trips by great circle distance between origin and destination for French national passenger transport surveys 1981–82 and 1993–94

Great circle *Distance*	Daily Mobility *1981–82*	Daily Mobility *1993–94*
< 5 km	30 217	48 721
5–14 km	7 527	18 709
15–49 km	3 393	10 238
50–79 km	366	1 361
80–149 km	226	1 021
150–349 km	157	633
350–499 km	19	148
≥ 500 km	17	97
Total trips	41 922	80 928
Sample size (persons)	21 358	38 455

Sources: Adapted from Madre and Maffre 2001: 356, 357

circle distance between origin and destination recorded in French national passenger transport surveys in 1981–82 and 1993–94 (Madre & Maffre, 2001).

Surprisingly, such concepts have attracted relatively little attention in tourism studies (editor's note: the one major exception to this is Williams and Zelinksy's pioneering effort in *Economic Geography* in 1970), despite acknowledgement of the importance of distance and time relationships in destination and activity site selection (Fesenmaier & Lieber, 1987; Greer & Wall, 1979; Hall & Page, 2001; Malamud, 1973; McAllister & Klett, 1976; Murphy & Keller, 1990; Pearce, 1995; Smith, 1985, 1989); commuting, leisure and shopping activity (Levinson & Kumar, 1995); and second home location (Bell, 1977; Müller, 1999; Wolfe, 1970), as well as the availability of a range of models with which to describe such relationships (Baradaran & Ramjerdi, 2001).

Figure 5.2 presents a model for describing different forms of temporary mobility in relation to number of trips or movements, time and distance. The number of movements declines the further one travels in time and space away from the point of origin. Such distance decay effects with respect to travel frequency have been well documented (e.g. Holmes & Brown, 1981; Smith, 1985) (see Table 5.1) and have been used to describe the relationship between tourism and other forms of temporary mobility (Bell & Ward, 2000; Williams & Hall, 2002) as well

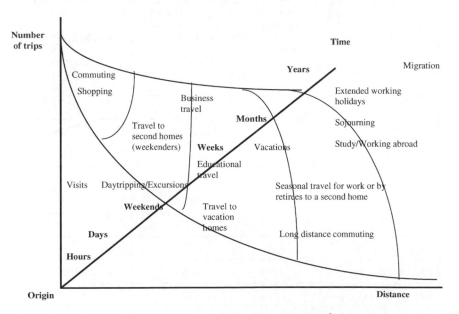

Figure 5.2 Extent of temporary mobility in space and time

as to critique Christaller's (1963) assertion that there is a concentration of tourism activity at peripheral locations (Cooper, 1981; Husbands, 1981, 1983; Krakover, 2002; Mansfield, 1990). In general, the long-distance trip making (e.g. journeys to destinations beyond 100 km from home or current base) usually associated with tourism constitutes a very small share of all journeys (about 0.5%), but represents a much larger share of the total kilometres or miles travelled (about 20%), and therefore of the commercial and environmental impacts of travel (Axhausen, 2001). For example, according to the *1995 American Travel Survey*, journeys over a 100 mile minimum distance threshold account for about 0.5% of all trips and cover approximately 25% of the person-miles travelled in the USA (Bureau of Transportation Statistics, 1997).

Perhaps most significantly Figure 5.2 highlights that tourism, defined as it often is in terms of overnight stay(s) away from the home environment (see Hall & Page, 2001), therefore tends to occur as a function of time-distance away from a central point of origin. Such an observation has significant implications for understanding TALC within the framework of tourism as a form of spatial interaction.

TALC as a Form of Spatial Interaction

Tourism does not occur randomly in space. The time-distance sensitivity of tourist-related travel leads to specific spatial patterns related to distance from origin. Space−time constraints exist for a range of accessibility relations between a point of origin and a destination (Burns, 1979; Hägerstrand, 1970; Pred, 1977). The space−time framework recognises that participation in activities, such as leisure, has both spatial and temporal dimensions, i.e. activities occur at specific locations for finite temporal durations. In addition, the transportation system dictates the velocities at which individuals can travel and therefore the time available for activity participation at dispersed locations (Miller, 1999).

Figure 5.3 presents an idealised model for leisure travel which extends from an urban core in relation to car-based mobility. The model not only highlights the nature of the distance decay effects of leisure travel, but identifies a zone of overnight stay within the hinterland of an urban centre. The zone of overnight stay refers to an area in which the tendency for travellers to stay overnight increases and the likelihood of same-day return trips decreases because of:

a. availability of time to travel (time budget) and engage in tourist related activities;
b. limitations related to the need for rest while travelling (i.e. tourists cannot continue to drive continuously without sleep); and
c. time-distance trade-offs between returning home to sleep and the travel time involved versus stopping overnight.

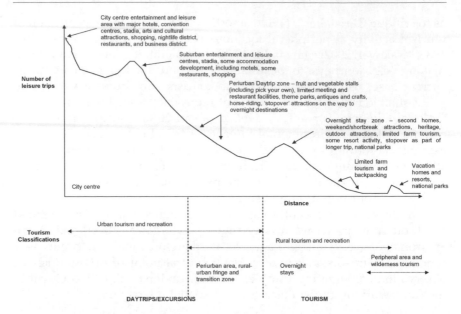

Figure 5.3 Spatial and temporal charateristics of leisure opportunities

The time sensitivity of leisure travel means that the location of overnight stays from a tourist-generating region tends to cluster at a location related to time-distance from a point of origin. Typically a tourism-generating area will be a large city, but a gateway may also act as such a point of origin. Figure 5.4 represents this clustering in terms of the density of overnight stays with respect to a highly simplified model of an isolated central tourism-generating location surrounded by a uniform plane. Individuals and households, possessing perfect knowledge of the distance costs, select a tourism area location that maximises their utility subject to their time-distance constraints. However, a uniform plane clearly does not occur in the real world and travel distances are highly affected by transport networks as well as the distribution of amenity areas which are sought by leisure tourists and weekend second-home purchasers. Such a constraint is accounted for by Miller's (1991) notion of Potential Path Space (PPS), defined in terms of the space–time prism that delimits all locations in space–time that can be reached by an individual based on the locations and duration of mandatory activities (e.g. home, work) and the travel velocities allowed by the transportation system. Assume an individual located at time t_1 at the point of origin (X_0, Y_0). Again assume that at time t_2 the individual has to be back at the origin. Then the available time for all activities is given by

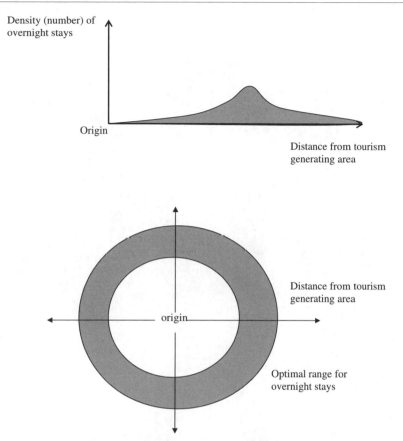

Figure 5.4 Location of overnight stays in relation to points of origin

$$t = t_2 - t_1 \qquad\qquad (4)$$

The projection of PPS onto two-dimensional XY-space represents the potential path area that an individual can move within, given the available time budget.

Figure 5.5 presents a hypothetical pattern of density of overnight stays in relation to optimal range for overnight stays and location of tourist areas given the presence of transport networks along the X and Y axes. Significantly, the figure postulates that the density of overnight stays will change overtime – presented as t_1 and t_2. Such changes can occur because of improvements in transport technology, e.g. a shift between or within technologies, or transport infrastructure, e.g. improvement in road quality allowing for faster travel. Although not represented here, it should also be noted that population growth and urbanisation processes

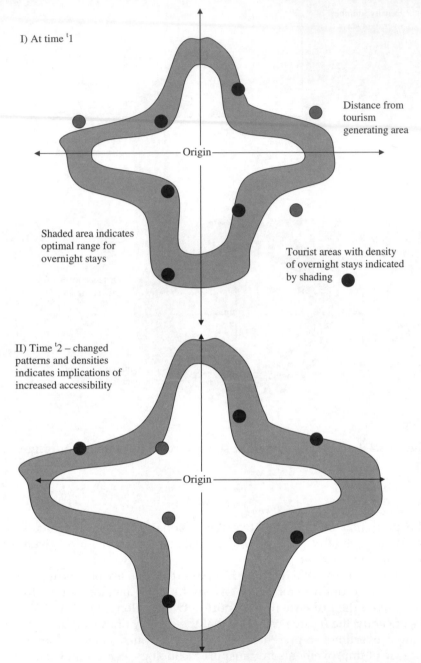

Figure 5.5 Hypothetical pattern of density of overnight stays in relation to optimal range for overnight stays and location of tourist areas

will also encourage such changes. These changes can also be represented as a wave analogue in which changes in time/distance from a central point of origin will lead to different densities d of overnight stay at a specific location L over times t_1, t_2, ... in relation to the overall distribution of overnight stays as a function of distance from origin (Figure 5.6).

Analogue Theory

The use of analogue theory – a formal theory of model building which provides for the selective abstraction of elements from an empirical domain and their translation into a simplified and structured representation of a particular system–was an important component of the quantitative revolution that existed in geography in the 1950s and the 1960s (Chorley, 1964). Within geography and elsewhere in the social sciences, the use of analogues is now so widespread that its implications are little considered (Livingstone & Harrison, 1981). Indeed, arguably TALC is itself such an analogue model.

Wave analogues have been used to describe phenomenon as distinct as urban density and the development of the urban fringe (e.g. Blumenfield, 1954; Boyce, 1966), and innovation (e.g. Hägerstrand, 1952, 1968). As noted above, in the case of TALC this chapter argues that within the context of the Butler model a tourist area/destination should not be primarily conceived of as a product in marketing terms. Instead, the destination should be primarily conceptualised as a geographical place, e.g. as a point in space which is subject to a range of factors which influence locational advantage and disadvantage. Most significant to these is the movement outward from a tourist-generating origin of travellers as a function of distance. Such travel movement

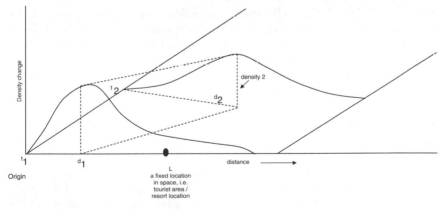

Figure 5.6 Wave Analogue

cannot be adequately represented in the classic linear form of a distance decay model whereby the location of numbers of travellers is highest closer to the generating area and diminishes in relation to distance. Instead, factors which influence travel behaviour, such as decisions relating to overnight stays and time to undertake leisure-oriented activities, creates a series of peaks and troughs in relation to distance from the generating area. Moreover, for any given form of transport there will be a different set of distance/time functions at which overnight stays will need to be made but all, out of the necessity of travellers to stop, can be represented through a series of peaks and troughs rather than a straight line. Given the above assumptions, changes in time-distance (cost-distance and other forms of distance would also be significant) between the tourist-generating origin and the surrounding hinterland will then lead to corresponding changes in the number of travellers for any given point in the spatial system.

However, locations within the spatial system are spatially fixed, towns and cities do not suddenly get up and move away in order to maximise advantageous distance functions, although they do change and adapt over time in relation to new networks and patterns of accessibility. Similarly, tourist areas/destinations are full of plant and infrastructure that are also spatially fixed. Therefore, as Figure 5.6 indicates, if the numbers of tourist bed-nights (or other measures of tourism-related density) at a spatially fixed point 'destination' (L) are drawn at t_1, t_2, t_3, ... in relation to the changing nature of distance from a tourist-generating origin(s), then this provides a representation of overnight stay density at a specific location which is analogous to that of the TALC when presented in its standard two-dimensional form (see Butler, 1980).

Clearly, the wave analogue approach to TALC is potentially far richer than that presented here. For example, as well as direct-line distance, the notion of distance can, and should be, expressed in terms such as network distance, time-distance, cost-distance, behavioural-distance (including perceived distance), and multidimensional measures combining time, money and effort spent in travelling between origin and destination. However, space–time functions can be developed for all these ways of considering distance both at the level of the individual and at the macrolevel. Perhaps more significantly there is the issue of multiple origin points as well as different forms of transport. However, in the case of both of these concerns it should be noted that given data availability, the relative role of different origin points in determining the accessibility of a given location should be assessable while different space–time prisms clearly exist for different forms of transport.

An additional criticism of the TALC model has been in relation to changing markets and tourist types recognised at different stages of the life cycle (Johnston, 2001, this volume). However, recognition of the spatial interaction of tourism areas with origin areas provides a potential powerful explanatory tool with respect to the characteristics of resort markets. According to Schafer (2000: 22), 'Aggregate travel behavior is determined largely by two budgets: the share of monetary expenditure and the amount of time that individuals allocate to transportation. However, neither budget is unique.' Given that a travel money budget represents the fraction of disposable income devoted to travel, a fixed travel money budget establishes a direct relationship between disposable income and distance travelled, provided average user costs of transport remain constant (see Schafer & Victor, 2000).

Data from the 1995 American Travel Survey and the 1995 Nationwide Personal Transportation Survey show that recreation trips (RTs) under-taken in a private vehicle (PV) make up about 14% of all local trips, 23% of all long distance trips and about 15% of total vehicle kilometres travelled in the USA (Mallett & McGuckin, 2000). However, recreation trips are not equally distributed among the population. For example, African Americans report about half the amount of recreation automobile trips and one-third the average kilometres as whites. Research by Mallett and McGuckin (2000) indicates that people in households earning US$75,000 or more made about 1.7 long distance PV-RTs each, more than four times the number made by people in households earning less than US$25,000 (0.4 trips per capita), although people in low-income households are more dependent on PV to make long distance RT than people in high-income households, with the gap widening as trip length increases. For people in households with an annual income over US$100,000, flying becomes a significant option for trips of 644–805 km (400–500 miles) away from home. About 30% of all PV and air trips combined for recreation are taken by air at this distance. For households with income less than US$25,000, this 30% threshold is not approached until trips of 1290–1450 km one-way (800–900 miles) or 2575–2896 km roundtrip (1600–1800 miles) (Mallett & McGuckin, 2000: 7–8). Similarly, from the same survey data Mallett (2001) also indicated that people in low-income households made less than half the annual number of long-distance trips (defined as a roundtrip to a destination at least 100 miles or more from home) per person than the population as a whole. On average, low-income people made 1.6 long-distance person trips in 1995 compared with 3.9 trips for the entire population. In contrast, persons in households with medium-low income made 2.6 trips a year, medium-high income 4.2 trips and high income 6.3 trips (Mallett, 2001: 170).

The US data also revealed that low-income individuals also travel shorter distances than people in higher income groups. The average (mean) trip roundtrip distance among low-income adults under 65 was 650 miles compared with 990 miles by high-income people. This is primarily related to the fact that the low-income individuals travel much less often by air because the average long-distance trip (excluding air) by all income groups was about the same (approximately 550 miles). Because they travel less often and less by air, low-income individuals travel less miles overall than other groups: low-income people travelled about 1350 miles in 1995 compared with 2300 miles by medium-low, 3650 miles by medium-high and 7250 miles by those with high incomes (Mallett, 2001: 173). Such data provide rich empirical evidence for the changing socioeconomic basis of markets for tourist areas with the relative cost-distance accessibility of destinations in part determining destination choice. As Stansfield (1978: 245), reported in his Atlantic City article, 'The socioeconomic orientation of a particular resort is thus often closely associated with its relative accessibility, as it exists, and as it had developed through the history of the resort.'

Travel time expenditures for leisure trips do not rise with trip distance and therefore roughly follow a budget-like development (Goodwin, 1981; Hupkes, 1982; Marchetti, 1994; Schafer, 2000; Schafer & Victor, 2000). Although the constant travel money budget leads to rising travel demand, the roughly constant travel time budget requires travel at a higher speed and thus shifts toward faster modes. For example, while the duration of leisure trips has remained constant in the USA between 1977 and 1995, trip distance has increased by almost 50% (Schafer, 2000). 'With rising incomes and a fixed travel money budget, people increase their mean speed and daily travel distance by allocating more money to travel. In the high income, automobile-dominated United States, 95% of all trips are made within a distance of 50 kilometers, the distance that can be covered by automobile within the travel time budget. With even greater income and a continuous supply of high-speed transport, 95% of all trips will be longer distance' (Schafer, 2000: 18). As this occurs, some tourist areas will rise and otherwise will fall in response to changing patterns and networks of accessibility between destinations and origins and the travel time and expenditure budgets of those that live there.

Conclusions

Butler's model has been extremely influential in tourism studies and in the subdiscipline of tourism geography. However, it is a model and not a theory. Theory provides a more general framework of 'connected statements used in the process of explanation' (Johnston, 1988: 483), while a model is 'an idealized and structured representation of the real' (Gregory, 1988: 301) or 'an experimental design based on a theory' (Harris, 1966: 258). Unfortunately, because much of the discussion of the cycle of evolution has been in terms of an aspatial product life cycle, the geographic underpinnings of Butler's model in terms of spatial interaction have not received the attention they deserved. Indeed, it is significant that in Stansfield's (1978: 238) paper on the resort cycle 'time-distance' and 'cost-distance' were listed as keywords.

This chapter has argued that an analogue model which incorporates distance as a variable within the spatial interaction between a tourist-generating origin and a tourist area provides a far greater degree of explanatory power than that provided in the original Butler (1980) model and subsequent (re)interpretations. As Smith (1985: 151) observed, 'it appears that the geographic variables are more important as predictors of vacation travel patterns that traditional aggregate socioeconomic variables'. Just as importantly, a spatial interaction approach highlights the fact that tourism areas need to be understood in relation to origin areas. Tourism areas do not occur in isolation. The dynamic magnitude and nature of tourism activity reflects the strength of interaction between origins and destinations and their associated environments. Changes in tourism activities which are reflected in changes in spatial interactions may lead to qualitative and/or quantitative economic, environmental and social change at destinations. Changes in the environment, such as changes in amenity values, may induce changes in tourism activities and consequently the interactions between origins and destinations. New networks and patterns of connectivity and accessibility will also affect the interaction between origins and destinations and corresponding changes in the tourism activities and their impact.

The understanding of accessibility and amenity values is regarded as critical to identifying and predicting the actual and potential patterns of tourism development at specific locations in space. Indeed, the product life cycle so influential in consideration of TALC is itself a space–time wave analogue related to innovation diffusion processes (Hägerstrand, 1952, 1968), a point seemingly lost in nearly all of the discussion which has taken place on tourism destination product life cycles. Such an observation also highlights the potential for spatial interaction modelling to provide a better understanding of the development of information regarding potential destinations through the analysis of information fields, a technique long established in the geographical literature (Morrill & Pitts, 1972).

A rich range of analytical tools already exists with which to analyse spatial interaction. Five major theoretical approaches for measurement of accessibility indicators can be readily identified in the relevant literature: travel-cost approach, gravity or opportunities approach, constraints-based approach, utility-based surplus approach and a composite approach. Accessibility measures in these approaches differ with respect to theoretical foundation, complexity of construction and demand on data, with availability of data an important factor in the choice of the appropriate measure in an accessibility study. Other significant issues include measurement of attraction masses, choice of demarcation area, unimodality versus multimodality and agglomeration effects (Baradaran & Ramjerdi, 2001; Miller, 1999; Wu & Miller, 2001). Unfortunately, while cognate fields such as regional science, transport studies and geography, especially Geographic Information Systems (Miller & Wu, 2000; Müller, 1999), have a long core tradition of studying travel-related spatial interaction problems, Tourism Studies does not. This may, in part, relate to how tourism is perceived within the academy as a whole (Hall & Page, 2001). However, it may also relate to how tourism researchers perceive their field of study. Arguably, if tourism is seen as a specific form of leisure-oriented temporary mobility within the range of human mobilities (Figure 5.2), then new possibilities emerge for the empirical understanding of tourism phenomenon in a manner which might not only lead to the development and improvement of models of tourism development, such as TALC, but which might also allow tourism to contribute to recognition of the concept of mobility as a central paradigm within the social sciences (Urry, 2000; Williams & Hall, 2002), rather than remaining in the academic periphery.

Acknowledgements

The general contents and approach of this paper have been utilised in my teaching in tourism, particularly at the graduate level, since 1989. However, although these arguments and ideas have been discussed in in-house research seminars and in conversation with colleagues, they have never seen the light of day, despite threats to the contrary, until now. Apart from thanking Richard Butler for the opportunity to publish this material and for discussions surrounding it, I would also like to thank the following colleagues with whom lengthy discussions have occurred on TALC and the tourism geography of spatial interaction: David Duval, Thor Flogenfeldt, Alan Lew, Dieter Müller and Stephen Page. Naturally, no blame can be attached to them for the contents of this chapter.

Part 3

Alternative Conceptual Approaches and the TALC

RICHARD BUTLER

There have been several versions of the TALC used in the literature; some of the more significant and widely quoted ones are included in the other volume. For the most part, however, those examples were modifications rather than conceptual alternatives to the TALC. In this section of this volume are chapters that propose alternative models or conceptual variations of the TALC, thus carrying the discussion a stage further by linking the original model to other concepts and theories, some in tourism and some from other bodies of literature.

In the first of her two chapters in this section, Russell discusses the contributions of theory on entrepreneurship to the TALC. This chapter serves two purposes, one is to introduce this body of theory, well known to many in the business world but much less discussed in the tourism literature, and the second is to elaborate on one of the areas of the original model, the triggers of development, a topic which has not been explored in great detail to date. Tourism, hospitality and travel, as many other areas, have benefited greatly from the efforts of early pioneers, Cook, Hilton, Flagler and Disney are obvious examples, but as Russell notes, there also have been major contributions in the area of destination development from small-scale entrepreneurs, as befits an industry characterised by a large number of small- and medium-sized enterprises. Russell's discussion of entrepreneurship at different scales is illustrated by the effect of individuals on specific destinations and their influence on the patterns of development modelled by the TALC.

In a very different setting, Weizenegger conceptualises the application of the TALC to protected natural areas, using a sample of such areas in Africa to illustrate her concepts. She argues for such areas to be regarded as destinations and as such, appropriate for consideration in the light of the stages of development proposed in the original model. In her chapter she discusses the trigger effect of designation as a protected natural area on a destination, along with the subsequent and inevitable changes in infrastructure, and the commencement of a new development cycle. The African examples, she argues, follow a wave movement with different gradients, a pattern discussed by Hall (this volume) and also illustrated by Lundgren (other volume) in his discussion on resorts in Quebec.

As with these authors, Weizenegger returns to a spatial perspective and the issues involved in this in her conclusions.

Lundtorp and Wanhill also apply the model in a local context, in order to explain how local features, including location and history, cause divergence of the pattern of development from the theoretical path. They propose a demand-based TALC model, and by taking the number of tourists as a measure of the time path of the model, they examine the theoretical underpinnings of the cycle from the visitor perspective.

Using differential equations to model the growth of visitor numbers, based in part on the spread of knowledge of the destination as it is developed, they identify breakpoints in the pattern of growth of numbers and thus stages in the development.

They go on to test the model through a time series analysis of the Danish island of Bornholm for which data on visitor arrivals has been available for over half a century. They argue that while the life-cycle curve can only be truly representative in an aggregate manner if all visitors are repeat, in a location such as Bornholm, which has a high proportion of domestic tourists, the model fits the observations on visitor numbers fairly well. The advantages of dealing with small islands as research laboratories because of their natural boundaries are demonstrated clearly.

The chapter by Ravenscroft and Hadjihambi also applies the TALC and an alternative theory to an island location, in this case, Ayia Napa in Cyprus. They choose not use the analogy of the life cycle but instead argue that the development of such resorts is better understood as being a process of evolution, in the sense that development has a number of iterations, each reflecting modifications and improvements from the previous pattern. In this they disagree with others such as Johnston (this volume) that the TALC implies multiple generations. Using Lamarck's theory of the inheritance of acquired traits, they suggest it has resonance with at least cultural and technological evolutionary processes, ones particularly pertinent to tourist destinations. They note that Ayia Napa has already proceeded through a number of stages in its development, but argue that it is continuing to evolve into yet another modified form, reflecting the influence of planners. Not unlike the influence of entrepreneurs argued by Russell, Ravenscroft and Hadjihambi propose 'change management' as being of particular importance in destination change and development. They argue that the life cycle of destinations is much more the result of planning and development decisions or interventions than inevitability, and reflects also the influence of exogenous forces. They conclude by acknowledging that the TALC is a reasonable 'post hoc analogy' of the development pattern of a destination but that tourist destinations need to be examined through different and multiple dimensions if we are to fully comprehend their patterns of development.

This theme of multiple dimensions and apparent often unrelated actions which impinge upon tourist destinations is the theme of the last chapter in this section, that by Russell on the application of Chaos Theory to the TALC. She argues that the adoption of Chaos Theory in many subjects has meant a reappraisal of the fundamental and traditional ways of looking at processes, particularly with respect to stability and change. The realisation that things are far more complex than many originally thought has been a long time coming, but recent events in the world (11 September 2001, the Bali bombing and SARS as examples) make the acceptance of unanticipated and uncontrollable exogenous forces much more easy than may have been the case in earlier times. Russell's discussion of tenuous equilibrium and the 'butterfly' effect have much more meaning after the events in the first two years of this century. She argues that the 'edge of chaos' state does not necessarily mean the demise of systems or destinations, and one can see the spectacular success of budget low-cost airlines following September 11, while traditional flag carrier airlines suffered major financial losses. Linking chaos and turbulence and the stages of the TALC model as Russell does harks back to an earlier paper by Keller (1987), who argued that immediately before a shift to another stage, a destination would be in an uncontrolled state. In many ways the linking of the TALC, which implies stability and continuance of a process with Chaos Theory, might be thought of as incongruous or impractical. In fact, as Russell shows, there are sound reasons for arguing that the two concepts can be related in the way that destinations are affected by exogenous forces in their pattern of development.

Chapter 6
The Contribution of Entrepreneurship Theory to the TALC Model

ROSLYN RUSSELL

Introduction

Entrepreneurship, from the earliest times, has been a major factor in the development of tourism. And yet, unlike other industries, it has not received the attention it deserves (Russell & Faulkner, 1999; Shaw & Williams, 1998). The innovation, flair and vision of entrepreneurs like Thomas Cook and Walt Disney shaped modern tourism and provided examples of the significant differences individuals can make to an economic sector. While these particular individuals have impacted tourism on a global scale, entrepreneurship also plays a major role in destination development at a regional and local level. Entrepreneurs are often crucial change agents in destination development, having a major influence on the shape of the TALC curve. 'Indeed, the defining moment in most tourism destinations can be attributed to the actions of rogues who actualised its tourism potential' (McKercher, 1999: 427). 'Rogues' because in refusing to squeeze into the mould by which the traditionalists had restricted themselves, they were perceived by them as not playing by the rules, and therefore as outlaws.

Why is it then that entrepreneurship has not been more visible in the tourism literature? It is probable that the traditional reductionist research methods inherited by tourism have made it difficult for the behaviour of entrepreneurs and the entrepreneurial process to be dealt with adequately. Entrepreneurs fall into the 'outlier' category, their individual arrivals, visions and impacts are impossible to predict and may be dismissed as aberrant noise. Russell (this volume) discusses Chaos and Complexity Theory, a research framework that actually highlights that which is unpredictable and therefore allows greater understanding of entrepreneurial behaviour. This chapter will focus specifically on the role of entrepreneurs – a chaotic element in the TALC.

Entrepreneurship in tourism is most likely when induced by favourable conditions in the macroeconomic, social, political cycles (Argawal, 2002; Haywood, 1998; Lerner & Haber, 2000). 'Favourable' not only in the sense of buoyancy but also in circumstances that are stimulating, challenging, demanding. Both tourism and entrepreneurship react with greater vigour and immediacy to the unexpected events that are occurring with increasing frequency and intensity. Bombs in Bali, oil spills off Spain interrupt the tenor of tourism and elicit the kind of imagination and daring that aims for recovery and beyond. The macroenvironment impacts tourism. Entrepreneurial responses recipro-cate by transforming impinging circumstances into opportunities. Understanding something of the web of intersecting influences would be a useful means of comprehending the role of entrepreneurs in destination development.

Entrepreneurs are uniquely individual. Therefore there can be no stereotypical concept of *the* entrepreneur. Nor can the individual, successfully entrepreneurial in some other field, necessarily be successful in tourism. Tourism too is unique. Its purposes, needs, products and sensitivities are different from those of business generally. However, a pool of characteristics selectively shared by entrepreneurs can be isolated. This chapter will give examples of a number of entrepreneurial categories that are essentially a function of the TALC stage, macro-environmental conditions and the individual characteristics of the entrepreneur.

The Nature of Entrepreneurship: A Background

Although the concept of entrepreneurship emerged initially from the discipline of economics in the 18th century, the amount of attention given to the role of entrepreneurs in economies has waned in modern economic theory, despite the growth in significance of entrepreneurial activity (Minniti & Bygrave, 1999). There are several explanations for this. Firstly, early studies revealing the inherently complex nature of entrepreneurs and the entrepreneurship process did not sit comfortably with classical economic theory. Secondly, there has been in the past an unwillingness by universities to recognise entrepreneurs, many of whom represent the antithesis of the philosophies of the established education system. Thirdly, at varying times, there has been public hostility towards entrepreneurs, which at its worst inhibits entrepreneurial activity, and at best makes it unpopular to research.

The term 'entrepreneur' was coined by the French economist Richard Cantillon in 1755. He saw the distinctive characteristics of the entrepre-neur as 'the willingness to take risks in the face of uncertainty' (Hartwell & Lane, 1991). In 1800, J.B. Say, another French economist, saw entrepreneurial activities as shifting economic resources from an area of low productivity into a situation where higher yields can be gained. John Stuart Mill brought the concept into English economics, describing an entrepreneur as an 'adventurer' (Hartwell & Lane, 1991). In general, the early theories of entrepreneurship were concerned with three functions – risk taking, provision of capital and managing operations.

It was not until after the Civil War in the USA that the concepts of entrepreneurship were dealt with by American economists. They too focused on entrepreneurship as having a managerial role and as being distinctive from that of capitalists. In 1921, Frank Knight made a significant contribution to the theory of entrepreneurship by separating the concepts of risk and uncertainty. He saw risk as being identifiable and therefore insurable, but uncertainty being determined by unpredictability and therefore uninsurable. Knight (1921 in Hartwell & Lane, 1991: 32) attributes entrepreneurs with the courage to take risks associated with uncertainty. Their decisions 'involved committing resources to future use in a world in which the future cannot be predicted with certainty'.

However, the true complexity of the entrepreneurship process was brought to the forefront by the works of an Austrian economist, Joseph Schumpeter (1934), who was responsible for one of the most significant contributions to the concept of entrepreneurship. In doing so, however, he unwittingly stunted the progress of entrepreneurship research within the discipline of economics. Schumpeter introduced the concept of innovation. At the time this concept was seen to be radical, especially to economists, because it suggested that entrepreneurial activities brought dynamic disequilibrium to a world which, according to economists, was characterised by stability and equilibrium (Drucker, 1985).

Although economists recognised the obvious facts that entrepreneurs were 'innovators' and 'change instigators', they could not slot them comfortably into their theoretical constructs, whose rigidity rested on their view (albeit blurred) of Newtonian scientific principles. Consequently, the significance of entrepreneurs was played down, their role was dismissed as external noise, a spasmodic phenomenon of little impact. Because entrepreneurs disrupted the neat models and did not comply with the equations and complicated predictions, the study of entrepreneurship was stifled (Minniti & Bygrave, 1999). It carried too many forebodings of discord (Drucker, 1985). It seems that tourism research has inherited genes from the same belief system and hence has suffered similar consequences.

Thus, Schumpeter's (1934) seminal contribution brought new concepts to the modern theory of entrepreneurship. Since then, entrepreneurship research has included concepts such as creativity, innovation and change as core ingredients to the entrepreneurial process. Schumpeter's notion of the 'creative entrepreneur' is described in the literature as being itself a 'doctrinal innovation' (Cauthorn, 1989) and is now entrenched in contemporary theory. He saw innovation as the 'creative response'

(Hartwell & Lane, 1991) to change and saw it as the act of 'combining productive factors'. Schumpeter proposed five categories of innovation:

- production of new goods;
- devising new methods of production;
- creating new markets;
- discovering new sources of supplies;
- creating new types of organization.

(Cauthorn, 1989)

A tourism researcher cannot help but notice the striking similarities of the above processes to the core elements of tourism development – producing new tourism products, introducing new methods of providing tourist services such as the internet, creating niche markets, increasing new sources of supply and developing new types of tourist organisations. Schumpeter himself did not realise some of the more important implications of his contribution to entrepreneurship theory at the time. The benefit of hindsight often reveals greater significance to research than original intention. As an economist, he saw entrepreneurship as only a developmental part of the capitalist process, which he thought would become obsolete as capitalism moved forward. It appeared that although he had an amazing insight for his time, the blinkers of classical economics led him to conclude that 'entrepreneurs and "true" innovative activity would disappear as "trustification" proceeds' (Cauthorn, 1989: 18). In other words he saw it as a temporary and dispensable developmental interlude. He was not a prophet and, therefore, failed to foresee the coming surge of insight into the entrepreneurial process.

Paradoxically, even subsequent critics of the Schumperian theory reaffirm the core assumptions as being highly relevant today. Wright (1951) voices his objection to the view of the entrepreneur being an historical phenomenon only:

> But I believe that in every generation of every culture there will be found at the least a few people who speculate about possibilities of doing things – both technologically and socially and who are not content to rest at mere speculation... If we make men 'free' they become creative (questioning), and if they become creative they create trouble, and also, in many cases, growth ... I almost wholly dissent from Schumpeter's doctrine of the obsolescence of the entrepreneurial function. (Wright, 1951: 134)

Quite correctly, Wright acknowledges that entrepreneurs can indeed sometimes cause 'trouble' and also growth. Tourist destinations have experienced both scenarios. The challenge for destinations is to create the right mix of conditions that limits the opportunity for entrepreneurial 'trouble'. Wright also encapsulates very well the nature of entrepreneurial activity in tourist destinations – they speculate, they act on speculation and they create.

Who is an Entrepreneur?

While research in the entrepreneurship field has struggled unsuccessfully to develop a comprehensive, accurate definition of an entrepreneur, there are some elements that appear to be common to all entrepreneurs. An entrepreneur is generally seen as someone who sees a business opportunity and gathers together the resources to realise it. However, over time, the literature has developed a deeper profile of an entrepreneur to include concepts that describe more clearly entrepreneurial behaviour and process. Schumpeter (1934) describes an entrepreneur as someone that 'destroys the equilibrium with a perennial gale of creative destruction'. This implies a greater involvement in bringing about change to create opportunities rather than sitting back waiting for opportunity. Kuratko and Hodgetts (1998: 5) describe an entrepreneur as 'the aggressive catalyst for change' in the world of business. Timmons' (1989) description creates a vivid image that describes many tourism entrepreneurs.

> Entrepreneurs work hard, driven by an intense commitment and determined perseverance. They burn with the competitive desire to excel and win. They use failure as a tool for learning, and would rather be effective than perfect. They respond to setbacks and defeats as if they were temporary interruptions, and rely on resiliency and resourcefulness to rebound and succeed. They have enough confidence in themselves to believe they can personally make a difference in the final outcome of their ventures, and in their lives. (Timmons, 1989: 1)

In imagining the hurdles and obstacles that faced tourism entrepreneurs like Thomas Cook for example, in his early endeavours in creating tourism innovations such as travellers 'cheques', package tours – concepts that contributed to the emergence of mass tourism, it is apparent that this could only have been achieved by someone with the traits described above by Timmons. His innovations were bold, completely discontinuous from the past, and created phase changing outcomes.

Entrepreneurs can be found within organisations – these are known as intrapreneurs and they are increasingly in demand. Organisations know that they need the specific characteristics and behaviour of entrepreneurs in order to gain a competitive advantage. The ability of entrepreneurs to use their creativity to exploit change, find opportunity and develop innovative products and strategies for the organisation need to be encouraged within the tourism industry as a whole and in government departments especially in the wake of the challenges to tourist destinations induced by the latest round of terrorist activities.

In summary, entrepreneurs, although highly individual, are generally likely to embody a number of the following behaviours.

An entrepreneur:

- Has the ability to perceive circumstances and needs.
- Has the resourcefulness to evaluate, respond to and create opportunities.
- Has the confidence and creative mind-set to envision beyond convention.
- Lives with and is confident in his dream.
- Has and constantly expands knowledge relevant to his field.
- Is goal-oriented, success-driven.
- Is not deterred by temporary set-backs, perseveres, thinks positively.
- Has people skills, is persuasive.
- Can cement organisational and financial backing.
- Is restlessly energetic.
- Has a social environment, including at the family level, that if not supportive does not impede.
- Has the ability to use to advantage or at the very least is not distracted by the presence of unpredicted occurrences.

The Entrepreneurial Environment

Successful entrepreneurship is dependent on a certain 'climate' or environment conducive to nurturing the spirit of entrepreneurs (Smilor & Feeser, 1991). Although there is a preponderance of literature focusing on the entrepreneur as a person, it is recognised that 'entrepreneurial activity does not occur in a vacuum. Instead, it is deeply embedded in a cultural and social context, often amid a web of human networks that are both social and economic' (Krueger & Brazeal, 1994: 92).

Interestingly, the environmental characteristic that is most conducive to entrepreneurial behaviour is turbulence. Not necessarily wild chaos, but instability, disequilibrium or when the system is at the 'edge of chaos' are the most favourable conditions for entrepreneurial activity. Tourism is certainly an industry that provides these conditions more often than most due to its sensitivity to external factors and events and market fickleness.

The ability of a destination to attract entrepreneurs from outside is often dependent upon the level of entrepreneurship already present (Krueger & Brazeal, 1994; Minniti & Bygrave, 1999). Minniti and Bygrave (1999: 42) refer to entrepreneurship as a 'self-reinforcing phenomenon' and Shapero (1981) discusses entrepreneurship as a vital element in 'self-renewing' communities. Incidentally, both of these terms describe Chaos Theory principles, highlighting the inextricable links between chaos, entrepreneurship and destination development. Minniti and Bygrave (1999: 43) go further in their explanation by suggesting that if entrepreneurship is indeed self-reinforcing, then 'as a result, the process of its development throughout a community is not predictable'. This would explain some of the problems that researchers have found in viewing the TALC as a predictive tool (Berry, this volume).

The necessary environment will of course depend on the developmental stage of the region, the industry sector being focused on, and the type or scale of entrepreneurship being encouraged. In addition, in considering the 'environment' ideal for entrepreneurial activities, several interdependent components need to be looked at: social, political and economic.

Social

One of the most pervasive impediments to entrepreneurship and entrepreneurship research has been the varying degrees of hostility felt by society towards entrepreneurs and their activities. Hartwell and Lane (1991) suggest that society's discomfort with entrepreneurship predates the existence of the term, beginning with Christianity and further reinforced by two other social movements, the Enlightenment and socialism. Christianity, from its emergence and continuing to today, purportedly scorns wealth accumulation on earth, preferring to emphasise the importance of 'riches' in heaven. On the other hand, the parable of the talents taught that multiplying one's resources had heaven's approval. This provided the drive that led to the Protestant work ethic and the British and Dutch maritime, economic and imperial ascendancy. However, this latter realisation was comparatively recent. For centuries the former emphasis was predominant. Poverty was virtuous – a condition which the established church happily facilitated.

Equality was a major theme of the Enlightenment and used as a vehicle for righting many social wrongs. However, it is also used as a basis for society's tending to prevent individuals from achieving economic success that puts them apart from the rest of the community. Australians especially, prefer to have their outstanding individuals, their heroes, achieve their success on the sports field rather than in the economic arena. Popular sentiment tended to be on the side of underdogs of humble order. The pretensions of 'tall poppies' and boat-rockers were not in favour. With the advent of socialism, the flag for equity was raised even higher in the fight for the downtrodden.

> It is difficult to imagine a more powerful combination of moral and intellectual forces than those generated by the old religion, the new egalitarian theory and later socialism. These three assailed the market system for its inefficiency and inequity and provided an enduring basis of hostility to business and business people, including entrepreneurs. (Hartwell & Lane, 1991: 39)

Studies have confirmed that in addition to seemingly ideal economic and political conditions for entrepreneurial activity, a supportive culture must be present in order to 'cultivate the mind and character of the potential entrepreneur' (Mueller & Thomas, 2000: 52). The culture must be such that an entrepreneur is motivated to act and feel capable and supported sufficiently to face the challenges that will arise in new venture creation. Busenitz *et al.* (2000) found that in countries where entrepreneurs were admired, there was a greater likelihood that people would attempt an entrepreneurial venture.

Although, by their nature, entrepreneurs have the determination and the motivation to succeed in even the most difficult environments, a destination that wishes to gain the benefits from entrepreneurship needs the encouraging mindset of the community and to portray a spirit of facilitation.

Political

Although political factors globally are significant to the growth of entrepreneurship, the political mix and their effects will be unique to specific countries, based on the nation's heritage, structure and social aims. Globally, however, there is a growing recognition that entrepreneurial activity and small business are becoming powerful forces in all industry sectors. Governments are ensuring that they are seen to be encouraging the growth of entrepreneurship, knowing that higher levels of innovation accompany higher levels of entrepreneurship.

The political environment, especially at a regional level, is particularly significant in the connection between entrepreneurship and the TALC. One of the primary roles of the state is to regulate. The entrepreneurial energy in a region is likely to be somewhat proportional to the inducements fostered by the extent and style of bureaucratic regulation. The degree to which the entrepreneur–regulator relationship is symbiotic or confrontational, that is the degree to which entrepreneurial behaviour is officially accommodated or discouraged, affects the degree to which it is functionally present. High tension between regulators and entrepreneurs will bring a low level of entrepreneurship. One of the key characteristics of entrepreneurs is their hatred of 'red tape', bureaucratic controls or obstructions. When governments attempt to encourage entrepreneurship, the first thing they claim to do is reduce the amount of 'red tape' that entrepreneurs have to deal with. A destination in its early stages of development is naturally low in formal policies and 'red tape', making this a very attractive environment for the entrepreneur. As a destination grows and formalises its structure, serial entrepreneurs, drawn by the prospective thrill of another hunt, will often move on to other destinations where they are again free to achieve their goals.

If the State is particularly keen for a tourist destination to develop, it can provide attractors to tourism entrepreneurs – from outside and within, by offering tax incentives on investment, incubators and other business support, government loans and infrastructure development (Lerner & Haber, 2000).

Economic

The relationship between entrepreneurship and the economy is well established. It was economists who first discovered its force within the economic environment. The earliest definitions involved the concept of shifting resources from a low yield to a higher yield. But what is the nature of the relationship between entrepreneurship and the economy?

The economic climate can act as a promoter or inhibitor of entrepreneurship, but sometimes in surprising situations. A downturn in the economy, or recession, can have a positive effect on entrepreneurship. This is, to a certain extent, attributable to the nature of entrepreneurs and their ability to turn a seemingly negative situation into an opportunity. Redundancies, either forced or voluntary, can be the trigger for those with entrepreneurial tendencies to start their own business (Morrison *et al.*, 1999), while the demise of competitors in a period of economic downturn can open up new opportunities for entrepreneurial business. This seemingly counterintuitive situation has been seen in the example of the spectacular success of short-haul budget airlines in Europe following the September 11 disaster. The passenger numbers of airlines such as Easy Jet, Ryanair and Southwest Airlines increased by 25–40% over the following 12 months as they went on the attack compared to drops in numbers for the established airlines such as British Airways and even bankruptcy in Swissair.

Most literature will claim that it is entrepreneurship that has the more powerful effect on the economic environment than the other way around. By driving innovation, entrepreneurship facilitates and revitalises economic growth (Busenitz *et al.*, 2000; Reynolds, 1997; Schumpeter, 1934). Timmons (1994: 3) sees the effect of entrepreneurship in the 21st century as being equal to, or greater than, the industrial revolution of the 19th century. 'This [entrepreneurship] revolution is revitalising economies, creating millions of jobs and forging new prosperity'. Tourism needs to be more strategic in harnessing and promoting entrepreneurial activity.

Entrepreneurship offers a cost-effective strategy for economic development, employment growth and innovation in a region (Ray, 1988). It is the entrepreneurs that have to obtain the resources, bear the risk and put in the long hours for often low return initially. Ray (1988: 3) has compiled a succinct list of ways that entrepreneurship contributes to economy.

Entrepreneurship:

- raises productivity through innovation (commercialising new inventions);
- creates jobs;
- facilitates technology transfer;
- plays a critical role in the restructuring and transformation of economies;
- helps reduce the ossification of established social institutions and the concentration of economic power;
- breathes life and vitality into large corporations and government bodies;
- creates turbulence in markets and reduces market inefficiencies;
- stimulates redistribution of wealth, income and political power;
- harnesses dormant, overlooked social capacity thereby improving social capital;
- creates new markets locally and internationally.

Entrepreneurship and Unpredictability

At this time, with increasing incidence of unpredictable events that continue to throw many organisations and industry sectors into chaos, it is pertinent to consider unpredictability as a variable that impacts entrepreneurial behaviour. As a destination evolves, it is often faced with unpredictable external and internal events that can either be detrimental to its growth or provide unexpected benefits. Most often it is the entrepreneur using creative energy, speed and resourcefulness who is able to mitigate the negative effects and exploit good fortune. Bouchikhi (1993) sees chance as an equal factor in the entrepreneurial process, along with the individual traits and the environment (see Figure 6.1). The role of chaos and unpredictability in the TALC is discussed in more detail in Russell (this volume).

Entrepreneurship and the TALC

Entrepreneurship has long been recognised as a vital ingredient in most industries. Entrepreneurship is being nurtured to bring about continual innovation and competitive advantage. The tourism industry is

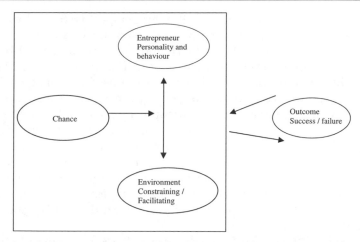

Figure 6.1 The role of chance in the entrepreneurial process
Source: Bouchikhi, 1993

a natural attractor to entrepreneurs. Its uncertainties and volatility are provocative of alertness, innovativeness and dynamic change. It is highly competitive, survival dependent and image related. Because a number of interlinking industries – day touring, catering, entertainment – attach to tourism, the scope for entrepreneurial visioning is greater than in most areas of enterprise. This is likely to be greatest in newer destinations where stagnation and rigidity are remote.

One of the earlier acknowledgements of the role of entrepreneurs in the development of a tourist destination came from Butler (1980) in the description of his TALC model. When visitor numbers begin to increase in a destination, locals see the need to provide businesses and services to cater for the visitor needs and the economic opportunities presented. Hence this stage of the cycle is termed 'involvement' stage, indicating the involvement of the residents as entrepreneurial agents in the destination's development (see Weaver, other volume).

While an extensive application of entrepreneurial process was outside the scope of Butler's (1980) paper, other authors have since taken the concept further. Din (1992) expanded on the entrepreneurship process in the involvement stage using a case study of a region in Malaysia. Barr (1990) also focused on the involvement stage and observes how, during this phase, small-scale local entrepreneurial initiatives contributed to the growth of tourism in the Whitsundays in northern Queensland. He noticed that it was not until the later stages of the TALC that 'outsider' entrepreneurs were attracted to the region. It is often the external entrepreneurs in the later stages that really make the difference. Perhaps it is their objectivity, fresh approach, lack of emotional attachment and their ability to see things from a different perspective that allows them to see opportunities that those within the community cannot.

Lewis and Green (1998), in their study of entrepreneurial behaviour among developers and operators in the European Alpine ski resort, highlight the point that entrepreneurs as opposed to managers thrive on chaos. Their creative response to new opportunities predisposes them to an approach that endeavours to circumvent constraints imposed by the managers, who aim to maintain a steady state through regulations designed to control change. Therefore if a destination has an over-abundance of managers or regulators aiming to control change, the destination would not be able to move through the different growth stages. Lewis and Green's (1998) findings suggest that entrepreneurs can have an impact in all stages of the destination if there is enough chaos present.

Gormsen (1981) refers to entrepreneurial activity taking place early in the development life of a destination. However, unlike Butler, Gormsen postulates that it is outsiders who initiate the entrepreneurship process. Both scenarios are possible. Entrepreneurship can be manifested in different ways within the TALC. As Hovinen (2002) notes, many destinations, especially mature destinations, exhibit many of the stages of the TALC simultaneously. Also, 20 years on, researchers have developed a greater understanding of the variety of patterns of destination development and also the complexity of the process has been brought to the forefront.

While the following categories of entrepreneurship may be more prominent at certain stages of the TALC, it is possible that a mix of these entrepreneurial typologies is active in the same stage. The categorisation is only a means to highlight the variety of entrepreneurial activity that can impact the shape of a destination, and is not meant to be prescriptive. The categories are not mutually exclusive nor are they a complete classification.

Phase-changing entrepreneurship

Change is an essential prerequisite for innovation. Change, positive or negative, is both an ingredient and an outcome of innovation. When a destination collectively encourages change strategies it may be the cumulative input of a number of entrepreneurial minds that trigger change. It may be sufficient, for example, to impel the destination to another development phase – from stagnation to rejuvenation for example.

In their discussion regarding crises and disasters in tourism, Faulkner and Russell (2001) propose three ways in which the tourism entrepreneur might be a phase-changing catalyst. Firstly, by shrewder management of externally generated disasters or crises, he may diminish his competition. Again, a case in point is the example of the success of European budget airlines in the wake of the 11 September 2001, disaster, which demonstrates superior entrepreneurial strategies that have perhaps contributed to the downfall of traditional competition. Secondly, by superior tactics he may induce crises for his competitors that render them less viable. The Gold Coast, Australia experienced this in the early days of the development of two of its key tourist nodes – Coolangatta and Surfers Paradise. Coolangatta, on the southern end of the Gold Coast, had superior natural beauty, but was surpassed by Surfers Paradise in tourism activity because of greater entrepreneurial vitality contributing significantly to the stagnation and decline of Coolangatta (Russell & Faulkner, 1998). Thirdly, by excessive expansion beyond the carrying capacity and environmental sustainability limits, an entrepreneur may induce a negative circumstance, detrimental to the resort's image. This last possibility is present if the entrepreneur's capacity to dream greedily overshadows his capacity to plan rationally. The prospect of short-term gain, cost cutting and greed leads the less intelligent entrepreneurs to ignore environmental carrying capacities resulting in unsustainable outcomes and a demise of the destination or parts of it. At many coastal destinations, development too close to the shoreline has in some instances suffered untimely and sudden destruction with the arrival of an unpredictable cyclone, king tides or erosion of the sandy and unstable earth beneath inadequate foundations.

On a more positive note, Kokkranikal and Morrison (2002) provide a wonderful example of entrepreneurial activity in Kerala, India that has revitalised indigenous cultural enterprises and also initiated a phase change in a region that was suffering negative environmental and sociocultural effects of tourism development. This case study is an example of innovative, indigenous entrepreneurship that is leading the way in sustainable tourism strategies (Kokkranikal & Morrison, 2002). In the early 1990s, a local tour-operator revived the traditional houseboat of Kerala – the Kettavullams, and offered tours in the backwaters of Kerala. The entrepreneur employed the use of other locals and local materials to build the houseboats, helping to revive traditional craftsmanship and to provide socially responsible tourist experiences to domestic and international tourists. This entrepreneurial activity sparked a growth in houseboat tourism in the area and also has encouraged a healthy economic multiplier effect helping to alleviate the economic and social problems in the region. In this respect, this entrepreneurial activity has caused a phase shift in a couple of different ways. In one sense it was a phase change at the beginning of the TALC by bringing a new tourism product and attracting a new market to the region and in another sense it has revitalised the destination by bringing economic growth – with minimal leakage, employment and new infrastructure. More importantly, it has attracted a new type of tourism to the region, one that displays principles of environmental sustainability and social responsibility.

Organic entrepreneurship

Christaller (1963), one of the earliest pioneers in research on destination development, described the process that supports the TALC model as being a gradual development. He focussed on the emergence of a destination whose magnet was artistic activity rather than climate or scenery. Early 'painters' or explorers discover the untouched destinations and then it becomes a 'colony', word spreads and poets, other artists, and gourmets follow (Christaller, 1963). The 'discovery' of the destination by more tourists opens it up to early entrepreneurial activity. More accommodation is needed, shops, transport and other supporting enterprises develop to capitalise on the tourism activity. In this scenario, this innovative development is demand initiated. In Chaos Theory terms, such a system is self-reinforcing. Positive feedback accelerates change and the development appears to take on a life of its own. Often, entrepreneurial enterprises 'compete' with each other in flair, vision and innovativeness fuelling the development cycle. This can be seen in places such as Las Vegas and the Gold Coast for example. In cases where regulations are lax, and development is left to grow uncontrollably, it can have a detrimental effect on the long-term sustainability of the destination.

As tourist expectations change over time, niche markets emerge, entrepreneurial initiative responds by not only meeting their expectations but also by sometimes creating expectations (Lundgren, other volume). For example, where coastal destinations were once dominated by tent cities, fishermen and pubs, their streets are now lined with plush hotels, shopping and entertainment complexes. Entrepreneurship style also changes as the complexity and financial stakes increase. Individual entrepreneurs are usually more dominant in the early stages of the TALC, but as the destination develops in sophistication, corporate entrepreneurship is usually more common. Also, as Argawal (2002), Hovinen (2002), and Russell and Faulkner (1999) have noticed, partnerships between entrepreneurs and government bodies often form fruitful synergies.

Tooman (1997) observed in his study of tourism development in the Smoky Mountain region in the USA that smaller-scale enterprises initiated within the destination that develop at a slower rate can be more beneficial especially in the earlier stages of the TALC than the grand-scale entrepreneurship. He noticed that this type of entrepreneurship (organic) allows a greater number of local linkages to be created to support the local economy. Also, smaller enterprises require less capital investment, allowing greater ease of entry for the local market.

Perhaps organic entrepreneurship is the recommended entrepreneurial model if destinations wish to move towards sustainability and retain control over natural and cultural assets, thereby increasing the likelihood of maintaining longer-term economic benefits that arise from tourism.

Grand-scale entrepreneurship

The most dramatic variations to the shape of the TALC come about when the actions of entrepreneurs are planned, purposeful and introduce elaborate grand development schemes to the region. These entrepreneurs often bring instant change to the destination, attract bigger or different markets and provide an instant trigger for the destination to enter a new development phase.

One example of a destination that has experienced this type of entrepreneurial activity is Orlando with the introduction of Disney World in 1971. The attraction single-handedly brought instant tourism to Orlando. There was nothing accidental about it. Disney had complete control over every detail, even the governing bodies.

> The company's desire to escape from popular as well as govern-
> mental control is ... Apparent in their application for a '701' planning
> grant from the federal Department of Housing and Urban Develop-
> ment in 1966. There they proposed an experimental city that would
> 'always be in a state of becoming' requiring that the city be 'freed
> from the impediments to change, such as rigid building codes,
> traditional property rights, and elected political officials.' The Disney
> company recommended a bifurcated government, in which planning
> and development would be under landowner control and only the
> remaining functions of government entrusted to elected officials.
> (Foglesong, 1999: 93)

It takes extraordinary vision, energy, boldness and forcefulness to undertake such a project. Disney was indeed an extraordinary entrepreneur. He was also well positioned to fund his dream. Attractions of this magnitude are certainly at the upper end of the examples of calculated, grand-scale entrepreneurship.

Smaller scale theme parks are more common examples of attractions that are created purposefully to dramatically increase tourist numbers to a region. The Gold Coast, Australia, has experienced a number of entrepreneurial activities of this nature. Incidentally, all these theme parks experience life cycles of their own, adding to the cyclic mix within a region (see Bao, other volume). On the Gold Coast, grand-scale entrepreneurship soon overshadowed the organic entrepreneurial activity as the involvement stage turned to development. There seemed to be one bold development after another being carried out by individual entrepreneurs: speedways, marine parks, luxurious hotels – all of which in the 1960s were innovative and ahead of their time, especially in a regional part of Australia (Russell & Faulkner, 1999).

It is often the grand-scale entrepreneurship that causes the most controversy in a destination, especially with the strong growth in recent times of environmental conservation groups. Port Hinchinbrook Resort in North Queensland is a case in point. Australian tourism entrepreneur Keith Williams, a major tourism shaper on the Gold Coast in the 1960s and 70s, moved his efforts in the 1990s to Port Hinchinbrook, a quiet North Queensland coastal site. Williams planned to transform it into Australia's largest integrated resort township. However, this time he did not enjoy the 'free hand' he had decades earlier while on the Gold Coast. Although entrepreneurs are known for their fighting spirit, nothing prepared Williams for the years of battles with environmental groups and government departments in attempting to get the resort established. Even though the majority of locals wanted the development to go ahead because of the employment it would provide to an area that has suffered high levels of unemployment and low socioeconomic status, the perceived damage that tourism would bring to the wildlife seemed to be the louder argument. Williams' persistence prevailed in the end and the resort has opened and it seems that the environmental groups have turned their attention elsewhere. The dream is still grand although it is taking substance at a more restrained rate than the dreamer had hoped.

Serendipitous entrepreneurship

Entrepreneurial studies abound with examples of individuals who 'stumble' across opportunity and can't resist the urge to exploit it. Again, the Gold Coast is an example of a destination that was heavily influenced by serendipitous entrepreneurial activity. In the 1950s many entrepreneurs from the southern states arrived on the Gold Coast with the intention to retire but could not resist the opportunity that was presented to them. They found a region with an overabundance of natural assets including some of the best beaches in the world, access to major cities, a temperate climate and a changing society that was ready for the sun, sand and sea holiday experience. The serendipitous entrepreneur has most effect on the TALC in the early stages. Word of mouth and the entrepreneurial network reaches far and wide and soon the activity turns organic and then often becomes grand scale.

In a different time and setting, Thomas Cook is an obvious example of a serendipitous entrepreneur. While Cook's activities were not specific to one specific destination, his innovations opened up many previously inaccessible destinations to tourists, kick-starting the TALC in many regions. Cook, by exploiting new technology, the steam engine, made travel available to the masses. He describes the moment the idea came to him as a 'revelation'. His entrepreneurial activity was the culmination of good timing, new technology and a perceived need in an unrelated industry. Upon his death, the following was a tribute that encapsulated his achievements very well.

> The late Mr Thomas Cook...was a typical middle-class nineteenth-century Englishman. Starting from very small beginnings, he had the good luck and the insight to discover a new want, and to provide for it. He saw that the great new invention of the railway might be made, by the help of a new organization, to provide large numbers of people with pleasanter, cheaper, and more varied holidays than they had ever been able to enjoy before. (Pudney, 1953: 19)

Revitalising entrepreneurship

Entrepreneurs have been noted for their enjoyment of turning failed products or organisations into success stories. Perhaps it is the challenge and visible reward that attracts them to seemingly impossible projects. In recent times, industrialised countries are putting efforts into increasing entrepreneurial activity in order to 'revitalise stagnating industries and provide new jobs to compensate for employment problems created by corporate restructuring and downsizing' (Mueller & Thomas, 2000: 52).

They also are known to have a significant effect on the TALC in the rejuvenation stage of the destination (Russell & Faulkner, 1999). They can provide the trigger that awakens stagnating destinations and launches them into a period of rejuvenation either by undertaking new projects that provide attractions or discovering new markets or opening up the potential of existing assets of the destination. Snepenger *et al.* (1995) suggest that business migration to parts of the Greater Yellowstone Ecosystem of Montana has ameliorated impacts of stagnation in that area. Hovinen (2002: 226) describes entrepreneurial activity as giving 'chaotic vibrancy' to Lancaster County when it reached a stage of maturity. Hovinen (other volume) believes that entrepreneurial activity is vital if a destination is to stave off decline.

The revitalising effect on destinations is not a new phenomenon. A historical account of Bath, England, one of the earliest of organised tourist destinations, portrays the activities of Beau Nash and the impact he had on revitalising Bath as a resort spa town. In the early 1700s, Bath was experiencing severe seasonality and downturn in market type so Nash, an entrepreneurial rogue (in fact, also a rogue in the general sense), set about updating everything in the town from the lodgings to the entertainment. He provided 'package' deals of accommodation, entertainment and relaxation at the spas. It wasn't long before news spread to London of the revitalised Bath and attracted an elite market including Dukes, Duchesses and royalty (Connely, 1955). Nash appears to have been a remarkably powerful figure capable of overriding the existing ennui by motivational presence and a bit of bullying. Rebirthing a destination locked into stagnation is not for the faint-hearted.

Conclusion

These five categories are certainly not intended to be exhaustive but to illustrate that entrepreneurship has a significant role to play in shaping the TALC and will often be manifested in a variety of ways. The categories are also broad generalisations as each instance of entrepreneurial activity is a function of the individual characteristics and traits of the entrepreneur, the environmental conditions – macro and micro under which it occurs, and the particular stage of the destination. The amorphous nature, the unpredictability and complexity of entrepreneurship should not be a deterrent to further research into entrepreneurship within tourism, but it should instead inspire investigation into the often

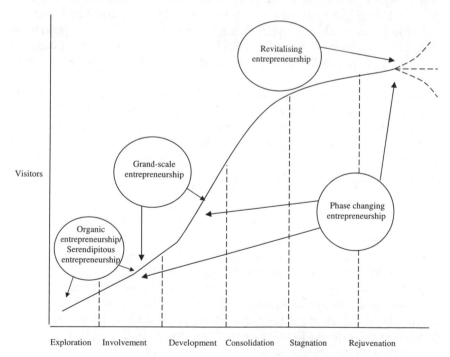

Figure 6.2 Entrepreneurship categories and the TALC

very colourful and interesting world of the entrepreneur. It is the uniqueness and creativity that makes the research all the more valuable.

Figure 6.2 is a simple diagram representing how and when the above categories can impact on the TALC.

Entrepreneurs, although highly individual, share common attributes. Each represents a unique composite of some or all of those attributes. They may or may not have managerial roles. They may be insiders or outsiders. Although individual, they may act in concert with those with similar goals and allied skills. An attempt has been made to glimpse the environments, political, social and economic, that enable or inhibit entrepreneurial activity. Further, this chapter has initiated consideration of the types of entrepreneurial behaviour and entrepreneurs most appropriate to the various stages of the TALC model. Examples have been provided to illustrate the different manifestations of entrepreneurial activity that may be found within tourist destinations. Phase-changing, organic, serendipitous, grand-scale and revitalising entrepreneurship are formed by the function of the macro- and microenvironmental conditions present at the time of the activity, the individual attributes of the entrepreneurs and the particular time or stage of the TALC.

Chapter 7

The TALC Model and Protected Natural Areas: African Examples

SABINE WEIZENEGGER

Introduction

'Destination areas carry with them the potential seeds for their own destruction, as they allow themselves to become more commercialized and lose their qualities which originally attracted tourists' (Plog, 1972; in Butler, 1980: 6). Destinations are no longer just a matter of where to go. Extensive concepts have been developed around those 'competition units' (Bieger, 2000: 73; Rubies, 2001) and a variety of different types of destinations on different spatial levels have been researched.

Protected areas are defined by the IUCN as an 'area of land and/or sea especially dedicated to the protection and maintenance of biological diversity, and of natural and associated cultural resources, and managed through legal or other effective means' (IUCN, 1998: xiv). The world's first National Park, Yellowstone National Park in the USA, was established in 1872. Since then not only have different types of protected areas been established, but the number of protected areas also has increased considerably. The UN List for Protected Areas comprises 13,321 protected areas (of over 1000 hectares) worldwide, among which 972 are located in Africa. The 7% of all protected areas found in Africa cover (due to their generally large size) more than one-third of the total global protected area territory. National Parks, management category II in the IUCN nomenclature, are represented at an above-average level on the African continent: more than a quarter (260) of all African protected areas fall under this category, while worldwide National Parks make up only 15% (2013) of all protected areas (see Figure 7.1).

Protected areas not only play a major role in conservation, but also in tourism. The World Conservation Union (IUCN) declares tourism and recreation as management objectives for most types of protected areas and as a primary management objective for categories II (National Park), III (Natural Monument) and V (Protected Landscape/Seascape) (IUCN, 1994: 8). Especially in Africa with its abundance of exotic wildlife, many of the protected areas function virtually as visitor magnets, some of them receiving more than 200,000 visitors per year (Republic of Kenya, 1999: 165). This raises the questions of whether this makes a protected area a

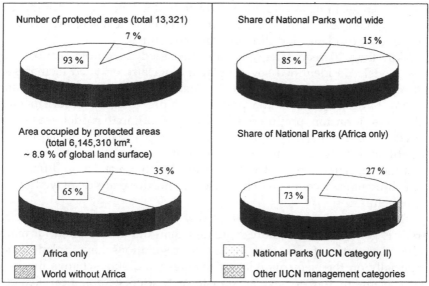

Source: own calculations on the basis of the 1997 United Nations List of Protected Areas

Figure 7.1 Protected areas in figures (UN list)

tourist destination, and if so, does Plog's apprehension cited above also apply to protected areas?

The World Tourism Organization defines a destination quite simply as a 'location of a cluster of attractions and related tourist facilities and services which a tourist or tour group selects to visit or which providers choose to promote' (WTO, 1993: 22). This definition can easily be applied to protected areas: protected areas offer attractions such as undisturbed landscape, attractive scenery, wildlife, and facilities such as visitors' centres, lodging, campsites or guides. They are visited by individual travellers as well as by organised groups. Often visits can be booked as a part of a package tour, and protected areas are promoted by different means such as leaflets, brochures or via the Internet. After this very brief examination and discussion, we can propose a working hypothesis that protected areas (at least the ones in which tourism takes place) are one type of tourist destination.

As protected areas are considered here as a type of destination, it is reasonable to argue that Butler's TALC model should be applicable to them (see Boyd, other volume, for an application of the TALC to national parks in Canada). The reflections in this chapter are based on the works of Butler (this volume) and Johnston (2001). In 1980 Butler linked earlier works on the growth and development of tourist areas with the product life cycle model and concluded that a tourist area would go through specific stages in its development. Not only does the number of tourists vary, so too do different types of tourists, different levels of involvement of the local residents and different infrastructures.

More than 20 years later, Johnston discussed the ontological basis of this model. He identified seven epistemologically oriented elements of life cycles and applied them to destinations (2001, this volume), and amongst these he noted the presence of pre- and post-tourism eras. Although Johnston proposed that Butler's original model was most suitable for resorts, in Figure 7.2 an attempt is made to apply the identified life cycle elements (left column) to an alternative type of destination, namely protected areas (middle column). Some differences and difficulties become quickly obvious, and these are displayed in the right column.

The most striking observation is that the development of protected areas is generally much more regulated than the development of many other destination types, and that those regulations have an influence especially on the elements relating to stages and stage change mechanisms (elements four to seven). Johnston's first epistemological element, the unit or entity undergoing the cycle, determines how all other elements are perceived. As we will see below, this is true in particular for the development of tourist numbers (element three, quantity of users), which make up for the ordinate in Butler's TALC model. The clear definition of the entity needs more sophisticated consideration.

While Johnston (2001: 9) lists examples for the examination of several *types of destinations* (criteria for differentiation include types of tourists' experiences, institutional development and others) as well as research conducted at different *spatial scales* (from theme parks up to the comparison of island regions in the Caribbean Sea with the ones in the Pacific Ocean), this work differentiates entities by using different levels of aggregation in a typology, which are displayed in Figure 7.3.

TALC and the Protected Area Concept

The overall research subject in this discussion is the destination (called tourism area in Butler's terminology from 1980). In this study a specific type of destination, namely protected areas, is examined. The highest level of aggregation is the protected area concept as a whole, and within this specific protected area types such as National Parks, Ramsar Wetlands or Biosphere Reserves are distinguished. The third entity, with the lowest level of aggregation, is the individual protected area. The triple appearance of 'W du Niger' in Figure 7.3 illustrates the fact that a specific area may appear in multiple classifications.

Numbers of internationally recognised protected areas have increased considerably worldwide, and continue to do so, which would be one

Epistemological elements of life cycles (cf. Johnston 2001: 7)	Application to protected areas as destinations	*Observations and problems*
Unit-entity - nature of destination entity and type of destination - spatial scale	- levels of aggregation: destination type, protected area type, protected area individual - protected area, protected area and its surroundings	*Entity determinates other epistemological elements. Applicability of life cycle model differs with entity regarded. Protected areas can not be regarded without surroundings.*
Internal characteristics - base resource - service resources - government	- natural features - tourist facilities: lodging, guides - development plans	*Facilities development is regulated or restricted (by international law or protected area administration).*
Users - quantity - quality	- visitor numbers - visitors' activities (hunting or photo-safaris, non-tourist-use by local population)	*Visitor numbers may be restricted (carrying capacity) Competition with non-tourist use (often consumptive) exists.*
Recognition of stages - features - type and level of activity	- induced instead of organic development - variety of activities ('Aktionsräumliches Verhalten')	*Depends on regulations and entity regarded (and not necessarily on stage). Often individual characteristics more important than type ones.*
Mechanisms of stage change - critical juncture or blurry transitions (occur as events): additions, alterations, cessations	critical junctures: new or reclassifications, new regulations added, (non-restricted visitor numbers): blurry transition	*Depends on regulations and entity regarded. Often macro-structural conditions as stage change mechanisms.*
Typical sequence and variation in stages - adaptation strategies: facilitation, inhibition, tolerance	- Pre- and post-tourism stages - Adaptation by hosts outside protected area	*Depends on regulations and entity regarded.*
Macro-structural conditions - external events - level of aggregation	- e.g. international conventions, political situation, security - upper level of aggregation influences the lower one	*Depends partly on entity regarded. Not necessarily protected-area-specific.*

Figure 7.2 Johnston's (2001: 7) epistemological elements of life cycles and their application to protected areas

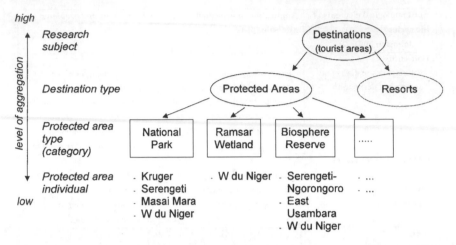

S. Weizenegger 2002

Figure 7.3 Entities undergoing the life cycle

indicator of the 'success' of the protected area concept. But instead of protected area numbers, the model uses protected areas' *visitor* numbers. Those are not easily available, except for single protected areas or, more rarely, on a national level.

Nevertheless, when looking back in history, an approximation of the idea can be given. By the end of the 19th century, tourism in Africa was characterised by a very specific group of visitors, namely hunters. While for many of the local populations edibility was the major criterion of attractiveness of wildlife, for international hunters, the sporting character of hunting became more and more important. Although this form of tourism was quite exclusive, hunting was excessive. In 1883, Africa's first game protection association was founded in Natal (MacKenzie, 1988: 232). At this time the first protected areas were institutionalised, starting in South Africa. Proclaimed in 1898, Sabi-Reserve in Transvaal was established, the continent's most famous protected area, today called Kruger National Park. Initially the intention of regulations was to protect game *for* hunting.

Nevertheless, the hunters' activities led in some areas to severe decline or even the extinction of certain species (Regensberg, 1911: 54). For example, in Somaliland a drastic decline in the game population, even after the promulgation of the game regulations a few years earlier is noted, attributed entirely to the importation of modern rifles. This is why now protected areas aim at protecting wildlife *from* hunting. Following several international conferences ('Conference on African Wildlife' in London 1900, 'International Conference for the Protection of Nature' in Paris 1931 and 'Agreement for the Protection of the Fauna and Flora of

Africa' in London 1933), conservation policies changed and protection measures became quite strict. For example, the Paris conference prohibited hunting from motor vehicles, motor boats and airplanes, and applied controls on the trophy, ivory and horn trade. Many Game Reserves were converted into National Reserves or National Parks. Most of the latter ones were established from the 1950s onwards (MacKenzie, 1988: 226), and after independence the protection idea was upheld by the new African governments. National Parks permitted another form of tourism, one that is nonconsumptive. Photo safaris developed and improved transport allowed a broader range of travellers to visit Africa. The main criterion of attractiveness for this type of user of protected areas is the ability to view wildlife.

The interpretation of the TALC in this context is that through *induced* stage change mechanisms (e.g. establishment of a different type of protected area as a reaction to overuse), facilitated by macrostructural influences (e.g. improvement of transport facilities), a rejuvenation would take place and a new cycle would begin. Hence cycles follow one another, the first one consisting of hunting tourism, the second one of photo safaris (Lundgren, other volume). They constitute a wave movement that can take different shapes and have different gradients, according to the circumstances. With continued (uncontrolled) hunting, wildlife would most probably have diminished even more, leading to a further decline in species numbers which would finally have led to an *organic* decline of (hunting) tourism in protected areas (Figure 7.4).

With the transformation from hunting tourism to photo safaris, a different type of tourist (*quality of users*) has entered the arena. The fact that at the same time visitor numbers (*quantity of users*) increased is independent. A contrary effect could be generated, e.g. by reorientation to controlled hunting with strictly limited distribution of hunting permits or a shooting quota (development option D in Figure 7.4). This would lead to a smaller number of tourists, but nevertheless represent a process of rejuvenation and not a decline. Countries like Tanzania, Botswana and South Africa have decided to follow this philosophy for a number of their protected areas, using hunting tourism as a high price segment instead of 'photo-safari mass-tourism'.

Towards the end of the 20th century, management paradigms for protected areas changed again, the main reason being conflicts with people living adjacent to protected areas. Those conflicts, due to population growth and subsequent land use pressure, are to be met by the sustainable and wise utilisation (instead of strict preservation) of protected areas and by the application of the concepts of participation and integrated management (Brown, 2002; Job & Weizenegger, 1999). This development has been enabled and enforced by the World Conservation Strategy (IUCN/UNEP/WWF, 1980) and the Convention

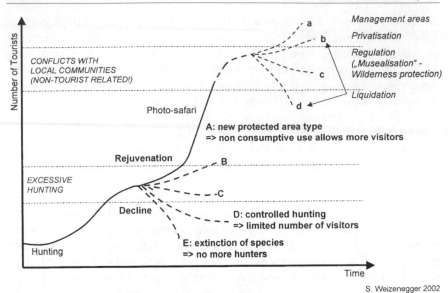

S. Weizenegger 2002

Figure 7.4 TALC and the protected area concept

on Biological Diversity adopted at the 1992 Earth Summit in Rio de Janeiro. In the context of this changing protection philosophy, new types of protected areas began to emerge.

When imagining different development options for protected areas, one extreme would be their liquidation (Weizenegger, 2002). This form of decline would result in a post-protected-area era, an equivalent to Johnston's (2001: 13) post-tourism eras, but again, this development is not caused by tourism-related factors. Even if the legal status as a protected area no longer exists, tourists may continue to visit the former protected area. On the other hand, if visitor numbers go down, the protected area status as such may persist – without being a tourist destination any longer. Therefore the two dimensions of the 'destination protected area', namely the official protected area status and the fact that the area is visited by tourists, need to be distinguished. The orientation towards visitor numbers in the TALC model may be problematic as it does not take into account qualitative factors such as the type of tourist (hunter or on photo safari) in the visualisation of the model.

TALC and Protected Area Types

A second approach is to consider life cycles of *protected area types* such as a certain IUCN category, a Biosphere Reserve or a World Heritage site. The 'World Conservation Union' (IUCN) was founded in 1948. Stating that at least 140 different expressions for protected areas exist, the IUCN set up the first preliminary classification system for protected areas in

1973, which became viable in 1978. At that time it comprised 10 categories of protected areas, including Biosphere Reserves (category IX) and Natural World Heritage Sites (category X). Although this system of 10 categories spread quickly and was widely used, it is in need of review and update. 'The differences between certain categories are not always clear ... Categories IX and X are not discrete management categories, but international designations generally overlain on other categories ...' (EUROPARC and IUCN, 2000: 9). It therefore was changed in 1994, distinguishing six management categories, which follow roughly a gradient of increasing degree of human influence from categories I to VI. For those six categories, a set of nine management objectives, including scientific research, wilderness protection, tourism and recreation, has been defined. Depending on the respective categories, primary, secondary and relevant management objectives are distinguished (IUCN, 1994: 5f.).

The 'World Heritage Convention' was signed in 1972 and the first sites on the World Heritage List were inscribed in 1978. In 2001 there were 721 World Heritage sites of 'outstanding universal value', among which were 143 natural, 555 cultural and 23 mixed ones. The African continent holds 91 sites (12.6%), among which slightly more than a third are natural ones (UNESCO, 2001).

In 1976 the UNESCO launched the Biosphere Reserve network, which endeavours to realise the objectives of the 'Man and the Biosphere' programme. Biosphere Reserves aim at nature protection, conservation of genetic resources, development of sustainable land-use, research, environmental monitoring and environmental information. Typically, each Biosphere Reserve has a core area, a buffer zone, a transition zone and, optionally, can have a regeneration zone. In those zones, different management objectives are followed. In 2001 there were 393 Biosphere Reserves among which 55 (14%) were located in Africa (UNESCO, 2002).

Another type of protected area is the Ramsar Wetland. The 'List of Wetlands of International Importance' was established in response to the 'Convention on Wetlands' (1971) and comprises 1069 sites of significant value for humanity as a whole. An additional 'category' that is becoming more and more important in some countries, but has rarely been considered in research to date, is that of private protected areas. The fact that these new protected area classifications and types were established was due to new management needs. Those needs evolved not only through tourism (when transforming from hunting tourism to photo safaris, for example), but also from the wish to enhance sustainable development in general and for practical reasons.

A reasonable approach would be to investigate possible interrelations between protected area type and attractiveness for visitors. In reality this task is a very difficult one, not only because of the problem of data availability, but also for the reason that even with a reclassification into a new protected area type, the former protective category may not be given up. The respective lists show that out of the 393 Biosphere Reserves, 69 are at the same time World Heritage sites and 70 are Ramsar Wetlands. Some areas fall under all three categories and most of them in addition are classified under one of the IUCN categories of protected areas. For example, the W du Niger or parts therein are at the same time a National Park under IUCN category II (since 1954), a Ramsar Wetland (since 1987), a Biosphere Reserve (since 1996) and a World Heritage site (since 1996).

The situation becomes even more complicated by the fact that national and international classifications often do not coincide. South Africa's Pilanesberg is, for example, classified as a National Park by national authorities and as category IV (Habitat/Species Management Area) by the IUCN. Kenya's Masai Mara is classified as a National Park by the IUCN and as a National Reserve by the Kenyan government. This means different management practices and results in different development. In Kenya, National Parks are managed by the national authority (Kenya Wildlife Service – KWS), while National Reserves are managed by district authorities. One major difference in this example is the flow of income: National Park entrance fees are managed by KWS, National Reserve income is managed on a decentralised basis by the respective County Councils, which also decide on how this money is spent. It is likely to be spent within the district, while KWS covers the whole country in its actions and may withdraw income from the area in which it had been generated for use in another area.

The first edition of the UN List of protected areas only came out in the 1960s, about half a century after the first protected areas had been gazetted and before National Parks had been defined at the international level for the first time. Although it lists the date of inscription of each protected area (under its current category), it does not contain information about past protected area types (e.g. Samburu National Reserve in Kenya has a date of 1985 by the IUCN, although it was already a Game Reserve in 1948). This leaves a gap of about half of the length of time of the area's existence in the time line (abscissa in the model), during which the protected area territories have varied a lot. For the period for which data are available, the problem with the time line is that of the comparability (or the lack of it) of the two IUCN classification systems, one from before and one after 1994.

It is not only the nonavailability of visitor numbers by protected area type and designation to a specific type over this century-long period and the multiple classifications that constitute a problem. It is equally difficult to visualise the situation for protected area types. Comparing visitors to more than 13,000 IUCN types or 2000 National Parks with some 143 Natural Sites on the World Heritage list exemplifies the need to transform the model's ordinate label from absolute to relative numbers.

TALC and Individual Protected Areas

Even for the lowest level of aggregation, the situations may vary widely *within* a protected area type. That means that the specific features of a protected area may play a more important role for visitors' attractiveness than the fact that it belongs to a certain protection type. The protected area individual life cycle would represent the empirical study of a specific protected area undergoing the cycle. This entity is the most suitable approach by which to explore the observations on the influence of regulations.

In Butler's model a 'critical range of elements of capacity' occurs when a certain number of tourists is reached. Without action, this process finally leads to stagnation because of reasons such as loss of attractiveness due to overcrowding, loss of authenticity and environmental degradation. One popular kind of regulation in tourism is to set capacity limits by restricting access for visitors, using the concept of carrying capacity borrowed from biology (Romeril, 1989: 108; Wall, 1982: 190). In most protected areas this happens implicitly by means of limited numbers of accommodation facilities within the protected area. Some protected areas reduce or control visitor numbers by elevated entrance fees. Tanzania's Gombe Stream National Park, for example, charges 100 $ US per person per day for an entry permit. An extreme example with explicit visitor limits would be Bwindi Impenetrable National Park in Uganda, where only 12 persons per day are allowed to visit the Mountain Gorillas. Such limitations may easily prevent the anticipated decline in, for example, environmental quality resulting in a decline of attractiveness for tourists. The (natural) critical point where the visitor number rises above the critical range of elements of capacity may never be reached (Figure 7.5). This means that consequently the curve cannot take its regular shape when the carrying capacity (determining visitor numbers) is set below the critical range of elements of capacity (development option F in Figure 7.5). However, if the carrying capacity is set at a very (too) high level (carrying capacity II in Figure 7.5), the life cycle is permitted to go through its regular stages. The level at which the 'optimal' carrying capacity is to be set can vary with (internal) management instruments. For example, the identification of zones of different intensities of use may allow a higher number of visitors with less negative effects. Using the hunter example to illustrate the idea, it should become quite obvious that several thousand hunters have a completely different effect on wildlife than several thousand tourists on a photo safari.

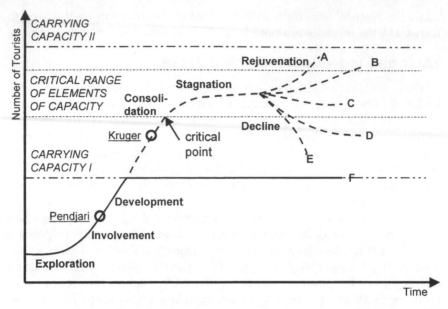

S. Weizenegger 2002

Figure 7.5 TALC and individual protected areas

It should be mentioned that individual protected areas (whether belonging to the same or to different protected area types) may have reached different stages of development in the life cycle over the same time period, depending very much on macrostructural conditions. Visitor numbers at Benin's Pendjari National Park are well below capacity. Tourists rarely visit the country due to the nonavailability of charter flights, high prices for airline tickets, weak infrastructure and transport facilities, and strong currents at the coast that make swimming a dangerous undertaking. These are but a few unfavourable conditions for an otherwise very enjoyable, safe and culturally rich country. Pendjari National Park is thus to be found somewhere between the 'involvement' and 'development' phases.

Better known and more easily accessible protected areas such as Masai Mara National Reserve in Kenya or Kruger National Park in South Africa are likely to be close to the critical point or in the 'stagnation' phase already. For Kenya a general decline in visitor numbers can be noted (macrostructural condition), but overcrowding (internal conditions) may be one of the motives for tourists to avoid certain parks and visit other, more unspoilt ones. Park fences and a prohibition on visitors leaving vehicles represent forms of regulation that may be unattractive for visitors. At the same time, a potential new competitor may enter the market. Differences between innovative offers in event parks, such as

Disney's Animal Kingdom, with 'Kilimanjaro Safaris' in an open pick-up-truck and pursuit of poachers, and the real park with a fence, begin to dissolve. If and to what extent such artificial or virtual offers are able to diminish the demand for an actual visit to destinations themselves, or how far they induce journeys to the real parks, remains to be seen (Dewailly, 1999).

A Spatial Perspective

Several authors indicate that destinations can be defined on different spatial levels. Although most works refer to resorts, Bieger (2000) stresses that destinations as (geographical) spaces offering a set of goods and services do not necessarily have to be villages or towns, but rather that they are defined from the user's perspective. He identifies as set of spatial levels, such as resort, place (respectively village or town), region, country and continent, and holds the hypotheses that (1) the more distant the destination, the bigger the destination is perceived by the guest, and that (2) the more focussed the travel motive, the smaller the destination for the guest.

How can a 'destination protected area' be delimited, where does it end for the tourist, at the borders of the protected area, e.g. the fence of Kruger National Park? The answer is not always as simple as that. One of the observations in Figure 7.2 relates to different kinds of users. Although when dealing with destinations the research focus is often on the demand side (the tourists), there is no doubt that the two principle groups of actors within a destination are hosts and guests (Smith, 1978), while other actors include mediators such as tour operators and transport service companies. In the specific case of protected areas, the situation is again somewhat different. The example of conflicts with local populations has shown that those living adjacent to protected areas are sometimes even more likely to determine the future development of protected areas than tourists. At the same time, since many types of protected areas are not inhabited, there are no hosts *within* the protected area, so that effects such as acculturation or income through trade do not specifically take place there on a large scale.

The limits of any protected area defined as a tourist destination depend heavily on the spatial structure around the protected area itself. This structure is defined by the hosts' economic situation as well as the guests' leisure activities and their movement in space. The destination can easily extend beyond the immediate local level of the protected site, for example when tourists are not only attracted by the protected area, but also by surrounding features such as waterfalls or archaeological sites. Visitors often arrive by car from the nearest international airport, allowing them an opportunity to come into contact with the hosts on the journey. Consequently, when regarding a protected area as a destination, such an area cannot be regarded as isolated or precisely limited within its formal boundaries, but account must be taken of its surroundings. That means that, from the spatial perspective, the *protected area* itself does not equal the *destination* (Figure 7.6).

In North America, Europe and Australia, in protected areas a shift from tourism to recreation has been observed (Butler & Boyd, 2000: 6), and a tendency to increasing domestic tourism can be noted in several developing countries (illustrated by G3 and G4 in Figure 7.6). Different tourists (G1, G2, G3, G4 in Figure 7.6) have different preferences. All those factors influence the spatial context of the protected area as a destination, along with other actors like the park administration and tour operators, which are not discussed here.

Conclusions

Protected areas cannot, in all cases, be treated simply as tourist destinations; sometimes other functions are of major importance. To distinguish clearly between the functions of protected areas as *sites for preservation* and protected areas as *tourist destinations* is a necessity, as protected areas can exist without tourists and vice versa. Even those types of protected areas that state providing opportunities for tourism and recreation to be their primary management objective do not necessarily depend on visitors for their existence. Protected area management in Benin, for example, is to a great extent financed by bi- and multilateral

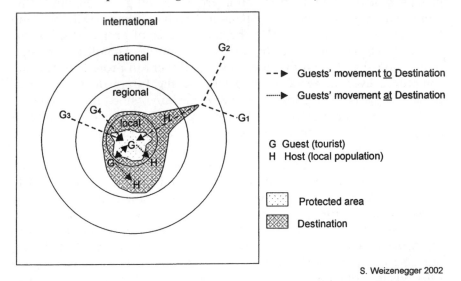

S. Weizenegger 2002

Figure 7.6 The spatial delimitation of destination protected areas

development co-operation, while in Kenya better visited Parks support the overall protection concept and operation. Tourism itself is just one factor among others in the development of protected areas, and thus the TALC model can be applied to protected areas to a limited degree only.

The limits of the applicability of the TALC model differ depending on the entity that is being regarded. Application to the protected area concept itself is difficult, because the distinct situations at lower levels of aggregation are not easily taken into account. Application of the TALC to protected area types poses a practical problem – even if visitor numbers were available, the question would arise as to how to assign a specific area to a particular category because of the widespread practice of multiple classification. The individual protected area is the most suitable to illustrate how, because of regulations, a specific protected area's life cycle is characterised by either induced stage changes (instead of organic ones) or by an irregular shape of the curve. A modification of the model that is sometimes necessary is to substitute the ordinate label with relative numbers. It would also be possible to go into more detail (arrivals or overnights) or even work with different variables, such as income generated through tourism. This latter would partly cover the quantitative aspect, for example the fact that income generated by having a single hunter visit is much higher than income from several tourists on a photo safari.

Nevertheless, TALC can contribute to some conclusions. One is that for protected areas the concept of the *longue durée* seems more applicable than for other types of destinations: 'as long as the resource underlying the destination's attractiveness remains intact and important, the institution of tourism can last for centuries' (Johnston, 2001: 19). By means of the described regulations, the loss of attractiveness (especially because of environmental degradation) should be prevented or slowed. It is particularly highly desirable to make use of the option to system-atically identify and apply limits of capacity to all protected areas. A second finding is of a more practical nature. The differentiation of levels of aggregation was shown to be very helpful in this work, thus it is argued that a clear definition of entities is essential for research on other types of destinations such as resorts or virtual destinations.

The spatial delimitation of protected area destinations is a difficult task (see also Johnston, this and other volume), because one of the two major groups of users, the local population, is often not living within the protected area. Not viewing protected areas as sealed off islands but regarding them in combination with their surroundings supports the opinion of progressive conservationists and their concept of integrated protected area management. It is clear that the spatial perspective of destinations needs further investigation in order to obtain a more detailed and differentiated picture.

Chapter 8
Time Path Analysis and TALC Stage Demarcation

SVEND LUNDTORP and STEPHEN WANHILL

Introduction

Since Butler (1980) wrote his original article on destination development, the TALC model has been widely discussed, applied, and accepted as a conceptual framework for analyzing the historical progression of resorts from a variety of perspectives (Buhalis, 2000). The general conclusion appears to be that the model is useful as a portrayal of resort development, but it is more descriptive than normative (Haywood, 1986; Oppermann, 1998). The several attempts that have been made to test the model describe aspects of development other than those predicted by the theory. However, the pure model is still used as a descriptive framework and, with that background, it is possible to explain how local features cause divergence from theory.

Case examples in the literature and those contained within this section of the book reveal that departures from the theoretical structure occur on both the demand and supply sides of resort expansion. Thus, from the demand perspective, the profile of the tourists may alter with time, which can give rise to discrete shifts in the curve as new markets are penetrated. On the supply side, a number of activities have been identified as being capable of interrupting the growth path of the cycle, in particular, political and commercial decisions, which include: planning regulations; public investment in, say, infrastructure; partnership development; competition, both local and global; and matters such as financial incentives. Thus, different decisions among public and private organizations are important for the speed and shape of the life cycle process and are acknowledged by Butler (1998), but more as 'variations on a theme' than challenges to the general concept. Because many of the case studies in the literature have been dealing with mature destinations, the stagnation period, with the implication of a growth ceiling, has been given most attention. In practice such a ceiling has been difficult to identify as the available evidence indicates that public and private initiatives for mature resorts may put off any stagnation phase before it occurs, so making it unobservable in the data.

A Demand-based TALC Model

In general, the descriptive aspect of the resort cycle has its focus on the tourism product. The advantage of looking at the 'tourism offer' is the implied challenge for product improvement, particularly when the stagnation stage appears to be looming. However, the number of tourists is the measure of the time path of the destination and it is the examination of the theoretical underpinnings of the cycle from visitor perspective that is developed here.

To formulate a demand-generated explanation of the life cycle model, we assume a destination, D, which is at the outset of the evolutionary process. By assumption, the number of tourists to D is stable before embarking on the growth path and the few tourists that are there, are of no significance, as D has no image as a resort. The development begins when the first 'explorer' tourists start to appreciate the qualities of D. Now, to discover an area as a tourist destination, knowledge of place must spread outwards. Communication channels may be overt through active marketing or may simply be word of mouth. The market or segment of a wider market, within which knowledge of D is growing, is assumed to have a positive likelihood of visiting D, when information about the resort has been received. This defines the potential market, M.

At time t, M_t persons within M will have knowledge about D, thus defining the actual market at time t. Let h express the velocity by which awareness of D expands, so that information will spread to $M_t \times h \times dt$ persons in the period dt. However, this is only a part of the total potential market; there are some $(M - M_t)$ persons yet to hear about D, which implies that the share of people who have not heard about D will be $(M - M_t)/M$. Hence, the total increase in the group of people knowing D during the time dt will be

$$dM_t = M_t h \frac{M - M_t}{M} \, dt \cdot M_t < M \tag{1}$$

The solution of this differential equation traces out the time path of the actual market as

$$M_t = \frac{M}{1 + e^{-ht+c}}$$

where c is a constant. Let $c = ht_0$, then the trend for the actual market is

$$M_t = \frac{M}{1 + e^{-h(t-t_0)}} \tag{2}$$

and because $e^{-h(t-t_0)} = 1$, for $t = t_0$, then t_0 is defined as the time where $M_t = M/2$. Equation (2) follows the pattern of a logistic curve and when the function is graphed it shows a curve replicating the life cycle path.

As noted above, M_t is the number of people who at time t have information on D and so, by insertion in equation (2), it is a simple matter to show that $M_t \rightarrow M$ for $t \rightarrow \infty$. When this situation is reached, market penetration of D is complete. At the outset, M_t rises slowly because only a few tourists have experienced D and information spreads gradually. But as M_t increases, knowledge will disperse more rapidly as the pool of tourists to D expands. By the time knowledge of D is widespread, there will be only a few people receiving the message for the first time and so the increase slows down, and will finally stop when M_t approaches M asymptotically.

It is assumed that each individual in the actual market, M_t, has a probability p for visiting D at time t. The probability p may be regarded as the average visit probability in the potential market. So, from Equation (2), the number of tourists (v_t) at time t will be

$$v_t = pM_t = \frac{pM}{1 + e^{-h(t-t_0)}} = \frac{m}{1 + e^{-h(t-t_0)}} \tag{3}$$

where $m = pM$.

The logistic curve (3) approaches m asymptotically for $t \rightarrow \infty$, which implies that m is the number of tourists at the stagnation stage. If the destination has had tourists long before it became a recognized resort, the model may be adapted by adding a constant a, where a is the (fixed) historical number of tourists, giving

$$v_t = a + pM_t \tag{4}$$

For the analysis that follows, the simplified Equation (3) is used rather than Equation (4), but without any loss of generality.

From Equation (3), the TALC model now is determined through the demand side and expressed in the form of a logistic function that may be manipulated to explain Butler's development progression (Lundtorp & Wanhill, 2001). A further simplification may be made by working with the relative number of tourists (w_t) (the actual number divided by the maximum number m), which avoids being dogmatic about absolute values. Thus

$$w_t = \frac{v_t}{m} = \frac{1}{1 + e^{-h(t-t_0)}} \qquad 0 < w_t < 1 \tag{5}$$

The full properties of the curve given by Equation (5) are presented in Figure 8.1. Time runs along the bottom axis and relative tourist numbers

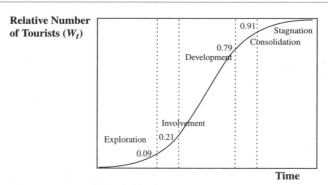

Figure 8.1 Stages of the TALC model

are measured vertically. Distinctive mathematical break points occur when the curve reaches 9%, 21%, 79% and 91% of the expected long run value or ceiling, which in turn can be identified with Butler's five stages. It is accepted that there will be, in practice, an amount of 'fuzziness' in the transition between one stage and another, but Butler's stages are linked to changes in the behavior of the curve, which the mathematics can elicit as operational points at which the stages begin and end as indicated on Figure 8.1. For example, at the consolidation stage, it will be observed that growth has significantly slackened. The destination is now well known in the market and tourists have risen from 79% of the possible maximum to 91%. Finally, with expansion ebbing away, the resort arrives at the stagnation stage, leaving it with Butler's two options for the future, decline or rejuvenation.

Some conditions

In deriving Equation (3) it was assumed that each individual in the actual market has a probability p of visiting the destination D, which implies that there could be multiple visits by the same tourist. However, there is often a segment of the market that visits a destination only once, a factor that can be significant for individual products, such as attractions and events. In what follows, it is assumed that a tourist in the 'non-repeat' segment of the market will visit D when knowledge of the resort is first obtained, but will never visit later. This simplification can be justified by looking at Equation (1): in these circumstances, the velocity h is a measure of both the spread of awareness about D and an indicator of the strength of the tourism offer in determining the decision to visit. It follows from what has gone before that the number of tourists in this group, say, u_t is equal to the increase in the market dM_t. Thus, from Equation (2)

$$u_t = \frac{dM_t}{dt}$$

which gives

$$u_t = \frac{hMe^{-(t-t_0)}}{(1 + e^{-h(t-t_0)})^2} \tag{6}$$

and is the first derivative of the logistic curve. Figure 8.2 compares the time path generated by repeat tourists (the familiar TALC shape) with the plot of Equation (6) that is produced by the 'one time only' tourist. The latter rises in a manner that is very similar to the logistic curve until a maximum is reached. From there on the number of tourists declines rapidly. If the entire market consists only of nonrepeat tourists, the

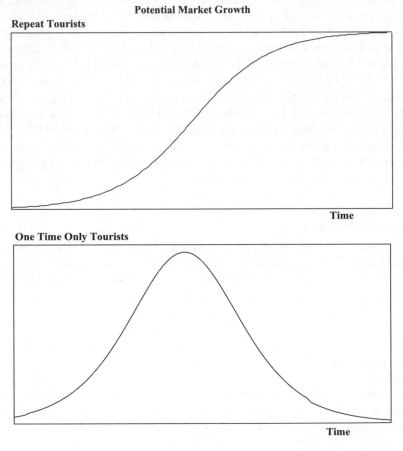

Figure 8.2 Different TALC profiles

destination will find itself in serious difficulties when the peak has passed, as there is no floor level at which the market will settle and a very different TALC pattern can be observed.

A mixed market model

In a market where there are two segments: one for repeat tourists M_1 and one for nonrepeat tourists M_2, the repeat segment, from Equation (3), will be

$$v_t = \frac{pM_1}{1 + e^{-h(t-t_0)}} = mL_t$$

where m is redefined for the repeat segment only and l_t is the logistic function,

$$L_t = \frac{1}{1 + e^{-h(t-t_0)}}.$$

The number of nonrepeat tourists will, from Equation (6), develop as

$$u_t = \frac{hM_2 e^{-h(t-t_0)}}{(1 + e^{-h(t-t_0)})^2} = hM_2 L_t (1 - L_t)$$

In this combined market, the time path of tourist numbers, y_t, will follow

$$y_t = v_t + u_t = mL_t + hM_2 L_t(1 - L_t) = mL_t(1 + rh(1 - L_t)) \tag{7}$$

where r is the ratio of the two segments, namely

$$r = M_2/m$$

The first aspect to note about Equation (7) is that although the underlying processes for both market segments are logistic and therefore conform to TALC specifications, the result for the combined market is not logistic and so any observed data will not trace out the pattern illustrated in Figure 8.1. On the other hand, as the nonrepeat segment is exhausted in the longer run ($u_t \to 0$ as $t \to \infty$), repeat tourists will dominate the market at this stage, which implies, mathematically, that $y_t \to v_t \to m$ for $t \to \infty$. Thus the size of the nonrepeat market can cause early 'blips' in tourist numbers before demand settles down. The extent of these 'blips' is directly proportional to the value of r, the ratio of nonrepeat to repeat visitors. Examples of this are shown in Figure 8.3; as the proportion of nonrepeat tourists increases, so the TALC model shows greater amounts of 'peakedness'.

Repeat plus Once Only Tourists

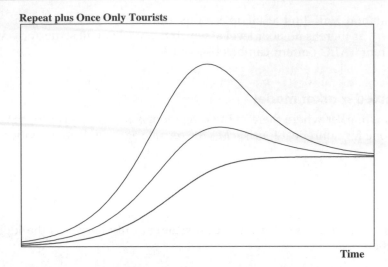

Time

Figure 8.3 Mixed TALC models

The implications of this analysis for the resort cycle paradigm are clear. Even under the assumption of a uniform market that ignores the shifting patterns of tourist arrivals cited by other authors, the life cycle curve could only be a truly representative aggregation if all tourists are repeat visitors. Once nonrepeat tourists are included in the market, the TALC model becomes only a statistical approximation or caricature of reality, departing from the 'ideal' model in Figure 8.1 according to the significance of 'one time only' tourists in the marketplace. Applying further segmentation to the market and allowing movements in the underlying parameters would result in a family of curves existing at any one time. The observed effect of this would be to produce a scatter diagram of data from which it might be impossible to discern anything, because logistic curves do not sum to a logistic curve. Therefore, it is not surprising that researchers have found it difficult to observe the TALC model in practice when moving beyond the general framework. Once this is recognized, then there are a number of polynomial trend curves that may be used to fit the data, but they lack any theoretical underpinnings and their interpretation depends on the skill of the researchers involved.

Testing the TALC Model

The tourism literature and the examples in this book indicate that the resort cycle model has been the focus of many empirical studies, though mainly in terms of qualitative research, using Butler's concepts for interpretation. What is especially interesting are long term data series, as used by Cooper and Jackson (1989) for the Isle of Man. The application here concerns the Danish island of Bornholm, in the Baltic Sea, some 7 hours journey time by ferry to Copenhagen. For more than a hundred years, it has been a long holiday destination for Danes and, in recent times, the neighboring countries of Germany and Sweden. As Bornholm is an island, it is relatively easy to record the number of arrivals and departures. Only a small proportion arrives by air and this is relatively new, so the number of ferry passengers is a good indicator of visitor flows. These figures have been recorded since 1912 and are listed in Table 8.1, giving a long data series. These are displayed on Figure 8.4, where the observations are plotted against the estimated function

$$v_t(\text{Bornholm}) = 35 + \frac{985}{1 + e^{-0.11(t-1960)}} \tag{8}$$

where v_t is again measured in thousands of passengers.

The logistic curve is a maximum likelihood estimate of the observations from 1912 to 1967. The figures from the World War II (WWII) period 1940–1945 are excluded, because Bornholm was occupied by German and then Soviet troops until the spring of 1946. The observations for Bornholm do not differ significantly from the spread of a normal distribution positioned around the estimated function. Outside WWII, only the years 1925, 1937 and 1938 exceed the upper significance limits, though the fitted curve underpredicts during the 1920s because there is a definite shift in the pattern of visitor flows downwards during WWI, although Denmark was not a combatant. The Bornholm function has an estimated spread of awareness, $h = 0.11$. The exploration stage continues until 1939, with the 'explorers' being the few Danish tourists who can afford to travel and are prepared to take the long and sometimes stormy ferry journey. The involvement stage begins in the late 1930s, but first becomes visible after WWII. In 1948, this stage passes into the time of development, which continues until 1972. It is a time when still more Danish families are taking seaside resort holidays. At the peak in 1960, the annual increase in passenger arrivals was more than 25,000. The development phase of the fitted model turns into the consolidation period in 1972 and the final chapter of stagnation commences in 1980.

However, only the observations up to 1967 are taken into consideration. Many of the observations from 1968 to 1998 differ very significantly from the trend and it has not been possible to generate a plausible function able to explain the erratic growth since then. This does not mean that explanations are not possible: on the contrary, there have been a number of shift factors that are likely to have altered the positioning of the curve. From 1967 to 1975, the decline in the number of tourists to Bornholm has been attributed to competition from the fast-growing

Table 8.1 Passenger flows to Bornholm (thousands)

Year	Numbers	Year	Numbers
1912	33	1957	399
1913	42	1958	418
1914	32	1959	445
1915	30	1960	488
1916	30	1961	506
1917	36	1962	555
1918	41	1963	579
1919	56	1964	630
1920	55	1965	712
1921	55	1966	718
1922	58	1967	696
1923	59	1968	654
1924	68	1969	665
1925	73	1970	667
1926	70	1971	672
1927	70	1972	685
1928	70	1973	638
1929	69	1974	647
1930	80	1975	587
1931	78	1976	602
1932	80	1977	665
1933	90	1978	688
1934	97	1979	715
1935	101	1980	780
1936	121	1981	849
1937	140	1982	842
1938	155	1983	887
1939	140	1984	893

Table 8.1 (*Continued*)

Year	Numbers	Year	Numbers
1940	30	1985	863
1941	32	1986	888
1942	33	1987	900
1943	41	1988	945
1944	46	1989	1079
1945	52	1990	1276
1946	200	1991	1326
1947	205	1992	1442
1948	242	1993	1262
1949	243	1994	1277
1950	240	1995	1201
1951	255	1996	1145
1952	297	1997	1252
1953	327	1998	1351
1954	357	1999	1272
1955	389	2000	1304
1956	356	2001	1487

Source: Bornholm Ferry Traffic Company

charter market, which caused many Danes to take their long holidays abroad. Thus, the situation in the early 1970s can be compared with the stagnation phase of the lifecycle, although it appears 13 years before the predicted trend in Figure 8.4. However, this stagnation then ceases and an apparent rejuvenation stage begins in 1976. From 1976 to 1988, passenger numbers increase steadily, but a detailed examination of the data show that this was entirely due to an increase in the number of tourists from Germany and Sweden, as the Danish market was still falling away. So the reason was not rejuvenation of the product, in the TALC sense, but shifts in demand patterns due to growth in alternative markets for the island.

Between 1989 and 1992, the growth in passengers to Bornholm accelerated, only to be followed by a decline of almost equal magnitude. This peak was due solely to tourists from East Germany and a few from

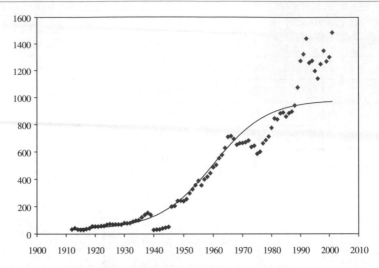

Figure 8.4 TALC model and passengers to Bornholm

Poland, as the disappearance of the iron curtain gave the East Germans the possibility of visiting a neighboring Western country and the proximity of Bornholm made it an attractive destination. But they were a nonrepeat market and just caused a 'blip' in the statistics. The number of Danish tourists actually declined during this peak, as the island became more expensive on the domestic market. This was compounded by difficulties with accommodation and ferry ticket availability. Finally, the decline after 1992 was reinforced by the Swedish devaluation, which almost closed down the Swedish market. There is a further upward move after 1996, which may be partly explained by an increasing flow of same-day tourists, a market that was then affected by the closure of tax-free shops on the ferries from mid-1999, as a result of European Union legislation. In the summer of 2000 a new bridge link was opened between Denmark and Sweden, which, together with a fast ferry link to Bornholm from Ystad in Southern Sweden, reduced the journey time Copenhagen–Bornholm by car or public transport to around 3 hours. This opened up a short-break market from the rest of Denmark, which is reflected in the boost in passenger numbers in 2001. Thus, in the period when Bornholm had a fairly uniform tourist market, it is possible to apply the TALC model. This was the situation up to 1967, when visitors were primarily domestic tourists who came year after year.

Conclusions

The TALC model has been one of the most significant paradigms used in research concerning the development of resorts. The applications of the model have been more descriptive than normative, proceeding by way of relating information from case studies to stages on the life cycle curve. The examples in the literature indicate that departures from the theoretical structure shown in Figure 8.1 occur on both the demand and supply side of resort development. This is because on the one hand the market is not uniform and on the other, the tourist product is an amalgam of a variety of different activities.

Starting from first principles, we show how the mathematical processes evolve to form the 'ideal' model supporting Butler's theory. By developing the model in this manner, it is also possible to mark precisely when the five stages of the resort cycle occur, though in practice the transition from one stage to another is unlikely to be so clearly observed. It turns out that even under the assumption of a uniform market that ignores the shifting patterns of tourist arrivals cited by various authors, the life cycle curve can only be a truly representative aggregation if all tourists are repeat visitors. It is possible to conclude that finding resort data that exhibit the properties of uniformity and replication are critical to the empirical testing of the life cycle model. Such data exist for the Isle of Man in Britain from 1884 to 1912 and for the Danish island of Bornholm from 1912 to 1967 (excluding WWII). In both cases, domestic tourists taking their traditional seaside holidays year after year dominate the market and the model fits the observations tolerably well. In later years there are too many shift factors in the data to find any plausible generating process within the scope of the TALC model. In such situations, there are several polynomial trend curves that may be used to fit the data, but they lack any theoretical structure and their interpretation depends on the skill of the researcher.

Acknowledgements

The authors wish to thank the Bornholm Ferry Traffic Company for their help in providing data to carry out the empirical testing of the TALC model.

Chapter 9

The Implications of Lamarckian Theory for the TALC Model

NEIL RAVENSCROFT and ION HADJIHAMBI

Introduction

In this paper we seek to probe the underlying rationale of the Tourism Area Life Cycle (TALC) model and its adherence to the increasingly discredited concept of the Product Life Cycle (PLC). Despite recent attempts to underpin the use of the PLC (Johnston, 2001, this volume), and recognising that Butler uses the biological life cycle in a heuristic rather than an ontological sense (Aunger, 2001; Hodgson, 2002), we suggest that the long-term maturity and explicit management of many tourist areas (Bosselman *et al.*, 1999) undermines the very construct upon which the TALC is based. While accepting that the time-mediated dimensions of the TALC are a useful analogy for the growth and (sometimes) decline of resorts, we argue that time is a weak and unreliable referent upon which to base the model.

Rather than the analogy of the life cycle we argue, following Tellis and Crawford (1981), that the development of resorts is better understood as a process of evolution. Interestingly, Butler (1980) refers to evolution in the title of the original TALC paper, although he does not develop this construct in the paper itself. By evolution, we mean that rather than consider a single 'generation' (the implication of the life cycle), the development of resorts takes place over a number of iterations, each reflecting a change (improvement) on the last. Use of this broader analogy has a particular appeal, given that few resorts stay the same over time, but instead evolve to reflect different market opportunities and trends. In making this distinction, we explicitly reject the contention of some authors (particularly Johnston, 2001), that the PLC implies multiple generations.

Most applications of the evolutionary model reflect the work of Charles Darwin (Darwin, 1859; Dawkins, 1986). For Darwin, evolutionary development was a function of two complementary constructs: random variation and natural selection. Thus, rather than a single strain of organism developing through a 'rational' process of improvement, Darwin argued that improvements to the genome occur randomly, with only the most suitably adapted being able to survive. This understanding has been applied to product development, on the basis that the market determines which of the many products offered for sale will be successful (see Katsanis & Pitta, 1995, for example). However, Cooper and Kleinschmidt (1993) and Massey (1999) have found this difficult to credit, on the basis that few products are developed without a market analysis, while the 'natural selection' of the market tends to take place prior to production. This is certainly the case with most tourist resorts, where development is usually regulated by a plan, to ensure that 'selection' is anything but random and 'natural' (Gunn, 1993; Hall, 2000; Priestley & Mundet, 1998).

As a result of these apparent shortcomings of the Darwinian model, we consider the relevance to the TALC of the work of Jean-Baptiste Lamarck and, in particular, his theory of the inheritance of acquired traits (Lamarck, 1809). This theory has been discredited for much of the time since it was first published. However, recent interest (Jablonka, 2000; Lenoir & Ross, 1996; Massey, 1999; Steele *et al.*, 1998) has suggested that it may have a particular resonance to cultural and technological (if not biological) evolutionary processes (Aunger, 2001; Gould, 1980), especially in denying the Darwinian inevitability of decline and death (Tellis & Crawford, 1981).

In attempting to determine the applicability of Lamarckian evolutionary theory, we consider the planning and development of Ayia Napa in Cyprus. Having been predominantly a relatively low-key family resort, Ayia Napa has recently been faced with an influx of young 'clubbers' from all over Europe, seeking to find a 'new Ibiza'. While initially welcoming the new demand, and the wave of development activity that followed, the local authority in Ayia Napa felt that the situation was getting out of control and that, as fast as the action had moved from Ibiza to Ayia Napa, it would move on again, thus seemingly 'fulfilling' the TALC model. As a result, actions have been taken, based on knowledge of what has happened elsewhere (Lamarck's acquired traits), to prevent clubs and clubbers dominating the resort to the exclusion of the more established visitors.

The experience of Ayia Napa suggests that Butler's TALC model may, at the very most, be a broad analogy of a rather deeper and more complex process. There have been definite 'stages' in the development of the resort, although it is not yet quite clear what they are. Indeed, notwithstanding claims to the contrary (Priestley & Mundet, 1998; Russell & Faulkner, 1998), this is argued to be one of the chief weaknesses of the TALC construct: it can only really be apparent what the stages were when the 'life' of the resort is over. Yet there is every indication that the 'life' of Ayia Napa is far from over. Indeed, following evolutionary theory, it seems to be evolving into a new and modified form, at the very least informed and mediated by the planners.

Yet, while reflecting that the apparent ability of Ayia Napa's planners to influence the development of the resort suggests an interventionist, non-random evolutionary model, we conclude by questioning how far this is actually the case, certainly in a Lamarckian sense. It is not clear quite what the lineage of the resort is, or how heritability occurs outside the biological world (see Stankiewicz, 2000). Equally, it is far from clear to what extent individual developments conform to Lamarckian rather than Darwinian theory. This is particularly with respect to the extent that some nightclubs and other developments are clearly more successful than others (see di Benedetto & Bojanic, 1993 for an application of the TALC to an individual attraction).

TALC, Biology and the Product Life Cycle

As Graham Massey (1999) has argued, the attraction of the biological life cycle as an analogy for the 'life' of a cultural or technical artefact is not hard to understand. With elements corresponding to birth, growth, maturity, decline and death, the 'life' of such artefacts seems every bit as inevitable as their biological model implies. This intuitive appeal certainly underlies Butler's development of the TALC, just as it has many areas of product development and marketing (Avlonitis, 1990; Catry & Chevalier, 1974; Kotler, 1997). Academic work on tourism development has, as Pearce (1989) recognises, certainly been informed by the PLC (see di Benedetto & Bojanic, 1993; Haywood, 1998; McElroy *et al.*, 1993). Indeed, while offering cautions about the empirical foundations of the TALC and other models, Pearce appears to accept the utility of the life cycle analogy. Similarly, Cooper *et al.* (1998: 114) suggest that the TALC is a suitable '... framework for understanding how destinations and their markets evolve'.

Yet, as Butler and Pearce certainly recognise, the biological model is – in most cases – little more than a heuristic, useful in reducing complex relationships to a simple linear form in which changes (developments) are predominantly a function of the time elapsed since 'birth' (Massey, 1999). This reliance on time as the key variable introduces an inevitability that, while biologically valid, is often contrary to the trajectory of cultural and technical artefacts and institutions (Giddens, 1984; Tellis & Crawford, 1981). Indeed, it is apparent that one of the characteristics of successful products and developments is managed longevity, with few signs of decline or death:

> The goal of any sensible community should be to maximize the benefits and minimize the risks of tourism. We believe that this can be done and that tourism can be 'tamed' by carefully managing its growth. ... the goals of each destination are the same: to secure those benefits that the community most desires; to avoid those impacts that

the community deems harmful; to share the benefits and burdens in an equitable way; and to be resilient enough to adapt the chosen strategy to future changes. (Bosselman *et al.*, 1999: 10–11)

While this type of sentiment is almost axiomatic in tourism texts (see Cooper *et al.*, 1998, for example), it would seem that it has rarely led to a sustained critique of the life cycle analogy or its application in the TALC. Quite apart from questions about the inevitability of decline, Dhalla and Yaspeh (1976) have found that some products have 'second lives', in which their sales plateau at maturity and then grow again (see also Agarwal, 1994, 1997, this volume). To some extent, Butler allows for this through his 'rejuvenation' stage, although maintaining that this is doing no more than lengthening the life of the tourist area (rather than questioning the ontological foundation of the life cycle analogy itself).

Yet both Dhalla and Yaspeh (1976) and Tellis and Crawford (1981) remain critical of the assumed inevitability of the PLC, arguing that if promotion ceases once a product reaches maturity, it will decline, certainly in relation to new products that are being heavily promoted. Thus the 'inevitability' of the life cycle becomes self-fulfilling, regardless of the potential creativity of managers to enhance and rejuvenate existing products. As Tellis and Crawford (1981) suggest, the key issue is not so much the time elapsed between 'birth' and maturity, as the resources and creativity put into developing the product to stimulate the subsequent growth in sales.

This has much resonance with Butler's observations encapsulated in the TALC. Many tourist areas do rise and fall in cycles of popularity and investment, while more resources are often applied to new rather than existing resorts. Yet, as Tellis and Crawford (1981) argue, this is neither natural (biological), nor inevitable. Rather, it is the result of deliberate investment strategies that seek to maximise short-term returns, allied to an adherence to the 'false' metaphor of the PLC. For, in theory at least, products do not have biological lives, or even gene equivalents (despite Dawkins, 1986, who attempts to construct the 'meme' as a technological copy). This has caused Tellis and Crawford (1981) to question the actual existence of the PLC, suggesting that it is more properly viewed as 'an artifact of an inappropriate analogy'.

Evolutionary Adaptation and Tourist Area Development

In their work, Tellis and Crawford (1981) note that products rarely stay the same over time, but evolve (or more correctly are developed) into more efficient forms, often with greater complexity, to meet changing customer requirements. So it is with tourist areas (Bianchi, 1994; Cooper, 1992; Laws, 1995; Morgan & Pritchard, 1999; Urry, 1997). Rather than the descriptor of the life cycle, this form of product development has been likened to biological evolution, to the extent that organisms (products or tourist areas) evolve over time, while retaining lineal connections to earlier generations (Aunger, 2001). For Steadman (1979), the evolutionary process involves a sequence of repeated copyings (inheritance), with small changes made at each step (variation) that are subsequently subjected to testing (selection). The level of analysis thus shifts from the individual organism or product to the intergenerational study of entire populations.

Such Darwinian thinking has been applied to research in architectural innovation (Daru *et al.*, 2000), marketing (Katsanis & Pitta, 1995) and organisational change (Romanelli & Tushman, 1994). In all these cases the departure from the former emphasis on the life cycle has been related to the adaptive design and redesign of artefacts, products and organisations (see Stankiewicz, 2000), thus shifting from an epistemology of ideas to one of lineal adaptation, development and proliferation. This has similarly been the case in tourism development, with 'change management' an increasingly key concept and continual investment necessary to maintain tourist numbers and consumption patterns (Laws *et al.*, 1998; Swarbrooke, 1995).

However, even advocates of such Darwinian evolutionary ontology concede that the biological metaphor does not easily translate to culture and technology. In particular, the Darwinian model assumes that changes to the genome of an organism occur independently of the environment it is inhabiting, thus randomising its survival in that environment (Darwin, 1859; Massey, 1999). Neither of these conditions hold in market environments, where developments are based on market research rather than the forces of natural selection (Cooper & Kleinschmidt, 1993). Indeed, the development of tourist areas and other cultural and technological innovations would seem to invert Darwinian orthodoxy. Instead of being developed randomly and then exposed to natural selection – as the biological analogy suggests – it is usually the case that selection would occur at the design and planning stage (Daru *et al.*, 2000), with only the best design being developed. In addition, the criteria for selection will, through rigorous market research, be the very antithesis of biological randomness.

Equally problematic for cultural and technological development, are questions about what actually evolves: is it the product itself (Basalla, 1988), or the technical knowledge required to make changes to that product (Constant, 2000; Mokyr, 2000)? In addition, as Aunger (2001) has identified, there are issues about how heritability occurs and how 'lineage' should be understood in nonbiological applications (Stankiewicz, 2000). These are important issues for tourist area development, and ones that are not addressed by the conventional Darwinian evolutionary model.

The Application of Lamarckian Evolutionary Ontology

Although widely discredited in biological sciences, the work of Jean-Baptiste Lamarck has found increasing resonance with those seeking to develop the evolutionary ontology of cultural and technical development (see, for example, Massey, 1999; Steele *et al.*, 1998). Working some 50 years before Darwin, Lamarck was credited by Darwin and others as the first naturalist to understand that changes in the organic world conform to identifiable 'laws' rather than random events. Lamarck developed his theories while working at the National Museum of Natural History in Paris, where he specialised in the study of invertebrates. Indeed, his theories of evolution were largely drawn from his study of invertebrates, particularly in his best known work, *Philosophie Zoologique* (Lamarck, 1809), in which he set out two 'laws':

(1) That changes in the environment cause changes in the needs of organisms living in that environment, which in turn cause changes in their behaviour. These behavioural changes lead to greater or lesser use of particular structures or organs, causing the physical characteristics of the organism to change over generations.
(2) All such changes are heritable.

In this way Lamarck's work distances itself from Darwinian selection, by embracing environmental influences as one of the principal catalysts for change and adaptation. This, for Gould (1980) and Massey (1999), represents a more plausible analogy for product development and survival than does conventional Darwinism. For, rather than survival of the fittest, Lamarck offers a model for the survival of the best adapted organisms – that survival and proliferation is the direct result of physiological intervention rather than statistical chance.

So it is with tourist area development. What superficially appears to be the inevitable result of a time-mediated life/death process is, we argue, much more the result of a complex series of planning and development decisions (the analogy of environmental and physiological interventions). Thus, just as the decision to develop a resort is neither random nor the result of natural selection, so its subsequent 'life' and eventual decline is similarly the result of entrepreneurial intervention (Cooper, 1992; Haywood, 1998; Russell, this volume). While reference to the phenomenology of tourist behaviour (Cohen, 1972, 1996; Plog, 1973) might imply the intervention of forces beyond the control of the individual resort, changes in the popularity of resorts are much more closely connected with the broader interplay of tourism demand and supply.

Thus, rather than representing an inevitable and deterministic 'life cycle', we suggest that the TALC is more appropriately viewed as part of a larger evolutionary epistemology (Zimon, 2000), in which *parts* of a tourist system increase and decrease in importance as the external environment alters. This has been recognised with respect to tourist resorts (Digance, 1997; Formica & Uysal, 1996; Priestley & Mundet, 1998). We suggest that those parts that prosper do so according to Lamarck's first law, in developing a utility that is superior to other areas or resorts. We furthermore suggest that, in maintaining this superiority, specific resort planners and managers are able to harness Lamarck's second law of heritability.

This undoubtedly raises a number of questions, not least how the lineage of heritability is formed and maintained, between which organisms and over what time periods? We now seek to explore these and other questions through a study of one resort that is seeking to acquire heritable traits in developing its tourist offering.

The Case of Ayia Napa Within the Context of Tourism in Cyprus

Prior to 1960, tourism on the island of Cyprus was limited, with the majority of the 25,700 tourists being attracted by the hill resorts. There were only 4000 tourist bed spaces, 30% of which were located along the coastline around the country (Ioannides, 1992). Forty-five years later, tourism plays a major role in the economic prosperity of Cyprus. Nearly 2.4 million tourists visited Cyprus in 2004, contributing an estimated CYP982 million ($1.8m) of gross receipts to the national economy. Revenue from the tourist sector accounted for 45.3% of the total foreign exchange earnings. There are currently approximately 90,000 beds in licensed establishments throughout the country.

This pattern of development has been particularly pronounced in the once sleepy fishing village of Ayia Napa, located in the South-eastern corner of the island, which together with the surrounding area, now accounts for almost half of the tourist arrivals to the country. Contemporary tourism development in Ayia Napa commenced in 1974, as an alternative to Turkish-controlled Famagusta (Theodoulou, 2000). It began as a family resort, with visitors attracted by the mix of coast and heritage. In recent years, however, this traditional market has increasingly been supplemented by younger people seeking out a club scene that is now thought to rival Ibiza as the 'holiday clubbing capital of Europe' (Theodoulou, 2001a). Rather than its former staid image, Ayia Napa is now a recognised 'party town':

> Welcome to Ayia Napa, the wild and gaudy party town that is reinventing itself as the new Ibiza, a clubbers' paradise where most venues charge under a tenner (*£10 sterling*) for admission and cocktails cost little more than a coffee. (Theodoulou, 2000)

Although not entirely planned as a centre of youth culture, it is apparent that the town's authorities encouraged a range of tourist development in and around Ayia Napa. This included allowing former property owners in the town to sell their land for development and move to new homes away from the town centre. This has led to a mixed tourist resort, in which the pub and club scene occupies one central area of the town, while luxury hotels, golf courses and visitor attractions are located along the coast, outside the town. For the authorities, this represents a sustainable planning mix, with wealthier and family visitors able to enjoy the amenities in Ayia Napa while staying in quieter resorts to avoid the night-time noise and crowds. It is widely claimed that this approach to tourism has allowed the resort to remain largely crime-free while accommodating large numbers of visitors (Theodoulou, 2000), in contrast to some Greek resorts where crime is an increasing problem (Press Association, 2002).

The Cyprus Tourism Organisation (CTO) has identified that in order for Ayia Napa to ensure its continued success, it should be viewed within the context of the country as a whole, rather than as an independent attraction. Regional strategies need to conform to the national framework for tourism whilst focussing on their individual strengths that enhance the profile of the island as a whole. It is this collaborative relationship that is essential for the future success of the resort. Central to this view is an understanding that there is a fine balance to be maintained between the mass of young clubbers and the wealthier, predominantly family market (Bryan-Brown, 2000).

The CTO Strategic Tourism Plan 2010 (CTO, n.d.) highlights that the success of the tourism industry is not dependent exclusively on the improvement of visitor numbers, but rather, on maximising revenue through increasing per capita tourist expenditure, improving seasonality, increasing the length of stay and increasing repeat visitation. In order to achieve this, there has been a realisation that the island needs to reposition itself through the development of its product base in a manner that attracts higher income visitors, extends the tourist season, and adopts a more intensive and focussed marketing strategy. Although much emphasis has been placed on building better high-class accommodation, it is apparent that, for some tour operators, this intervention has come too late:

> An upmarket tour operator has dropped Ayia Napa from its brochures, saying the resort's raucous reputation is causing a decline in high-spending travellers to Cyprus. Over the past few years, Ayia Napa has steadily grown in popularity among clubbers ... But images of debauchery and tales of drug-use ... have tainted the overall image of the island. (Bryan-Brown, 2000)

While the CTO and other Cypriot authorities claim that the clubbing scene is not damaging Cyprus' image (Theodoulou, 2000), it is clearly perceived as having the potential to be a negative influence on the area's tourism profile. In this respect, the authorities have chosen deliberately to identify the problems that Ayia Napa faces with those already experienced in Ibiza. These revolve around the predominance of one tourism submarket, and its association with drugs, drinking and crime (Theodoulou, 2001a, 2001b). In addressing this issue it is apparent that the authorities have been able to mobilise a large part of the state and civil society, in a concerted effort to reduce the impacts of the clubbers. These measures include:

- *Confining the club scene to a specific area.* Most of the night-time activity takes place in and around the central square adjoining the monastery of Ayia Napa. By restricting the sprawl of related activities beyond this area, the authorities have managed to confine the problem to a manageable size, thereby allowing for effective monitoring and regulation of the activities taking place here. In addition it offers more respectable establishments outside the immediate area the opportunity of attracting the more traditional clientele and maintaining a positive image of the destination.
- *Zero-tolerance on both the use and distribution of drugs.* A range of authorities have prioritised the 'drug problem', in a move that Theodoulou (2001b) sees as an attempt to prevent Ayia Napa becoming a new version of Ibiza, where he claims drugs are readily available. This has led to the police enlisting the foreign embassies, tour operators, bar tenders and club owners in spreading the word that drugs will not be tolerated. Indeed, it is accepted that most of those in the local tourist industry co-operate with the police in identifying drug users. The judiciary are equally involved, through imposing tough sentences on drug users and dealers (Paschalides, quoted in Theodoulou, 2001b).
- *Limiting pollution levels.* Increased levels of competition resulted in clubs and bars trying to outdo each other in any manner possible. This included the distribution of flyers offering free drinks and discounted entrances to clubs, the exterior façade of the establishments being designed in an over-the-top and often unattractive manner and unprecedented noise levels emanating from the establishments' sound systems. The local authorities have addressed this through the enforcement of curfews on the respective bars and nightclubs, in terms of both sound and light pollution, building regulations for new establishments and the confinement and proposed eradication of flyer distribution. Even though these issues have yet to be resolved, the authorities are progressively

implementing measures to regulate levels of pollution, and in the interim have been successful in keeping the area clean during respectable (non-clubbing) hours.

- *Pedestrianisation of the central Ayia Napa area.* In order to ensure the safety of the tourists visiting the resort, and to make the centre of Ayia Napa more attractive to all tourist groups, the local authority has opted to pedestrianise the area within the heart of the resort. During the day this affords the tourist the freedom of walking through the centre of the town, appreciating the shops, food and beverage outlets and attractions offered by the destination. In the evenings this has enabled tourists to move with ease throughout the centre and has alleviated problems such as congestion (by discouraging the use of motorised vehicles) and the safety of pedestrians, and at the same time has created a more relaxed feel in the centre.

Yet it is apparent that even these measures have been insufficient in reversing perceptions of the resort. The authorities in Ayia Napa understand the importance of the tourism industry and have prioritised its development and continual improvement within the national context. As a result, the decision was taken early in 2002 to rein in the activities of the clubs and clubbers, as described by Barbara Pericleous, the Mayor of Ayia Napa:

> If clubbers come here and misbehave, drinking and dancing in the streets and doing goodness knows what, then we'll find a democratic way to send them away if they're not put in jail first. (quoted in Smith, 2002)

Rather than continuing to be 'fashionable' to young clubbers, the Ayia Napa authorities are seeking to re-engage with their more traditional tourism markets, especially families who are seen to enjoy the natural resources that the resort has to offer. This has widespread support from local people and is reflected in national tourism planning. Indeed, Cyprus is one of a surprisingly few countries where the government (at all levels) takes tourism seriously (Seekings, 1997) and this has proven to be beneficial in terms of product development, income generated and visitor arrivals. Development in Ayia Napa may have been sporadic and at times unplanned. However, the intervention of the authorities and the cushioning effect that tourism on the national scale has had, has enabled a new vision and approach to be adopted by the resort in order to align and integrate its development with the national context.

Discussion

The case study of Ayia Napa – particularly the interventions of the town's officials – suggests that the ontology of the PLC is an inappropriate way in which to study resort development while it is actually occurring. While it is apparent that the early stages of the resort's 'life' have been experienced, it is far from clear whether Ayia Napa has yet reached maturity, whether it is into a rejuvenated 'second life', or whether the arrival of the club scene reflects a different stage and process altogether. There is a suggestion by some observers that the resort's newly rediscovered emphasis on family tourism neatly coincides with its eclipse as a clubbing capital. Indeed, there are claims that Faliraki, on Rhodes, is already attaining the status of the 'new Ayia Napa' (Press Association, 2002).

It might thus be argued that the recent actions of the local authorities amounts to the types of stage 'marker' suggested by Priestley and Mundet (1998) and Russell and Faulkner (1998). In particular, the official intervention would seem to have marked a watershed, from the largely supported hedonism of the clubs back to a family-oriented conservatism (Smith, 2002). However, this certainly does not signal decline, as much as it does a shift in policy emphasis. Indeed, the actions of the town's officials would seem to indicate long-term stewardship rather than a single and relatively short-term 'life'.

Butler certainly recognises the ontological problems posed by the model, particularly in linking the TALC with *ex post* observation rather than diagnostics. However, as we have argued, it is doubtful whether this is really a sustainable position, given the continuous development and change that Ayia Napa (and all resorts) has experienced. Indeed, what characterises Ayia Napa and many other resorts is the continual creativity of the planners and other officials, both in promoting and supporting new developments and – as in the current case – restricting adverse trends and themes (see Cooper, 1992). This implies a level of intervention and design that certainly challenges the temporal inevitability at the core of the life cycle. Thus, to view the entire existence of the resort as equivalent or analogous to a single life of a single biological organism seems an unreasonable proposition.

Yet, of course, at another scale Butler is undoubtedly right. The increasingly globalised flow of capital and labour means that investors can switch in and out of markets, products and resorts with comparative ease. Thus, as many resorts have found, capital will flow into new schemes with high financial returns, and flow out again when even newer schemes become available elsewhere. To this extent, each resort has a 'life' that is largely determined by capital and labour markets far removed from its control (Haywood, 1998). There is certainly evidence to suggest that this capital flow was experienced between Ibiza and Ayia Napa. It might, even without any intervention from the officials in Ayia Napa, be experienced again, as the clubs seek a new location such as

Faliraki (see McElroy *et al.*, 1993 for a study of this phenomenon and also Butler, other volume).

Yet, even in this case, planners and resort officials have the potential ability to lure capital back with new schemes or, as is now happening in Ayia Napa, by redeveloping and improving existing facilities. As a result, we have argued in this chapter that the TALC is less a reflection of a life cycle, and more an analogy of biological evolution. By shifting to the metadimension of evolution, the actions of planners and officials can be understood as developmental interventions, such that the resorts improve and adapt through each successive iteration (life). This removes, or at least plays down the temporal inevitability of the life cycle model, in favour of an open-ended approach that links survival to adaptation. It also supports the types of 'pre' and 'post' tourism stages of the TALC model posited by Agarwal (1994, 1997, this volume), Juelg (1993) and Young (1983).

What is rather less clear, certainly with regard to Ayia Napa, is how far the evolutionary analogy relates to Darwinian selection or Lamarckian adaptation. The case has been made by Aunger (2001) and others that, while Darwin's construct is probably a more accurate reflection of biological evolution, Lamarck's work resonates with the development of cultural and technological artefacts. Yet, while tourist resorts certainly belong in this latter category, it is far from certain that Lamarck's theorem is superior to Darwin's. In particular, there is little evidence that the Ayia Napa officials initiated the arrival of the club scene. Rather, they exploited it when it arrived and, belatedly, have attempted to regulate it when it threatened to get out of control. This is really much more analogous to the random variation and natural selection of Darwin, than to the inherited traits of Lamarck.

However, despite the officials' lack of intervention in the arrival of the clubs, it is equally clear that, once the clubs had arrived, the officials sought to ensure that the resort capitalised on their presence. As a result, the resort began to evolve, from a largely family orientation to one in which parts of it were redeveloped to cater for a younger clubbing market. Further recent intervention has sought to restrict the impact of this shift on the traditional family market. These developments are very much more analogous to Lamarck's construction, with the officials responding to the new environment by deploying a range of enhancement and proliferation strategies that are anything but random in their application. What is rather less clear is quite how far the interventions count as inherited or learned traits, in Lamarck's terms.

To conform to Lamarck's construct, there would need to have been some explicit process of adaptation and inheritance. However, as Stankiewicz (2000) has observed, it is far from clear just how this process happens in technological development, and at what level. In contrast to biological inheritance, where it is the genome that varies internally, the resort development process is largely externally initiated and mediated. While Dawkins (1986) has proposed the 'meme' as a 'technological genome', it does not have the same characteristics, nor function. Rather, the learning function in Ayia Napa is largely related to the human actors, who impose particular regulatory formats on the built environment (largely in opposition to what they perceive to have happened in Ibiza).

For some observers, including Steadman (1979) and Daru *et al*. (2000), this is the very point of the evolutionary analogy: the ability of planners and designers to develop a series of improvements to the built environment that allow it to evolve (literally) according to the changing use requirements. Thus, rather than residing in the built environment itself (as is the case with biological heredity), it would seem that technological heredity lies in the work of the planners and officials – and is merely articulated through the technological forms of the resort. In this case, as Zimon (2000) recognises, the planners (and other inhabitants) are an essential (cultural) component of the resort system, such that they, rather than the built form, represent the 'meme'.

If this is the case, the lineage so important in establishing heredity lies in the training and development of the planners, police, judiciary and other officials, such that they 'inherit' an understanding of how the resort works and the positive influence they can have on its future. In addition, and so fundamentally important to sustaining the resort, their inheritance can include learning from what has happened elsewhere, such that Ayia Napa's lineage is increasingly linked to the evolution of other similar resorts – particularly Ibiza. Thus, in making the decision to restrict the development of the club scene in Ayia Napa, the officials learned (inherited) from what had previously happened in Ibiza. Similarly, officials from other resorts will be taking a keen interest in the development of Ayia Napa, so that they will be better equipped should they have to deal with similar issues in the future. Early evidence suggests that this may not be happening yet in Faliraki (Press Association, 2002).

To conclude, we can certainly make the case that the TALC is, in Tellis and Crawford's (1981) terms, 'an artifact of an inappropriate analogy'. That is, because the popularity of some resorts appears to rise then fall does not mean that the underlying processes have any relationship with biological life cycles. Nevertheless, it is quite possible that the TALC is a reasonable *post hoc* analogy of the development history of a resort. Despite this limitation at the metascale, the TALC remains an appealing model of the 'life' of the individual elements (memes) of a bigger system (Digance, 1997; Formica & Uysal, 1996; Priestley & Mundet, 1998). This might be at a more global level, mediated by capital flows

(McElroy *et al.*, 1993), or at a more local level, relating to individual attractions (di Benedetto & Bojanic, 1993; Swarbrooke, 1995).

At the tourist area level, in contrast, it is apparent that there may well be appropriate linkages between development and biological evolutionary processes. Again, this relationship is currently largely analogous rather than diagnostic, in the sense that tourist areas are fundamentally different from the biological genomes that they supposedly reflect. Notwithstanding this caveat, there are echoes of both Darwinian and Lamarckian theory evident in the Ayia Napa case study, in the way in which clubbers 'arrived' at the resort (Darwin) and the ways in which the development and disciplinary processes have subsequently been managed (Lamarck). Following Gould (1990) and Steele *et al.* (1998), we suggest that this is a defensible proposition, in which the two evolutionary constructs operate in tandem, at different levels and at different times.

In refiguring the TALC to take account of this proposition, we suggest that the primary requirement is for tourist areas to be understood across multiple and differentiated dimensions. At the lowest level, the individual attraction, the life cycle analogy, may still hold as a descriptor, particularly in the case of night clubs and other predominantly short-lived uses of buildings. In such cases, time remains a key mediator of success. However, at the tourist area level we argue that changes are best viewed from an evolutionary perspective in which the external environment is understood in relation to Darwinian selection, while changes to the built environment are mediated according to Lamarckian inherited traits. This rather implies a system of 'models within models', such that individual attractions are represented by conventional TALC models, which are themselves framed by a broader evolutionary paradigm. However, it is apparent that more work needs to be done to develop the evolutionary model into anything more complex and appropriate than the life cycle model it is seeking to replace.

Chapter 10
Chaos Theory and its Application to the TALC Model

ROSLYN RUSSELL

Introduction

The Tourism Area Life Cycle (TALC) model has, over the last 20 years, proved to be a valuable heuristic tool in understanding the development of tourist destinations. Like any good theoretical model it has been applied, applauded, criticised and modified over the years. The most valuable recommendations for improving the TALC have been in relation to exploring further the change processes underlying the evolution of a tourist destination (Prosser, 1997). Butler himself (1998: 4) admits that the idea of 'triggers, factors which bring about change in the destination ... were, perhaps not given the focus they might deserve' in the original paper.

Other criticisms have been aimed at the quasi-linear depiction of a model that purports to represent a process that is anything but linear (Faulkner & Russell, 1997). However, at the macroscale the development of many tourist destinations does appear to progress through the S-curve or a mutation of it, quite predictably as suggested by Butler. But when zooming in on the evolution of a destination it is evident that the process is not as straightforward as it appears in the macro view. The very term 'life cycle' suggests a paradox. Life is commonly perceived as a linear progression through events and developmental stages – in human terms, birth, infancy, childhood, adolescence, adulthood and ultimately death. However circumstances may intervene along the way to initiate cycles that may radically modify and redirect development, providing unexpected outcomes. Linearity and cyclical complexity, opposite as they appear, are coexisting elements of any dynamic system, and few systems are more dynamic than tourism. So while not disagreeing with the original TALC model, this chapter will provide additional theoretical concepts that will enhance the power of the model to provide a greater understanding of the evolution of tourist destinations. The principles of Chaos Theory and Complexity have been meshed with the TALC to bring to the forefront the underlying forces of change and the importance of triggers at critical times in the evolution of a destination.

The emergence of Chaos Theory and Complexity has brought a different perspective to many disciplines that have found the traditional research frameworks inadequate for explaining complex phenomena. The physical sciences have discovered, mainly through enhanced technological capabilities, that things are far more complex and less stable and predictable than was first thought. The value of Chaos and Complexity is not so much in the creation of new tools but in the new perspective that it brings to research – being able to look at the same problem and issues but from a new angle, which of course brings into focus elements that were previously obscure. The Chaos and Complexity theories have been established on very different premises than those of traditional scientific methods. While traditional methods assume stability, and constancy of impacts – that is, all things remaining equal, chaos and complexity assume change and instability. Uncertain circumstances, chaotic states and unpredictable outcomes are inherent attributes of apparently linear systems.

This chapter, in demonstrating the usefulness of viewing destination development from the chaos and complexity platform, will first highlight the problems inherited from sustained use of traditional linear and reductionist models.

The Nature of Traditional Research Methods

Tourism study is indebted to many disciplines that have been founded on traditional scientific methods which trace back to the Newtonian/ Cartesian paradigm of the 16th century. The traditional modes of enquiry have been amplified from their Judeo-Christian and Greek genesis through Copernicus, Kepler, Bacon, Galileo, Descartes, Newton and others becoming synthesised into what became known as the scientific method (Capra, 1982). It incorporated the twin rational functions of induction and deduction (Smith, 1995). Induction involves discovery through problem sensitivity and definition, data gathering, testing and generalised codified explanation – all this with much looping back to earlier stages of the total process. Thus it involves a linear progression through a series of stages that incorporate returning to accepted under-standings to revise concepts to accommodate emerging data.

On the other hand, deduction is a complementary process in which the formalised theory produced by induction is applied to similar situations for predictive purposes. Both aspects of the process can be dynamically creative. Deduction need not imply a mechanical, somewhat moribund application of rules. Indeed, the technological revolution owes much to the imaginative, flexible utilisation of principles, of 'surfing' the possibilities and finding the best match to the problem.

This complementary inductive/deductive relationship is not universally recognised. Faulkner (1999: 12) discerns that a fundamental impediment of the inductive procedure emerges from the logical anomaly associated with inferring general statements from a limited number of instances. 'A fundamental impediment seen by Harvey (1969, p.87) in more extreme terms as "speculative fantasy"'. Deductivists argue for the superiority of deduction on the basis of it being a more orderly process carried on within an established frame of theory with testable propositions developed about the relationship between the theory and the specific phenomenon.

On the other hand, it may be argued that to denigrate scientific method, essentially inductive, as inviting indulgences of fancy, is to question the objectivity and integrity of many scientists who have used it to establish many understandings, the veracity of which cannot be questioned. Faulkner (1999: 11) recognises that, 'the distinction between the inductive and deductive routes to explanation is obviously somewhat blurred' because 'it is difficult to imagine any process of measurement which does not rely on some apriori framework.' The initial review of literature in the induction process provides that base. Both induction and deduction imply flexibility. In each, hypotheses are adapted to accommodate new data. Nor are most principles derived via the inductive route other than tentative, to be revised as more instances, newer scholarship and improved technology make them more sophisticated. Each has open-ended potential. There are, however, some absolutes. Apples are likely to continue falling downwards but all conclusions have provisional status that permits periodic overhaul so that truth generally moves in an evolutionary progression in which only that fit to survive, does.

The Newtonian concept of physical reality, in its strictest sense, assumes that all things continue as they were, behaving as they have in the past, following previous patterns. It incorporates the idea that all things behave with the same predictable constancy, as do falling apples. It assumes both implicitly and explicitly that systems are stable and in equilibrium.

Newton visualised tangible reality as a gigantic clock with each component transferring energy systematically – from spring, to cogs, to hands – along a predetermined, mechanical path according to rules ordained by God. As an adjunct to this, emerged the reductionist view that each component in the cosmic process could be theoretically disassembled from the rest and examined in isolation. An understanding of each part in isolation can be summed to produce an understanding of the whole. Reductionism and determinism were consequential partners of Newtonian thinking.

Some later researchers recognised the clockwork, linear hypothesis as being too simplistic, in that it failed to take account of the synergy in what were indeed exceedingly complex, multivariable networks. Data that did not fit into the mechanistic paradigm was assumed away by reductionists who abandoned it as aberrant 'noise'. For examples, 'meteorites were thrown out of the Vienna museum because there was no place for them in the description of the solar system' (Prigogine & Stengers, 1985: 307). Such apparently atypical data became more common as superior research technology and scholarship opened up a plethora of complexities, exceptions, surprises and order from disorder. Disequilibrium, nonlinearity and transience coexisted with the evolution of pattern.

Chaos Theory: The Radical Phase Shift

Chaos Theory emerged as a response to the perceived deficiencies of the Newtonian/Cartesian model to be hailed by some as, along with the theory of relativity and quantum physics, a part of a triumvirate of 20th-century triumphs in materials science scholarship (Nijkamp & Reggiani, 1995). Although ranked third in this trio, it exists partly as a spin-off from the other two (Tsonis, 1992) and although its ascendancy has been relatively recent, its conception goes back as far as the previous century when a mathematician, Henri Poincare, recognised and provided the intellectual impetus for accommodating nonconforming phenomena. Technical innovation, especially in the form of powerful computers, has combined with scholarship as enabling factors for the development of the Chaos Theory perspective. Its use has clarified our understanding of phenomena that were previously unfathomable, but has at the same time brought to light new perplexities.

Poincare had demonstrated the possibility of erratic or 'chaotic' behaviour in planetary orbits, an area usually associated with predictable regularity (Markworth et al., 1995). 'Apparently', comments Tsonis (1992: 3) cynically, 'the founders of Chaos Theory, had a very good sense of humour, since "chaos" is a Greek word for the complete absence of order'. But 'chaos' in the new, scientific sense does not represent absolute, formless disarray. Instead, according to Ward (1995: 629), it refers to systems that are in a state of flux. Also, 'Chaos' in the Chinese language refers to a form emerging from the turbulent void. Briggs and Peat (1989: 19) claim that all cultures believed in 'chaos as something immense and creative ... From which beings and things burst forth'. Chaos describes a situation where a system is dislodged from its steady state after being conditioned by a catalyst that is as random and unpredictable as the outcome. It involves the regrouping of the elements of the system, from which a new order eventually emerges incorporating vestiges of the old.

Gleick (1987: 299) describes the chaotic systems as having 'life-like' characteristics and having the ability of self-organisation – 'Life sucks order out of a sea of disorder'. According to Peat (1991: 196), Chaos can beget 'a new order so rich and subtle that it lies beyond any pattern of periodicity' and so infinitely complex as to be inexhaustibly puzzling. This feature of life-like or self-organising systems partly explains the paradox of the Second Law of Thermodynamics. According to this law, there is an inexorable increase in entropy, whereby the universe is supposed to run down as atoms randomise. Yet, as observed by Waldrop (1992: 286), if we have increasing levels of randomness and disorder at the atomic scale, why is matter constantly becoming more and more organised on a large scale? Clearly, if simple rules of behaviour governing individual particles (agents) can give rise to astonishingly complicated and highly structured arrangements at the macrolevel, the random perturbations of individual particles simply become initiators of the constant flux of structures (emergence, coalescence, decay) that can be observed at this level.

Different fields manifest varying tendencies to chaotic symptoms. Nilson (1995) identifies the broad behavioural types included in Table 10.1.

Pure physics can cite many examples of the stable predictable system, which comply faithfully with the Second Law of Thermodynamics, dissipating their stored energy, running down, entropying at a calculable rate. 'Some systems are linear in their operation. That is, their action can be predicted by information about their starting point and their rules of operation' (Ward, 1995: 629). In the context of these systems therefore, the mechanistic Newtonian view is appropriate and not redundant in certain contexts. Mathews *et al*. (1999: 446) see nonlinear systems having the dual capability of either 'low-dimensional' or 'high-dimensional chaos'. It 'is justified to some extent', claims Capra (1982: 286) 'because living organisms do act, in part, like machines' just as mammoth, impersonalised corporations do from time to time (p. 233). But the rigid conformity is qualified because corporations are as capable of 'a high degree of internal flexibility and plasticity' (p. 289) as living organisms are as well

Table 10.1 Behavioural types of systems

Stable systems	Dynamic chaos systems	Totally turbulent systems
Predictable, no change	Change within boundaries	Out of control

Source: Nilson, 1995, Figure 3.2

as tourist destinations, and are indeed 'subject to forces of instability which push them toward chaos' (Thietart & Forgues, 1995: 19). But perhaps there is no system so stable that it is totally immune to perturbations that would unsettle its equilibrium. The delicate pendulum has its oscillating rhythm distorted by a puff of breeze and any attempt to measure subatomic particles destroys their organisational patterns. Big Ben, London's famous clock which became an international symbol of 'business as usual' during World War II might have had its regularity radically disturbed had one well-aimed bomb found its chiming mechanism. At that time it was (at least) markedly chaos prone to the extent that, as few if any functional entities are insulated against disruptive energy, stability is tenuous. Not since World War II has there been a time greater than now, when chaos conditions have been more prominent. New York did experience what Big Ben avoided, a well aimed attack that sent the city, temporarily at least, into the category of the third type of behavioural system, totally turbulent and out of control. Even though order has been restored somewhat, and the system has subsided into dynamic chaos, global stability is still highly tenuous, experiencing an edge-of-chaos state.

However, totally turbulent systems are relatively uncommon – perhaps extreme volcanic activity, terminal cancer or intertribal turmoil in Central Africa approach this state. Nor are there definable boundaries between the types. A continuum based on the susceptibility of systems to chaotic behaviour is a more likely configuration. Indeed, Pinfield (1986) demonstrated the complementary functions of 'structured' and 'anarchic' processes in a single system. Nevertheless, it is broadly agreed that most systems are potentially chaotic, especially those that relate to human interaction.

Stehle (1994) noted an upheaval in scientific thoughts in the last one and a half centuries in which the flaws in the cherished views of many branches of science were laid bare and found wanting. 'And the path from the old to the new was unmarked and booby trapped' (Stehle, 1994: xiii). The transition to newer and better understandings has been lurching with fluctuating vigour between the roundabouts towards a retreating destination. For example, 'In business we deal with human beings, incredibly more complex than studying friction or the weather . . . and it is not unreasonable to assume that all interactions in the business world are based on non-linear relationships' (Nilson, 1995: 27, 28). In an understated fashion, Brown (1995: 1) observed, 'there is no apparent reason, intuitive or otherwise, as to why human behaviour should be more linear than the behaviour of other things, living and non-living'. If in the animate sphere, the linear paradigm corresponds to the kind of unfolding orderliness in a ceremonial parade or a church mass, the chaotic states have attributes of a game of football (Australian Rules presumably, editor's comment) as seen by the uninitiated. To the alien, such a match degenerates spasmodically into the brawling of petty anarchists, regulations and regulators notwithstanding. Out of the 'confusion', a move of individual spontaneity – a feint, an intercept – can be the 'break' that makes the underlying combination and coordination evident. This 'new' order may be some previously untried manoeuvre or the creative adaptation of some rehearsed move. And the confusion out of which it erupted may have been more illusory than actual – i.e. 'creative confusion'.

'The "order-through-fluctuations" model introduces an unstable world where small causes can have large effects, but this world is not arbitrary' (Prigogine & Stengers, 1985: 206). The climactic repercussions of small initiators are illustrated by the exaggerated 'butterfly' metaphor of Lorenz (1963) and others – the initially undiscerned fluttering of the butterfly in the Amazon basin that can theoretically cause a swelling ripple that becomes a gigantic dust storm in Texas.

Another analogy borrowed from Per Bak by Waldrop (1992: 304, 305) adds a further dimension. Tenuous equilibrium is visualised as a pile of sand heaped on a table to the limit of capacity. When sand is added to the pile, the point of criticality cannot be exactly determined, nor can the magnitude of the response be predicted. The pile of sand can be in an apparently stable phase (dynamic equilibrium in terms of General Systems Theory) as the supply of sand from the top is balanced by a spill over at the bottom allowing a stable pile to be maintained. Or there may be a period of chaos; an avalanche that reshapes the pile, depending on how near the pile was to the edge-of-chaos. It implies a critical ceiling like the straw that breaks the camel's back; a single grain dropped on to the pile under maximum stress will cause a sudden phase-shift into dramatic chaos manifest in the collapse of a face of the sand pile. It implies a readiness for change, or an 'edge-of-chaos' state in which the adhesive friction between the sand grains is taxed to the limit of tolerability.

Essential to the concept is the self-organising capacity of the pile. It is a bottom-up adaptive synthesis that contrasts with the top-down, pro-grammed manipulations which impose compliance. Bottom-up self-organisation is seen as characteristic of dynamic systems and is followed by a new phase of periodic or punctuated equilibrium. Within the self-organising concept belongs the paradox of how highly complex and complicated systems can produce rich and organised patterns and how large-scale ordered structures can house elements which are 'swimming in a sea of chaos' (Ruthen, 1993).

Edge-of-chaos tentativeness may be seen not as the precursor of the system's demise but as the gateway to renewed vibrancy and therefore as a condition to be desired. An organisation may cultivate 'creative conflict' to achieve productive change. Stewart (1993: 3) agrees that systems in this edge-of-chaos state are the ideal. Success arises from systems that are

> ... at the transition between order and chaos. A central tenet of complexity theory is that selection or learning drives systems towards this edge of chaos. Systems that are too simple do not survive in a competitive environment because more sophisticated systems can outwit them by exploiting their regularities. But systems that are too random do not survive either. It pays in survival terms to be as complicated as possible, without becoming totally structureless.

Tourism could not provide a more ideal example of a system that is complicated, but not structureless, often in an edge-of-chaos state and thereby creating a great deal of opportunity for emergent adaptive behaviour.

The range of response possibilities varies with the nature of the system. Like all models, the Per Bak metaphor had few possible outcomes and these were largely foreseeable. Chaos Theory stresses the openness and unpredictability of outcomes. Applications of Chaos Theory to management research highlight how the organisation plans for foreseeable contingencies and attempts to channel chaos effectively by drawing from a 'catalogue' or 'repertory' of responses (Thietart & Forgues, 1995). However, in the context of the totally unexpected, the thief-in-the-night take-over bid or the terrorists' bomb, the enterprise may flounder as it searches for a survival response.

'Systems which exhibit the "butterfly effect" do not exhibit proportional sensitivity to changes in the initial conditions' (Smith, 1995: 25). Smith illustrates, through the use of 'hard' data that, 'the outcome state is extremely sensitive to minor variations in the initial conditions' (p. 22) by citing two studies carried out using the same mathematical model and the same computer. In replicating Lorenz's (1963) initial work, the objective was to calculate the position of the planets 850,000,000 years in the future. The only difference between the first and second set of data was that the second set moved the position of each planet 0.5 mm. For all but one planet the calculated future positions were identical to the first-set of findings, but in the case of Pluto there was a 4 billion mile discrepancy. This experiment was seen as providing a surprising manifestation of the 'butterfly effect's' power, while incidentally confirming that although short-term predictions are possible, 'long term outcomes of chaos are not' (Markworth et al., 1995: 24).

On the other hand, others (Lorenz, 1963; Nijkamp & Reggiani, 1995) detect a likelihood that some systems will make 'smoothing adjustments' so that 'wild fluctuations' of the short term may be partially nullified in the long term, possibly through the effects of negative feedback mechanisms. One would expect that such a reversion to the norm, however limited, would make long-term outcomes more predictable, at least for those particular systems. Mandelbrot (1977) found that particles continuously magnified appeared to experience pattern decay but had apparently infinite capacity to reform into new patterns that are both unique while at the same time being similar to the original. The further the process was pushed, the greater this similarity became. However, identical replication is impossible, especially in human science. 'When the course of human events comes full circle it does so on a new level' (Stewart, 1990: 1). Toohey (1994: 276) borrows the words of Herachtus, 'it is not possible to bathe in the same river twice.' New York and the world will never be the same again after 11 September 2001.

In addition, initial conditions, although not unalterable, tend to have residual pervasiveness, a behavioural stubbornness that makes them less vulnerable to the effects of similar forces than later additions to the system. This primacy factor may account for the continuing supremacy of Coke over Pepsi and the predominance of VHS over Beta in VCR formats (Arthur, 1990). In both cases, the brand or technology that was first introduced had a sustainable head start, irrespective of its merit relative to the competition. In any case, the 'similar forces' can only be a rough approximation. In Chaos Theory, the time-irreversibility quality precludes the replication of stimuli and responses or a return to base conditions. Geographers are also well aware of this, as in the locational advantage accorded by primacy and agglomeration effect – e.g. Plymouth Rock perhaps was not the best site that could have been chosen by the pilgrims in 1620, but it became a major focal point by merit of its status.

The persistence of individual innovations irrespective of changing circumstances has been described as a form of 'lock-in' effect (Waldrop, 1992). This term usually refers to some quirk of heritage that is so entrenched and unwieldy or so immune to even catastrophic forces, or of such time-honoured appeal, or so inconsequential that it survives regardless. The configuration of QWERTY keyboards, cumbersome currency classifications, the Ten Commandments and the Declaration of Independence, for example, are islands of constancy in the turbulence caused by ongoing technological innovation, values drifts and political change.

Also relevant to this topic is the concept of bifurcation. When a system is pushed farther from its steady state and ultimately beyond endurability into chaos, alternatives emerge (Prigogine & Stengers, 1985). These are analogous to a Y junction from which the path taken leads to more Y junction bifurcations and an extension of discontinuous change punctuated by periods of relative rest. In tourism it can represent critical points in a destination's development. The most obvious bifurcation point in the TALC is at the point of stagnation when the destination can either rejuvenate or decline. Keller (1987) proposed a theoretical model that highlights four critical points in peripheral tourist destinations where changes in decision-making bodies and sources of investment – ranging from local to international, lead to significantly different development trajectories for the peripheral destinations.

In summary, all these concepts, the butterfly effect, bottom-up synthesis or self-organisation, lock-in effect, edge-of-chaos, self-similarity patterns and bifurcations have become the tools of an alternative perspective which can further our understanding of aspects of tourism systems in general and the development of destinations that are inherently complex and nonlinear. By the very nature of these elements, the laws and methods of conventional, Newtonian science, as we have known it, are revealed as deficient. The deterministic, reductionist, top-down analysis principles established by Newton and Descartes centuries ago, whilst applicable to phenomena characterised by linearity, do not explain the true nature of many systems which are nonlinear. Further, it is becoming increasingly apparent that these methods can be misleading, especially if used for predictive purposes. Table 10.2 provides a summary of the contrasting nature of the fundamental properties of the Cartesian–Newtonian and the Chaos–Complexity models.

Chaos and TALC: A Synthesis

While many disciplines within the sciences and social sciences have embraced Chaos and Complexity as a perspective which has fostered a better understanding of aspects of their domain that were previously poorly illuminated, it has only just begun to creep into the area of tourism. Faulkner and Russell (1997) introduced the concept and continued its application to entrepreneurship in tourism (Russell, this volume; Russell & Faulkner, 1999). Faulkner and Russell (2001) have also used Chaos and Complexity in furthering the understanding of crises and disasters in tourism. McKercher (1999) has developed a framework using Chaos Theory to enhance our understanding of how tourism functions as a system. His model accounts for and appreciates the complexity of tourism, highlighting the importance of the relationships between the elements, not just the characteristics of the elements themselves. Tinsley and Lynch (2001) have discussed the merits of the Chaos and Complexity framework in understanding the role of small tourism business networks and destination development.

In combining the TALC model with the principles of Chaos and Complexity it allows the somewhat paradoxical view of the evolution of destinations being both linear and complex, having both predictable and unpredictable outcomes. It also embraces that which is unique in a destination's development, allowing for unpredictable events and

Table 10.2 The Cartesian–Newtonian versus Chaos–Complexity models (Faulkner & Russell, 1997)

Cartesian–Newtonian model	*Chaos–Complexity model*
Based on 19th century Newtonian physics (deterministic, reductionist clockwork model).	Based on biological model of living systems (structure, patterns, self-organisation).
Systems seen as structurally simple, with a tendency towards linear or quasi-linear relationships between variables.	Systems viewed as inherently complex, with a tendency towards nonlinear relationships being more prevalent.
Systems tend towards equilibrium and are driven by negative feedback.	Systems are inherently unstable and positive feedback-driven processes are more common.
Individual differences, externalities and exogenous influences that create deviations from the norm are exceptional, noise-generating factors.	Individual differences and random externalities provide the driving force for variety, adaptation and complexity.

Source: Adapted from Toohey (1994: 286) and Waldrop (1992: 37–38)

triggers to be seen as significant to the development process and subsequent outcomes.

Faulkner and Russell (1997), by reinterpreting Butler's model using the perspective of Chaos Theory, suggest that the successive stages of the cycle can be seen as being triggered by seemingly random events, which cause a positive feedback process culminating in a new plane of tourist activity, and periodic equilibrium. For example, the involvement stage is characterised by a high level of contact between tourists and locals. This could be brought about by random encounters between a small number of visitors and local residents that induces the increased development of services on a commercial basis. This in turn opens up new opportunities for others and before long there is a complex web of tourism-oriented service providers enhancing the attractiveness of the destination. This attracts a greater number of tourists to the area.

Each phase of the cycle represents a period of instability, which is being driven by fundamental shifts in relationships between the various parties involved. An intense process of mutual adaptation among individual agents occurs as old niches become redundant, new opportunities emerge, markets shift and competitive relationships change. Meanwhile, specific manifestations of the butterfly effect and lock-in phenomenon at individual destinations will either impede or facilitate the growth of tourism, and add to the varying patterns of tourism development at this level.

In one respect, Butler's stagnation stage epitomises the point of criticality referred to in the description of 'edge-of-chaos' or phase shift phenomenon, as this stage represents a point of tenuous equilibrium at which the system (tourist destination) is at the edge of a dramatic transformation which could have distinctly different outcomes (i.e. ranging from rejuvenation to absolute decline). However, it might be that destinations are at the edge-of-chaos at all stages of their evolution. That is, there is an ever-present prospect of events precipitating dramatic transformations at individual destinations, irrespective of the stage reached according to Butler's model. In other words, tourist destinations are perpetually in a state that resembles Per Bak's pile of sand. The sequence depicted in the model is therefore not inevitable and, accordingly, cases where the cycle is truncated might be just as numerous as those that conform to the expected pattern. Destinations that undergo a precipitous decline immediately after reaching the involvement stage owing to some random political or natural event, for instance, are hardly likely to attract much research attention. Table 10.3 provides examples of four of the basic concepts of Chaos Theory and how they are illustrated in destination development.

It seems anomalous that Butler's theory, although essentially cyclic, is always depicted graphically as a quasi-linear progression. It seems appropriate, not only to represent it diagrammatically as a cycle, but also to superimpose on it the Chaos concept of a succession of cycles (see Figure 10.1). (There is some similarity between this figure and one which appeared in a paper which was the predecessor to the 1980 TALC article, as discussed in Butler, other volume, editor's note). Although the evolution of the target areas will thus be seen as a progression in the biological order of things, any attempt to represent diagrammatically the complexity of chaos, given all the unpredictable impinging factors, can be no more than a token attempt that oversimplifies reality. It seems warranted however to regard each phase of the Butler model as a cycle with triggering mechanisms determining the timing and intensity of the phase shifts.

The resulting model of the synthesis of TALC and Chaos is intended to crudely represent at least the major phases within the cycle. Rather than always being a smooth linear blending into the next phase, each transition is more likely to be marked by turbulence occasioned by a critical combination of circumstances often unforeseen and/or unforeseeable. Out of the disequilibrium a new set of circumstances emerges, most likely with input from outside the system, to usher in a new phase of relative stasis or tenuous equilibrium.

The butterfly metaphor, for example, recognises that circumstances unplanned, unexpected, often unpredictable, and sometimes apparently random and remote can cause a chain of reactions that are climactic

Table 10.3 Basic concepts of Chaos and Complexity and corresponding examples
in destination development

Concept	Tourism elements/examples
Bottom-up synthesis: individual agents driven by simple rules of transaction give rise to complex, dynamic systems.	• Host–guest relationship between visitors and residents • Client–service provider relationship between tourist and tourism industry • Competitive relationships between providers of similar services/product • Co-operative relationships between vertically integrated providers or coalitions of providers at a single destination • Regulator/regulatee relationship between public and private sector agents
Butterfly effect: initial small random or remote change or perturbation induces a chain reaction that precipitates a dramatic event or shift of considerable magnitude.	• Relaxation of legal restrictions on gambling in Nevada initiates development of Las Vegas as major tourist destination (Moehring, 1995) • Terrorist activities in Europe in the 1980s boosts international arrivals in safe destinations such as Australia (Faulkner, 1990)
Lock-in effect: where accidents of history have a lasting effect long after the conditions that influenced their initial impact have subsided or where innovations have a lasting effect despite being superseded by new technology.	• The Las Vegas example (i.e. in the sense that this destination has maintained and enhanced it position in spite of Nevada no longer being the only state in the US to have legalised gambling).
Edge of chaos (phase shift): a state of tenuous equilibrium whereby small changes ('mutations') involving individual agents may be enough to precipitate evolutionary change in the system through mutual adaptation of its constituents.	• Displacement of railway-based system of tourist services by car-based network. • Phase shifts in the life cycle of destinations.

Source: Faulkner & Russell, 1997

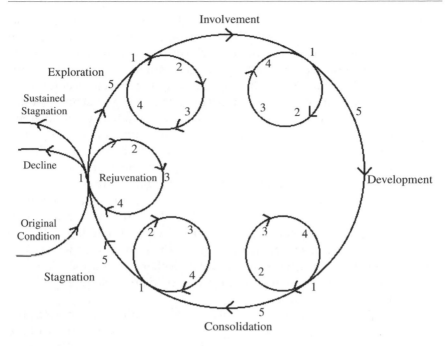

1. Triggering circumstances, disequilibrium
2. Deregulated chaos
3. Positive feedback, self-healing enablers
4. Transition to a new phase that reflects the old
5. Regulated chaos renewed tenuous conditional equilibrium

Figure 10.1 Synthesis: TALC and Chaos Theory

enough to bring about a phase shift to a degree that is as unpredictable as the stimulus. This may occur at any of the TALC stages but could be expected to be most pronounced in the stagnation stage when the system is run-down, tottering on the edge of chaos, or in the early stages when things are in a stage of fast growth, and instability and uncertainty are characteristics of the environment. Triggers are more effective when regulations have not been formed and direction is not clear.

However, it needs to be noted that the butterfly analogy reflects Plog's (1973) concept of every enterprise carrying the seeds of its own demise. In the sand-on-the-table illustration, the sand always falls downward; only the extent of the slide is in question. There is an obvious element of pessimism that sits uncomfortably with the notions that optimistic but realistic vision is one of the ingredients of sound management in the tourist or any other arena.

Compounding the butterfly and the sand pile, the distant flutterings can initiate slides of varying dimensions. The fall of the existing outmoded state may clear the way for the rise of the new and better.

The living organism model confirms that although cells deteriorate and die, they are, at least in a healthy way, constantly replaced. Although the external whole is apparently at rest, inside it is a complex vitality of buzzing interaction. But chaotic? Apart from mutations, which may turn out to be rejuvenating for the species, and cancers, accidents or decrepitude, which would hasten decline, the living system operates within infinitely precise rules. Using again the football game analogy helps explain the chaos-regulation paradigm (dynamic Chaos). The ultimate objective is clear. The rules are clear as elaborated in an extensive document, as defined by the goal posts, the lines, the linesmen and monitored by the referee, precedent and if necessary by a disciplinary tribunal. Without question it is a regulated, disciplined activity but the on-field spontaneity – the ducking, dummying, manoeuvring – give appearance, at least to the uninitiated, of reflexive chaos. Certainly a not-so-remote butterfly in the form of an intercept can rapidly transform the game. One accidental chance (or a Joe Montana, editor's comment) can snatch victory out of defeat. Randomness can prevail as the deciding factor.

In revisiting some of the past applications of Butler's model from the Chaos and Complexity perspective, new light can be shed on some of the previously unexplained deviations highlighted in the cases. For example, in Harrison's (1995) case study of Swaziland he discusses the significance of the 'initial conditions' in the evolution of Swaziland. What he describes is a 'lock-in' effect that inhibited Swaziland's development of international tourism. 'Swaziland's evolution was initially conditioned by its status as a British colony and later constrained by close links, which still remain, with the Republic of South Africa' (Harrison, 1995: 136).

Harrison also mentions events which were of an unpredictable nature that caused disruption and turbulence to the tourism development process. Terrorist activity such as arson at two hotels in 1987, assassinations and kidnappings caused instability and decline in tourism numbers. Strict cholera inoculation requirements on all arrivals to Swaziland deterred tourists and demonstrated again how external, and seemingly unrelated incidents can significantly impact on tourism development.

Choy (1992), in applying the TALC to the Pacific Islands, also discusses the impact of external triggers and unique factors in the development of the destinations and how these are unaccounted for by the S-shaped curve. The Pacific Islands, like many mature destinations, are an agglomeration of destinations and cannot be successfully measured as one single entity. Each of these separate destinations have all been affected by either political turmoil, natural disasters or both that have been unpredictable and caused dramatic distortions to the S-shaped curve.

Argawal (1997), in her studies of British seaside resorts and the TALC has concluded that unpredictability and extreme variations in internal and external factors limit the use of the model in most destinations. Interestingly, Argawal noticed the significant impact of local entrepreneurs, a topic that is dealt with in her chapter in this volume. In Argawal's earlier article (1994: 206), the cyclical concept is highlighted when she is describing the 'critical juncture' at the point of stagnation or rejuvenation when the destination makes repeated efforts to stave off stagnation. Argawal notes that the process is more likely to be turbulent rather than a smooth transition as depicted in the TALC.

Even from these few examples, the concepts of Chaos and Complexity are evident and provide the necessary additional framework to account for the significant incidents that impact on a destination's development.

Conclusion

Chaos and Complexity theory over the last decade has continued to gain recognition as a valuable research framework in an ever-increasing range of disciplines – from physical sciences and medicine to social sciences. Indeed the principles of Chaos and Complexity have never been more apparent. The events of 11 September 2001 and the Bali bombings of 2002 have brought to the forefront, in the most shocking manner, the impact of unpredictable events and the subsequent ripple effect. As the world remains poised on the edge of chaos, the tourism industry is once again bracing itself for turbulence, self-adapting to the new conditions, seeking out areas in which it might gain and trying to reshape to fit the circumstances that evolve.

Like tourism generally, the development of tourism destinations is inherently complex because it is dependent on the most complex entity – human. It also impacts on and is impacted by the surrounding biological and ecological systems – also inherently complex. Both the study of humans and the study of ecological systems have benefited greatly by the development of Chaos and Complexity theories and hence the study of tourism will be enhanced too.

By blending the TALC with the principles of Chaos and Complexity, the understanding of the evolution of destinations is greater, more complete and accounts for some of the previously 'unaccountable' factors in the many applications of the TALC. While the TALC model as it stands provides a valuable foundation for understanding destination development at a certain level, the overlaying of the Chaos principles reveals the full richness and complexity of the evolutionary process and illuminates the elements that Newtonian science tries to hide.

Part 4

Renewing or Retiring with the TALC

R.W. BUTLER

One of the key features of the TALC model is the element of rejuvenation, and its inclusion builds upon the belief of this author that appropriate intervention can enable a destination to change its fate from inevitable decline. It is accepted that it may not be able to permanently avoid ultimate decline, but there are examples, of which Atlantic City (see Stansfield, other volume) is probably the most cited, of destinations that have renewed at least elements of their function as a tourist resort. It was never claimed that renewal, rejuvenation or revisioning could ever solve all of the problems which mature destinations were likely to face, but it was felt that those in charge of destinations should be able to identify strategies and actions which would allow the destination to maintain elements of its attractiveness and add new features in order to continue to attract tourists, recognising that the market segment(s) thus attracted may be different to the original or traditional market segment(s) on which the destination had first developed.

The three chapters in this section discuss ways in which destinations have responded and might respond to such a challenge. Cooper, who has written widely on the development process, reviews the parameters and elements involved in the 'rejuvenation' stage of the TALC. He draws on examples and policies from a number of settings and lays out the process necessary for appropriate rejuvenation. In doing this he reviews the more generic management literature and processes utilised to revitalise products. Cooper discusses potential strategies for destinations, relating these to reorganisation and reformation at different scales of operation and planning. He reviews these in the context of the competitiveness of the destination and its components and products. He concludes with a discussion of the elements needed for successful rejuvenation, and his chapter contains a considerable number of examples of issues and destinations that have attempted or are attempting to reverse their process of decline. Leadership and vision, and the appropriate tools and resources are noted as being of particular significance if a destination is to achieve a significant measure of success.

Agarwal's writings (1997 and 2002 in particular) on restructuring of destinations have been widely quoted, and she was one of the first researchers in tourism to draw extensively on the generic restructuring literature (for example, Bagguley *et al.*, 1990) and apply this to tourism destinations. In her chapter she reviews this literature and its relevance to destination renewal and rejuvenation at considerable length and provides an excellent theoretical base to the subsequent discussion of resorts. In the chapter she brings together the concept of deliberate change in order to achieve renewal from both the restructuring theories and from the TALC and notes how these relate to each other. Agarwal then discusses the strategies that have been used by those in charge of developing destinations to change the focus and appeal of the resorts in order to benefit from changes in market forces and tastes. On the basis of her study of destinations that have attempted renewal and rejuvenation, she argues for the inclusion of an additional stage in the TALC, a 'reorientation stage', which would be positioned between the stagnation and poststagnation stages of the original model. This is a stage that, Agarwal argues, can be repeated more than once in a destination and reflects a stage before rejection of traditional approaches.

If rejuvenation is not attempted and decline appears and continues, then the future of a destination in terms of its attractiveness to tourists may be bleak, and as Baum argues, it may well be more appropriate to exit tourism than to attempt to stay in an unsatisfactory situation. He argues that the origins and nature of tourism at many destinations means that almost inevitably such destinations fail to see beyond tourism and to recognise other opportunities and the possible ending of tourism as a viable industry for that location. Baum argues that reinvention of the location is often necessary, and discusses the critical importance of the identification and application of a strategy for exiting tourism where this is the most appropriate step to be taken. He uses the example of Lloret de Mar to illustrate how a specific destination has moved towards such a strategy and the process undertaken.

Depressing though it may be to consider that some traditional destinations may have to exit tourism, it is almost inevitable. Few products retain their attractiveness and market appeal indefinitely, and those which recognise this and prepare for an exit under their own control and in the direction of their own choice are more likely to emerge successfully from tourism than those who let exogenous forces make the decisions for them. There was no 'flat-line' in the original TALC model to reflect abandonment of tourism, only a continuing decline to, presumably, zero visitation or development. Baum's argument would support further modification of the original model to reflect what may be an alternative 'life-after-death' divorced from tourism.

Chapter 11

The Anatomy of the Rejuvenation Stage of the TALC

C. COOPER

Introduction

As the tourism market matures, many tourism destinations world-wide are facing the challenge of revitalising their product and repositioning themselves in the marketplace. The recognition of the need to constantly review and adjust the destination formula began in the mid-1980s and accelerated in the 1990s with a range of destinations committing both politically and financially to the need to manage change. It is these destinations that are often cited, with hindsight, as having gone through each stage of the Tourism Area Life Cycle (TALC). This is partly due to the fact that tourism markets have reached maturity, with many mass tourism resorts developed in the late 1960s and 1970s reaching stagnation in the 1980s and seeking strategies for rejuvenation. It is these latter stages of the cycle – decline and rejuvenation – that have begun to receive attention in the literature as governments and the tourism sector have strived to adjust to changing market demand. Such is the level of public sector concern that many resorts are now seeing a surge of investment and strategic thinking to combat the problem. The issues faced by destinations in the latter stages of the cycle are therefore both real and pressing. In Butler's original (1980: 5) paper, he recognised that the final stages of the lifecycle involved:

> the possible replacement of physical plant and facilities, and the change (or even disappearance) of the original natural and cultural attractions which were responsible for the initial popularity of the area. In some cases while these attractions remain, they may be utilized for different purposes ...

He continued:

> ... rejuvenation may occur, although it is almost certain that this stage will never be reached without a complete change in the attractions on which tourism is based ... In many cases, combined government and private efforts are necessary and the new market may not be the allocentric section of the population ... but rather a specific interest or activity group. (p. 9)

183

Destinations in need of rejuvenation have reached the decline stage of the life cycle, a stage characterised by declining visitor numbers, low yield, domestic and repeat visitors. The decline stage is brought about by the interplay of forces outside the destination's control, and a range of issues related to the destination's built fabric. For example, on the demand side, changing tastes and expectations of the tourism market-place lead to the growth of competing destinations that can service demand more effectively. Yet, for the declining destination, responding to changes in the marketplace is problematic. Destinations normally are comprised of fixed plant, capital investment in tourism infrastructure and superstructure that is difficult to change. Indeed, reduced visitation to many destinations places their environmental quality, including unique architectural and townscape resources, in jeopardy (Cooper, 1997a; Malcolm-Davies & Russo, other volume).

Some destinations effectively exit tourism at this stage and become dormitory towns or a centre for services (Baum, this volume), although often destinations are located in regions where economic alternatives are scarce, hence the need for rejuvenation that is often public sector-led. It is this fundamental choice that faces failing destinations – effectively, the deterministic nature of the life cycle dictates that, if corrective action is not taken, then the resort will continue to spiral into decline.

This deterministic element of the TALC has sparked debates about its usefulness as a framework for understanding the development of tourism destinations. Some argue that the utility of the TALC lies in helping us to understand the process and constraints upon decline and rejuvenation (Cooper & Jackson, 1989). In a sense though, the tourism literature has followed on from the business literature on the Product Life Cycle (PLC). The PLC concept was greeted with enthusiasm on its introduction in the 1950s and 1960s as an early element of managerial research. It continued strongly in the 1970s and early 1980s, characterised by an enthusiastic statement by Hofer (1975: 798): '...the most funda-mental variable in determining an appropriate business strategy is the stage of the product life cycle.'

However, despite the fact that the cycle is one of the best known concepts in business, touching upon almost every variable from the mid-1980s onwards, the literature peters out as many authors recognised the limited value and application of the concept (Coles, this volume; Crawford, 1984; Gardner, 1987). The disillusion is expressed by Gardner (1987: 183) who suggests that the PLC looks 'for rather simplistic and uni-dimensional answers when in fact marketing phenomena are complex, multi-dimensional and non-deterministic'.

Ten years later, in the tourism literature, these criticisms of the cycle were echoed by Bianchi (1994) and Ioannides (1992) who called for a more integrated system for the understanding of resort dynamics, particularly taking into account the context of development and the network of institutions, agents and entrepreneurs who shape the development of a destination. Other authors have criticised the cycle for failing to provide an explanatory framework. Haywood (1986, this volume, other volume), for example, sees the cycle as difficult to operationalise in terms of identifying stages, turning points, difficulties in the level of aggregation to adopt and the fact that the cycle is only really effective with hindsight. Whilst this debate continues in the tourism literature (see Agarwal, 1999; Oppermann, 1999), in business it seems to have been played out.

One solution to this impasse was provided by Crawford (1984) who noted that in the biological sciences the life cycle is only applied to individual species – the equivalent here of companies or enterprises in destinations (see also Ravenscroft & Hadjihambi, this volume). For groups of species – the equivalent of destinations – they use the evolutionary life cycle. Crawford (1984: 6) feels that this evolutionary cycle is more appropriate for business settings as it is:

- cumulative: each change builds upon previous ones;
- directional: each change moves towards greater complexity, efficiency and diversity;
- motivated: each change is motivated by genes, the environment and mediated factors; and
- patterned: change increases the divergence of new species, increases the numbers of species, increases variation, experiences long periods of stabilisation and demise occurs through the loss of species.

The evolutionary approach recognises that for new products, the rejuvenation stage should be seen as part of the evolutionary process of continuous adoption, and not as a one-off new development (Tellis & Crawford, 1981; Gardner, 1987). As such the new product literature is not as closely linked to the life cycle literature as might be expected, a view supported by Johnston (2001), who states that rejuvenation changes the destination to a fundamentally new and different place. Choy (1995), on the other hand, sees them as linked in his classification of strategic responses to decline:

- Life cycle extension
  - expand and or modernise existing facilities to increase the market; and
  - reposition the destination to attract new markets.
- New product development
  - Supply new and different attractions to modify the appeal of the destination to new markets.

Evolutionary thinking requires an understanding of the basic causal factors at work (Crawford, 1984: 10), and it is here, it can be argued, that the life cycle provides a useful explanatory framework (Cooper & Jackson, 1989). Rejuvenation is influenced by the same forces that drive a resort though the earlier stages of the cycle – namely market, technological and competitive forces (Di Benedetto & Bojanic, 1993).

The Rejuvenation Stage

Once a destination is in decline, it is common to have a public sector-led planning process to decide the future direction of the destination. Such destination planning initiatives tend to be in the domain of the public sector, where traditional approaches and short-term budgeting and political agendas have held back the strategic view that is needed for effective rejuvenation. A further problem is the composition of destinations, with the private sector dominantly comprised of small businesses, who have traditionally held a short-term, tactical view of tourism and rejected all-embracing attempts to draw together the industry at a particular location. Yet, evidence later in this chapter shows that the holistic approach is one of the keys to successful rejuvenation. Equally, in the past when a destination has been in the growth stages of the life cycle, success has obscured the longer-term view, whilst a declining destination may have difficulty in justifying the overhead of an expensive planning exercise. These problems are compounded by the difficulties of implementing strategic planning in communities. In companies, hierarchies and reporting lines are clear; in destinations the political battleground of varied stakeholders may hinder the process. However, the benefits of a strategic planning approach to rejuvenating destinations are clear: a plan provides a sense of ownership for both the industry and the public sector and in so doing gives a framework for cooperative action and policies at the level of the destination. This coherence of approach sharpens the guiding objectives of the destination and forces myriad stakeholders to determine their role. In addition, the approach delivers a range of key performance indicators against which the sector can be judged in the future.

In such planning exercises for destinations in the decline stage, two basic options for the future are available– abandonment and life cycle extension through rejuvenation.

Abandonment

The first option for a failing destination is to consciously exit tourism. Baum (1998, this volume) terms this as 'abandonment', but stresses that emotionally this is a difficult decision for destinations, particularly given the domination of small businesses – such as guesthouses, restaurants.

Such a strategy demands that stakeholders no longer see the destination as in the tourism business and facilities and resources are allocated to new uses.

Other reasons for abandonment can be:

- natural disasters (such as the volcanic eruptions on Montserrat);
- terrorism;
- war (examples here include the demise of the resorts of northern Cyprus following the invasion by Turkey) (Weaver, 2000); or
- the creeping urbanisation of neighbouring larger settlements as has happened at Ayr, Southport and Margate in the UK, where resorts become residential suburbs for neighbouring cities.

Life cycle extension

The second option, taken by many destinations, is a conscious decision to rejuvenate and thus extend their tourism life cycle. As Russell and Faulkner (1998a) say, 'Getting Cinderella out of the Kitchen' is the key to rejuvenating a destination through developing a new strategy or vision. Here, the tourism literature has focussed upon strategic options, initiatives and the restructuring of tourism (Agarwal, 2002, this volume). Strategic responses can vary from purely public sector initiatives, to the more popular public/private partnership, to the purely private initiatives. In all of these cases, the decision to rejuvenate represents a significant shift in thinking towards the strategic and the long term. Whilst there is a range of individual options including environmental improvements, addition of new attractions and diversifying/repositioning in the market place, increasingly destinations recognise the need for a holistic response that embraces all elements of tourism and the broader economy. Destinations function through complex environmental, economic and social systems and it is impossible to disentangle these systems when rejuvenating. At the same time, strategic responses for resorts are destination specific, determined by the resort's product mix, location and its place in the wider regional economy.

In classifying the available strategic responses, the strategic management literature is useful. For example, Jain (1985) sees the choice of strategic options as complex and determined by two key factors that can be applied to tourism (Cooper, 1995):

(1) The destination's competitive position in the market place; and
(2) the life cycle characteristics of the destination. These will include:
   - demand-side variables
      i. consumers – the changing nature of clientele and markets
   - supply-side variables
      i. industry structure

      ii. competitors
     iii. suppliers
     iv. environment
      v. organisation
     vi. rate of development
    vii. access

In tourism, a number of authors have classified responses to life cycle extension. For example, Diamond (1988) suggests four possible strategies:

(1) A turnaround strategy. This represents a concerted public and private sector effort to reverse falling visitor numbers by investment in development and substantial planning and promotional efforts (Stansfield, other volume).
(2) A sustainable growth strategy. Here the destination's external conditions are unfavourable, perhaps in terms of access, and the strategy concentrates on maintaining existing markets and achieving a low level of growth by new recruitment of visitors to supplement a loyal repeat clientele (Hovinen, other volume).
(3) An incremental growth strategy. This strategy adopts a phased approach to resort development with limited use by test marketing of new products and phased development projects as the destination seeks new markets. This is similar to Baum's (1998) reinvention stage where he sees the rejection of the original formula that attracted tourists and the creation of new models by gradually letting one product 'die' and replacing it with another alongside existing products – in effect the destination may have various elements of the destination mix at various stages of maturity, decline or rejuvenation (Hovinen, 2002; Johnston, 2001; Lundgren, other volume).
(4) A selective tourism strategy. Here only certain market segments are targeted to capitalise on the destination's strengths (Martin, other volume).

Tourism Rejuvenation Strategies

As increasing numbers of destinations have adopted rejuvenation strategies, it is possible to identify common elements across these strategies, and to identify examples of their use. From her studies of UK resorts, Agarwal (2002) provides a useful framework with which to classify these elements:

(1) Product reorganisation – investment and technical change, centralisation and product specialisation.

(2) Product transformation – service quality enhancement, environmental quality enhancement, repositioning, diversification, collaboration and adaptation.

Product reorganisation

Investment and technical change

An early example of a resort targeting investment in new facilities to attract new market segments is Atlantic City, where casinos were introduced (Del Viscio, no date; Stansfield, 1978, other volume; The Atlantic City Convention and Visitors Authority, no date). Another example of casino development is Scheveningen, the Netherlands (van de Weg, 1982). A second approach adopted in early rejuvenation strategies has been the development of convention centres as at Brighton and Bridlington in the UK, and Boston and Waikiki in the USA. Later investment strategies include the introduction of new attractions to update tired resorts. Examples here include aquaria at Rhyll, Wales and both Atlantic City and Long Beach, USA (Harmon, 1999), a ten-pin-bowling complex at Torbay (Agarwal, 1997) and major investment in theme parks as at Acapulco in Mexico with a refurbished water park, Port Aventura adjacent to Salou, Spain and Benidorm's addition of a water park in Spain (Curtis, 1997; Priestley & Mundet, 1998).

Centralisation

As economic and tourism policy makers begin to recognise the significance of the decline and rejuvenation stages of destinations, regional, national and international initiatives have emerged to coordinate investment and to create learning organisations and consortia to build on the experience of destinations undergoing rejuvenation.

Regional level

At the regional level, COAST is a marketing grouping of southern English resorts cooperating in marketing and rejuvenation initiatives (COAST, 1993).

National level

At the national level, the British Government has initiated a comprehensive review of resort revitalisation, following on from pioneering earlier initiatives in the 1980s. The review forms a key part of the government's tourism plan, and the focus of European funding for resort revitalisation (DCMS, 2000a). Regeneration of traditional resorts was one of the key 15 action points set out in the UK government's policy paper – *Tomorrow's Tourism*, recognising that UK seaside resorts are facing challenges both from new attractions within the UK and overseas tourist destinations. The report addresses the ways in which tourism can make a difference to the economy, society and the environment and encompasses action by the British government (DCMS, 2000b). Many tourism-dependent areas such as seaside resorts are eligible for the European Structural Funds, particularly through the Single Regeneration Budget.

In Wales, the Wales Tourist Board has coordinated financial assistance towards six coastal resorts to achieve a comprehensive scheme of tourism regeneration. Since the implementation of the program a total of £80 million has been generated in investment in the coastal resorts, creating the equivalent of 487 full-time jobs (Wales Tourist Board, 2000).

In Ireland (Irish Tourist Board, 2001), the government introduced a coordinated investment scheme to encourage and facilitate the redevelopment of many of Ireland's traditional seaside resorts including:

- a range of tax incentives for investment in qualifying tourist facilities in designated traditional resort areas;
- capital works budget allocation to address infrastructure deficiencies around the coast that will promote socioeconomic wellbeing in peripheral coastal regions; and
- additional funding to upgrade harbour infrastructures and allow for the exploitation of important marine tourism and leisure opportunities.

In Spain, the government has devised a national strategy to readdress its whole outlook towards tourism and reinvent itself in order to survive (Fayos Sola, 1992). Funds were made available at a national level for local renewal initiatives empowering local authorities to address all aspects of their resorts including the beach, accommodation and infrastructure (Green Globe News, 2000).

International level

At the international level there are two notable initiatives:

(1) The European Union has funded ECoNETT – a demonstration project to provide resort areas with a methodology for managing revitalisation in a practical, cost-effective, comprehensive and coordinated way. Countries involved are the UK, Ireland, Spain and France. The project provides planning templates for reports in seven key stages:
   a. creating a Vision
   b. political ownership and commitment
   c. data collection
   d. ideas generation and data interpretation
   e. issues identification
   f. policy formulation
   g. action
   h. monitoring

(2) The World Tourism Organization's (WTO) initiative in this area sees destinations focussing on 10 key areas in the rejuvenation process, with a strong sustainable management focus (WTO, 2001). The WTO's project is designed to facilitate information exchange on the management of mass tourism destinations and to build a cooperative learning network of resorts. The ten key areas are:

   a. *Integral sustainable management strategies*. Creation and implementation of sustainable development strategies in tourism destinations (Agenda 21 type strategies), integral tourism destination planning (physical planning, resources, products, seasonality, feasibility, etc.) and initiatives geared to integrating tourism in the economy, culture, territory and landscape.

   b. *Management of the local cultural and natural heritage*. Initiatives for using, evaluating and conserving the most valuable natural and humanised areas of the destination, as well as the tangible and intangible cultural heritage, for tourism purposes.

   c. *Coastal strip management*. Initiatives geared to preserving the natural quality of beaches, coastlines and seas, activity planning (sports fishing, scuba-diving, sailing, etc.) and infrastructure planning (marinas, etc.) as per the carrying capacity of each subsystem.

   d. *Access and management of tourist movements*. Sustainable management, adapted to carrying capacity, of tourist flows and tourism infrastructures, and steps to promote collective transport and alternative means of getting from one place to another.

   e. *Integral quality of tourism centres*. Measures geared to creating attractive urban frameworks, the sustainable management of natural resources (land, water, energy, materials), sustainable waste management, and the benefits to be derived from creating a healthy and safe environment.

   f. *Integral quality of tourism products and services*. Initiatives geared to guaranteeing quality and the sustainable management of tourism accommodation and commercial services (including refurbishment and rehabilitation), congress centres, golf courses, marinas, theme parks, etc.

   g. *Information, awareness raising and social participation*. Initiatives geared to facilitating the dissemination of information, raising the awareness of visitors and local populations, and increasing the involvement of businesses, entrepreneurs and representative social organisations in the sustainable and quality tourism management of the destination.

   h. *Human resource training and incentives to boost local enterprise*. Experiences relative to basic vocational training and local human resource training, measures to boost entrepreneurship and local tourism or diversification initiatives.

i. *Tools for promoting quality.* Innovation and sustainable tourism management: use of the systems that have emerged in the field of sustainable management in tourism destinations: local statistics and information, certification systems and product and service quality clubs, financing and fiscal instruments, entities and enterprises that specialise in boosting tourism development, new technologies, means and systems of social communication.

j. *Tools for evaluating and monitoring the quality and sustainability of tourism and local development*. Use of indicators for evaluating scenarios and programmes, the creation of observatories for monitoring the quality and sustainability of tourism development and local development

Product specialisation

Jain (1985) identifies one strategic response as the development of niche products. For tourism this includes the development of health care and beauty facilities and the development of events and festivals. This has been evident in Sitges, Spain, where events have been developed alongside the existing sun, sea and sand product (Priestley & Mundet, 1998). A similar approach has been used in Waikiki, USA with spa and duty-free retail developments (Centre for Policy Studies, 1998), whilst the development of 'wellness' products is being used to supplement health prevention approaches in the spa resorts of central Europe (Cooper *et al.*, 1996).

Product transformation

Service product quality enhancement

A key area of rejuvenation strategies that has been developed in more recent initiatives is the enhancement of service quality in destinations, particularly through the medium of training. For example, in County Mayo, Ireland, the approach has been to provide a package of financial incentives for accommodation, product improvement and training (anon, no date). Training is also being provided to encourage a more coordinated and professional approach to the tourism industry in Bali. Bali has focused on quality issues, particularly in terms of service, environment, health and safety (Bagus Oka, 1992). A major training initiative has been developed in Hawaii by the Native Hawaiian Hospitality Institute. Their 'Revitalization and Re-enhancement of Waikiki' report includes training initiatives for the revitalisation and re-enhancement of Waikiki, through guiding and information services. This will be achieved through the training of visitor information guides focussing on the history of Waikiki and the Hawaiian tradition of *ho'okipa*. Once trained, these guides will serve the public at visitor information centres established by the City and County of Honolulu (Native Hawaiian Hospitality Association, 2000).

Environmental quality enhancement

Almost all rejuvenation strategies contain an element of environmental enhancement from the 'greening' of resorts, to the redevelopment of resort townscapes and recreational business districts. The following exemplify the huge scale of investment that is now occurring to revitalise destinations around the world.

Spain In Torremolinos, a physical town plan has coordinated environmental improvements – the Pilot Plan for the Recuperation of Tourist Areas – focussing on environmental redesign, beautification and preservation (Pollard & Rodriguez, 1993). In both Salou and Benidorm, environmental and quality improvement has been undertaken (Curtis, 1997). In addition, in many plans increasing priority is given to environmental upgrading – in Majorca for example, one of Europe's major tourist destinations, 30% of the island's area has been set aside as a natural preservation area.

USA In Hawaii, both Honolulu and Waikiki have focussed on physical master plans. In Waikiki this includes detailed improvements such as pedestrian areas, landscaping and green spaces, as well as traffic planning and management (Patoskie, 1992). A number of other changes to Waikiki's streets and open areas are either government funded or partnerships between business and government (Apo, 2000; Foster, 2000; Waikiki Improvement Association, 1999). The city and county of Honolulu's 'Goals for a Livable City' project includes a series of improvements to make the central resort area a landscaped pedestrian recreation experience. Some of the improvements include spot ponds, landscaped pathways, increased park areas and public entertainment venues that have improved recreation space (The City and County of Honolulu, no date).

In Atlantic City, developers are enhancing the town's look and facilities, including new housing, better roads and a number of municipal beautification projects, whilst major casino renovations and additions of hotel rooms are occurring. Transportation facilities have also been improved, including a new bus terminal and airport expansion (Del Viscio, no date; US Department of Housing and Urban Development, 1995).

In Long Beach, California, the Queensway Bay Project involves the redevelopment of 300 acres of oceanfront land including a 2000-foot esplanade, a new aquarium, and a large entertainment and retail area (Harmon, 1999).

Mexico In Acapulco, the Acapulco Beautification Program implemented in 1992 has led to an increase in investment and allowed for diverse infrastructure that appeals to a range of visitors.

Australia In Cairns, the City Council, supported by the State of Queensland and the private sector, has committed funding to three major environmental improvement projects – foreshore improvements and developments; city port development; and central business district streetscaping.

Repositioning

Every rejuvenation strategy contains an element of repositioning. For example, the repositioning of northern European coldwater resorts, such as Torbay and Weston Super-Mare (Agarwal, 1999; Cooper, 1997b) and Mediterranean resorts – Benidorm, Magaluf and Palma Nova (Curtis, 1997) has been away from mass-market low-spend tourists and toward high-spend special interest visitors. The same is the case for the Gold Coast and Coolangatta, Australia (Russell & Faulkner, 1998a) where the destination is repositioning to attract international as well as domestic visitors and moving the resort upmarket. One of the most comprehensive studies of this repositioning approach has been the Gold Coast Revisioning Project, where significant funding has been provided to research the key dimensions of both tourism demand and supply, before visioning the future of the destination through a series of 'revisioning' workshops involving all stakeholders (Faulkner, 2003; Faulkner & Tideswell, other volume).

Similarly, the Spanish Balearic islands have looked at a comprehensive repositioning strategy including environmental improvements (funded in part by a somewhat controversial 'Ecotax' payable by visitors using officially registered accommodation, editor's comment), improvement of the product, community engagement and major marketing initiatives to reposition the islands (Salva Tomas, 2000). The rejuvenation of large resorts such as Benidorm, Salou, Torremolinos and Lloret de mar has been achieved largely through a committed programme of resort renewal with both public and private finances and initiatives designed to preserve the best aspects of the resort while gradually introducing significant quality improvements.

In Hawaii, repositioning has emphasised the preservation of the distinctiveness that draws people to Hawaii and Waikiki. The investment in and the repositioning of Waikiki's tourism product have aimed to attract the corporate traveller, primarily drawn to Waikiki by the convention centre.

Diversification

Agarwal (2002) identifies the development of previously untapped natural cultural and built resources to attract new markets such as business and conference tourism and domestic short breaks. Examples include Bournemouth and Brighton, UK; Benidorm's drive to attract the growing Spanish domestic market and Palma Nova's development of niche markets such as walking, cycling, golfing and yachting (Curtis, 1997). In Ireland, funding is provided to enhance general tourism marketing efforts and to extend niche product and special interest marketing (Irish Tourist Board, 2001).

Collaboration

A key element of rejuvenation strategies is collaboration across all destination stakeholders. For example, the improvement of Waikiki has required collaboration and cooperation from the state and city and county governments, private sector, and nonprofit organisations (Centre for Policy Studies, 1998). In Thailand, at Pattaya Beach, the government is spending 30% of the city's budget on tourism-related projects, which include infrastructure improvements that also benefit residents. In the resort, industry representatives and experts are meeting with local government officials to develop a consensus on how to manage the resort's redevelopment (Goad & Crispin, 1999).

Adaptation

Rejuvenation strategies require market information and forecasts that are difficult to generate and access. For example, Priestley and Mundet (1998) note the undertaking of market studies with the aim of forecasting future trends and facilitating adaptation to changing markets for the resorts of l'Estartit, Sitges and Lloret de Mar in Spain. In Blackpool, UK there has been an urgent need to understand changing market trends as holiday tastes have changed and domestic competition has grown. As part of the adaptation to these new markets, the resort recognises that it is hindered by old infrastructure, seasonal business and the fact that the town's traditional attractions have not invested sufficiently to meet today's demand for high-quality services. A regeneration strategy has acknowledged that the resort has to improve its facilities and infrastructure if it is to survive.

Elements of Successful Rejuvenation

A body of knowledge is now emerging from the experience of the destinations mentioned above, and other destinations, in terms of the key elements of successful destination rejuvenation. Clearly each destination has its own particular set of issues, partly as a result of the centralised approaches mentioned above. There is of course a danger that a 'recipe' approach to rejuvenation leads to the standardisation of products, environments and landscapes that in turn will fail to attract visitors (Urry, 1990).

An early attempt to analyse success factors in rejuvenation emerged from the British experience of the mid-1980s. In a belated effort to reverse the declining fortunes of resorts in the UK, the first significant initiative in rethinking the direction of resorts was taken by the English Tourist Board in 1985 (Cooper, 1990). This was in response to declining domestic markets, a tired and outdated product and heightened competition from other destinations. The Board introduced a competition for resorts to come up with the best rejuvenation strategy. The competition distilled the success factors of such strategies in the judging criteria as:

- level of local authority commitment;
- level of political support;
- the extent of 'corporate' thinking and involvement;
- evidence of partnerships with other public agencies, voluntary bodies and commercial interests;
- attitude and commitment of the local tourism industry;
- potential and ability to capitalise on strengths and opportunities;
- the need for tourist board involvement;
- professional public sector leadership; and
- coordinated promotional and product development strategy.

This supports Agarwal's (1997) statement that restructuring of resorts is conditioned by factors such as the degree of cooperation across the local authority, the size of the resort and the importance of tourism to the economy. Following on from this early attempt to distil success factors, the following three key success factors can be identified from both the plans and strategies examined above and the tourism literature.

Vision, planning and leadership

Vision, planning and leadership are critical – particularly in the early stages of rejuvenation. A local champion for the process is the single most important success factor identified in the literature, as it is the champion who drives the process of creating a vision. A strong political will to succeed is also critical (Russell & Faulkner, 1998b). This involves managing the political process of regeneration by engaging with the resort community, involving constituencies who often have no tourism interest – such as those in rural resort hinterlands (Hovinen, other volume), and managing the conflicting interest groups in the resort (Cooper, 1995). Leadership is also required from the public sector in terms of adopting professional approaches to planning and management (Agarwal, 2002). However, acceptance and take up of such programmes is patchy due to the fragmented and small business nature of tourism in destinations.

Taking a holistic approach

A number of writers support the imperative of taking a holistic view. For example, Farrell (1992: 123) defines sustainability as 'essentially an exercise in the optimisation and finer tuning of all elements and sub elements of the development system so that in its operation the system as a whole maintains direction and one or more of the elements does not surge or is not enhanced to the detriment and impairment of others'. In other words, the destination formula is constantly reviewed and adjusted with differing strategies appropriate to particular stages of the TALC. At the rejuvenation stage it is vital to have strategies that take a broader approach than simply focusing on tourism. In one sense it is here that the TALC fails to adequately explain the rejuvenation phase, with Agarwal (2002) suggesting that other theoretical approaches, such as restructuring, provide a more all-embracing explanatory framework. A planned relationship between tourism and the rest of the economy and social fabric of the destination is essential.

A further success factor here is the need to holistically integrate physical product development (convention centres, new attractions, environmental upgrading) with the promotion of the destination. As noted above, there is increasing attention being given to the quality of the built environment through the planning process of landscaping, streetscape, heritage considerations with design briefs, integration of green spaces in resort business districts etc. Yet it is essential that this 'product' element is carried through in the promotion and positioning of the destination.

The holistic approach also applies to integrating tourism and residential development. Sheldon and Abenoja (2001) for example, in their analysis of residential attitudes in the mature destination of Waikiki, found that preferences are for improvements that will be of benefit to the residential community as well as to the rejuvenated tourism markets. Whilst the need for physical improvement of the built fabric of many destinations is clear, the English Tourist Board (1991) observes that resort planning strategies often treat tourism as a sector separate from the rest of the town's economy. This has resulted in the lack of a planned relationship between tourism and other forms of development (Cooper, 1997a; Davies, 1992; Smith, 1991; Turner, 1993). For example, low-quality day-visitor amusement arcades and low-cost fast-food traders attracting and catering for a heavily seasonal low-spending market often characterise key visitor locations. Such facilities have little relevance to residents and create both visual blight and resentment. They also serve to convey a particular image of resorts that detracts from their potential appeal to other market segments, thus inhibiting and reducing the effectiveness of marketing expenditure on repositioning. At the same time it may reduce commercial interest in both tourism investment and other, nontourism uses (English Tourist Board, 1991).

The English Tourist Board (1991) identifies the concept of core visitor areas in an attempt to address this problem. Core visitor areas provide the sense of place for visitors lacking in many resorts. In effect it is recognition of the need to provide differently landscaped and developed areas where the focus is on visitor use of, say, speciality retailing, food and beverage, entertainment and interpretation. These areas will need to be sustained year-round and will reflect the needs of both visitors and residents. Recognition that visitor use is unlikely to sustain development on a year-round basis demands that mixed use of leisure and other activities is more viable and therefore developments must attract both residents and visitors. In other words they provide for an integrated provision for visitors and residents alike. In these areas, increasing attention is being given to security issues to manage issues such as visitor safety and alcohol abuse, through the use of tourist police and CCTV installation.

Securing the tools to succeed: Budgets and marketing

Budgets

Accessing regional, national and international funding to augment local sources has become a critical element of destination rejuvenation. This is particularly the case in Europe where European monies are available through the structural funds for regional development. A further key element is the development of public/private sector steering committees to ensure that various groups buy into the process, and the formation of partnerships for marketing, development and investment. Destinations can access public sector funds for rejuvenation from four key sources:

(1) *International funds* accessed from the European Union (EU) Structural Funds and applied to coastal and resort regeneration. The European Union's COAST fund in particular is utilised for infrastructure and environmental upgrades (COAST, 1993). In both the UK and Ireland, EU finding has been accessed for regeneration.

(2) *National funds* for coastal and resort regeneration exist in many countries. European countries, in particular, have been putting resort regeneration initiatives in place at a national level. In the UK considerable funding has been set aside for regeneration for coastal resorts under the 'Tomorrow's Tourism' imitative (DCMS, 2000b). Also in the UK, lottery funding has been an important source of funding since the mid-1990s. These initiatives may also include tax incentives for investment, environmental improvements and product upgrading (as in Ireland – see Irish Tourist Board, 2001). In

Wales, the funding is disbursed by the Wales Tourist Board from central government to resorts (Wales Tourist Board, 2000). In Spain a major government initiative to reintroduce a competitive Spanish tourism product delivered considerable funding, particularly for marketing, to the provinces and resorts (Fayos Sola, 1992).

(3) *State level funding* is less common, though this depends upon the political organisation of the country. In Spain, for example, devolution has placed considerable autonomy in each of the Spanish provinces – Catalonia, Valencia and Majorca (Calvia) for example. They are dominantly sourcing state level funds and applying them to individual resorts in the state. Large resorts – Benidorm, Salou, Lloret de Mar, Magaluf and Palma Nova – have benefited considerably from an injection of funds at this level. At both state and local level the capability of raising regeneration funding is dependent upon the local taxation base. In Atlantic City, USA, for example, this is considerable due to the gambling revenues in the resort (Stansfield, other volume).

(4) *Local authority funding* initiatives are found across the world, often with private sector partnerships (particularly in US resorts). The local level tends to be active in sourcing funds and driving initiatives, although in some countries, such as the UK, this was not done until the national government raised concerns about the economic, social and environmental state of resorts.

Marketing

The marketing element of destination rejuvenation strategies commonly targets new markets (such as conferences), whilst also protecting existing markets, even though such markets may be in decline. Target market selection is critical here and drives the decisions about promotion and distribution of the destination as well as the question of developing the right facilities to attract and cater for the selected target markets. This involves a disciplined process of goal setting, annual and multiannual plans and relevant budgets. Key success factors here are the need for cooperative marketing across destinations in the recognition that they are not competing with each other, but with other types of destination both domestic and international (Travis, 1992). However, as the English Tourist Board (1991) state, a consistent underinvestment in marketing at the decline stage debilitates attempts to derive such strategies (Malcolm-Davies, other volume). They call for increased expenditure on marketing initiatives, which to be cost-effective must be based on the development of better marketing data. Destinations must clearly identify for whom visitor facilities will be developed and marketed. This requires a market-led understanding of current and potential markets and the identification of target groups. However, there is a serious lack of data on tourism demand and supply at the destination level. This holds back attempts by destinations to effectively reposition their products and for securing the support of prospective commercial developers.

Conclusion

The rejuvenation stage of the TALC is receiving considerable attention from both academics and policy makers. With the realisation that mass tourism destinations around the world are often in need of revitalisation, this issue has attracted considerable funding and investment, and as this chapter has shown, there are a number of attempts to coordinate and learn from the experiences of destinations undergoing rejuvenation. The TALC provides a useful framework within which to locate these ideas, but the tourism literature appears to be following that of business management with the PLC in recognising that diminishing returns set in with yet more and more case studies attempting to reverse-engineer visitor numbers into the cycle. This chapter has shown that, whilst many of the destinations examined have gone through the life cycle, it is more important to understand the causes of change in destinations, the triggers that initiate rejuvenation, and to understand the political and developmental processes at work. If tourism research can begin to move in this direction, create true 'learning partnerships' of destinations, and draw together the underlying success factors of rejuvenation, then we can build on the explanatory framework of the TALC and yet avoid going down intellectual *cul de sac* of the PLC.

Acknowledgements

I am grateful to Lisa Ruhanen for her background work on this chapter.

Chapter 12

Coastal Resort Restructuring and the TALC

SHEELA AGARWAL

Introduction

Tourism restructuring in coastal resorts has attracted increased research and policy attention (Shaw & Williams, 1997). Much of the academic attention this issue receives occurs in relation to the TALC model which proposes that decline and restructuring are associated with two of the model's advanced stages of resort development, these being stagnation and poststagnation (Agarwal, 2002; di Benedetto & Bojanic, 1993; Getz, 1992; Priestley & Mundet, 1998). Decline may occur during either of these stages; on the one hand, it may signify the onset of stagnation and on the other hand, decline may continue into poststagnation as attempts to compete with newer destinations and regain market share are unsuccessful. Restructuring meanwhile is associated with the model's poststagnation phase and may result in varying degrees of life-cycle extension. The TALC model provides a useful analytical framework for understanding coastal resort decline and restructuring and, in particular, it highlights the dynamism of resort evolution and the different development scenarios that may be experienced once it has reached the stagnation phase.

However, there are limitations when viewing resort restructuring within the context of the TALC model alone, as it emphasises structure over agency (Milne, 1998), and fails to consider adequately the potential interdependencies between the external forces of change that are driving resort evolution and human interaction. According to Gordon and Goodall (2000: 301), developing an understanding of decline and restructuring 'is a precondition for thinking about how such a system may be managed in the interests of its long-term sustainability'. This may be achieved by the application of other bodies of theory, such as the restructuring thesis, as this not only provides insights into decline and alternative restructuring strategies but highlights the importance of contingent factors which may influence resort trajectories.

This chapter draws on the restructuring thesis and discusses the theoretical insights and relationships that exist between this construct and the TALC model within the context of mass tourism coastal resorts.

Particular emphasis is placed on resorts that are in the later stages of the life cycle and which appear to have reached the postmature stage of development. The chapter begins with a brief account of the restructuring thesis and its relevance to resort development generally and to the TALC model specifically. The theoretical insights and relationships between the two constructs are then documented, drawing on examples from Northern and Southern European postmature mass tourism coastal resorts, and some planning and management implications of these theoretical insights and relationships are highlighted.

The Restructuring Thesis: Meaning and Nature

Explaining what constitutes restructuring is extremely difficult as it is an imprecise and complex body of theory that has been developed from the contributions of several different elements, including Marxism, Realism, Time, Space and Society, Flexible Accumulation, Agency, Locality and Postmodernism (see Table 12.1).

Table 12.1 The elements and substance of the restructuring theory

Marxism: emphasises the manner in which capital makes use of particular places for production in the pursuit of capital accumulation and the ways that as production processes are transformed, they change and force corresponding changes in the places that host them.
Realism: emphasises the 'spatiality of social phenomena' and not only recognises the significance of causal entities engaged in social processes, but also the importance of the spatial range over which they operate, and exert their powers.
Time, Space and Society: emphasises the importance of social processes and of the spatial features of, and constraints on, social phenomena.
Flexible Accumulation: connects the analysis of capital accumulation and labour process issues to the qualitative aspects of production and consumption.
Agency: emphasises the important role of local groups, interests, institutions and coalitions in responding to strategies of accumulation by capital in a global context.
Locality: emphasises the importance of detailed investigations of how places as agency can modify the distribution and effects of major social and economic forces and the place provides the arena for this to occur.
Postmodernism: emphasises Western society's desire for specialised, differentiated and targeted products which acts as a vehicle for capital accumulation.

Source: Adapted from Bagguley *et al.*, 1990: 2–8

According to Bagguley *et al.* (1990), Marxism has perhaps made the most significant contribution to the theory's development as it emphasises the space-economy and highlights the processes and consequences of the pursuit of capital accumulation for particular places. This view, according to the latter authors, produced one of the clearest and strongest statements of restructuring theory, that: 'the social and economic structure of any given local area will be the complex result of the combination of that area's succession of roles within the series of wider national and international divisions of labour' (Massey, 1978: 116). Moreover, this view has subsequently been reinforced by Soja (1989: 158), who states that "The restless formation and re-formation of geographical landscapes that is triggered by the dynamics of capitalist development has been the most important discovery arising from the encounter between Western Marxism and modern Geography.' However the contributions of Realism, Time, Space and Society, Flexible Accumulation, Agency, Locality and Postmodernism are important also, as they highlight the fact that context generally, and place specifically, matter as the key to restructuring is understanding the inter-relationships between various past and present activities and processes that are shaping the future economic potential of places. A concern for the spatial dynamics of social phenomena and of the dynamism and influence of capital is a broad theme that binds all these different elements together to form the restructuring thesis (Bagguley *et al.*, 1990).

The restructuring thesis is therefore a complex and amorphous body of theory and because of this it is perhaps best understood as a set of theoretical propositions about the widespread economic and social changes that are taking place in society, which involve deep changes in the geography of production and consumption. It may be regarded as having two interpretive elements. First, restructuring may be represented as part of the process of change in capitalist economies and societies (Boyer, 1986; Coriat, 1979) and as conveying the notion of change towards a 'significantly different order and configuration of social, political and economic life' (Soja, 1989: 159). There is a fundamental tension between the stability of a specific spatial fix of capital and the constant need for capital to go beyond these and create new landscapes of accumulation. In this respect restructuring thus places great emphasis on continuity and change and upon decline and regeneration, as Harvey (1989) and Massey (1978, 1984) see the ceaseless formation and reformation of geographical landscapes as vital moments in the reproduction and transformation of contemporary capitalism. Based on this interpretation, in recent years the restructuring theory has been used to 'examine the spatial aspects of widespread economic and social changes that are taking place in society' (Bagguley *et al.*, 1990: 1). These changes pivot around the contention that there has been a shift from one capitalist stage of development, Fordism, that focuses on economies of scale and on the mass production of standardised goods, to post-Fordism, a more advanced stage of capitalism, which is characterised by economies of scope, flexible production techniques and product differentiation (Dicken, 1998; Harvey, 1989; Piore & Sabel, 1984; Storper & Walker, 1989).

Second, the restructuring theory may be related to the 'changes that have occurred or are occurring in and between constituent parts of the economy' (Johnston *et al*., 1986: 411) in response to the alleged shift from Fordism to post-Fordism (Welch, 1993). These changes may involve the geographical redistribution and/or switching of capital between sectors, reorganising labour or changing the scale of production (Agarwal, 2002). In this respect restructuring represents the outcome of managerial strategies pursued to improve accumulation and it is the analysis of the processes and strategies through which capital seeks expanded accumulation that lies at the core of the restructuring thesis (Harvey, 1989).

Overall, these two interpretive elements of restructuring enable a clear distinction to be drawn between the restructuring of a given sector that is partially an unintended outcome of an exceptionally diverse range of circumstances, and industrial restructuring that results from a strategy pursued by a given firm following a logic of accumulation (Bagguley *et al*., 1990). The second interpretative element of restructuring was in fact first used extensively by Massey and Meegan (1982) to describe the processes of change that were occurring within the manufacturing industry in an attempt to enlighten on-going debate on uneven development and regional restructuring in Western countries (Martin, 1989, Rodriguez-Pose, 1994; Soja, 1989). The authors identified product reorganisation as a restructuring strategy and three related forms – intensification (whereby increased labour productivity is encouraged through the social reorganisation of production as opposed to technical change), investment and technical change (whereby capital investment leads to the design and use of new techniques of production), and rationalisation (which is equivalent to labour reductions) – as central to industrial restructuring. Since this study, a host of similar and different restructuring forms and strategies have been identified within the manufacturing and public services sectors. Other related product reorganisation strategies that have been identified (Bagguley *et al.*, 1990; Nilsson, 1995; Nilsson & Schamp, 1996; Savary, 1995; Urry, 1987) include consolidation (direct and indirect vertical integration bet-ween sectors is sought to capitalise on economic benefits and to extend market reach), internalisation (business transactions kept within the firm/corporation provide ownership advantages such as lower costs), commodification (competitiveness and market efficiency is increased by market demands), market encirclement (forced operation within a competitive environment) and budget centre fragmentation (creation of directly accountable cost centres).

In addition, other restructuring forms and their related strategies have been identified within manufacturing and some service industry sectors. In response to the development of new technology, computer-controlled machinery and the growing volatility of product markets in the manufacturing industry, Atkinson (1984, 1986) for example, notes the occurrence of labour reorganisation and its associated restructuring strategy of labour flexibility. Spatial relocation, which is comprised of concentration (whereby costs are reduced by the geographical clustering of production units into larger units) and decentralisation (the relocation of firms to sites where there is cheaper land, property and/or labour) is another restructuring form that was noted by Aglietta (1979), Hudson (1992), Oberhauser (1987) and Sabel (1982). Finally, product transformation which involves change to the product itself as opposed to change in the way in which the product is produced is another restructuring form that has been observed in certain service sectors. Observed product transformation strategies (Bagguley *et al.*, 1990; Finch & Groves, 1983; Gershuny & Miles, 1983; Levitt, 1976) include partial self-provisioning (shift to consumer self-reliance and labour reductions), domestication (whereby parts of a service are deliberately relocated to home environments), materialisation (transformation of a service product into a material object that can be bought) and enhancement of quality of service (achieved through an improved labour input that is more skilled and/or better trained).

More recently, a number of similar restructuring forms and strategies have been identified in selected sectors of the tourism industry and in a variety of contexts (Table 12.2).

For example, within the hotel and restaurant, the airline and tour operations tourism industry sectors and the mass coastal tourism market sector, the restructuring forms of product reorganisation, spatial relocation and product transformation and the restructuring strategies of investment and technical change, rationalisation, labour flexibility, partial self-provisioning, quality enhancement of the service product, internalisation, centralisation and replacement of the existing labour input with cheaper, younger, female and/or non-white personnel have been observed (Agarwal, 1997, 2002; Bagguley, 1987; Bagguley *et al.*, 1990; Bywater, 1992; Clegg & Essex, 2000; Mak & Go, 1995; Tarrant 1989; Twinning-Ward & Baum, 1998; Urry, 1987; van den Weg, 1982; Vellas & Becherel, 1995; Williams, 1995).

However, a number of different restructuring strategies have been identified, primarily within the mass coastal tourism market sector and specifically in relation to resorts that are in the postmature phase of development. Agarwal (2002), Marchena Gomez and Vera Rebollo (1995),

Table 12.2 Studies of tourism industry restructuring

Restructuring forms/ strategies identified	Context	Author/date of publication
Product reorganisation:		
Rationalisation	• UK hotel and restaurant sectors • UK hotel sector	• Bagguley et al. (1990) • Clegg and Essex (2000); Tarrant (1989)
Technical change and investment	• UK hotel and restaurant sectors • Northern European coastal resorts	• Bagguley et al. (1990); Clegg and Essex (2000) • Agarwal (1997); Van den Weg (1982)
Internalisation	• Airline, hotel and tour operations sectors	• Williams (1995)
Consolidation	• UK hotel sector	• Clegg and Essex (2000); Tarrant (1989)
Centralisation	• UK hotel sector	• Urry (1987)
Product specialisation	• Southern European coastal resorts • UK hotel sector	• Priestley and Mundet (1998) • Clegg and Essex (2000)
Labour reorganisation:		
Labour flexibility	• UK hotel sector	• Bagguley et al. (1990)
Replacement of existing labour	• UK hotel and restaurant sectors	• Bagguley et al. (1990)
Spatial relocation:		
Concentration	• European suppliers of travel and tourism-related services • Airline sector	• Bywater (1994) • Mak and Go (1995); Vellas and Becherel (1995)
Decentralisation	• Airline sector	• Mak and Go (1995)
Product transformation:		
Partial self-provisioning	• UK hotel and restaurant sectors	• Bagguley et al. (1990)
Service quality enhancement	• UK hotel and restaurant sectors • UK hotel sector • Northern European coastal resorts	• Bagguley et al. (1990) • Clegg and Essex (2000) • Agarwal (2002); Twining-Ward and Baum (1998)

Table 12.2 (*Continued*)		
Restructuring forms/ strategies identified	*Context*	*Author/date of publication*
Environmental quality enhancement	• Southern European coastal resorts • Northern European coastal resorts	• Jordon (2000); Marchena Gomez and Vera Rebollo (1995); Morgan (1991) • Agarwal (2002); Turner (1993); Smith (2002)
Repositioning	• Southern European coastal resorts • Northern European coastal resorts	• Curtis (1997); Knowles and Curtis (1999); Jordon (2000); Morgan (1991) • Agarwal (1999, 2002)
Diversification	• Southern European coastal resorts • Northern European coastal resorts • UK hotel sector	• Jordon (2000); Morgan (1991) • Agarwal (2002); Smith (2002) • Clegg and Essex (2000)
Adaptation	• Southern European coastal resorts • Northern European coastal resorts	• Priestley and Mundet (1998) • Agarwal (2002)
Collaboration	• Northern European coastal resorts	• Agarwal (2002)

Source: Adapted from Agarwal, 2002

Morgan (1991) and Turner (1993) identify the occurrence of environmental quality enhancement within many Northern and Southern European mass tourism coastal resorts. This strategy focuses on the improvement of key areas within a resort through environmental redesign, beautification and preservation and has been implemented, for example, in the Spanish resort of Torremolinos, and in the southern English seaside resorts of Bognor Regis, Ilfracombe, Minehead, Ramsgate and Weymouth. Product specialisation which involves targeting 'a limited number of market segments by offering a specialised and differentiated product and a series of complementary sub-products' within the general scope of the existing tourism product (Priestley & Mundet, 1998: 105) is another previously unidentified restructuring strategy that has been observed in many postmature mass tourism coastal resorts including the Northern European resorts of Minehead, Scarborough and Weymouth (Agarwal, 2002), and the Southern European resort of Sitges (Priestley & Mundet, 1998). Also repositioning (realigning and strengthening a destination's image towards potential target markets and existing holiday and business markets), diversification (development of a destination's product range), adaptation (use of market research to inform future planning and management) and collaboration (joint involvement of public and private sectors) are other restructuring strategies that have been identified in Magaluf, Palma Nova, Benidorm, Lloret de Mar and L'Estartit (Curtis, 1997; Morgan, 1991; Priestley & Mundet, 1998), all of which are in Southern Europe, and in the Northern European coastal resorts of Scheveningen located in the Netherlands (van den Weg, 1982), and Torbay, Bournemouth, Brighton, Weston-Super-Mare and Bridlington, all of which are situated in England (Agarwal, 1997; Knowles & Curtis, 1999; Turner, 1993).

Restructuring and the TALC: Theoretical Associations?

So far, the preceding discussion has detailed the meaning and nature of the restructuring thesis and has discussed this construct in the contexts of the manufacturing industry and some service and tourism industry and market sectors. Given its emphasis on firstly rebirth and secondly decline, the restructuring thesis has an obvious theoretical association with the later stages of the TALC model – stagnation and poststagnation – as these stages possess also decline and rebirth characteristics. Thus, although the restructuring thesis and the TALC model are two separate constructs, they are of relevance to each other as they are both concerned with the occurrence of decline, and with responses to decline. According to Agarwal (2002: 32), both constructs are based on the 'the premise that decline will continue unless corrective measures are initiated'. In the case of the TALC model, unless the onset of the stagnation phase is recognised and responded to, tourist areas will progress to poststagnation, of which varying degrees of decline is a real option. For the restructuring theory, industry sectors will become uncompetitive and decline unless remedial action is undertaken. The restructuring thesis and the TALC model therefore provide theoretical insights into the causes and consequences of decline and the responses to it. Agarwal (2002: 32) states that when viewed together these insights are 'potentially very useful to destinations experiencing decline and/or restructuring, as they inform and improve the efficacy and effectiveness of planning and management responses'. This knowledge is particularly valuable to many Northern European and some Southern European mass tourism coastal resorts which, according to Butler (1980: 11), have 'passed steadily through all the postulated stages' and appear to be in poststagnation.

The restructuring thesis and the TALC model thus indicate important information pertaining to the causes and consequences of the decline of mass tourism coastal resorts that are in the postmature phase of development. With regards to the restructuring thesis, this construct clearly highlights that postmature mass tourism coastal resorts may be considered to be victims of the supposed transition from Fordism to post-Fordism as several key processes associated with this transition, these being the search for capital accumulation, consumption changes, shifts in production mode and production flexibility, may have contributed to their decline by reducing their competitiveness. For instance, in the search for capital accumulation, the tourism industry has become internationalised and globalised, resulting in the creation and development of a large number of previously unexplored destinations that are competing with mass tourism coastal resorts for a share of the global market. Consumption changes are reducing the popularity of some mass tourism coastal resorts, just as mass produced, standardised goods are being rejected in favour of customised products that are geared to the individual and in this respect are perceived to be unique. Alongside this, shifts in production mode have resulted in the increased popularity of rural and urban areas, thereby intensifying the competitive conditions within which resorts operate, and production flexibility has created opportunities to customise products that appeal to a differentiated clientele. This is threatening the appeal of standardised, rigidly packaged and mass-marketed holidays such as those offered in postmature mass tourism coastal resorts.

The consequences of these external forces of change are highlighted by the TALC model, which associates a number of characteristics or 'symptoms of decline' (Agarwal, 2002: 33) with the stagnation and poststagnation stages. These characteristics include a diminishing share and volume of the holiday market, a lack of investment, the loss of bed-spaces through the conversion of holiday accommodation to residential homes for the elderly, and a deteriorating physical environment. Many of these characteristics have been observed in Northern European and some Southern European mass tourism coastal resorts. For example, in the context of Northern European mass tourism coastal resorts, Agarwal (1997) highlights the similarities between the model's specified decline characteristics to those exhibited by Torbay, a Southern English seaside resort. In addition, Cooper (1997) notes several features of decline in the supply environment of UK resorts that correspond with those specified in the TALC model. In the context of some Southern European mass tourism coastal resorts, Marchena Gomez and Vera Rebollo (1995), Morgan (1991), Pollard and Rodriguez (1993) and Priestley and Mundet (1998) all discuss the decreasing economic viability and the poor environmental quality of these tourist destinations.

Important theoretical insights into the responses to decline are provided also by the restructuring thesis and the TALC model. The implementation of corrective measures to address decline is an important characteristic of both constructs. The restructuring thesis highlights the fact that the external environment within which resorts operate has become highly competitive as opportunities for pleasure, leisure and tourism are no longer confined to coastal resorts. Consequently, if these tourist destinations are to survive in the global tourism marketplace, they must respond in ways that recapture their competitiveness and market appeal. Perhaps the best testament to the nature and importance that is attached to coastal resort restructuring is the wealth of restructuring forms and strategies that are being implemented (see Table 12.2; for a fuller discussion, see Agarwal, 2002). Responding to decline is an important feature of the TALC model's poststagnation stage. It proposes that life-cycle extension may be achieved by diversification and suggests two ways of achieving this: first, by adding a built attraction, and second, by taking advantage of untapped natural attractions. There are many examples within Northern and Southern European mass tourism coastal resorts to illustrate the implementation of these strategies. For example, Agarwal (1997) observes the development of previously untapped natural, cultural and built resources in Torbay that is enabling the resort to attract new markets such as business and conference tourism and domestic short breaks. Benidorm and Palma Nova are two Spanish examples of coastal resorts that are utilising diversification as a means to gain life-cycle extension. According to Curtis (1997), both are working hard to capture a share of the developing Spanish market by developing niche markets such as walking, cycling, golfing and yachting.

However, it is important to highlight a number of difficulties that arise with the use of the restructuring thesis and the TALC model to provide theoretical insights into the causes and consequences of decline and the responses to decline. These difficulties are summarised in Table 12.3.

Inter-relating these two conceptual frameworks raises some complex, philosophical problems that stem from the fundamental difference between the theoretical underpinnings of the restructuring thesis and the TALC model. The restructuring thesis relates decline and restructuring specifically to the capitalist stage of post-Fordism, while TALC is a universal model in which decline and the responses to decline may occur at any stage in capitalist society. Moreover, according to Agarwal (2002) both constructs fail to distinguish between the causes and the consequences of decline and as a result it is not clear whether decline is caused by changing patterns of consumption or production or whether the consequences of decline are changed consumption or production patterns.

Table 12.3 Theoretical insights and relationships: Problems and difficulties

1. Causes and consequences of resort decline	
TALC:	Restructuring thesis:
• Difficult to identify the poststagnation phase (Agarwal, 1997; Cooper & Jackson, 1989; Haywood, 1986; Strapp, 1988) • Difficult to distinguish between the stagnation and poststagnation stages • Nonlinear sequencing of stages	• Theorised shift to post-Fordism is widely contested (Aglietta, 1979; Harvey, 1989; Lash & Urry, 1987; Lipietz, 1986; Scott, 1988; Soja, 1989) • Undervalues the role of consumption in shaping production (Piore, 1986) • Failure to account for the spatial unevenness of resort decline • Resort decline occurred before post-Fordism
2. Responses to decline	
TALC:	Restructuring thesis:
• Difficult to ascertain resort trajectory once poststagnation has been reached	• Lack of applicability of restructuring forms and strategies to tourism • Restructuring forms and strategies are destination and sector specific • Variation in responses between resorts

Source: Compiled from Agarwal, 2002

Theoretical Relationships and Beyond

Based on the insights into the dynamics of resort areas that are provided by the restructuring thesis and the TALC model, Agarwal (2002) identifies two theoretical relationships that exist between the latter constructs which, despite some difficulties with their individual and combined application, when taken together, provide a conceptual framework for interpreting local economic trajectories and development possibilities. Decline underpins the first of these theoretical relationships, while the second is underpinned by the responses of resort planners, managers and private operators to decline. These theoretical relationships highlight that 'resort decline is best conceptualised as the complex interaction of internal–external forces, which underpin development irrespective of life-cycle course or capitalist stage of development' (Agarwal, 2002: 40). In addition, according to Agarwal (2002), they draw attention also to three key issues that have important implications for future resort restructuring. First, that decline is the outcome of interaction between internal and external forces of change. Second, the threat of decline is constantly present and is not necessarily associated with the course of the TALC model or with a particular capitalist phase. Third, the process of restructuring is continuous and must be based on regaining uniqueness and individuality.

In terms of the first of these issues, that decline is the outcome of interaction between internal and external forces of change; the recognition of this fact is of obvious importance to the potential success of resort restructuring as it highlights the need for resort planners, managers and tourist operators to understand and appreciate a range of abstract processes and their likely impact. In particular, careful consideration must be given to the role of the postmature mass tourism coastal resort in a global political economy and of the extent to which these destinations are able to exert an influence on their fate, given that so much of their present situation has been caused by global political and socioeconomic forces. There is much evidence to suggest that many Northern European and some Southern European mass tourism coastal resorts are responding vociferously to decline as their respective local states appear to be playing a pivotal role in initiating and co-ordinating development in the pursuit of life-cycle extension (Agarwal, 1997, 2002).

However, the evidence of success achieved is extremely contradictory, at least in the case of English resorts, as there is spatial variation in their economic performance, which suggests that some resorts appear to have been more successful than others in engaging with exogenous forces. This differential economic performance may be observed in three English seaside resorts, these being Bournemouth, Scarborough and Weymouth. Bournemouth, a large Southern English coastal resort, typifies economic vibrancy as it has a diverse economy, attracts consistently 5.5 million visitors each year (Bournemouth Borough Council, 2002) and was bestowed the English Tourism Council's accolade of 'Resort of the Year' in 2000. In contrast, the two medium-sized seaside resorts of Scarborough, located on the North-east coast of England, and Weymouth, situated on the Southern English coast, struggle to maintain existing levels of tourists despite energetically implementing a wide range of restructuring strategies. These strategies include product specialisation, product quality enhancement, repositioning, diversification, preservation, adaptation, professionalism and collaboration (Agarwal, 2002). The spatial variation of resort economic performance thus raises two fundamental inter-related questions; first, to what extent is human agency able to overcome structure? and second, in what context(s) does this occur, if indeed it does at all? In order to address these questions it is important to establish in a theoretically informed manner the ways in which places and their associated agents, setting and structure successfully combat global forces. Thus, further research is required that enhances knowledge and understanding of the economic performance of resorts, and of the underlying reasons that determine the relative success or otherwise of the resort economy.

Despite the apparent lack of understanding of the differential economic performance of resorts, it is clear that local response and interaction with broader external forces has produced 'place-specific' outcomes (Massey, 1984). Tourist destinations including those that are in the postmature stages of development are not passive victims of global forces as the impact of local politics on decision-making and actions (Martin, other volume; Urry, 1981), the existence of collective action (Cheshire & Gordon, 1996; Gordon & Goodall, 2000), networks (Garmise & Rees, 1997; Lundvall, 1994; Putnam, 1993) and institutional capacity (Amin & Thrift, 1994; Evans & Harding, 1997) are factors that have been reported to encourage local competitiveness. The significance of the local arena has clearly been heightened and consequently, the nature of global–local interaction and the extent to which local restructuring strategies are shaped and influenced by exogenous forces (Agarwal, 2002) are two issues that require detailed local investigation. The recognition of the need to understand local-level change has, in part, led to renewed calls for the resurrection of locality studies, a social science approach that was widely used during the late 1980s and early 1990s to study local differences in response, and to evaluate changes on the ground (Gordon & Goodall, 2000). The locality studies approach was developed originally to examine the interaction between global and local processes of restructuring (Cooke, 1989; Massey, 1984). It is based on the premise that localities articulate internally to wider socioeconomic processes, and change, modify and transform the effects of global, international and national processes (Cooke, 1987). According to Gordon and Goodall (2000: 306), 'its emphasis on local interaction between various activities and processes shaping the future character and economic potential of places is particularly apposite for an economic sector which is so crucially dependent on a wider range of place characteristics'.

However, the use of the locality studies approach to examine the processes and outcome of restructuring has been strongly questioned as it is associated with a number of conceptual and methodological problems. For example, it has been argued that the concept lacks firm definitional foundations (Pratt, 1991) and 'plays a variety of functions in different scientific discourses' (Urry, 1988: 441). In addition, there are difficulties with its operationalisation as it is plagued by scale of analysis and boundary delimitation problems. With regards to the latter, Pratt (1991) argues that the spatiality of social relations will not necessarily be expressed by neatly contiguous areas. In terms of the former, the scale of a locality may change according to the object of analysis and as scale varies, so does its significance. Thus, the vital connection between setting and interaction remains unspecified, leading to uncertainty about how precisely a setting actually determines interaction (Duncan & Savage, 1991). According to Duncan and Savage (1989: 212) the danger here is that 'locality research simply produces a description albeit a rich one of particular localities rather than an analysis of processes that underlie evolution and development'. Unresolved questions of philosophy, theory and methodology (Peet, 1998) are hampering the study of places and yet developing an understanding of particular places and of the relationships between the contingencies of place and external and internal forces of change is an essential precondition for informing how resorts may be managed in the interests of their long-term sustainability. Place is critical to the tourist experience and therefore the challenge is to 'understand in a theoretically informed way how the processes of interaction between tourism and sets of place characteristics operate and develop over time in different contexts' (Gordon & Goodall, 2000: 292).

Agarwal's (2002) second contention, that decline is an ongoing threat that is not necessarily associated with the stagnation and poststagnation stages of the TALC model or with a particular capitalist phase, has important implications also for postmature coastal resort restructuring. It suggests that continuous corrective measures are vital in order to counter the impact of negative spatial externalities, and that restructuring plays a much more important role during the later stages of the TALC model than it has previously been credited with. Indeed, the TALC model itself has been criticised for overemphasising structure over agency (Milne, 1998; Williams & Shaw, 1998) and Agarwal's (1997) study of the public sector's role in planning for renewal and her study (2002) of three English postmature coastal resorts (Minehead, Scarborough and Weymouth) reinforce this criticism by highlighting the fact that the model downplays the role of human interaction. In both studies, there was not only evidence of strong local state commitment to restructuring and of the implementation of different restructuring forms and strategies, but also that the nature and extent of restructuring depends primarily on the size of the resort, the importance of tourism to the local economy, the amount of support given by local authorities and the degree of co-operation that exists between public and private agencies. In any case, Agarwal argues that given the economic dependence of resorts on tourism, combined with the amount of capital investment that is tied to the resorts' physical and built fabric, it would be economically and politically unacceptable not to at least attempt to restructure.

The importance of restructuring during the later stages of the TALC model when it is applied to postmature coastal destination points to the urgent need for its theoretical reformulation and the insertion of an additional stage, in order to take into account the series of restructuring efforts that are inaugurated before decline sets in (Agarwal, 1994). This stage, termed as 'reorientation', should be added between the stagnation and the poststagnation stages of the TALC model to represent continued efforts at restructuring (see Figure 12.1).

Unlike Butler's original idea of rejuvenation, during the reorientation stage in the short term, the option of decline is not contemplated, as instead efforts are concerned with reviving and renewing the dwindling tourist industry. It is this feature that makes the reorientation stage fundamentally different from the TALC's poststagnation phase. Greater emphasis is placed on encouraging growth and market maturity, rather than on accepting decline. At this critical juncture, Agarwal (1994) proposed that the smooth transition from the stagnation stage to the poststagnation stage is suspended; in the short term the reorientation phase can be repeated as many times as necessary. This reflects continued efforts at catering for changes to the structure of visitor markets and changing consumer tastes, thereby capturing the dynamic nature of restructuring. This pattern will continue until, inevitably, circumstances change and the poststagnation stage is finally entered. From this point onwards, the events associated with the poststagnation stage resume. In the medium to long term, the resort can now continue to regenerate indefinitely, or enter a period of long-term decline. However, Agarwal (1994: 206) states that 'it must be remembered that long-term

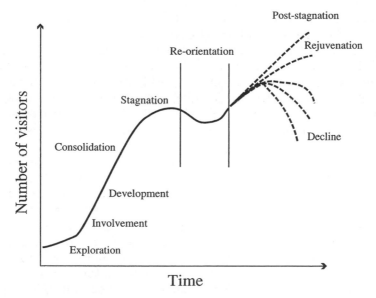

Figure 12.1 Modification of the Butler Tourist Cycle of Evolution Model

development of a resort is by no means inevitable and that, consequently it may be possible for a resort to re-enter at other stages within the cycle'.

The third issue that Agarwal (2002) highlights relates to the need for a greater appreciation of the uniqueness of place. This was emphasised in the TALC model as decline relates specifically to a loss of uniqueness and product competitiveness. This suggests that the challenge for many postmature mass tourism coastal resorts is to restructure in ways that recapture 'place specificity' (Massey, 1984) so that they are able to compete with an ever-increasing range of tourist destinations that are more attuned to contemporary consumption practices. By and large, many mass tourism coastal resorts that are in the postmature phase of development are trying to recapture uniqueness through product specialisation that attempts to develop and exploit a sense of place (Lundgren, other volume). This may be illustrated by Agarwal's (2002) study of three English seaside resorts, Weymouth, Scarborough and Minehead, which found that all three were attempting to reinforce their role as unique seaside resorts by developing subproducts such as conference and activity tourism.

In addition however, many of these tourist destinations are trying to establish uniqueness by capitalising on their 'symbolic capital' or 'cultural capital'. This concept was developed originally by Bordieu (1977, 1984) to describe the consumption and collection of culture intended to demonstrate explicitly tastes, style and status and is of relevance to postmature destinations as culture is increasingly being used as a tool or a catalyst for restructuring (Smith, 2002). Within England, local authority cultural strategies have been piloted in a number of coastal destinations (DCAL, 2001), and there are numerous examples of destinations that are attempting to take advantage of their symbolic capital. For example, culture is playing a key role in the restructuring of Southend-on-Sea, a resort located on the Southeast coast of England (Smith, 2002). Meanwhile, according to Jordon (2000), there are recognisable attempts at image creation for local cuisine, souvenir and handicraft products in Croatia's postmature mass tourism coastal resorts.

But restructuring in this way is arguably inherently problematic for most postmature mass tourism coastal resorts. In attempting to regain uniqueness, these destinations are ironically becoming more standardised as they are restructuring in similar ways. Agarwal (2002: 46) in particular warns of the similarities in responses to decline and states that 'restructuring is not occurring in ways that best creates competitive advantage'. This reiterates earlier warnings by France and Barke (1991) and Urry (1990, 1997), who question whether resorts are ever able to recapture uniqueness. Urry (1997) states that although there is plenty of evidence to suggest that resorts have manipulated their cultural dynamics in an attempt to create objects that are more culturally appealing, resorts are contaminated and there is little or no way that they can be reconstructed successfully. Moreover, he contends that in attempting to regain uniqueness, resorts have contributed to the production of a standardised landscape and to the eradication of distinctive places. In many cases, restructuring focuses on 'problem definition, pinpointing of strong points of existing structures and strategic action to correct defects' (Priestley & Mundet, 1998: 108), and consequently, the appropriateness of this action has been criticised, particularly by Agarwal (2002: 47), who states that such action is more concerned with 'the symptoms of decline rather than the internal mechanisms which cause decline'.

Conclusions

Life-cycle extension is complex, but several academics (Cooper & Jackson, 1989; Getz, 1992; Haywood, 1986; Ioannides, 1992) claim that the key to recapturing competitiveness is adequate planning (see also Papatheodorou, this volume). A phased planned approach to resort restructuring is vital in order to ensure that new products are developed before existing ones have reached decline (Gordon & Goodall, 1992). However, this is not a straightforward task, as there are clearly heavy financial costs involved. There are implications also for the co-ordination of tourism development as it requires a degree of institutional flexibility and cross-organisational co-operation and collaboration, but often it is thwarted by industry fragmentation, multiple ownership and scarce financial and human resources (Thomas & Thomas, 1998).

Many postmature mass tourism coastal resorts suffer from these problems as they are characterised by small businesses with low levels of capitalisation and managerial experience and there exists a weak culture of trust among firms (Cooper, 1997; Shaw & Williams, 1997). While some academics suggest that the shift from a system of local government which has narrow responsibilities for service provision, to a system of local governance which is responsible for a broader range of activities involving contracting, regulating enabling, problem-solving and leadership (Brookes, 1989; Stoker, 1995, 1999), may overcome some of the difficulties of securing co-operation and collaboration between the public and private sectors by fostering a culture of collective action, others suggest otherwise. For example, Thomas and Thomas's (1998) study of the impact of local governance on local tourism development in Britain reveals misplaced expectations that tourism development would be one of the beneficiaries of changes in local governance. The authors found that inertia and vested interests in the status quo not only retarded organisational change, but also exploited the relatively marginal nature of tourism development in local governance to the extent that tourism development was often indefinitely delayed or abandoned. Consequently, public sector intervention and the establishment of effective mechanisms that encourage and facilitate co-operation and collaboration with the private sector are imperative for the restructuring of postmature mass tourism coastal resorts.

This chapter set out to review the restructuring thesis and to detail the theoretical relationships that exist between the latter construct and the TALC model, which, when taken together, provide a conceptual framework for interpreting the potential economic trajectories of postmature mass tourism coastal resorts. In addition, this paper discussed in-depth three key issues for future resort restructuring: first, that decline appears to be the outcome of interaction between internal and external forces of change; second, the threat of decline is not necessarily associated with the course of the TALC model or with a particular capitalist phase; and third, restructuring is continuous and must involve attempts that recapture the uniqueness of resorts. In doing so, this discussion has highlighted a number of future research avenues that relate broadly to the need to understand the role of these destinations in the global market-place, the nature, extent and success of local interaction with global forces of change, reasons for resort differential performance, the appropriateness of restructuring strategies and the most effective mechanisms that encourage co-operation and collaboration between the public and private sectors.

Chapter 13

Revisiting the TALC: Is There an Off-Ramp?

TOM BAUM

Introduction

Traditional destinations in many developed countries have matured to a point where critical assessment is required with respect to their future in the tourism sector. Their earlier role in meeting the leisure needs of the urban population of industrialised Europe and North America has been superseded by changes in consumer demand and expectations, developments in transport and technology and the emergence of new destinations. The need to reassess the future roles of mature coldwater destinations has been well recognised in the UK, elsewhere in Europe and the USA (Cooper, 1997; Shaw & Williams, 1997) but is becoming an increasing requirement for Spanish and other Mediterranean locations as well (see Lloret de Mar case example below). How destinations respond to the challenge of change is a critical issue, and the focus of much academic and practitioner attention has been on reinvention or rejuvenation of the existing concept and product (see Agarwal & Cooper, this volume; Faulkner & Tideswell, other volume; Stansfield, other volume). Less consideration has been given to a strategy within which the abandonment of traditional tourism is considered as a viable way forward or where new tourism resources are substituted for those which have failed within the traditional model. This paper, building on earlier work (Baum, 1998a), seeks to explore an elaboration of the established Tourism Area Cycle of Evolution (TALC) (Butler, 1980) as a means of exploring alternatives to the rejuvenation of existing products and markets. The paper is intended as a conceptual rather than empirical extension to the considerable literature which already exists on the TALC. However, one Mediterranean case study is included to illustrate how thinking with respect to resort planning is moving to acceptance of the principle of alternatives to the rejuvenation of existing products and markets.

Mass tourism to purpose built destinations (coastal, mountain) in Europe has evolved over the past 150 years in two waves. Resorts were developed in, primarily, coastal regions of Northern European countries such as Britain, France and Germany from the early 19th century and gained mass appeal with the growth of the railways in the 1850s. The second spur to development came in the early 1960s when low-cost jet travel permitted large numbers of visitors to access Mediterranean destinations in, initially, Spain, Italy, France and Greece and subsequently, other coastal countries. These locations drew Northern European visitors away from domestic coastal locations and modelled their facilities upon the resorts that they replaced. Resorts from both cycles focused on the provision of low-cost, value accommodation and facilities with the coastal strip as the main attraction. In the British Isles, 'first wave' resorts of this kind include Ayr, Blackpool, Morecambe, Skegness, Portrush, Southend and Weston Super Mare. In the Mediterranean, their second wave successors include Magaluf, Benidorm, Torremolinos and Lloret de Mar in Spain and Constantia on the Romanian Black Sea. None of these destinations were built with concepts of sustainability in mind. Their design and the nature of facilities and accommodation that were built reflected the needs of the times (late 19th century and 1960s) in which they were developed.

International tourism, since its inception, has proved to be highly 'predatory' in nature. It has developed on the assumption that there will always be new locations willing to accommodate visitors once traditional markets grew tired with existing facilities. In practice, this has proved to be the case, with new destinations emerging first domestically, then throughout the rest of Europe and, ultimately, in long-haul 'third wave' destinations such as the Caribbean, Dubai and Thailand to meet the appetite of tourists from developed countries for sun, sea and sand. These new waves of investment took place without any significant reinvestment in 'redundant' locations with the result that they have become less and less attractive and relevant to contemporary tourists. They were only able to continue to compete in the tourism marketplace on price, by cutting the amount charged to visitors more and more in face of new destination competition. This, in turn, created a vicious circle of fewer visitors, lowering prices, underinvestment and fewer visitors again (see Russo, other volume). This process fits, classically, within Butler's TALC model.

One of the big challenges facing contemporary tourism is how to handle its redundant or decaying 'plant'. In a sense, this is a challenge faced by all industries that require upgrading in their use of technology and factory premises. Abandoned heavy industrial sites can be found throughout Europe. In some case, these 'brown field' sites have been developed for alternative use – new industrial units, housing or leisure. In other cases, they remain monuments to an industrial past. Tourism destinations are somewhat different to industrial locations in that they tend to cover a far greater area and are, by definition, sited in what are also prime natural environments. They often front prime beach areas, as is the case in a number of the Spanish locations noted above, or are in desirable mountain terrain – Aviemore in Scotland is a good example. Unlike factory sites, they also integrate the private homes of local residents with the tourist resources. The tourist facilities are also, generally, privately owned by a large number of operators. Bulldozing the totality of a tourism brown field site is rarely a realistic option.

Rejuvenation is by no means impossible but may not be the only option. Major public sector investment has borne fruit in a number of major seaside destinations in Britain, notably Blackpool, Bournemouth and Brighton. All three have invested heavily in conference and convention facilities as a means to reduce dependence on traditional family vacations. In the Mediterranean, the island of Majorca is a mature destination that has faced issues of decline. Focused public sector leadership, in partnership with major private sector organisations, has driven significant change in the destination, which now acts as a role model for integrated destination change management.

Butler's TALC model provides a useful theoretical model through which to review the development of resorts and to consider how mature destinations can develop effective strategies for their future survival. The TALC has a number of features which give it robustness despite its longevity and these are identified by Butler (1998) in terms of its flexibility and capacity to accommodate a diversity of destination contexts.

The TALC, as Butler (1998: 4) notes, has been subject to considerable scrutiny and modification over the years, 'much of it producing reasonable comment and criticism, improvements and modifications, and alternative models' and he lists a range of contributions to this debate covering the period from the mid-1980s to the present day. Examples of work in this area are particularly plentiful where they draw upon evidence from 'first wave' coldwater destinations, and include Cooper and Jackson (1989), Cooper (1990, 1992, 1995, 1997), Twining-Ward and Twining-Ward (1996), Twining-Ward and Baum (1997) and Baum (1998b). The TALC is useful in interpreting and explaining the past and this is one of its prime attractions in the context of 'first wave' destinations and, as we shall see, increasingly those in the 'second wave' as well. In coldwater destinations in Britain, the model has been played out over 100 or more years. In this mature destination context, the model can be used strategically to stimulate action against decline. This is even more the case with respect to 'second wave' destinations of the Mediterranean, with a history of perhaps 40 years, as we shall see in the case of Lloret de Mar. It is, however, arguable that the model may have less value, except perhaps of a cautionary nature, to newly emerging 'third wave' destinations in the developing world. Here the development period has been much more rapid and, with the added force of globalisation and multinational investment, may well have 'jumped' one or more stages within the model cycle.

Butler (1998) argues that some of the criticism levelled against the TALC has been based on the application of detail rather than upon recognition of more general attributes and strengths. Nevertheless, he acknowledges the contributions that writers such as Choy (1992), Getz (1983, 1986, 1992), Haywood (1986, 1992) and Prosser (1995) have made to the debate about the model, and the criticisms of validity and application that are at the heart of their concerns. A number of criticisms (Hovinen, 1981, 1982) postulate 'the possibility of alternative and additional stages after the stagnation stage of the original model' (Butler, 1998: 6) and considerations of this nature are at the essence of the discussion which follows here.

The TALC and Alternative Scenarios Beyond Decline

This paper develops the author's arguments (Baum, 1998a) relating to two possible development scenarios to the TALC which, at that point, had not been given consideration in the literature. One is of a community exiting tourism altogether and the second, of 'starting from scratch' with an entirely new tourism product while accepting the decline of the traditional product and market. These scenarios appear to have been neglected because they lie outside the product paradigm that appears to shape the TALC in its most common interpretations. This paradigm, simply stated, is that tourism development occurs within broadly fixed tourism product (supply-side) and market (demand-side) parameters and that development strategies operate within these constraints. It also focuses on growth in arrival numbers and revenues as the key indicator and objective of tourism development respectively. Any other outcome is seen as indicating failure. This paradigm mindset can make it difficult for traditional seaside resorts, as an example, to think beyond their specific coastal resource and the family market to which they may appeal. In many respects, the reluctance to think beyond the exiting tourism paradigm is understandable, given the heavy capital investment in tourism infrastructure in both financial and emotional terms. A seaside pier, for example, can represent a statement of civic pride, part of a town's heritage and a well loved visitor attraction. A seafront guesthouse in Douglas, Isle of Man, likewise represents a family's commitment to a style of tourism and market which, while it may be in decline, is all that the family knows and is their home and financial security for the future. In this sense, then, abandoning tourism may be rather more involved than is the case in some manufacturing sectors. An evident parallel to abandoning family agricultural investment can be seen – the emotional and historic family ties which many farmers face in relinquishing their land can also be seen in tourism. The link is, perhaps, the small business structure of tourism (Morrison, 1998) which influences decision making at both the individual operator and the destination level.

Underpinning the application of the TALC model in the context of mature destinations is a notion that a decline in tourism, in a similar way to agriculture, is a 'bad thing' (Cooper, 1997), representing a 'whig' view of tourism history which argues for the need to reinvest in order to reverse such decline. The TALC model, in its original form, does not acknowledge the possibility of further stages beyond decline or rejuvenation, or indeed, a way forward after periods of attempted rejuvenation or marked decline. In the context of this paper, additional stages to the TALC constitute the partial or total abandonment of traditional tourism as an economic activity, change driven by the collective will of the community within which it has traditionally been located. While Butler, in his original analysis, acknowledged that decline may be terminal, and lead to the end of tourism activity, this approach appears to be based on the assumption that decline will be gradual without any level of strategic intervention managing the end of tourism. Abandonment, in the context of this paper, is a deliberate and collective strategy by a destination or community. The community may have few options about ending its association with tourism but the decision is a conscious one nonetheless.

Exit stage

Abandonment, in this sense, can be total or virtually total and can be styled the *exit* stage. This means that the location and its existing supply-side profile, traditionally with a high level of tourism dependence, is no longer consciously perceived as a tourism destination by the community or those responsible for its marketing and image. Tourism resources, such as seafront accommodation, develop or are allocated new uses (commercial or residential) within the alternative land-use or economic strategy that has been adopted. Public sector resources are diverted away from tourism development and marketing to other community or commercial priorities. In many respects, this process represents the reverse of that which takes place when a location embarks upon a tourism development strategy when other areas of economic and social activity (agriculture, fishing manufacturing) may be abandoned in favour of tourism. Political decisions must be made with respect to land use and the management of resources and can lead to abandonment of one in favour of others.

An exit strategy may be forced on a community as a result of natural or human induced change or catastrophe (coastal erosion; volcanic activity; a mega environmental disaster; war or sustained civil unrest); as a result of changing patterns of human habitation; or industrial development (discovery of new rich mineral deposits) (see Russell, this volume). Within any of these scenarios, tourism may be marginalised or impossible to sustain. The abandonment of much of the island of Montserrat because of volcanic eruption, involving some of its main tourist areas, represents one example of enforced exit. Creeping urbanisation in the commuter-belt environs of major cities likewise means that traditional coastal resorts such as Bray in Co. Wicklow and Bangor, Co. Down, both in Ireland, have over time abandoned much of their traditional seaside resort role in favour of a new role as commuter and retail centres for prosperous hinterlands of Dublin and Belfast respectively. Such change may have been inevitable for market reasons as well but an evident alternative to tourism meant that attempts at tourism rejuvenation, found in other coldwater locations, did not take place. Such changes involving the urbanisation of traditional resorts are the result of competition for the use of scarce land.

Exit from tourism may not be enforced on destinations but may also be a deliberate strategy selected by communities for whom tourism no longer offers the best option in economic, social, cultural, environmental or lifestyle terms. Such strategies can be manifest in the withdrawal of economic and political support for tourism-related activities within the community (public parking, access to resources, land-use zoning, licensing) and through the active promotion of alternatives such as dormitory town status, a focus on attracting high technology or financial sector industries or, indeed, a return to earlier agricultural land uses. As deliberate and articulated policies, such exit strategies are difficult to identify on a large scale although there is growing evidence of the reality of such change. During the 1980s, a number of communities in Oregon adopted 'visitors not welcome' strategies (since reversed) and thus implemented a deliberate exit from tourism strategy even though they were by no means mature destinations in the TALC sense (see also Martin, other volume). Partial manifestation may be more readily identified as communities make it increasingly difficult to be a tourist in a specific area. This can be through the imposition of restricted or high cost parking or restricting access by casual visitors to key tourism resources such as the ocean front in Cape Cod. Niagara-on-the Lake in Ontario, Canada is one community that has sought to limit the impact of tourism through its access pricing and licensing strategies. Similarly, promotion of alternative land uses in the Northern part of Tenerife, for retirement homes and for high-value agricultural activity, has been at a cost to traditional tourism which is now increasingly segregated to the South of the island. Tourism, in some respects, is about seeing how other people live and part of the attraction of visiting communities is free access to villages and towns in order to experience the local culture. Increasing hostility to visitation, for security and privacy reasons, and the growth of gated communities in many countries means that, in practice, such communities are seeking to exclude visitors and are abandoning options for tourism.

Reinvention

Abandonment of tourism may, in theory, be total. Alternatively, abandonment may be directed at traditional tourism resources and markets while new forms of tourism are developed from first principles alongside or in close proximity to the original resort. This *reinvention* stage may be seen as a subset of rejuvenation, but may more usefully be understood to involve a process of exit and re-entry, including a rejection of the destination's original tourism paradigm and the creation of new tourism models, appealing to alternative markets. At a theoretical level as well as in the context of destination strategic planning, reinvention as a stage in tourism development fits comfortably into Handy's (1994) adaptation and extension of the product life cycle model. Described by Handy as the 'Sigmoid curve', this adaptation allows companies, in the case of products, to plan strategically for the decline of one line and to introduce other lines in tandem, each commencing at the earliest phase of the cycle. Figure 13.1 represents Handy's Sigmoid curves. Shay (1998) describes Handy's model as organic and proactive by comparison with the static and reactive characteristics of the traditional product life cycle.

If the Sigmoid curve model is applied to the context of the TALC, the opportunities for both natural and strategic reinvention of the destination become evident. If a destination is able to recognise traditional markets that are in decline and where the decline process appears to be irreversible for whatever reason, application of Handy's principles may be more realistic than attempting to reverse this decline within the traditional market. This could involve creation of entirely new products for alternative markets than those traditionally attracted. This process of reinvention has taken place in a number of locations, in full or partial form. Both Bournemouth and Prince Edward Island's (PEI) (Canada) traditional markets lay with family summer vacations. Both recognised the importance of maintaining this market, albeit at a time of on-going decline, while creating altogether new markets, in the case of Bournemouth in the conference sector and in PEI through golf. In both cases, the reinvented focus required strategic recognition that traditional markets and products were unsustainable and that the new tourism models would require a reinvented supply side rather than an adaptation of existing facilities. In both cases, major public sector investment in the new tourism model was required through the Bournemouth International Conference Centre and PEI's publicly owned and managed

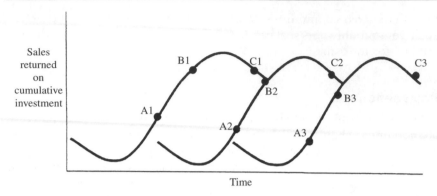

Figure 13.1 Handy's Sigmoid curves

golf facilities. In parallel with these new models, investment in traditional marketing and product reduced in both locations.

The Isle of Man also represents a good example of a destination seeking to reinvent itself and where public policy fully recognises this need (Isle of Man, 1996). Traditional family seaside holidays have declined in importance to a level where they have been virtually abandoned within the island's economic and tourism planning process and, to some extent, by the organised public sector as well. Seasonal activity continues in urban seaside centres such as Douglas but is in apparent terminal decline with little attempt to rejuvenate either product or markets. Reinvention, through the early stages of a new curve, can be seen in the form of 'high end' cultural, sporting and general activity tourism, located away from the traditional resort areas and, as such, much more rural in focus. The reinvented image has a strong Celtic cultural flavour, is designed to appeal to the short-break market and offers activities that are far less seasonal in focus.

The Isle of Man's reinvented tourism cannot and, indeed, does not wish to build upon the island's traditional tourism image. Therefore, the 'new' tourism has started again in marketing terms at the exploration if not the innovation stage because the destination has no market image for its reinvented product and, in addition, must overcome well entrenched market images of its 'old' tourism product. In this sense, the Isle of Man's 'new' tourism is clearly at the exploration or early development phase of the TALC. Unlike the traditional TALC model where rejuvenation challenges stagnation or reverses decline, reinvention assumes an almost clean sheet following exit from the destination's traditional tourism paradigm and abandonment of its existing resources and markets.

In this author's earlier paper, Baum (1998a) addressed exit and reinvention strategies in terms of mature, coldwater, 'first wave' destinations. The case study of Lloret de Mar, which follows, considers moves towards reinvention in the context of a 'second wave' Mediterranean destination where the approach appears to be a combination of the rejuvenation of existing tourism resources, exit to new areas of economic activity (residential) and reinvention through culture and heritage.

Case Study. Reinventing Tourism: Applying the Handy Model in Lloret de Mar, Catalonia

Lloret de Mar is a major coastal resort in Catalonia on the Costa Brava, situated some 70 km north of Barcelona and about 100 km south of the French border. It is located close to the main coastal motorway between Barcelona and France. Lloret is served by the charter airport at Girona (40 km) and the major international airport at Barcelona is 100 km away. Lloret is an ancient settlement and celebrated its 1000th anniversary in 2001. However, Lloret developed as a holiday resort in the 1960s and much of its accommodation and facilities stock dates from the period between the mid-1960s and the early 1980s. Lloret has some 30,000 hotel bed spaces in about 100 hotels and a large number of additional self-catering facilities and holiday homes. The main vacation facilities are Lloret's beaches and a concentrated collection of restaurants, clubs, bars and retail outlets. The town does have a number of historical and cultural resources but these are currently poorly presented for tourist purposes and do not attract much tourist visitation. Indeed, it is fair to say that Lloret has developed since the 1960s exclusively on the basis of its mass tourism appeal and other areas of potential economic activity were neglected.

Lloret's main tourist season extends for four to five months between May and September when good weather is a dependable resource. The main international tourist market during this period is budget to mid-market package holidays from Northern European countries, principally the UK, Germany, France and the Netherlands. Diversification into the Eastern European market has taken place in recent years, primarily focusing on the Czech Republic, Poland and Russia. Domestic visitors are from elsewhere in Catalonia, principally Barcelona, who make use of the range of holiday homes in the resort. Outside of the main summer season, Lloret has established a consistent market for third age visitors from France, Germany and elsewhere in Spain.

Lloret's tourist resources are, generally, of mediocre quality and lack significant culture and regional authenticity. Restaurants focus on international tastes and many provide British and German menus rather than local alternatives. Accommodation is predominantly in the two- and three-star range, although this represents a significant up-grade from about 10 years ago when much of the serviced accommodation was in hostels and one-star facilities. Lloret appears to be significantly underpriced for its accommodation. Rack rates for three-star hotel rooms are between $25 and $40 per person for half-board. Tour operator rates are significantly below this level.

The Town Council of Lloret de Mar and Lloret Turisme have recognised the consequences of permitting the resort's downward spiral to continue. The process started about 10 years ago, designed to gain competitiveness over other new destinations and to improve its international position. In 2002, a strategic rejuvenation plan was launched by Lloret Turisme on behalf of the community, entitled *Looking towards Lloret of the future*. This plan is characterised by comprehensiveness and the manner in which it integrates all dimensions of the destination and recognises a future for Lloret that goes beyond traditional tourism to cater for a new style of visitor interested in culture and health as well as a lifestyle resident. In other words, rather than just rejuvenating existing tourism stock, the plan seeks to create new economic activity alongside traditional tourism in the anticipation that, eventually, the pressure from 'monoculture' tourism can be relieved.

The plan is underpinned by principles of environmental management, quality services and re-evaluation of resources within the resort, all operating in line with sustainable tourism development criteria. *Looking towards Lloret of the future* is driven by the public sector and includes the following features:

Relieving the town centre

This aspect includes further pedestrianisation of the town centre and the provision of out-of-town parking for cars and buses, thus seeking to attract leisure visitors from the region and other resorts in Catalonia.

Town planning

This features planned purchase and demolition of redundant buildings, including older, town centre hotels and the use of the resultant space as public leisure space. Controlled growth of new development is also included, with the creation of new public spaces, the declassification of some existing building areas and control over the height of buildings, thus creating a more attractive residential living space beyond traditional tourism.

Hotel Quality Scheme

Hotels are strongly encouraged to join this Quality Scheme and some 60% of accommodation providers are currently affiliated. The scheme sets operational and service standards for all hotels. The hotel quality scheme is being extended to other sectors within tourism, including restaurants and travel agents.

Tourism Excellence Scheme

This scheme is intended to lead to very specific actions, aimed at improving both the quality of life for the people of Lloret and offering improved services to visitors. Demolition of redundant facilities and their replacement with quality public areas is one example of this objective in action. Enhanced and consistent signage systems will also be introduced to assist both local people and visitors.

Management plan

Lloret's management plan for tourism is the first of its kind in Spain. At its core is the creation of Lloret Turisme, under professional management and responsible for visitor services, the management of quality in the destination, promotion and marketing, the development of new tourist products and the management of new resources and facilities.

Transport

This area includes enhancement of public transport within the destination and the management of direct access routes to the motorway system. Parking for visitors, in designated and controlled areas, is also accommodated within the plan.

Drainage systems

This features the building of one of the most up-to-date sewage plants on the Costa Brava and the building of a new drinking water plant.

Agenda XXI

Sustainability is seen as an underpinning principle within the total plan. This is covered by a Local Agenda XXI, through which sectors of the local economy (including tourism) work jointly to determine the parameters of future development, based on criteria of balance and respect for the environment. Agenda XXI is seen as a valuable working tool enabling modernisation proposals for the town to be adapted to their geographic surroundings, without causing damage to the existing environment in Lloret. Several groups have been established in order to focus on key areas of noise, transport, cultural heritage and water control.

New Resources

New resources for tourism and resident leisure will focus on currently underused cultural and heritage resources, thus providing some diversification from Lloret's core product of sun, sea and sand. These include unique neoclassical gardens, ancient Iberian remains, mediaeval fortifications and coastal pathways.

Looking towards Lloret of the future represents a good example of integrated tourism planning by tourism's public sector in co-operation with private sector operators. It represents realisation that, without such actions, the prospects for the resort as a traditional tourism destination are relatively bleak. The plan focuses on the coastal resort alone but also recognises the need to address what is one of the main challenges for seaside resorts – how to link and integrate core coastal resources with the wider natural and cultural hinterland, in this case towns, villages and the countryside of Catalonia. Effective tourism planning needs to recognise this wider environment although the constraints of local government control are such that it can be difficult to plan outside of political boundaries.

The underpinning vision that is evident in *Looking towards Lloret of the future*, particularly its sustainable and environmental focus, is probably essential if mature and declining resorts are to reverse this decline. What is of particular pertinence in the context of this paper is that Lloret's plans are designed to create an environment within which traditional tourism will play a significant but not exclusive role. The 'new' Lloret de Mar is intended to provide quality of life for local inhabitants and for short-term leisure visitors as well as meeting the needs of traditional, long-stay tourists. In other words, it represents application of the Handy model within the context of tourism. Through this strategy, the 'new' Lloret is expected to attract a higher spend per visitation day and will, therefore, contribute to an alternative and more sustainable future for the resort.

Conclusion

Any model is an abstraction of reality and the two extensions of the TALC considered here, representing *exit* and *reinvention*, are not without their problems in terms of application. Deliberate and overt policy changes against tourism are less likely in reality than evolutionary change in that direction. From a political and strategic policy perspective, the options which these extension stages provide may be important agenda items for the future as destinations and their resident communities evaluate their future with or without tourism. Reinvention takes the courage to abandon what is in place and to start from scratch, in itself a challenging option for policy makers. What the two extensions to the TALC considered in this paper do is to place the overall model firmly back within the context of management decision making, something which Butler in his original paper stressed and which has become somewhat lost in subsequent interpretations. Finally, there is little doubt that these extensions to the TALC model require further empirical testing through analysis and case examples in much the same way that Butler's original contribution has been assessed since its inception in 1980.

Part 5

Predicting with the TALC

R.W. BUTLER

When the TALC was first conceived, it was thought of as both a predictive and a descriptive model (Butler, other volume), but this former aspect was not pursued beyond a very preliminary discussion. One of the questions asked at the end of the first presentation of the model at the meeting of the Canadian Association of Geographers in Vancouver was whether the model could be used in a predictive sense. The response given was affirmative. It was felt that if the curve could be graphed on the basis of data such as visitor numbers or numbers of bed-nights for sufficient destinations over a considerable number of years, then the nature of the curve could be determined and it could be modelled for the future by the application of a relatively simple formula (Butler & Brougham, 1972). This proved to be easier to contemplate than to implement and in most discussions and applications since then the TALC has not been thought of as a model with predictive capacities, but rather as a descriptive model.

One of the major problems to using the model in a predictive way has been the often-quoted lack of time series data on which to base a destination life cycle curve, given the general lack of accurate and consistent data on tourism in most places. There is little incentive to keep track of tourism data when tourism is barely present in a location and by the time it has become well established, the common problems of fragmentation and multiple competitive private ownership of facilities mean that limited data are made available to researchers. It was with considerable delight, therefore, that I came across two examples of destination forecasting using a life cycle approach. Manente and Pechlaner base their model, an Interactive Destination Evaluation System, on a life cycle, and the influences on this of four categories of variables; demand, supply, destination resources, and innovation and organisation. They note 'the importance of the TALC approach as the basis to develop a warning system prototype of decline' (Manente & Pechlaner, this volume). Manente and Pechlaner describe a study undertaken for the European Commission, the purpose of which was to analyse the decline of tourist destinations in order to define an 'early warning system' using indicators to anticipate decline. The decline of tourist destinations is a major issue in Europe and elsewhere, none more so than in many of the poorer parts of the European Union where there is often little alternative to tourism to support populations. While tourism may be criticised by many academics on the grounds of its impacts on culture and society, its environmental effects and its inflationary economic impacts, the fact remains that it is often the only alternative to abandonment of many communities. Being able to anticipate when decline may occur and take intervening action is therefore of considerable importance and has always been a key element in the TALC model. The authors set up a diagnostic system of the evolution of a destination using a series of selected variables. They begin by discussing the factors that influence the decline of destinations, and then examine the feasibility of monitoring destinations to anticipate such decline. They go on to suggest specific indicators and the relationship between them, and then formulate best practice for upgrading and rejuvenating a destination. They conclude by proposing a model with seven variables, which can be applied to the TALC phases from maturity onwards.

The second example used the TALC much more directly (Berry, 2001), and is based on identifying indicators (predictive and lagging) for the specific stages in the TALC model. This study is a part of a much more comprehensive analysis of the TALC (Berry, 2001), which involved a great deal of empirical primary and secondary time series data and the testing of over 50 criteria in the application of the model to Cairns, in Queensland. Berry uses the principal of 'leading' indicators to explore the potential future direction of development of the destination region, and 'lagged' indicators to confirm that a stage has occurred. An important part of Berry's argument is that the absence of a plan to deal with what was felt to be an anticipated decline in tourism in Cairns was a major problem and that utilising the TALC in a predictive way might have made alleviation of decline more practical. Using newspaper searches, existing statistics and a business questionnaire, Berry identifies 'criteria' or indicators of the stages of development of the destination. He also incorporates some of Cooper's (1990) threats to destinations, and Haywood's (1986) indicators of the stagnation stage. Berry then tests the existence of each stage and the appropriateness of the indicators identified. He found that over 80% of the indicators suggested in the original model were positive, with others partly so, and that those of Cooper and Haywood also had a high success rate. He concludes that it is possible to utilise the TALC in a predictive manner as well as a *post hoc* tool and that it could have considerable benefit to destination planners and managers. The amount of data required to use the model in this way may help explain why few, if any, researchers have undertaken such a comprehensive empirical application of the model, but Berry's results are confirmation of the suitability of the model to predict as well as to describe the pattern and process of destination development.

In the final chapter the TALC is reviewed by this author and through a personal assessment of the relevance of the TALC to tourism in the future. It proceeds by summarising what are felt to be the elements of the original model and their relevance to the development of tourist destinations in the 21st century. Perhaps not surprisingly the conclusion is that the TALC does have continued relevance, in part for many of the reasons discussed earlier in this volume and elsewhere. These include its ability as a predictive tool, its relationship with other models and theories of development and restructuring, its links to Chaos Theory and increasing turbulence in the world, and perhaps above all, the close relationship between TALC and the concept of sustainability. While sustainable development has been much more talked about than implemented, especially in mainstream tourist destinations, the basic principles such as a long-term viewpoint, the necessity of living with (capacity) limits and being proactive in resource management relate strongly to the arguments expressed in the original TALC model. The fact that an increasing number of destinations appear to be approaching the end of their growth and facing rather uncertain futures suggests that, unfortunately, the predictions of inevitable decline (in the absence of intervention) of the 1980 model and by Plog (1973) are likely to continue to become true in many locations.

This is particularly likely in those situations where local decision makers are reluctant to accept that exogenous changes may have made or are making their destinations uncompetitive. Those in charge of destinations need to look both backwards and forwards if they are to exert effective influence over the future of the destinations they control and realise the 'implications for management of resources', as noted in the title of the original TALC article a quarter of a century ago.

Chapter 14

How to Define, Identify and Monitor the Decline of Tourist Destinations: Towards an Early Warning System

MARA MANENTE and HARALD PECHLANER

Introduction

The recent trends towards globalization, which are presently characterizing the tourist market and the development of emerging tourist destinations both in and outside Europe, are at the basis of the need for traditional European destinations to effectively manage their product in order to keep a competitive position in the tourist market and prevent decline. This chapter summarizes the results of a study carried out for the European Commission aimed at analyzing the decline of tourist destinations with regard to the definition of an early warning system based on appropriate indicators that would allow the identification of tendencies of decline.

In case of definitions, the term 'declining destination' brings Butler's (1980) model of the Tourism Area Life Cycle (TALC) to one's mind. According to this model, the decline phase, subsequent to the stagnation phase where maximum capacity is likely to be reached, implies a decrease in the number of tourist arrivals to a certain destination.

Although, at an advanced stage, the decline of a tourist destination normally results in economic losses or failure, even those destinations which are still profitable might already be declining or may be under acute threat of decline. It would, therefore, be insufficient to define 'decline' merely by actual decreases in guest numbers and turnover. This is why in this study the authors propose a set of indicators in order to monitor the evolution of the destination according to the TALC phases, and redefine a declining destination as a 'destination with a certain tradition in providing tourism, but characterized by one or more negative trends'. These negative trends can be anticipated by a number of different signals before the destination reaches a decrease in demand.

For instance, signals of decline can be represented by:

- a decrease in the elements defining former quality of the destination;
- a decrease in the competitive success of the destination (market share);
- a difficulty in assuring sustainable tourism;
- a decrease in the average per capita tourist expenditure.

Effective planning and management of a destination imply the use of any available tool in order to detect early signals of decline and take preventive measures with the purpose of leading the destination itself to a rejuvenation phase. Of course, policies used may differ a lot depending on the nature of the factors which lie at the basis of the decline. Some of them, especially external factors, are not predictable, and therefore not controllable in advance. In such cases, an effective communication process can be very useful in order to refocus the image of the destination among current and potential visitors. In other cases, it is actually possible to identify trends likely leading to a decline. The purpose of the early warning system developed in this study is to strengthen the importance of the TALC approach by setting up a diagnostic system of the evolution of the destination, based on selected strategic variables. Furthermore, it allows the actors involved to measure such trends in a wide range of situations and enables them to undertake suitable actions.

In the first part, the chapter discusses all kinds of factors that may influence the decline of tourist destinations. On the one hand, these factors may be divided into external and internal factors; on the other hand, it must be considered that in urban destinations for instance, different basic conditions apply to those in coastal, thermal or mountain destinations. In the second part, the authors focus on the monitoring of destinations with regard to an early warning system. The main question is whether it is possible to inhibit a decline of tourist destinations by means of an early warning system. The third section discusses criteria for the selection of the indicators and presents sets of indicators based on the possible causes of decline as well as dynamic relations between the destination's environmental, social, and economic structures and incoming system. According to the case study approach, the fourth part formulates best practices for upgrading and revitalizing tourist destinations. A survey among practitioners in tourist destinations provides some indications about variables recognized by local managers as decline indicators. Finally, the last section proposes a first warning system prototype on the basis of a seven-variable model, to be applied to each TALC phase, starting from 'maturity'.

Factors and Conditions of Decline

Reasons for decline can vary depending on the different situations. Decline can be caused both by external factors, basically linked to changes in the global tourism market or exogenous variables, and internal factors, particular to the specific destination.

External factors

- causes beyond one's control (e.g. wars, epidemics, earthquakes, climate or political changes);
- upcoming of new competitors for one or more of the tourist products supplied by the destination;
- negative publicity;
- failure to communicate the destination's image.

Internal factors

- product obsolescence with respect to requirements of demand;
- physical deterioration of the environment/heritage;
- congestion; reaching/exceeding of carrying capacity threshold.

Tourist flows to Europe are not spread evenly. There are areas which are intensely exploited, with major sustainability problems, and areas where tourism development has not yet reached large numbers.

In the light of such considerations, we can identify certain typologies which are most likely to be in a situation of maturity or decline rather than others. These typologies are:

- urban destinations
- coastal destinations
- mountain destinations
- thermal destinations

In *urban* destinations, major factors of decline are linked to congestion, visitor and tourist mobility, deterioration of heritage sites, and the potentially conflicting relationship between visitors and residents. Competition plays a less crucial role in cities than in other types of destinations as far as cultural tourism is concerned (this is particularly true for cities endowed with an important cultural and architectural heritage, due to the uniqueness of each destination), while it can be an essential issue if we are to analyze other categories of tourists (i.e. conference and business tourism).

Coastal and *mountain* resorts may be affected by congestion and deterioration of the natural environment, as well as by worldwide competition, which puts these resorts in the position of having to compete not only with similar resorts, but with any kind of resorts (the strong reduction of packages and flight rates, and the low level of tourist prices in some emerging countries put the potential tourist in the condition to be able to choose between, for example, a week in the Austrian mountains and a week on a Thai beach).

A major issue which many coastal and mountain destinations must tackle is the redefinition of their supply in order to make it more appealing to the visitor, therefore providing him/her with a more complex tourist product which implies the combination of simple products and/or types of tourism (e.g. sea & sand + culture, or mountain + sport).

As far as *thermal* tourism is concerned, traditional resorts are affected by growing competition deriving from emerging countries (especially Eastern Europe). Besides, the image that most of these resorts convey is still an old-fashioned one, basically linked to the health aspect and mainly addressed to an aged segment. Many spa resorts are presently repositioning in the market with a strategy of product differentiation, which allows them to address a wider range of segments.

Indicators Grids

An early warning system needs a systematic selection of indicators. The number of indicators which can be collected to monitor the dynamics of a destination is potentially very large. For selecting a framework of manageable size, it is useful to assess potential indicators against several evaluation criteria.

Criteria for the selection of the indicators should be:

- The data to build the indicator are obtainable. In case the data are available but difficult to retrieve, the usefulness of the indicator must be assessed with reference to the resources (in terms of both time and money) needed to build it.
- They are credible and easy to understand. Their goal must be to provide credible information to tourism managers who have varying perspectives, priorities, and knowledge. It is therefore preferable to ensure that chosen indicators are easily understood by the audience.
- Their significance in order to express the decline process of a mature tourist destination together with the conditions which allow the decline.
- The effectiveness in achieving awareness of decline risks and, therefore, the possibility of defining an early warning system.
- The temporality, i.e. the ability to detect destination trends over time.

- The comparability of the indicators in order to spread experiences throughout a large number of destinations.
- The possibility of summarizing different indicators with a few integrated, easily understandable, composed indicators and of communicating results by means of graphical tools (e.g. spider plots).

The sets of indicators proposed for the analysis are the following.

First set of indicators: State of the art

These indicators are meant to identify possible causes of decline and describe the 'state of the art' with regard to the examined destination.

S1.1. Destination functions

A first portrait of the destination is defined by means of tourist functions showing the main dimensions of the destination and allowing an easy comparison between different destinations (e.g. destination size, excursionist share, economic role of tourism, etc.).

S1.2. Tourism consciousness of the destination from the demand side and its evolution

The destination is evaluated in depth from the demand side by means of indicators related to life cycle, visitor flows, types of visitors, motivations, consumption behavior and its evolution. This is a funda-mental step to identify declining trends and possible factors of decline (e.g. destination life cycle, tourism demand, market share).

S1.3. Tourism consciousness of the destination from the supply side and its evolution

The destination is analyzed from the supply side. The related indicators describe local conditions of the tourist market and local responses to tourist demand (e.g. tourist attractions, tourist accommodation, restaurants).

S1.4. Tourism consciousness of the destination and its evolution according to indicators of the whole tourism system

Tourism and its development are analyzed with reference to the destination's whole economic environment (e.g. role of tourism on local economy, degree of co-operation).

S1.5. Quality of life

Quality of life in the considered destination is a joint product of citizen and visitor contribution together with public and private institutions' managing system (e.g. population growth rate, per capita revenue, consumer prices).

S1.6. Tourists' quality of experience

Tourists' quality of experience, even if depending on the selected tourist segment, is based on the destination's system as a whole (tourist resources and supply, urban, economic and cultural environments) and is related to general quality of life indicators (e.g. tourist prices).

Second set of indicators: Towards a dynamic analysis

These indicators describe the interactions between the destination's environmental, social and economic structures and incoming tourism. They also show the positive actions and rules adopted by the local community when facing decline.

S2.1. Quality of socioeconomic development

This section presents the characteristics of the destination, such as the structure and evolution of the local economy, consumer price dynamics, and planning process (e.g. consumer price dynamics, employment).

S2.2. Quality of tourism supply development

These indicators describe the destination supply from a resource-based approach (e.g. quality and size of commercial accommodation, degree of specialization).

S2.3. Tourism impacts

Tourism impacts on the local economy are presented. Many of the indicators are related to the first set of indicators (i.e. tourism conscious-ness of the destination from the demand side and its evolution, quality of life).

Early Warning in Practice

The use of case studies is an important way to produce and compile information on the phenomenon of declining tourist destinations and to examine, analyze, and outline best practice for upgrading and revitaliz-ing tourist destinations in decline or threatened by it.

A survey among practitioners in tourist destinations gives some indications about variables recognized by local managers as decline indicators. Ten destinations have been selected for the investigation: Gran Canaria (SP), Naples (I), Torremolinos (SP), Scheveningen (NL), Brighton (UK), Cornwall (UK), Biarritz (F), Achensee (A), Otzal (A), and Baden-Baden (D). For the selection the following four criteria have been used. (1) Signals of decline. Each destination should present at least one of these signals: decrease in tourist flows; decrease in the elements defining former quality of the destination (e.g. image, tourist expendi-ture, etc.); decrease in the competitive success (market share); difficulty in assuring sustainable tourism. (2) Situation regarding decline. Three major classes have been considered: (a) destinations which are presently in a decline phase; (b) destinations which have recovered from a decline phase; (c) destinations which are threatened by decline and need to prevent it. (3) Type of destination. The selected destinations should represent the following categories: urban, coastal, mountain, thermal. (4) Geographical balance among all the EEA countries. The ten selected destinations are located in eight European countries, characterized by stronger tourism tradition and larger amount of tourist flows within Europe, thus representing the whole area adequately. For methodological details concerning the selection criteria see: TNO-CISET (2001), DE-TOUR: An early warning system identifying declining tourist destinations, Final Report.

Figure 14.1 summarizes these decline signals. Some results can be drawn from this chart:

- Most destination managers are aware of the risk of decline: they perceive the threat but they have difficulties in effectively measuring it.
- They base their analysis mainly on visitor flow trends (31% category A), i.e. the most direct decline indicators.
- They also stress mainly the strategic role of inner factors (53% categories B plus C), but they miss a really integrated use of the indicators.
- Exogenous factors are viewed as less direct decline risk indicators as they cannot be controlled by the managers and sometimes are unpredictable (MFD, terrorism); however, market analysis on

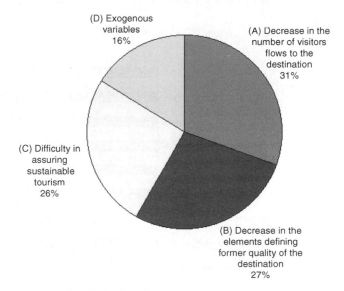

Figure 14.1 Signals of decline by macrocategory

competitors (which means destination positioning and market policies) is considered important.

Figure 14.2 shows the decrease in the number of visitor flows of the destination, which is the most represented category and a very direct signal of decline.

However, this could be the consequence of a decrease in the elements defining the former quality of the destination – mainly represented by varying composition of visitors flows, decrease in the quality of the tourists coming to the destination, decrease in the quality of the tourist product – or of difficulty in assuring sustainable tourism – mainly expressed by a physical indicator e.g. congestion, damage to the environment/heritage, traffic, etc., and by a lack of adequate infrastructures and supply. The need to invest in human resources is also an important signal and occupies 10th place. Exogenous factors are represented by the threat from competitors, the only variable, in fact, on which a destination can operate by means of targeted marketing actions.

There seems to be coherence between major signals of decline and indicators used by destination managers. In fact, the most voted indicators correspond to category A of signals of decline (tourist arrivals, nights, length of stay, seasonality); some of them are related to category B (expenditure, type of accommodation, visitor characteristics, visitor satisfaction), some others to category C (investment in tourist attractions) (Figure 14.3). Analysis of competitors, corresponding to signal category D, is in 11th position.

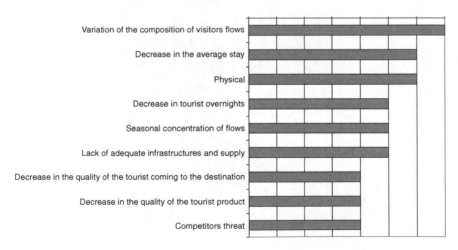

Figure 14.2 Top nine signals of decline

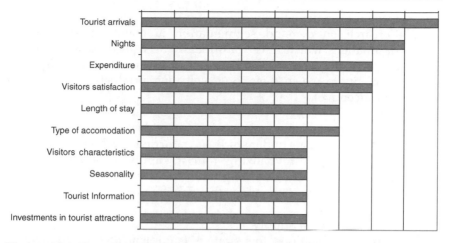

Figure 14.3 Top ten indicators currently monitored

Figure 14.4 describes the strategies by the four macrocategories within which the main strategic options implemented by most destinations have been summarized:

A. Demand
  • Regular surveys on tourism
    Surveys are carried out in most destinations, either on a regular basis or occasionally. As for the other destinations, data are often available on a broader geographical basis (regional or provincial). The surveys are mostly focused on the collection of information on tourists' characteristics and in some cases about tourists' expenditure, while excursionists are often neglected.

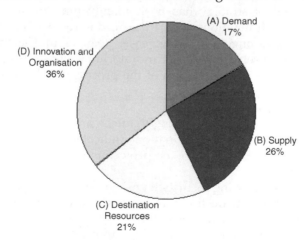

Figure 14.4 Strategies to face decline by macrocategories

- Demand segmentation
  Research on demand segmentation is mainly carried out in destinations which have traditionally been focused on a specific segment (e.g. sun & sand) and feel the need to identify new segments to which they could sell their products (e.g. congress and incentive).

B. Supply
  - Development of new or renewed attractions
    Many destinations under study have carried out this strategy, with the purpose of revitalizing tourist supply. Examples of new attractions are the building of a new conference center, the creation of new itineraries, the development of new packages and programs.
  - Increased tourist supply
    In some destinations, this strategy is implemented by an increase in tourist accommodation (in general or, more often, in a specific category and/or price range). In some other cases, this strategy translates itself into a general increase in tourist services.
  - Creation of special events
    This is a strategy often carried out by destinations in order to increase their appeal to different segments of visitors.
  - Quality certification and standardization processes
    The recent focus on quality has positively influenced the tourism industry. In some destinations, quality plans have been carried out with the objective of setting up a quality assurance system for services addressed to tourists.

C. Destination resources
  - Destination layout (e.g. master plans)
    This kind of strategy has been mainly implemented in highly congested destinations, where the need to regulate the destination layout is stronger. In some cases (e.g. Gran Canaria), it has translated itself in a tourist moratorium, whose objective is the strict control and regulation of the process of urbanization of the coastline.
  - Environmental protection
    Environmental issues strongly affect any kind of destination. Nevertheless, not all destinations indicated that they have taken appropriate measures for the protection of the environment.
  - Security
    Strategies regarding security have been successfully implemented, mainly in urban destinations with a negative image concerning crime (e.g. Naples and Brighton).
  - Residents' awareness of the role of tourists
    Residents play a crucial role in the whole tourist experience.

Therefore, programs focused on residents' awareness of the role of tourism have been developed in several destinations.

- Investments in public transport
  Accessibility and mobility are crucial for a tourist destination. Nevertheless, only a minority of destinations have indicated that they have taken actions on this note.

D. Innovation and organization

- Human resources training
  The training of human resources is essential to the improvement of services addressed to tourists. It is mentioned by a minority of destinations, especially the ones which are implementing tourist plans (in which human resources training plays a crucial role).
- Co-operation between different actors (public/public, private/public)
  The creation of partnerships between different categories of actors is very important for the success of a destination. All the destinations under investigation state that a certain degree of co-operation exists among stakeholders.
- Partnerships with other destinations
  Some destinations mention the possibility to create synergies with other destinations by the creation of special itineraries and packages and/or joint promotional actions.
- Destination promotion (information campaigns, communication policies, etc.)
  This kind of strategy is probably the most obvious in order to face potential or actual decline, therefore it is very common also among the destinations. Basically, all of them carry out promoting actions to current targets or potential ones.
- Clustering of functions
  This strategy, especially mentioned by Scheveningen, translates into a spatial clustering of functions to achieve agglomeration effects.
- Investments in new technologies
  Most destinations have introduced new technologies for the management of services addressed to visitors. This is a necessary measure for the modernization of the tourist supply and the improvement in service delivery.

The main conclusions from this section are:

- Innovation and organization strategies are dominant, and represent 36% of total strategies mentioned by local stakeholders.
- Some factors are considered strategic but are not sufficiently monitored (e.g. environment).

- Other factors are considered important but their importance is still underestimated (e.g. human resources training).
- Many of the approaches are detailed in some aspects but are lacking some strategic variables.
- A holistic vision and an integrated reading of data are often missing, because unique-dimension approaches are preferred.

The strategies can be ranked in a TOP 9 list on the basis of the feedback of stakeholders (Figure 14.5).

Major efforts seem to be developed in new soft measures such as destination promotion, creation of special events, regular surveys on tourism, tourist product differentiation; then in reorganizing the tourist system by means of co-operation between different stakeholders and investments in new technologies; finally some actions regarding the destination's physical structure such as new or renewed attractions, increased tourist supply and destination layout (Figure 14.5).

Tools for Visualizing Threats of Decline: Prototype of an Early Warning System

Within the study carried out for the EU, a first warning system prototype has been proposed by means of Interactive Destination Evaluation System (IDES), a holistic diagnostic system which can be used to simulate different scenarios.

From a set of selected indicators, a dynamic and user-friendly decision-making tool can be built which summarizes the following three functions:

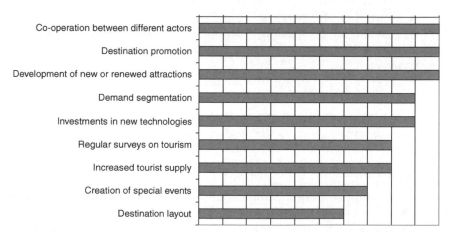

Figure 14.5 Top nine strategies to face decline

(1) giving destination managers strategic information about the current situation and risk of decline that can easily be interpreted;

(2) showing in a really effective way (by means of a series of snapshots) the evolution of the destination over time; and

(3) simulating by means of images (created with a simple interface) the effect of changes in variables.

IDES is therefore a Virtual Warning Machine which, once strategic variables have been selected (in this example, a seven-variable model is proposed) and appropriate decline thresholds have been adopted, helps to anticipate decline and gives an input for the implementation of practical measures to face it (Figure 14.6).

A threshold value, in fact, is a theoretical maximum value that must not be exceeded. The identification of a threshold is necessary in order to provide a benchmark against which the overall trend for a given variable can be assessed.

In the image above, proposed as an example, it is immediately clear that variables V6 and V7 exceeded their threshold and need therefore appropriate corrections, while variable V2 is risky (it is just on the border) and variable V3 must be kept under observation.

IDES is an internal and external benchmarking tool as it allows monitoring specific destination dynamics over time as well as a horizontal comparison between different destinations. (For more details on the seven-variable model and on thresholds estimation see: TNO-CISET (2001), DETOUR: An early warning system identifying declining tourist destinations, Final Report.)

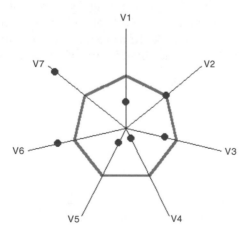

Figure 14.6 Interactive destination evaluation system (IDES)

This next section presents an example of the application of the IDES warning system to a hypothetical tourist destination (Utopia) monitored in the last periods of its life cycle: maturity, decline, and rejuvenation.

The following life cycle is assumed for Utopia: introduction (P1), development (P2), maturity (P3), decline (P4), and rejuvenation (P5) (Figure 14.7).

Five variables have been identified as adequate in order to achieve a successful implementation of IDES:

A. tourists/residents
B. excursionist share
C. economic role of tourism
D. Gini seasonality index
E. Gini demand structure index
    Two other variables have been added to this list in order to acquire more comprehensive insight into the destination:
F. Lack of co-operation. This variable can be expressed by the formula '1 degree of co-operation', where 'degree of co-operation' is measured by the percentage of operators and organizations involved in partnerships on total.
G. Environmental impact. This variable represents the physical pressure that affects the destination as a consequence of tourism, and can be expressed most easily by means of use intensity indicators (i.e. number of visitors/surface). Other indicators which could prove useful to express environmental impact, but with less availability of data, are represented by waste levels, water consumption and air pollution.

Due to its dynamic nature, IDES needs systematic data as an input in order to represent an effective warning system. The seven variables chosen for its implementation have been selected on the basis of their effectiveness (i.e. the amount of information they provide with reference to the destination) and the likelihood of finding systematic data

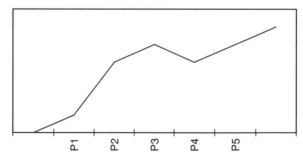

Figure 14.7 Utopia's lifestyle

necessary to build them. In order to build the IDES graph, a threshold for each of the variables considered must be established; if reached or exceeded, such values provide a warning of a potential decline. In our example, hypothetical threshold values for each of the seven variables have been identified.

The three pictures that follow show the dynamics of Utopia over time from maturity (P3) to decline (P4) and rejuvenation (P5). A joint analysis of these graphs and the TALC curve allows the evolution of the destination to be monitored effectively.

Particularly, the IDES graph referring to period P3 (Figure 14.8) shows a situation of maturity in which main issues are represented by seasonality and tourists/residents ratio, while the other variables are still within an acceptable range. P4 identifies a situation of decline (Figure 14.9), as the majority of the variables register a value which goes beyond the fixed thresholds. Nevertheless, the variables which claim for immediate action are linked to environmental and seasonality issues, as well as to strong excursionist pressure.

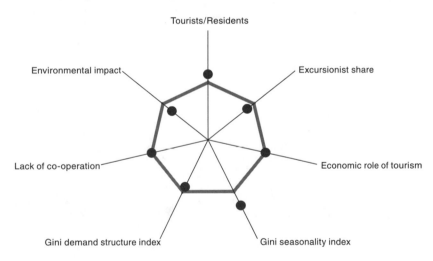

code	indicator	value	threshold	value/threshold
A	Tourists/Residents	17,14	15,00	1,14
B	Excursionist share	0,30	0,35	0,86
C	Economic role of tourism	0,25	0,25	1,00
D	Gini seasonality index	0,19	0,15	1,27
E	Gini demand structure index	0,32	0,35	0,91
F	Lack of co-operation	0,50	0,50	1,00
G	Environmental impact	2,40	3,00	0,80

Figure 14.8 IDES applied to Utopia (period 3)

The graph referring to period P5 (Figure 14.10), on the other hand, shows that most variables have returned within an acceptable range (implying that strategies and measures have been implemented in the destination), even if it is evident that the tourist/resident ratio must be carefully monitored, and that the destination is still too dependent on tourism (the economic role of tourism is now the only variable whose value exceeds the fixed threshold).

Even if only theoretically, this example clearly shows that a warning system prototype can be built on the basis of simple data, although data must be collected on a regular basis.

Conclusions

Monitoring decline or tendency towards decline in a tourist destination is a complex exercise which requires a strong interaction between theoretical and quantitative approaches, leading to user-friendly decision-making tools. This study stresses the importance of the TALC

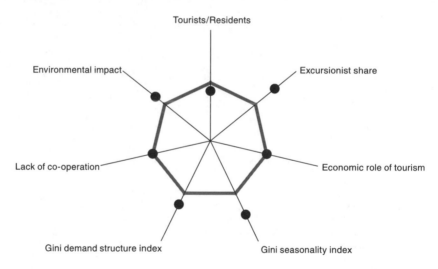

code	indicator	value	threshold	value/ threshold
A	Tourists/Residents	12,86	15,00	0,86
B	Excursionist share	0,50	0,35	1,43
C	Economic role of tourism	0,25	0,25	1,00
D	Gini seasonality index	0,21	0,15	1,40
E	Gini demand structure index	0,42	0,35	1,21
F	Lack of co-operation	0,50	0,50	1,00
G	Environmental impact	3,60	3,00	1,20

Figure 14.9 IDES applied to Utopia (period 4)

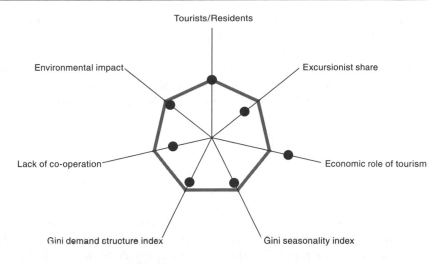

code	indicator	value	threshold	value/threshold
A	Tourists/Residents	15,00	15,00	1,00
B	Excursionist share	0,25	0,35	0,71
C	Economic role of tourism	0,33	0,25	1,33
D	Gini seasonality index	0,13	0,15	0,87
E	Gini demand structure index	0,30	0,35	0,85
F	Lack of co-operation	0,33	0,50	0,67
G	Environmental impact	2,70	3,00	0,90

Figure 14.10 IDES applied to Utopia (period 5)

approach as the basis to develop a warning system prototype of decline, which can be built from a set of selected indicators representing the strategic variables for the destination. The proposed prototype is a tool able to show in a really effective way the evolution of the destination over time and then to visualize threats of decline. Furthermore, it can help destination managers to anticipate decline and give an input for the implementation of practical measures to face it.

The compared analysis of the 10 selected destinations indicates that 'decline' is still a 'fuzzy' concept, one that some destination managers and stakeholders do not completely understand. It is perceived to be more likely a theoretical concept than a threat and, even where perceived, no real warning system is in use. Even if limited in number and very different in size and structure (e.g. from a city like Naples, to a mountain region like Achensee, to a beach resort like Scheveningen, which is a district of The Hague), the case studies give a good overview of different kinds of destinations, and as a consequence, of the different roles that the destination managers play.

In detail, other important considerations emerge from the study, which confirm the relevance and topicality of the subject discussed here as well as the need to develop adequate tools for decision makers based on reliable theoretical guidelines and credible, systematic and effective data:

- Decline is basically perceived through 'manifested' and/or easily measurable phenomena. The decrease in the number of tourist flows (arrivals, nights, average length of stay, etc.) is the most evident signal – 4 out of the top 10 signals focus on the evolution of tourist demand – followed by the negative environmental impacts.
- There seems to be coherence between major signals of decline and indicators used by destination managers. In fact, the most voted indicators correspond to the major category A of signals of decline (tourist arrivals, nights, length of stay, seasonality).
- Many other variables regarding the tourism consciousness from the demand and supply side (e.g. excursionist flows, role of tourist activities, etc.) and the social and economic impacts of tourism (e.g. residents' quality of life, site stress, crowding out effects, etc.) as well as the quality of supply development (resource-based approach) are not monitored at all. The authors intend to stress the importance of such indicators, which are essential to the full understanding of the trend of a destination, and therefore recommend that they are collected on a regular basis.
- Furthermore, in fact, among the indicators used, some of them are not monitored constantly over time but derive from an occasional analysis (e.g. a specific survey).
- A range of strategies are available to destination managers in order to face potential decline. In theory, a variety of models exist which provide possible strategic options in different environments and situations. Most of these models originate from general marketing theories and are adapted to destinations, thus treating a tourist destination as a product (as with the TALC approach). Nevertheless, the practice of destination management does not always fit into such theoretical models. More often than not, strategies implemented in practice do not originate from a thorough analysis of the destination's situation, as they should. This is due to many factors, such as the lack of a vision and/or mission for a specific destination, the lack of regular data collection and so on.
- Not all destination managers show a clear vision of what has to be done to face or prevent decline. While in some cases there is a coherence between signals perceived and strategies implemented, in

other cases the actions do not seem supported by real under-standing of problems and causes, but by an undefined generic feeling that 'something has to be done'.

- In spite of that, there is growing awareness that 'soft' measures may be more effective than 'hard' ones. The reorganization of the tourism system as a whole, through the development of co-operation networks between all stakeholders involved (also using new technologies), is regarded as one of the most important strategies to overcome decline and gain competitiveness in the market.
- In most cases, the implementation of strategies and practical measures starts from the public sector, which is in the best position to ask for and administer funds from the state or other institutions. However, there are a few cases which show the willingness on the part of private operators and/or associations to finance some of those actions necessary in order to prevent or face decline.
- The lack of a systematic monitoring system makes it difficult to conduct a feedback analysis which can provide the measure of the effectiveness of the strategies implemented.

Acknowledgements

The research has been co-ordinated by Mara Manente and carried out by the CISET staff: Dr Laura Andreatta, Dr Emilio Celotto, and Dr Valeria Minghetti. Collaborators of the study included Mag. Günther Lehar from the 'Institut für Verkehr und Tourismus' and Prof. Klaus Weiermair from the University of Innsbruck.

Chapter 15
The Predictive Potential of the TALC Model

TED BERRY

In this chapter, data from the Cairns region, Australia, are analysed to demonstrate to what degree the TALC model can be used to identify indicators of stage development and how these can be used to suggest future trends. The study area is located in the wet tropics on the North East coast of the island continent. Natural attractions include the Great Barrier Reef, pristine tropical rainforest and a high, scenic, tableland rising from the narrow coastal plain. The purpose of this chapter is to emphasise the value of the model to government and business and how it can be used to avoid the negative aspects of regional economic decline. Examples of negative factors referred to include bankruptcy, unemployment and associated problems such as loss of family home, family break-up and all that follows.

This chapter also addresses what is seen as the serious under-utilisation of the TALC model in government and business (a point also discussed by Haywood, other volume, editor's comment). Correctly used, the model can provide a timely warning of possible deterioration in a region's tourism industry as well as suggest corrective strategies. The model does not suggest a predetermined cycle for all tourism-based economies such that 'stagnation' and 'decline' are unavoidable. However, it does suggest that without appropriate intervention from responsible policy makers, it is highly likely that some tourism regions will behave as the model suggests. On the other hand, not all intervention is appropriate, as we will see later on in this chapter; some forms of intervention, while appearing on the surface to be helpful, are merely normal symptoms of advancement along the TALC curve. To be aware of the difference between action by local authorities which is an economic stimulus, and that which is just part of the normal cycle, one must be aware of how the model works.

The predictive nature of the TALC model, explored in detail below, comes from 'leading' indicators that provide an idea of the general direction in which an economy is heading if nothing else changes. A common example of a leading indicator is the level of housing starts, often used by manufacturers and sellers of household goods to give advanced knowledge of possible future sales volumes for their products.

An underlying assumption is that houses are completed and sold to people with sufficient funds to buy household goods for their new homes. An economic downturn could change the whole picture. In contrast to leading indicators, 'lagged' indicators can be used to confirm that a TALC stage has actually occurred. In this chapter, indicators are not discussed until after Butler's 'involvement' stage when they have more relevance to recent events in the study region.

The research on which this chapter is based found that by 1998, the end of the study period, the Cairns region was about to enter the 'decline' stage (Berry, 2001). The study also found that indicators of 'stagnation' and 'decline' had been present for up to at least eight years prior to the end of the study period. Further, there was no indication of any policy on the horizon that would result in the region breaking out of the TALC cycle and avoiding inevitable 'decline'. Had a TALC model been in place and heeded, much of the hardship experienced by many businesses and individuals could have been avoided.

Application of the TALC Model to a Resort Region

First, the basic cubic TALC curve must be constructed. In many cases the curve will not be S-shaped because the region may be in the early stages of the cycle. In the case of Cairns the analysis starts with historical information relating back to the late 1880s, but data used to construct the TALC curve does not start until time-series data became available in 1977. Although Butler (1980) used visitor numbers as the basis for the TALC curve, it was decided to use accommodation takings for this study because of the direct relationship between the latter and regional economic activity. The data set was then adjusted for inflation using the Consumer Price Index (CPI) (Australian Bureau of Statistics (ABS), Cat. No. 6401.0, Table 15.1B). To find out if the data were cubic, a third order polynomial (cubic regression) was fitted using the Software Package for the Social Sciences (SPSS), giving an R^2 value of 0.918, shown by the dotted line in Figure 15.1. A slightly better fit of $R^2 = 0.9225$ was then obtained using a fifth order polynomial in Microsoft Excel. The latter is shown by the solid line in the figure. The formula used was:

$$y = 0.00005645x^5 - 0.01455x^4 + 1.2215x^3 - 35.254x^2 + 404.94x + 302.34 \quad (1)$$

The figure shows that accommodation takings peaked in 1997 and the 'decline' stage was imminent at the end of the study period in December 1998 although two or three more years of decline would be necessary to confirm the change of direction in the longer term. In the case of study regions found to be in the early stages of the TALC then various regression models may need to be used to try to get a good fit. Choice of data is surprisingly flexible. Basically, any data can be used which reflects

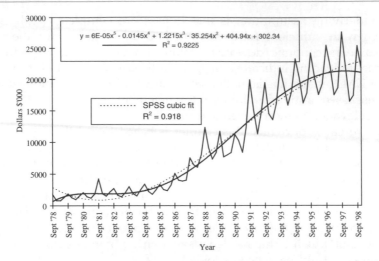

Figure 15.1 Inflation adjusted accommodation takings quarterly, ($'000)
1978–1989. Cairns region (base year 1978)
Source: Based upon data in ABS, Cat. No. 8635.3.40.001

tourism growth in the region. Examples include visitor numbers, arrivals
and departures, visitor spending, visitor nights and even the number of
tourism-related businesses. The Cairns study revealed that all of the
preceding data sets produced a cubic curve. The choice of data therefore
depends on what is available and suitable.

Stage Identification

For forecasting purposes, the TALC curve is incomplete without
establishing the timing of Butler's (1980) stages. It is the various
characteristics of the stages, referred to here as 'criteria', that are the
actual indicators. In the study region, criteria identification was
performed using data obtained from a local newspaper search, a business
questionnaire and published statistics. The newspaper search included
letters to the editor and articles, and the questionnaire was sent to
organisations which were members of the region's tourism industry
promotion body, Tourism Tropical North Queensland (TTNQ). It was
assumed that membership of TTNQ implied an interest in the tourism
industry. The questionnaire covered the period 1978–1998 and for each
time-series question, respondents were asked to draw a line on an empty
graph without reference to historical records. The aim was to obtain
respondents' perceptions of what happened. Results were unexpectedly
uniform. Responses containing conflicts between cross-questions were
discarded. The methods used to identify criteria could be applied to
almost any resort region.

The only addition to Butler's (1980) original criteria in the Cairns study was the use of some of Cooper's (1990: 63) 'threats' to the survival of coldwater resort regions and Haywood's (1986: 161) list of 'stagnation' stage leading indicators. Some examples of Cooper's 'threats' include the effect of political interference on decision making, diminishing domestic market share, poor access to the resort region and local government area amalgamation. Some examples of Haywood's stagnation stage leading indicators include a declining proportion of first-time visitors, declining profits of the major tourist businesses, the appearance of new and accessible destinations and a decline in advertising elasticity. Based on the extra reinforcement given to Butler's model in the case of the Cairns study, it is strongly recommended that both these authors' suggestions be incorporated into any serious use of the TALC model. The next few pages are largely descriptive and are intended to provide the reader with examples of criteria identification methodology.

Testing Criteria for the 'Exploration' Stage (1889–1912)

The 'exploration' stage is characterised by the presence of a few adventurous tourists who are attracted to the area because of its unique and different natural and cultural attractions (Butler, 1980: 7). There are little or no specific tourist facilities and contact between visitors and locals is high compared to the latter stages of TALC.

In the case of the Cairns region a number of historical records indicate the presence of a small number of tourist attractions between 1889 and 1912. These include Kuranda in the Atherton Tablelands and Green Island on the Great Barrier Reef. The year 1889 was selected as the start of the stage because that was the year that the rail link between Cairns and Kuranda was completed and evidence of tourism commenced. Whatever the region under study, evidence of tourism must commence at some time, even if it is not very significant. 1912 was selected as the end of the stage because of involvement by local people in the provision of transport and accommodation services. Table 15.1 lists three key 'exploration' stage criteria in the study region.

Table 15.1 Summary of Cairns region's compliance with Butler's (1980) 'exploration' stage criteria (1889–1912)

Butler's (1980) criteria	Compliance (yes/no)
Few, adventurous tourists	Yes
No specific tourist facilities	Yes
Contact between locals and visitors is high	Assume yes

Testing for the 'Involvement' Stage (1912–1984)

During the 'involvement' stage there is an increase in visitor numbers and local involvement in the provision of services for them. Contact between visitors and locals is still high and there will be some advertising to attract tourists. A market area can be identified. A tourist season develops and there will be some organisation in the travel arrangements made for tourists. Pressure will come to bear on governments to provide tourist facilities such as airports, roads and harbours (Butler, 1980: 7, 8).

Regardless of the resort region being studied, the object is to find and examine evidence with which to test the various criteria. In the case of the Cairns region, of eight criteria tested, all were positive. 1912 marked the beginning of this stage because transport was available in the Cairns region for people wishing to visit local beauty spots and there was some regional advertising. The one-day rail trip from Cairns to Kuranda and return was becoming popular and a number of tourist attractions were developed in and around Kuranda. From 1921 a local bus company offered passenger transport to places that the railway did not reach.

During the late 1920s and 1930s, the weekly arrival of passenger ships from the southern capital cities meant that the local tour bus company had a steady supply of tourists. Each ship carried up to 200 passengers, but actual visitor numbers are not known (Lander, 1937: 7; Pelgrave, 1994: 21–28). Visitor numbers more than likely increased during this period.

In the 1920s and 1930s the Great Barrier Reef was accessible to tourists via a number of local marine operators and return rail tickets were sold from Brisbane to Cairns indicating some organisation of travel arrangements (Qld. Govt. Tourist Bureau, 1939: 36). Advertising to attract tourists was first apparent as early as 1912 with the publication of a 70-page pictorial handbook on the region by Queensland (Government) Railways. The booklet also published timetables so that tourists could get around the region after arrival. Services were advertised to places as far inland as the outback towns of Irvinebank, Mount Garnet and Forsyth. A number of other tourism-related services, such as hotels, were also advertised in the same publication.

Regional advertising became institutionalised in the 1930s with the formation of a district promotion body, TTNQ's predecessor, for the specific purpose of promoting tourism in the region. By 1949, a tourist season was firmly established in the region. During the winter months, southern tourists would come north to escape the cold. This pattern was officially confirmed when the Australian Bureau of Statistics (ABS) commenced compiling statistics on accommodation takings in 1977 and 1978.

Evidence that there was pressure on government to provide tourism infrastructure was apparent from the 1970s, particularly in relation to the provision of an international airport at Cairns. Eventually, after numerous unsuccessful attempts to obtain federal and state funding, the Cairns Harbour Board took over the existing airport and built a new one adjacent to the old site (*Cairns Post*, 6 May 1981: 9). The new International Airport was completed in 1984 and non-stop flights to the USA commenced that year and to Japan two years later (*Cairns Post*, 7 April, 1986). The opening of the airport signalled the change to Butler's 'development' stage by encouraging a new wave of tourism infrastructure development, mostly financed with capital from outside the region. Table 15.2 contains a summary of the study region's compliance with Butler's (1980) 'involvement' stage criteria.

In any tourism region, the demarcation between the 'exploration' and 'involvement' stages depends on the criteria that are present. In terms of the usefulness of the model for forecasting purposes, this particular demarcation line is not very crucial. The region is still in its very early stages of tourism growth and a possible deterioration in an industry which has barely commenced to exist will not have much effect on the economic welfare of the region. However, the demarcation between the 'involvement' and the 'development' stages is slightly more important than the previous demarcation date because it sets the stage for rapid tourism-related development. Usually, it can be traced to one or more events which have the effect of attracting tourism investment to a region. In the case of the study region, that event was the opening of the international airport in 1984 which dramatically improved access to the region from markets such as Asia, Europe and the USA.

Testing for the 'Development' Stage (1984–1991)

This stage is characterised by a well defined tourist market area which is partly the result of heavy advertising. At the same time natural and cultural attractions will be marketed specifically and supplemented with human-made attractions. Local involvement and control of development will decline rapidly and locally owned facilities (particularly accommodation) will give way to large-scale facilities provided by external investors. Butler (1980) also noted that during the 'development' stage changes in the physical appearance of the region will be noticeable and sometimes these changes will not be welcome. Regional and national involvement in planning and provision of facilities will occur, and again, this will not necessarily be welcomed by the local residents. The number of visitors will exceed locals in peak periods and imported labour will be used. Auxiliary industries, such as laundries, will start to appear and the type of visitor will change towards Plog's (1991: 64) 'mid-centric'. Most

Table 15.2 Summary of Cairns region's compliance with Butler's (1980) 'involvement' stage criteria (1912–1984)

	Butler's (1980) criteria	*Compliance (yes/no)*	*If 'yes', when?*
1	Visitor numbers increase and start to assume regularity	Yes	From early 1920s
2	Limited involvement in tourism by locals	Yes	From early 1920s
3	Contact between visitors and locals is high	Assume 'yes'	During this stage
4	Some advertising of services to attract tourists	Yes	From 1912
5	Initial market area for visitors can be defined	Yes	From 1912
6	Pattern of seasonal visitation starts to appear	Yes	From 1920s
7	Organisation of tourist travel arrangements	Yes	From 1912
8	Pressure on government to provide tourism infrastructure e.g. transport and local amenities	Yes	Particularly in the early 1980s (e.g. airport)

importantly, at this point we are interested not only in 'development' stage criteria, but also any criteria from a higher stage which may be present. The existence of such criteria is an important leading indicator of different stages and is what gives the model its forecasting ability.

Before 1984, the main market area of the Cairns region was metropolitan Australia. After 1984, charter flights from the USA generated sufficient demand to warrant the introduction of regular direct services. For that year, the regional promotion organisation, TTNQ, almost tripled expenditure before dropping back again the following year. By 1991, the end of the 'development' stage, Japan had become the major international market. Japanese companies, led by Daikyo, had invested heavily in tourism-related infrastructure in the study area, and along with TTNQ and some of the other major tourism operators, commenced extensive advertising campaigns in that country.

Natural and cultural attractions marketed included the Great Barrier Reef, tropical rainforest, wildlife and Aboriginal culture. However, as predicted by the TALC model, human-made facilities supplement some natural attractions (Butler, 1980: 8). Examples of such facilities included additional floating facilities and boats for reef viewing; retreats, markets, tours to, through and over, the rainforest; wildlife theme parks and the Tjapukai Aboriginal cultural experience. Most of these facilities were introduced during this stage, but there was some overlap into the 'consolidation' and 'stagnation' stages.

Indicators of external involvement and control considered in this study included the place of residence of the owners of the businesses, the region from which the management was hired, and the city and country where the tourism bookings originated. The latter is particularly important, because tour organisers and travel agents have the power to redirect business elsewhere should the area be perceived as being out of fashion or not as desirable as alternative destinations.

Regardless of the region, the main point here is to verify that the event used as a starting point for the 'development' stage did actually stimulate rapid growth and development. In the study region, major tourism-related project starts and announcements peaked around 1986, two years after the new International Airport was opened. A period of rapid growth in the number of bed spaces available in the region occurred about two years after that (see Figure 15.2). The peak in development activity and the number of bed spaces are both lagged economic indicators. Their timing confirms that the opening of the

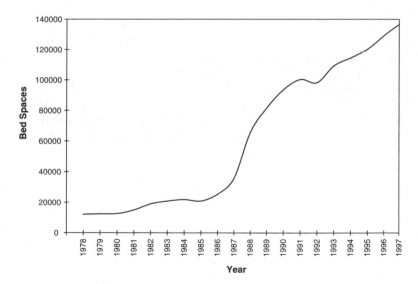

Figure 15.2 Annual number of available bed spaces in Cairns, Douglas, Mareeba and Atherton LGAs
Source: Calculated from ABS Cat. No. 8635.3.40.001

airport was the catalyst for the rapid tourism infrastructure development, much of it financed from overseas.

The business survey identified a clear long-term decline in the
percentage of locally owned businesses and a long-term increase in the
percentage of outside ownership. The survey also identified changes in
the sources of management that were similar to the ownership trends.
The proportion of locally sourced managers declined significantly over
the whole of the 'development' stage (1984– 1991). Meanwhile, the
proportion of bookings originating overseas showed a steady increase
starting in 1986, two years after the international airport was opened,
through the 'consolidation' (1991– 1993) and 'stagnation' (from 1993)
stages until 1998. Bookings arising from interstate agents moved in the
opposite direction to overseas bookings indicating that in percentage
terms, one gained at the expense of the other.

In all, eight 'development' stage criteria tested positive during that
stage (see Table 15.3). However, of significance are the early appearance
of two 'consolidation' stage criteria, local opposition and discontentment
about tourism and tourism facilities, and the appearance of a recreational
business district (RBD) in place of the former central business district
(CBD). Both are leading indicators. The former became apparent with the
appearance of a society called 'Australian Citizens Against Foreign
Ownership' in February 1989. In addition, during a '60 Minutes Open
Forum' national TV show recorded in Cairns at the time, fears were
expressed which included a Japanese desire to colonise Australia and the
need for Australians to take a stand and decide their own future. The
inflationary effect of the tourism industry on the affordability of land and
houses for the locals was also discussed, an argument not new to the
region's populace (*Cairns Post*, 7 May 1987: 1).

The appearance of a RBD in place of the former CBD was first
reported in The *Cairn Post* of 13 April 1989, although, as would be
expected, the term 'RBD' was not used. The paper reported that 'tourist
shopping was taking over the CBD' and that conventional retailing
would move out to the suburban shopping malls, particularly a
proposed $A400 million mall on the city railway station site on the
fringe of the CBD. In addition, plans were made to remove some of the
traditional CBD activities to the city fringe including the city hall, police
station, courthouse and newspaper printing facility. The transition from
CBD to RBD continued through the 'development', 'consolidation' and
'stagnation' stages and by October 1996, despite much opposition, most
of these removals from the CBD had become a *fait accompli* (*Cairns Post*,
19 October, 1996: 9).

The premature appearance of both of the above 'consolidation' stage
criteria means that they can be considered leading indicators. Had a
TALC model been in place at the time, experts would have been able to

Table 15.3 Summary of Cairns region compliance with Butler's (1980) 'development' stage criteria (1984–1991)

	Butler's (1980) criteria	Compliance (yes/no)	Criterion 'belongs' to which stage	Leading or lagged indicator?
1	Well defined tourist market area and heavy advertising	Yes	Development	
2	Local involvement and control of tourism declines	Yes	Development	
3	Old facilities (e.g. visitor accommodation) superseded by larger, more elaborate, more up-to-date facilities provided by external organisations	Yes	Development	
4	Natural and cultural attractions marketed specifically, supplemented by man-made facilities	Yes	Development	
5	Changes in the physical appearance	Yes, from 1984	Development	
6	Regional and national involvement in planning and provision of facilities	Yes, from 1992	Development	
7	Number of visitors will exceed locals in peak periods	N/A	N/A	
8	Imported labour will be used	Yes	Development	
9	Auxiliary industries, such as laundries, will start to appear	Yes, from 1985	Development	
10	Type of visitor will change towards Plog's (1991: 64) 'mid-centric'	Yes	Development	
11	Local opposition and discontentment about large number of tourists and tourist facilities	Yes, from 1989	Consolidation	Leading
12	A recreational business district (RBD) has taken shape	Yes, from 1989	Consolidation	Leading

predict that the life cycle was progressing and the next stage was not far away.

Testing for the 'Consolidation' Stage (1991–1993)

Butler's (1980: 8) first criterion for the 'consolidation' stage is that the rate of increase in visitor numbers starts to decline. Also, total visitor numbers will exceed local residents and a major part of the region's economy will be tied to tourism. Marketing, advertising and promotion will be far-reaching and efforts will be made to extend the tourist season. Major tourism franchises and chains will have a presence in the region, but there will not be many new additions during this stage. The large number of visitors and facilities provided for them can be expected to arouse some opposition and discontent among residents. There will be a well defined RBD and some older facilities will be regarded as second-rate and not desirable.

The point on the TALC curve where accommodation takings change from an increasing, to a declining, rate of growth occurs at the point of inflection which, for the study region, was in January 1991 (see Figure 15.1). This point therefore is the demarcation between the 'development' and 'consolidation' stages and occurs in every TALC study, regardless of the region, if it has reached this stage.

At this point in any TALC analysis it is not only important to examine in detail all criteria which test positive, it is also important to look at why some of them occurred and how they can be used to the benefit of the region. Given that the next stage is 'stagnation', it is important for any region in this stage to identify what is causing the slowdown in growth and what can be done about it. However, if there is no TALC model in existence for the region, the long-term significance of the slowdown could easily be missed. Any decline in the growth rate of the tourism industry is likely to be viewed as being a temporary setback and blamed on some phenomena outside the control of regional policy makers. In the Cairns case the setback was first blamed on a devastating domestic pilot's strike and later on the economic collapse of the Asian economies, particularly Japan, the region's major market. The perceived temporary nature of these two phenomena led policy makers to implement no long-term corrective strategies for the area's tourism industry and so the decline continued. Had there been a TALC model in place, the change from the 'development' to the 'consolidation' stage might have been seen as part of the overall picture and appropriate long-term corrective strategies could have been employed. The model suggested some alternative corrective strategies and these will be discussed as the chapter progresses.

The 'consolidation' stage criteria stating that total visitor numbers will exceed local residents, is likely to occur only in an economy which has few alternative economic activities. Using the Cairns example again, there are many and diverse forms of economic activity including a large boat-building and engineering company, fishing and a sizeable sugar industry. Consequently, this criterion does not apply to this, or similar, regions and can safely be ignored, illustrating the flexible nature of the TALC model. Application of the model is not an act of blind faith, it requires an operative who is well versed in the study of economics as well as the tourism industry.

The next criterion, involving far-reaching advertising and promotion efforts, is not difficult to measure. Tourism companies advertise and regional promotion organisations exist solely for that purpose. Efforts are best measured in percentage terms. For example, an organisation involved in tourism such as a resort, will spend a percentage of its budget on advertising. If this percentage increases it could safely be said that the marketing effort has been increased compared to the size of the company. Likewise, if the budget of the official tourism promotion organisation increases in relation to the data used to plot the basic TALC curve, then it could be safely said that there is an increase in promotional effort from that source. In the study region, there was a significant increase in the TTNQ budget relative to accommodation takings. At the same time, questionnaire respondents reported large increases in advertising relative to their organisations' budget. Both indicators can be calculated in percentage terms.

The change in advertising strategy recorded during this stage in the study region could have been a 'knee-jerk' response to the decreasing rate of growth in accommodation takings. Whatever the reason, considerable efforts were made to extend the market area to countries such as Korea, Taiwan, China and India. The term 'knee-jerk' is used because at that time most of the Asian countries were experiencing a prolonged economic recession and further advertising would therefore only have a marginal and short-term effect.

Growth in accommodation takings, however, continued to decline. Further analysis revealed that while marketing efforts were concentrated on nearby, economically depressed, Asia, the existing US market was neglected to the point that direct flights to that market were progressively abandoned because of reduced demand. Direct flights ceased altogether in 1994. Visitors from the USA were forced to come through Brisbane or Sydney or alternatively through Japan or Korea, both of which required stop-overs of up to a day. The trip to the study region from the USA, the world's biggest and richest market, now took up to two days and cost nearly double the direct fare. Given the elastic nature of tourism demand, the effect of the increased cost of access to the region had a more than proportional decrease in visitors from that market.

If a TALC model had been in place at the time, local policy makers would have been able to identify the problem and recognise their action as a 'consolidation' stage criterion and therefore hardly likely to break the region free of the 'S' curve. Meanwhile, local and state governments were making efforts to extend the tourist season with plans for a casino and convention centre. This latter point further confirms the region's progress toward 'stagnation' and again highlights the necessity to identify the cause of the reduction in the rate of growth.

The existence of old, poor or second-rate facilities could be considered a partially lagged indicator because it occurs in the last year of this stage and continues on into the next 'stagnation' stage. Of interest however, is that the tourism industry questionnaire revealed that nearly all such facilities cited by respondents were the responsibility of either local government or a statutory government authority. Exceptions included a small number of aging private motels and hotels. For a local government that is serious about attracting tourists, this criterion points to work which needs to be done. Often, such work involves inexpensive maintenance. The need to clean and maintain public toilets in places frequented by tourists is not costly and can make a big difference to the image presented to visitors.

Most of the remaining criteria are merely descriptive of the 'consolidation' stage and serve only to remind the region that it is heading towards stagnation and needs to search for appropriate remedies. The existence of a RBD, for example, is not in itself detrimental to the region. On the other hand, if the RBD is associated with an oversupply of retail space, there is a problem.

Overall, during this stage in the study region there was a high degree of compliance with Butler's (1980) model (see Table 15.4). Of the criteria shown in the table, eleven tested positive, two of which (numbers 7 and 8) occur in the 'development' stage and are therefore lagged indicators and highlight the overlapping or 'fuzzy' concept of the demarcation between the stages. The last three indicators in the table however, are leading indicators of 'stagnation' and therefore of much interest to the TALC analyst. The first leading indicator refers to the existence of 'environmental, social and economic problems' due to 'capacity levels' being reached (Butler, 1980: 9), all of which appeared in the study region during the 'consolidation' stage.

There are numerous capacity levels that can be looked at given time and resources. Some involve scientific techniques such as environmental capacity levels while others may include the ability of the local people to absorb more outsiders. The latter example could be reflected in the attitude of locals towards visitors. The essential point of Butler's

Table 15.4 Summary of relevance of Butler's (1980) consolidation stage criteria to the Cairns region (1991–1993)

	Butler's (1980) criteria	Compliance (yes/no)	Criterion 'belongs' to which stage	Leading indicator?
1	Rate of increase in tourism declines	Yes	Consolidation	
2	Total number of tourists exceeds the number of locals	N/A	N/A	
3	Tourism is the major part of the economy	Yes	Consolidation	
4	Advertising more wide ranging	Yes	Consolidation and stagnation	
5	Local efforts are made to extend the tourist season	Yes	Consolidation	
6	Major franchises and tourist chains will be represented but few, if any, additions will be made	Yes	Consolidation	
7	Local opposition and discontentment about large number of tourists and tourist facilities	Yes, from 1989	Consolidation	Lagged
8	A recreational business district (RBD) has taken shape	Yes, from 1989	Consolidation	Lagged
9	Some of the older, deteriorating facilities are second-rate	Yes, 1993–1998	Consolidation	
10	Environmental, social and economic problems	Yes, peaked 1991	Stagnation	Leading
11	Type of tourist changes to the organised mass tourist	Yes, peaked 1991–1993	Stagnation	Leading
12	Reliance on repeat visitation	Yes, since 1993	Stagnation	Leading

statement however, is not that capacity levels are reached, but that problems will result.

The natural and cultural attractions of a tourism region, often the reason the region became popular in the first place, can become in danger of being destroyed by overdevelopment or overuse. Accordingly, the Cairns region questionnaire asked respondents if they thought that the 'original physical attraction of the region was threatened in any way?' By far the majority (86.5%) believed that to some degree, the 'original physical attraction' was under threat. However, some respondents may have been thinking about the natural environment, while others may have been considering the city skyline and the intrusion caused by the new high-rise buildings. The newspaper search reinforced the questionnaire responses.

Indicators of social problems present during the 'consolidation' stage included high unemployment, financial hardship caused by the high cost of housing and crime rates. Indicators of economic problems were assessed using three separate methods. First, the degree of tightness of organisational budgeting was tested, followed by profit as a percentage of capital invested and last, profit margin per client. All pointed to a high degree of economic stress during the 'consolidation' stage.

The second leading indicator involved the percentage of mass tourism relative to total tourism. According to the results of the business survey, this indicator rose from about 18% in 1979 to 31% of total tourists in 1991 and then fell slightly after that year. This criteria, therefore, is premature by at least three years and would have been a valuable leading indicator of 'stagnation' had policy makers been using the model.

To test the last leading indicator in Table 15.4, business survey respondents were asked, 'What is the percentage of first-time visitors over the time period handled by your business?' The results showed that the percentage of first-time visitors increased steadily until 1993 when it reached 67.5% and from then on there has been a levelling off or even a small decline. Whilst this does not represent heavy reliance on repeat visitation, there is a move in that direction from 1993 onwards. Later in the cycle it is probable that this trend would have been more pronounced had it not been for the completion of the new Cairns Convention Centre in 1996. The opening of the Cairns Casino in 1995 would also help counter the trend towards reliance on repeat visitation. Coincidentally, the appearance of these two establishments also conforms to Butler's statement about increased reliance on 'conventions and other forms of traffic' (Butler, 1980: 8).

Testing for the 'Stagnation' Stage (1993–1998)

During this stage, tourism numbers peak and, as mentioned above, the type of visitor changes to the organised mass tourist while capacity levels are reached, resulting in environmental, social and economic problems. The resort has a well established image, but is no longer fashionable and there is a reliance on repeat visitation. There is an increase in conventions and older property ownership turnover rates are high. New developments are still occurring, but on the periphery of the original tourist area. Large numbers of imported attractions start to outnumber the natural and cultural attractions and local people consider visitors annoying (Butler, 1980: 8).

The main point about this stage is that at some time visitor numbers (accommodation takings in the case of this research) will peak (Butler, 1980: 8). In the study region the TALC curve peaked around September 1997 (see Figure 15.1). Stage demarcation timing depends on the presence of appropriate criteria according to the original TALC model as proposed by Butler in 1980. Under these rules it is possible for a region to have enough 'stagnation' stage criteria to be said to be in that stage but at the same time have a number of criteria belonging to say, the 'decline' stage. As with other stages, these 'decline' stage criteria become leading indicators of 'decline' because of their presence in the 'stagnation' stage.

Probably one of the most import criteria for this stage is that the region has a well established image but is no longer fashionable. If this criterion tests positive it means that agents will not be sending many new tourists and so the region has to rely more on repeat visitation. A high percentage of repeat visitors can therefore be quite unhealthy for the region and this had already occurred in the study region by 1993. Once identified, the problem of a low level of fashionability can be addressed. Rather than spend more money on advertising to the same market, which was mainly Japan in the case of Cairns, this criterion suggests that new markets should be found where the region is not unpopular. The obvious market would have been the USA, but direct flights would have been necessary and these had stopped due to lack of demand, in part due to lack of marketing by the region. Charter flights would have been necessary as had occurred in 1984 when the international airport was opened.

This question was tested in the study region using the business survey but at best the result is the opinion of businesses which are members of TTNQ. A more appropriate approach would be to obtain the opinion of prospective tourists or agents located in different parts of the world, but logistics and cost precludes such methods. In 1996, however, there was a survey of 100 North Queensland tourists, 40 of whom returned negative opinions about what they found in the Far North. This survey came immediately after the release of a Japanese report expressing disappointment with the city (*Cairns Post*, 9 September 1996: 44). The report also quoted an Australian Tourist Commission report quoting Japanese calls for the city to be scrapped as an international air hub (*Cairns Post*, 9 September 1996: 44). These reports would appear to reinforce the questionnaire results.

Other criteria, such as 'surplus bed capacity will be available' (Butler, 1980: 8), can easily be tested in any tourism area using a tourism business questionnaire or existing statistics. In the Cairns region, bed-occupation rates tended to increase until 1994, but, for the last four years of the data series there was a steady decline. On the other hand, bed occupancy rates in some areas of the economy, say backpacker hostels, may well be healthier than for five-star hotels. TALC, however, is a holistic model and it is important not to get bogged down discussing individual market segments or their characteristics. The purpose of the model is to look at the economy as a whole and then, if action is warranted, the next step in the planning process is to examine specific issues in finer detail.

Another stagnation stage criterion, which is almost as important as lack of fashionability, is that strenuous efforts, as measured by advertising expenditure, are needed to maintain the level of visitation. Using the study region as an example, between 1993 and 1998, TTNQ expenditure was increasing exponentially, while at the same time the rate of increase in accommodation takings declined significantly. In this five-year period, TTNQ expenditure tripled. The results of the business survey also indicated that private expenditure on advertising and promotion expressed as a percentage of total expenditure increased exponentially. This rapidly increasing expenditure represented a concerted effort to attract more visitors.

Table 15.5 shows that in all, ten 'stagnation' stage criteria tested positive, three of which had occurred in previous stages as leading indicators of 'stagnation'. Of more importance is the existence of three 'decline' stage criteria. The first of these is that there is increased competition from other resort areas. At the beginning of the study period the most common response was that there was a low level of competition from outside the region. As the cycle progressed, however, competition steadily increased to the point where respondents considered it to be high.

The next 'decline' stage criteria which tested positive was that the viability of tourist businesses was becoming questionable. An increasing percentage of businesses were recording negative profits, decreasing profit margins and tighter budgeting. All three of these indicators are easily measurable in any region and will give an uncomplicated indication of just how healthy the industry is.

The next leading indicator which tested positive in this stage is perhaps a little more subtle. During the 'decline' stage there is a

Table 15.5 Summary of responses to Butler's (1980) 'stagnation' stage criteria (1993–1998)

	Butler's (1980) criteria	*Compliance (yes/no)*	*Criterion 'belongs' to which stage*	*Leading indicator?*
1	Peak of accommodation takings reached	Yes, peaked 1997	Stagnation	
2	Environmental problems	Yes, peaked 1995	Stagnation	
3	Social problems	Yes, peaked 1991	Stagnation	
4	Economic problems	Yes, peaked 1991	Stagnation	
5	Well established image but resort region is no longer fashionable	Yes 1996	Stagnation	
6	Reliance on repeat visitation	Yes since 1993	Stagnation	
7	Decrease in occupancy rates	Yes since 1994	Stagnation	
8	Strenuous efforts needed to maintain the level of visitation	Yes, progressive throughout this stage	Stagnation	
9	Type of tourist changes to the organised mass tourist	Yes, trend started 1991	Stagnation	
10	Natural and cultural attractions superseded by man-made attractions	No	Stagnation	
11	Resort image is divorced from its geographic environment	Not tested	Stagnation	
12	New developments still occurring but on the periphery of the original tourist area	Yes, progressive throughout this stage	Stagnation	

Table 15.5 (*Continued*)

	Butler's (1980) criteria	Compliance (yes/no)	Criterion 'belongs' to which stage	Leading indicator?
13	Frequent changes of ownership	No	Stagnation	
14	Locals consider visitors annoying	No	Stagnation	
15	Increased competition from other resort areas with newer attractions	Yes, since 1990	Decline	Leading
16	The viability of tourist businesses becomes questionable	Yes, since 1993	Decline	Leading
17	Local involvement in tourism will increase	Yes, since 1994	Decline	Leading

reduction in the degree of outside influence because some companies leave the region and others file for bankruptcy. The increase in the supply of tourism businesses and property relative to demand meant that local people could buy back in at very reasonable prices, thus increasing their influence over the tourism industry. This occurred in the study region during the whole of the 'stagnation' stage in the areas of ownership, management and the place of origin of the bookings. The decrease in demand for property goes a long way towards explaining the noncompliance of item 14 in Table 15.5. On the other hand, the buy-back by locals could also refer to the turnover of properties suggested in the original article (Butler, 1980: 8).

Testing for the 'Decline' Stage

Butler's (1980: 9) 'decline' stage is characterised by a declining market and an inability to compete with newer attractions. Holiday-makers will stay away, but the number of day-trippers will increase if the region is located close to a centre of population. Property turnover is high and tourist facilities are converted to other uses. Hotels may become apartment blocks, retirement or convalescent homes. Local involvement and control increases as residents are able to buy back into the tourism industry at reduced prices. In the study region, only three 'decline' stage criteria were present at the end of 1998, not enough to be able to say that the area is in that stage. Accordingly, the region was still classified as being in the 'stagnation' stage at the end of the study period.

For TALC model purposes, the value of most 'decline' stage criteria is that, like some 'stagnation' stage criteria, they can be used as a means of identifying factors which need to be addressed as part of a rejuvenation effort. Examples include at least two of the three leading indicators of 'decline' discussed above in relation to the 'stagnation' stage. Item 15 of Table 15.5 involves the problem of increased competition from other resort areas with newer attractions. Item 16 involves the lack of economic viability of tourist businesses. The former must be addressed in order to solve the latter. In the study region, a major part of the solution would involve changing the focus of marketing efforts from the mature Japanese market to the relatively untapped North American market.

Item 17 of Table 15.5, stating that local involvement in tourism will increase as 'decline' sets in, is a special case. Whereas this criterion is a symptom of 'decline', it can also be a key to 'rejuvenation'. Previous research, most notably in Grand Cayman and Antigua, has shown that increased local involvement can help in the planning process and is a positive influence on a region (Weaver, 1988, 1990, 1992). It may well be the case that this criterion should be developed and encouraged, instead of eliminated, to help smooth the rejuvenation process. Used in this way the TALC model serves to highlight criteria that are a reminder, or a pointer, to what has to be done so that 'rejuvenation' can take place.

Testing for the 'Rejuvenation' Stage

Butler's (1980: 9) 'rejuvenation' stage will almost certainly not be achieved without a complete change in the attractions on which tourism in the region is based. Such a change can be done by introducing human-made attractions like theme parks and casinos or by making better use of previously untapped natural resources. Winter sports at Aviemore in Scotland is an example of the latter. Another alternative strategy involves finding a new market which has not yet experienced the existing attractions of the region. Ideally, a combination of these and other strategies could be used. As with other stages, criteria which test positive, point to possible 'rejuvenation' strategies.

In the study region, of five 'rejuvenation' stage criteria tested, two tested negative and three had partial compliance (see Table 15.6). All of those with partial compliance occurred during the 'stagnation' stage, which in itself is perhaps an indication of some recognition by local authorities that things are not all that they should be. There is no doubt that the interpretation given to all five criteria is subjective and is open to argument. The main point, however, is to identify areas where improvements can be made rather than to argue about compliance or otherwise

Table 15.6 Summary of responses to Butler's (1980) 'rejuvenation' stage criteria

	Butler's (1980) criteria	Compliance (yes/no/other)	Criterion 'belongs' to which stage?	Leading indicator?
1	Complete change of the attractions on which tourism is based	No	Rejuvenation	
2	Introduction of man-made attractions such as casinos and theme parks	Partial, 1996	Rejuvenation	Leading
3	Take advantage of previously untapped natural resources	Partial, 1996	Rejuvenation	Leading
4	Combined government and private efforts are necessary to look for new markets and encouragement of special interest groups	Partial, on-going	Rejuvenation	Leading
5	Beautification/urban renewal projects (response to 'old' and 'second-rate' facilities of 'consolidation' stage)	Not much	Rejuvenation	

with the various criteria. For example, it makes no difference whether the criterion regarding beautification and/or urban renewal tests negative or positive, the model suggests that any rejuvenation strategy should contain that element regardless.

Application of Suggestions by Haywood (1986) and Cooper (1990, 1994)

This section considers the use of leading indicators in addition to Butler's (1980) TALC model and these have been mentioned briefly earlier in the chapter. Two sets of indicators are considered, the first put forward by Haywood (1986: 161), and the second suggested by Cooper (1990: 63) as threats to the survival of coldwater resorts, some of which no doubt apply equally well to warmwater regions.

Haywood (1986: 161) suggested seven leading indicators of 'stagnation', four of which proved to be relevant to the study region and have

Table 15.7 Summary: Haywood's (1986: 161) leading indicators of 'stagnation'

	Leading indicator	*Yes/no*	*If 'yes', year of occurrence and stage*
1	A declining proportion of first-time visitors	Yes	1993, 'stagnation'
2	Declining profits of the major tourist businesses	Yes	1991, 'consolidation'
3	Appearance of new and accessible destinations	Yes	1990, 'consolidation'
4	Decline in advertising elasticity	Yes	1991, 'consolidation'

been discussed above. Three out of the four gave at least two years warning of impending stagnation (see Table 15.7). There is no doubt that Haywood's leading indicators add to the short-term forecasting capability of Butler's (1980) model and could be applied to most regions.

Cooper's (1990: 63) threats to coldwater resorts are not specific to any particular stage of TALC and are more in the nature of negative factors associated with the decline of resort regions (see Table 15.8). This research assessed the threats for their value as leading indicators of Butler's (1980: 8, 9) 'stagnation' and 'decline' stages. Some of Cooper's suggestions reinforce Butler's criteria and are similar to Haywood's (1986: 161) leading indicators and need not be discussed again.

Perhaps one of the most interesting of Cooper's (1990: 63) threats concerns political interference on decisions. The indicator does not include routine decisions made by public servants, but it does include one-off decisions made by politicians which affect businesses within the region. One example is the building of Cairns Central shopping mall on state government land on the edge of the CBD. The decision to build the complex was made by the government minister responsible and was not subject to local government scrutiny or approval. Once finished, the complex, which consists of more than a hundred shops, several cinemas and food outlets, took much of the CBD trade away from existing businesses. The Cairns mayor belatedly responded to this sort of political decision-making by demanding 'a guarantee from Queensland's political leaders that no more of the city's government owned land will be sold for retail use' (*Cairns Post*, 24 January 1998: 1).

Survey results clearly showed that respondents thought there was too much political influence on decision making. Many respondents provided specific instances indicating that these are not just vague accusations. It would seem that when politicians take the decision-making process away from the normal administrative institutions by

Table 15.8 Summary of Responses to Cooper's "Threats" (Cooper, 1990:63).

	Threat	Yes or No	If "yes", when?	Suitable as a leading indicator?
1	Political interference on decisions	Yes	Early 1990s	Yes
2	Diminishing domestic market share.	Yes	Since 1991	Yes
3	Poor Access and Traffic Problems	Yes	Since 1991	Yes
4	LGA amalgamation	Yes	1996	No
5	Confidence in tourism industry	Yes	Declining since 1990	Yes
6	Demands for Greater Efficiency in Local Government	Yes	From 1990	Yes
7	Lack of Professional, experienced staff	Yes	As at 1998, (not a time-series question)	No
8	Growth in low-spend tourists	Yes	Declined since 1988, identifiable from 1991	Yes

using ministerial privileges, it is in itself a leading indicator of stagnation or decline. The lesson here is to watch the politicians and try to curb their involvement, some of which may not be entirely legal and not difficult to stop in its tracks.

Cooper (1990: 63) also stated that a drop in a tourism region's share of the domestic market can be considered a threat to the survival of the region's tourism industry. The study region's share of the domestic market reached a peak in 1991/2. Since that year however, there has been a steady decline. Coincidentally, this was same year that the growth rate in visitor spending started to slow down and the region slipped from the 'development' stage into the 'consolidation' stage.

The resort region's domestic share of the international market does not appear in Cooper's (1990: 63) list of threats, however, it is equally useful. In terms of this statistic, the region reached a peak in 1992 and has since declined, indicating that there is increased competition from other regions within Australia.

Perhaps the most important of Cooper's (1990: 63) threats involves visitor access to the region. The term 'access' refers to the time it takes to get to the region, the number of stops and changes, and the cost. The high price elasticity of demand of tourism ensures a more than proportional reduction in visitors for each dollar increase in the cost of getting there. This is also a point legislators should be aware of when considering bed taxes and the like.

Another curious but none-the-less accurate threat to resort regions is that local government area (LGA) amalgamation poses a threat to the survival of a tourism region. This is because it dilutes the bargaining power of the tourism industry by making the local government larger and more powerful than it was previously (Cooper, 1990: 63). In 1996, the City of Cairns joined with the neighbouring Mulgrave Shire to form one large LGA containing the bulk of tourism activity. This was another leading indicator of decline that was ignored by the region's policy makers. Interestingly, the main reason for LGA amalgamation is to increase local government efficiency, the demand for which is itself one of Cooper's threats. Other threats which tested positive in the study area included: a low degree of confidence in the tourism industry expressed by operatives; lack of professional, experienced staff; and growth in low-spend visitors.

In the case of the Cairns region, eight of Cooper's (1990: 63) threats tested positive and could, therefore, have been considered as threats to the long-term survival of the region as a successful tourism area. Of the eight, six occurred at least two years prior to the study region entering Butler's (1980: 8) 'stagnation' stage and would, therefore, qualify as leading indicators (see Table 15.8). Cooper listed 20 possible threats, any of which could be used to assess the long-term viability of a resort region and some of which may well appear early enough to be used as leading indicators of 'stagnation' or 'decline'.

Summary and Conclusions

As stated at the beginning, the object of this chapter has been to emphasise the utility of the TALC model to the tourism industry and tourism regions as a whole. The most important aspect of the model is to know how to implement the model and how to use it for forecasting. First, a TALC curve has to be constructed using appropriate data. Not necessarily tourist numbers as originally suggested by Butler (1980), but the data must be complete for the review period and intuitively relevant. A large selection of data was tested for the study region and nearly all of it was found to be suitable. Next, as many as possible of Butler's, Cooper's (1990) and Haywood's (1986: 161) criteria must be tested at the same time. Stage demarcation lines can then be constructed and leading indicators identified, some of which will point to remedial action which

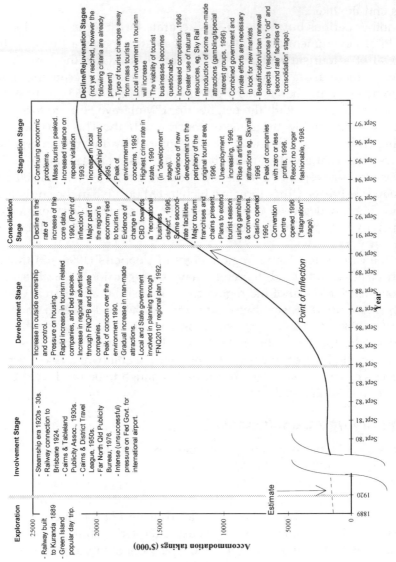

Figure 15.3 Summary of application of Butler's (1980) theory to the Cairns region: Major criteria only

can be taken to avoid stagnation or decline. Figure 15.3 provides an overall impression of the results of the Cairns study.

Fifty-six of Butler's (1980) criteria were tested in the study region, out of which 46 (82.1%) were positive and 3 were partially positive. Of those, 15 overlapped into other stages. Five tested negative and two were not applicable to the study region. The eight 'poststagnation' stage criteria can be used to provide guidance for strategic planners, the main aim being to reinforce the 'rejuvenation' stage criteria and eliminate the 'decline' stage criteria. The fact that not all of Butler's (1980) suggested criteria apply to the study region does not detract from the model. On the contrary, it serves to highlight the differences between regions.

Haywood's (1986: 161) leading indicators of 'stagnation' and Cooper's (1990: 63) threats to coldwater resorts have a high success rate in the Cairns region. Not all, however, have the same degree of significance and predictability and will differ between regions. Nevertheless their high success rate in the study region is of academic and commercial significance. Within this study there are numerous illustrations of how valuable the model could be to the tourism industry worldwide. One important example is that it took TTNQ three or four years to respond to the 1991 slow-down in growth rate of accommodation takings. This is perhaps one of the best arguments for having an on-going TALC model.

Part 6
The Future and the TALC

RICHARD BUTLER

Introduction

Given that the original TALC was not anticipated to have a future of the type which it has experienced since 1980, this author clearly was not blessed with a very effective crystal ball. Nevertheless, it is incumbent upon me to conclude these two volumes with an attempt to set the model within a potential scenario of what its relevance might be at the beginning of the 21st century and how it might be developed in the future. It seems appropriate to begin by discussing the principals and elements of the original model and what developments may be anticipated in the future. As noted earlier (Butler, other volume), the original model was developed at a time when conceptualisation in tourism was at a relatively early and primitive stage. While one may not be able to argue convincingly that the tourism literature is a hotbed of conceptual and theoretical application and development, things have certainly improved over the situation some three decades ago. Thus the applications of alternative theories and concepts discussed earlier in this volume and to a lesser extent in the other volume should leave their marks on the TALC and how it may be modified and redeveloped in the future. This concluding chapter reviews the key elements that comprise the model and the way they have been, and may be, addressed in the years to come, and then discusses the potential redundancy or continued relevance of the TALC for tourism destinations in this new century.

Key Elements and their Relevance

The overall purpose of a model is to provide a simplified and generalised version of reality in order that some sense can be made of the mass of detail and unique cases that exist in the real world. It is, therefore, a representation of reality and not reality in itself. If the TALC does not fit exactly every case and every tourist destination, that is not only hardly surprising, but to a degree, a measure of its suitability as a model. Despite that, in many of the reviews and applications of the original model, attention has often been focused on what does not fit the particular case being examined. In some cases the failure to capture the detail or the essence of reality has led to suggestions for modification to the original model, the work of Agarwal (this volume) and Weaver (other volume) are particularly good examples. In other cases some of the criticisms of the model seem to be based more on inappropriate examples being selected than any particular failing of the model. Choy (1992) applying the model to a considerable number of island microstates in the South Pacific could be taken to be a good example of this. The model as published in 1980 discussed the projected future pattern of development of a specific tourist destination or resort, rather than a set of very different destinations, sharing only an insular nature and southern Pacific location (a point noted by Johnston, this volume).

The 1980 article had a number of specific elements or attributes that perhaps should be reviewed if the present and future applicability and relevance of the TALC are to be discussed. To some degree it can be argued that at least some of these elements have been overshadowed by discussions of details relating to the cases to which the TALC has been applied. In its initial form the model was presenting the case that tourist destinations could be viewed as products, and that as such, they could be expected to experience a generic life cycle, proceeding through stages, and ultimately, without significant management intervention, ending in decline and even abandonment. Thus it attempted to bring together the elements of growth, change, limits and intervention in a tourism context, and to incorporate both the demand and supply sides of the equation in the process of destination development.

Dynamism

Of all the elements involved, the key one is that of dynamism, or change. In the present-day world this aspect may appear so obvious that one may think it goes without saying. Tourism has seen so many changes within the last few decades that we readily accept that it has great dynamism. We need to see also, however, that it has great inertia and stability, and that it is the interplay between these two forces that determines how a specific destination develops, and the rate at which it changes. Not all destinations experience the same forces of change at the same time, and some may benefit from innovations early and significantly, while others may not experience any advantages from such changes for a long time.

When the model was being developed, tourism was only just beginning to witness the fundamental changes that were to alter it so greatly in the last three decades or so of the last century. Modern package holidays, charter flights, jet aircraft, wide availability of credit, removal of travel restrictions and global peace (for the most part) all began to appear as global phenomena in the 1960s and 1970s. The market for tourism grew at a rapid rate, the Asian countries entered the tourist market for the first time on a large scale, and international tourism became truly global rather than continental. The effect on established tourist destinations by and large had not been foreseen and most were singularly ill equipped, physically, socially, culturally and financially to adjust easily and appropriately to these changes. One may wonder if many current destinations have such flexibility and capability even now. The fate of the first wave of 'new' resorts, in particular those on the Spanish Costa Brava, should give us pause for thought. They were anticipated and hailed as the resorts of the future, as they were in the 1960s, but were relatively quickly condemned as the resorts of the past by the 1980s. Places like Atlantic City, Brighton and Blackpool can feel they did rather better, given that it took about a century for them to become clearly out of step with what was happening in tourism. It was the failure to appreciate the fact that the world (tourism and tourists in the case of resorts) was changing and that they needed to change in anticipation or at least in reflection of these changes if they were to survive, that is at the heart of the TALC.

Process

Another major element was process. At the core of the model was the argument that there was an identifiable and replicable process that the changes in each resort went through. It was argued that this process could be described and modelled, and that it was not a random pattern of events for each destination. While the set of events and forces acting at each destination may be unique, it was proposed that the effects were similar and could be anticipated in general. The fact that the process may take longer in some places than others, that it may be caused by a different set of forces and that it may have different end results seems to have diverted authors of some studies from appreciating that the process still occurs. The introduction of transportation innovations, the efforts of individual entrepreneurs and local decision-makers, political instability, economic upheaval and especially the development of competition all intervene in the process of the life cycle of a destination (see Agarwal, Papatheodorou and Russell, this volume). It is still argued, however, that as Plog (1973) noted, destinations do proceed inexorably towards their ultimate state, whatever that may be, as the process or cycle runs its course. Like human mortality, old age is a reality for resorts as well as the people who visit them. Physically at least, most of us and most resorts become less attractive to the world at large as we get older. A few, Venice and Dubrovnik, for example, or Catherine Deneuve and Sean Connery, retain their appeal despite or because of their age, but they are the exceptions. While discussing old age, it is perhaps relevant to recall the contribution of Strapp (1988) to the research on the TALC. He incorporated the TALC into the process of conversion of second-home destinations from conventional tourist destinations into retirement havens, a process which is taking place in many established tourist areas with potentially serious implications for their future conventional tourism function. The conversion of tourist resorts to retirement settlements (a process hinted at by Gilbert (1939) a long time ago) may represent an alternative penultimate stage in the TALC (prior to exiting the tourist route) and warrants further investigation.

Carrying capacity

Another of the elements which is central to this process is that of the carrying capacity of the destination. This is a concept that was strong in the recreation literature in the 1960s, and which this author strongly believes to be equally relevant today (Butler, 1996), despite arguments to the contrary (see, for example, the *Journal of Sustainable Tourism* 5 (2) 2002). This is not the place to discuss in detail the development of the carrying capacity concept from its early articulation by Lucas (1964) and Wagar (1964) and its early application to tourism (for example, An Foras Forbatha, 1966), or the alternatives that have been proposed in its place, such as *The Limits of Acceptable Change* (Stankey *et al.*, 1985). Suffice it to say that while this concept may not have retained universal support, the issues of carrying capacity, congestion and overuse remain highly relevant still in many well developed tourist destinations. The TALC model had at its core the belief that if demand and visitation exceeded the capacity of the destination, however defined (physical, economic, environmental or psychological), then the quality of experience for visitors, quality of life for residents and the destination's physical appearance would suffer. In short, the destination would be less attractive, and this in turn would cause visitor numbers to eventually decline. If local residents began to react in a negative manner to what they perceived as too many tourists, this too would likely translate into a loss of attractivity and appeal. It is accepted that there is not a magic number for carrying capacity, particularly for something as multifunctional as tourist destination, which normally caters to a variety of markets that may be at different stages in their development. It is reasonable to assume that the stage of development of the destination will also affect the level of capacity. This is a view shared by Martin and Uysal (1990: 390) who argue that:

> It is impossible to determine tourist carrying capacity outside of the context of the position of the destination areas in the life cycle. The interrelationship of the two concepts is dynamic, with the idea of change implicit in both concepts.

While carrying capacity is, as noted above, a discarded concept in some quarters, an alternative has not been found. It would be a brave and perhaps overly optimistic observer of destinations who would argue that a resort cannot be overdeveloped or have too many visitors. As long as this remains the case, at some point each resort will have to face the decision of what is the maximum level of development it can or should accept, and begin to plan for that level and what to do when it is reached.

Management

This point leads to another critical element in the model and that is the one of management. The original article included in its title the phrase 'implications for management', yet one might argue that if there is one element that has been most often ignored in the discussion and application of the model, it is this. It has to be acknowledged that there was not a great deal of discussion of this component in the 1980 article (and even less in its predecessors), and this may explain in part why it has tended to be overlooked. This has meant that there has been criticism that the model argues for the inevitability of decline. In reality, it posits the view that such decline is only inevitable if management and appropriate action are absent. The whole point of the article and the identification of the resort cycle was to illustrate what would happen if development was allowed to continue at a destination in an unplanned and uncontrolled manner. Admittedly just what form such management and intervention might take was not discussed in any great detail. The examples of rejuvenation that were discussed (Atlantic City and Aviemore) were dealt with very briefly and the actions that had been taken in these resorts were not explored at all. Perhaps of all the elements in the TALC, this is the one that needs the greatest attention in the future. The chapters by Hovinen, Stansfield, and Faulkner and Tideswell (other volume) and Agarwal and Cooper (this volume) go some way to describing and analysing what is involved for a destination to achieve revisioning, restructuring or rejuvenation. This element is discussed again below in the context of sustainability.

Spatial components

In the introductory chapter of the other volume on the TALC, I drew particular attention to the role played by the spatial component of the first version of the TALC (Brougham & Butler, 1972). In this early form it was a major element, but it was much less prominent in the published version. The downplaying of this element in the 1980 article was because of the absence of subsequent research on the spatial patterns that had been discussed earlier. While the spatial hypothesis, that there would be a series of locational shifts as development at the initial site peaked and stagnated, is still felt to be correct, it remains an area that has not been adequately studied. The chapters by Hall, Papatheodorou, and Ravenscroft and Hadjihambi (this volume) and Lundgren (other volume) address certain aspects of this idea and hopefully other geographers will rectify this gap in our knowledge of the spatial spread of tourism development.

Triggers

One of the elements which was not made explicit in the TALC, but which is, of course, of crucial significance to the basic idea of the model, is that of triggers of development and change in a destination. Clearly, forces have to be at work beyond a growth in demand to cause the changes in destinations as they move through the cycle described by the TALC. These were not given the emphasis that they deserved, and certainly in terms of the shifting of a resort from one stage to another they are of particular relevance. The two chapters by Russell (this volume), dealing with the relevance and application of chaos theory, and the role of entrepreneurs, go some way to tackling this neglect. One might propose that actions by management (as discussed above) correspond to deliberately induced triggers, while unintentional and accidental triggers correspond to chaos and turbulence in the tourism system. Keller (1987) argued that an overlooked trigger of change, and one which could be related strongly to the stages of development, was control over development and sources of investment, and the issue of control was raised in a different context by Debbage (1990, 1992). Control over development and its relevance in local politics is the focus of Martin's chapter (other volume) and a topic which still needs further investigation.

These then, were the key elements of the original concept and model. I would argue that not only do they remain crucial elements in our understanding of the way that tourist destinations develop, but that this understanding is still far from complete. In the majority of cases researchers have tended to describe rather than explain the patterns observed, note differences from the model but not necessarily interpret the significance of such variations, and treat each case as a unique destination rather than one in a set of options available to the market. It was this situation that partly stimulated the idea of these two volumes, of getting those researchers who had made significant modifications and conceptual linkages with the TALC to contribute their ideas to one (or two as it turned out) volume. While there were other elements and issues raised in the original paper and in the subsequent literature, I see the above as still being the key components and concepts of the model. None of them have lost their relevance in research aimed at illustrating, interpreting, explaining and predicting the patterns and processes of tourism destination development. The remaining issue to be dealt with is the overall relevance of the TALC model some two decades or more after its introduction.

Continued Relevance of the TALC?

A few years ago Prosser (1995) succinctly summarised the criticisms of the TALC as falling into five categories, and in general I concur with his analysis:

(1) doubts on there being a single model of development,
(2) limitations on the capacity issue,
(3) conceptual limitations of the life-cycle model,
(4) lack of empirical support for the concept, and
(5) limited practical utility of the model.

Despite these quite profound criticisms and others raised by contributors to these volumes, the model is still being used, a point recognised by Prosser (1995: 9):

> The extensive criticism levelled at the resort life cycle concept shows no sign of dissuading researchers from adopting the model as a framework for their research ... the original model survives largely intact and according to some, offers the prospect of further development.

After 20 years, is the cycle still a valid model for the study of tourism development and can it still serve as a broad conceptual framework for the study of the development process of tourism destinations? Perhaps inevitably I have to argue that the basic tenets of the model and the concept are as, or perhaps even more, applicable today than 20 years ago. The reasons for coming to this conclusion include:

- the fact that there is still evidence that the idea that resorts cannot exist forever without deliberate management and control still exists;
- the fact that there are still few models in tourism that offer a viable alternative to the TALC;
- the fact that tourism management is, in reality, little understood and rarely practised at most tourist resorts, tourism promotion is usually substituted;
- as Plog (1973) pointed out three decades ago, there is a finite number of locations that can be developed as tourist resorts;
- the concept of sustainability has been widely adopted and has a great deal in common with the TALC, and if it is to be applied to resorts, then it is necessary to understand the process of resort development.

The late Bill Faulkner, in discussing the revisioning exercise that he was developing on the Gold Coast in Queensland before his tragically premature death (see Faulkner & Tideswell, other volume), noted that there was great reluctance, and even refusal, by local tourism industry representatives to participate in a revisioning exercise. They felt that this would imply there were problems and a need to change direction and vision (Faulkner, personal communication, 2001). Instead, they agreed to participate in a 'visioning' exercise, thus maintaining the illusion that nothing was going wrong and that there were no problems being faced by the region.

All too often, those responsible for destinations prefer to tinker with attractions on the assumption that there is nothing really wrong with what is on offer, and that if things could be tidied up, the crowds would return. The situation was nicely summed up by a cartoon which appeared in the London Free Press (London, Ontario that is) in the 1980s. It followed a statement by a federal minister with responsibility for tourism that all that was needed to reduce the Canadian balance of payments deficit in tourism was to promote Canadian tourism resorts to Canadians. The cartoon showed a plane heading south (in the winter) with the caption, 'How are you going to keep them on the Canadian farm when they've seen Miami'. While Canada has many superb attractions for visitors, if one is wanting sun and warmth in the winter, Canada does not compete effectively with Florida. In the early 21st century resorts are competing in a truly global marketplace with many alternatives for the potential visitor. Thus Iceland, for example, faces competition from New Zealand (especially for the market on the West coast of North America) as well as from Scandinavia, its geographically closest competitor. The sad fact of life is that some resorts have little or no future in modern tourism, at least at the global scale in their existing form, and need to 'read the signs'. As Baum (this volume) demonstrates, they may be best advised to prepare an exit strategy from tourism.

In contrast to those resorts whose appeal is declining, there are an increasing number of destinations that are experiencing problems of overdevelopment and overuse. Current difficulties aside, all projections are for continued tourism growth globally, in both international and domestic forms, and thus continued pressure on those destinations viewed as attractive. This is hardly a new problem; Wolfe commented with his usual farsightedness on such issues over five decades ago (Wolfe, 1952), and suggested an alternative curve of development and potential impacts shortly after the original TALC model appeared (Wolfe, 1982). It appears highly likely that the rate of consumption of tourist destinations is increasing, that is, the time taken to proceed through the cycle is diminishing. Improvements in transportation, reductions in cost, savings through economies of scale, innovations in marketing and societal changes in tastes and behaviour all serve to reduce brand and place loyalty and to encourage the desire for stimulation, novelty and change for the sake of change. The collection instead of enjoyment of destinations has the potential to speed the movement of places along Plog's (1973) curve. While many may like to think they are, and will remain allocentrics rather than psychocentrics (travellers rather than tourists), in reality one may argue that almost all travellers are on their way to being tourists (Wheeller, 1993), whether they like or realise it or not, and most traveller destinations are also on their way to becoming tourist resorts, management notwithstanding.

Implicit in the TALC is an argument for a taking a long-term viewpoint in the planning and management of destinations. If destinations are to avoid the pitfalls of overuse and subsequent decline in appeal, then looking forward from the beginning is of crucial importance, not to how to attract tourists in the first decade of the development, but how to keep them coming 50 or 100 years in the future. This line of thinking fits very well with one of the most important concepts of the late 20th century, that of sustainable development and its application to tourism development (Butler, 1999). It has been argued earlier that the TALC represents an early call for the principles of sustainable development in the context of tourism destinations (Butler, 1997). The original model contained within it virtually all of what are seen as the essential elements of sustainable development. These are the long-term view, the acceptance of limits to growth and development, and the need for responsibility and control over development. I believe, probably even more strongly than in 1980, that these principles are basic and essential if destinations are to be developed and maintained in an appropriate manner.

We may not be able, nor wish to prevent the process of development and subsequent decline of areas as tourist destinations, but surely we do have a responsibility to avoid Hardin's *Tragedy of the Commons* (1968) being repeated by accident or neglect in many tourist destinations (an argument discussed at more length by Healy, 1994). At the heart of the resort cycle model is the principle that the development of destinations is evolutionary rather than revolutionary, and control and responsibility over development are crucial if development is to be appropriate and the destination to survive over the long term. In the years ahead there is no reason why the TALC model cannot continue to serve as a call for such responsibility and intervention, and therefore as such, have continued validity. It is still being used to illustrate the process of the development of tourist places in a variety of ways (Wilkinson, 1996).

Because it is a generalised simplistic model, it is inevitable that the resort cycle model would not fit perfectly, or even closely, all of the many specific and unique cases to which it has been applied. The question best asked perhaps, is that partly answered above, namely whether it has applicability and validity at the beginning of the 21st century, rather than whether in its original form it successfully and completely explained the process of tourist destination evolution. The amount of use the model has received and the number of examples discussed in the literature would tend to support the view that the model does have validity in terms of being a descriptive tool that has applicability in a wide variety of spatial, temporal, cultural and economic situations. Until there is convincing evidence that those responsible for tourism destination planning, development, marketing and management and their political decision-makers have learned the lessons from past mistakes, the resort cycle model is likely to continue to have some validity in a predictive sense as well, perhaps unfortunately for many destinations and tourists.

References

Abernatthy, W. and Utterback, J. (1978) Patterns of industrial innovation. *Technology Review* 80, 41–47.

Agarwal, S. (1994) The resort cycle revisited: Implications for resorts. In C.P. Cooper and A. Lockwood (eds) *Progress in Tourism, Recreation and Hospitality Management* (Vol.5, pp. 194–208). Chichester: Wiley.

Agarwal, S. (1997) The resort cycle and seaside tourism: An assessment of its applicability and validity. *Tourism Management* 18 (3), 65–73.

Agarwal, S. (1998) Reply – What is new with the resort cycle? *Tourism Management* 19 (2), 181–182.

Agarwal, S. (1999) Restructuring and local economic development: Implications for seaside resort regeneration in South West Britain. *Tourism Management* 20 (5), 511–522.

Agarwal, S. (2002) Restructuring seaside tourism. The resort life-cycle. *Annals of Tourism Research* 29 (1), 25–55.

Aglietta, M. (1979) *A Theory of Capitalist Regulation*. London: New Left Books.

Aiken, K.G. (1994) Not long ago a smoking chimney was a sign of prosperity: Corporate and community response to pollution at the Bunker Hill Smelter in Kellogg, Idaho. *Environmental Values* Summer, 67–86.

Alford, C. (1962) *The Island of Tobago* (Vol. 7). London: The Ranelagh Press.

Alipour, H. (1996) Tourism development within planning paradigms: The case of Turkey. *Tourism Management* 17 (5), 367–377.

Allen, L., Long, P.T., Perdue, R.R. and Kieselbach, S. (1988) The impact of tourism development on residents' perceptions of community life. *Journal of Travel Research* Summer, 16–21.

Allen, L.R., Hafer, H.R., Long, P.T. and Perdue, R.R. (1993) Rural residents' attitudes toward recreation and tourism development. *Journal of Travel Research* Spring, 27–33.

AMBIO (1877) The Mediterranean, Special issue. Stockholm: Royal Swedish Academy of Science.

AMBIO (1981) The Caribbean, Special Issue. Stockholm: Royal Swedish Academy of Science.

Amin, A. and Thrift, N. (1994) *Globalisation, Institutions and Regional Development in Europe*. Oxford: Oxford University Press.

Amir, S. (1976) *Unequal Development: An Essay on the Social Formations of Peripheral Capitalism*. New York: Monthly Review Press.

Andereck, K.L. and Vogt, C.A. (2000) The relationship between residents' attitudes towards tourism and tourism development options. *Journal of Travel Research* 39 (1), 27–36.

Anonymous (no date) *Renewal Scheme for Traditional Seaside Resorts*. On WWW at http://www.mayo-ireland.ie/Mayo/CoDev/RenSeaRs.htm. Accessed 23.2.2001.

Ansoff, H. (1965) *Corporate Strategy*. Harmondsworth: Penguin.

Ap, J. (1990) Residents' perceptions: Research on the social impacts of tourism. *Annals of Tourism Research* 17 (4), 610–615.

Ap, J. and Crompton, J. (1998) Developing a tourism impact scale. *Journal of Travel Research* 37 (2), 120.

Apo, P. (2000) Waikiki: At heart a Hawaiian destination. *Waikiki News* July. On WWW at http://www.waikikinews.com/0700/0700apo.html. Accessed 22.3.2001.

A.R. (1883) The preservation of Mt. Desert. *The Nation* August 9, 116–117.

Arthur, B. (1994) *Increasing Returns and Path Dependence in the Economy.* Ann Arbor: The University of Michigan Press.

Arthur, W.B. (1990) Positive feedbacks in the economy. *Scientific American* 262 (2), 92–99.

Aspinall, A. (1928) *A Wayfarer in the West Indies.* London: Methuen.

L'Association des Vingerons du Quebec (1995) Prenez le chemin des vignobles du Quebec. Pamphlet et communications orales.

Ateljevic, I. and Doorne, S. (2000) Staying within the fence: Lifestyle entrepreneurship in tourism. *Journal of Sustainable Tourism* 8 (5), 378–392.

Atkinson, J. (1984) Manpower strategies for flexible organisations. *Personnel Management* 16 (8), 28–31.

Atkinson, J. (1986) *Changing Work Patterns: How Companies Achieve Flexibility to Meet New Needs*. London: National Economic Development Office.

Aunger, R. (2001) Review of technological innovation as an evolutionary process (Zimon, J., ed). *Journal of Artificial Societies and Social Simulation* 4 (4). On WWW at http://jasss.soc.surrey.ac.uk/4/4/reviews/ziman.html.

Australian Bureau of Statistics (1999) *Consumer Price Index: Table 1B. All Groups Index Numbers – Quarterly (Base Year 1989–90 = 100)*. Product number 6401.0. Canberra: Australian Government.

Avlonitis, G.J. (1990) Project dropstart: Product elimination and the product life cycle concept. *European Journal of Marketing* 24 (9), 55–67.

Babbie, E. (2000) *Practicing Social Research*. Belmont, CA: Wadsworth Publishing.

Backman, S., Patrick, J. and Wright, B.A. (2001) Management tools and techniques: An integrated approach to planning. In D.B. Weaver (ed.) *The Encyclopedia of Ecotourism* (pp. 451–462). Wallingford, UK: CABI Publishing.

Bacon, W. (1998) Economic systems and their impact on tourist resort development: The case of the spa in Europe. *Tourism Economics* 4 (1), 21–32.

Bagguley, P. (1987) *Flexibility, Restructuring and Gender: Changing Employment in Britain's Hotels.* Lancaster Regionalism Working Group Working Paper No. 24, University of Lancaster, Lancaster Regionalism Group.

Bagguley, P., Mark-Lawson, J., Shapiro, D., Urry, J., Walby, S. and Warde, A. (1990) *Restructuring Place, Class and Gender.* London: Sage.

Bagus Oka, I. (1992) Traditional tourist resorts; problems and solutions: The case of Bali. International Forum on Tourism to the Year 2000: Prospects and Challenges, Acapulco, Mexico.

Baird, R. (1850) *Impressions and Experiences of the West Indies and North America in 1849*. Philadelphia, PA: Lea & Blanchard.

Baker, M. (1991) One more time – what is marketing? In M. Baker (ed.) *The Marketing Book* (Vol.2, pp. 3–9). Oxford: Butterworth-Heinemann.

Bao, J. (1994) Big theme park distribution research. *Research of Georgraphy* 13 (3), 83–89.

Bao, J. (1998) Tourism planning and tourist area lifecycle model. *Architect* 12, 170–178.

Bao, J. and Peng, H. (1995) Tourist area expanding research: Case study of Danxia Mountain. *Science of Geography* 15 (1), 63–70.

Bao, J., Chu, Y. and Peng, H. (1993) *Tourism Geography* (p. 134). Beijing: Higher Education Press.

Bao, J. (1994) Tourism development of karst cave. *Geographic Sinica* 50 (4), 353–359.

Barker, J.A. (1992) *Discovering the Future: The Power of Vision*. Florida: Infinity Limited.

Barr, T. (1990) From quirky islanders to entrepreneurial magnates: The transition of the Whitsundays. *Journal of Tourism Studies* 1 (2), 26–32.

Barrett, J. (1958) The seaside resort towns of England and Wales. Unpublished PhD thesis. London: University of London.

Barrot, T-A. (1978) *Unless Haste is Made: A French Skeptic's Account of the Hawaiian Islands in 1836*. Kailua, HI: Press Pacifica.

Basalla, G. (1988) *The Evolution of Technology*. Cambridge: Cambridge University Press.

Baum, T. (1998a) Taking the exit route: Extending the tourism area life cycle model. *Current Issues in Tourism* 1 (2), 167–175.

Baum, T. (1998b) Tourism marketing and the small island environment. Cases from the periphery. In E. Laws *et al*. (eds) *Embracing and Managing Change in Tourism*. London: Routledge.

Baum, J.A. and Singh, J.V. (1994) *Evolutionary Dynamics of Organisations*. New York: Oxford University Press.

Beckford, G. (1972) *Persistent Poverty: Underdevelopment in Plantation Economies of the Third World*. New York: Oxford University Press.

Bell, M. (1994) Personal interview, Hilton Head Island Planning Office, Hilton Head, SC.

Benham, B. (1970) Kealakekua Bay remains 'unlisted'. Hawaii *Tribune Herald* 9 August, 2.

Bennett, R.C. and Cooper, R.G. (1984) The product life cycle trap. *Business Horizons* 27 (Sept–Oct), 7–16.

Benson, J. and Shaw, G. (eds) (1999) *The Retailing Industry. Volume I: Perspectives and the Early Modern Period*. London: I.B. Tauris.

Berman, E.M. (2002) *Essential Statistics for Public Managers and Policy Analysts*. Washington, DC: CQ Press.

Berry, E.N. (2001) An Application of Butler's (1980) Tourist Area Life Cycle Theory to the Cairns Region, Australia, 1876–1998. PhD Thesis, Tropical Environment and Geography, James Cook University, Cairns Campus. On WWW at www.geocities.com/tedberry_aus/tourismarealifecycle.html.

Beverland, M.B., Hoffman, D. and Rasmussen, M. (2001) The evolution of events in the Australasian wine sector. *Tourism Recreation Research* 26 (2), 35–44.

Beyers, W.B. and Nelson, P.B. (2000) Contemporary development forces in the nonmetropolitan West: New insights from rapidly growing communities. *Journal of Rural Studies* 16, 459–474.

Bianchi, R. (1994) Tourism development and resort dynamics: An alternative approach. In C. Cooper and A. Lockwood (eds) *Progress in Tourism, Recreation and Hospitality Management* (Vol.5, pp. 183–193). New York: John Wiley & Sons.

Bieger, T. (2000) *Management von Destinationen und Tourismusorganisationen*. München, Wien: Oldenbourg.

Bigelow, J. (1851) *Jamaica in 1850. Or, the Effects of Sixteen Years of Freedom on a Slave Colony*. New York: George P. Putnam.

Bird, I.L. (1966) *Six Months in the Sandwich Islands*. Honolulu: University of Hawaii Press.

Bird, J. (1963) *The Major Seaports of the United Kingdom*. Hutchinson of London.

Blamey, R. (1997) Ecotourism: The search for an operational definition. *Journal of Sustainable Tourism* 5, 109–130.

Blanchard, O.J. and Fischer, S. (1989) *Lectures on Macroeconomics*. Cambridge, MA: MIT Press.

Blazevic, I. (1994) Opatija Chronicle. In Proceedings, *150th Anniversary of Tourism in Opatija* (pp. 15–24). University of Rijeka, Faculty of Hotel Management, Opatija.

Boniface, B. and Cooper, C. (1987) *The Geography of Travel and Tourism*. Oxford: Butterworth Heinemann.

Booth, J.D. (1982) *Railways of Southern Quebec* (Vol.I, 1982; Vol.II, 1985). Toronto: Railfare Enterprises Ltd.

Bordieu, P. (1977) *Outline of a Theory of Practice*. Cambridge: Cambridge University Press.

Bordieu, P. (1984) *Distinction: A Social Critique of the Judgement of Taste*. Andover: Routledge and Kegan Paul.

Borenstein, S. (1992) The evolution of U.S. airline competition. *Journal of Economic Perspectives* 6 (2), 45–73.

Bosselman, F.P., Peterson, C.A. and McCarthy, C. (1999) *Managing Tourism Growth: Issues and Applications*. Washington, D.C.: Island Press.

Bouchikhi, H. (1993) A constructivist framework for understanding entrepreneurship performance. *Organization Studies* 14 (4), 549–570.

Bournemouth Borough Council (2002) *Tourism Facts*. Bournemouth: Bournemouth Borough Council.

Boyd, S.W. (1995) Sustainability and Canada's national parks: Suitability for policy, planning and management. Unpublished PhD thesis: Department of Geography, University of Western Ontario, London, Canada.

Boyd, S.W. (2000) Tourism, national parks and sustainability. In R.W. Butler and S.W. Boyd (eds) *Tourism and National Parks: Issues and Implications* (pp. 161–186). Chichester: Wiley.

Boyd, S.W. (2003) Marketing challenges and opportunities for heritage tourism. In A. Fyall, B. Garrod and A. Leask (eds) *Managing Visitor Attractions: New Directions* (pp. 189–202). Oxford: Butterworth-Heinemann.

Boyd, S.W. and Butler, R.W. (2000) Tourism and national parks: The origin of the concept. In R.W. Butler and S.W. Boyd (eds) *Tourism and National Parks: Issues and Implications* (pp. 13–27). Chichester: Wiley.

Boyer, R. (1986) *La Theorie de la Regulation: Une Analyse Critique*. Paris: Editions La Decouverte.

Bramwell, B. and Lane, B. (1993) Sustainable tourism: An evolving global approach. *Journal of Sustainable Tourism* 1 (1), 1–5.

Bramwell, B. and Lane, B. (2000) (eds) *Tourism Collaboration and Partnerships: Politics, Practice and Sustainability*. Clevedon: Channel View Publications.

Brassey, S. (1886) *In the Trades, the Tropics, & the Roaring Forties*. London: Longmans, Green, & Co.

Braunlich, C.G. (1996) Lessons From the Atlantic City casino experiment. *Journal of Travel Research* 34 (3), 46–62.

Briere, R. (1966) Le Tourisme au Quebec. Unpublished PhD dissertation, Geography Department, Universite de Montreal.

Briere, R. (1967) Les grands Traits de l' Evolution du Tourisme au Quebec, *Bulletin de l'Association des Geographes de l'Amerique Francaise* No. 11, Quebec.

Briggs, J. and Peat, F.D. (1999) *Seven Life Lessons of Chaos*. St. Leonards, NSW: Allen & Unwin.

Britton, S. (1991) Tourism, capital and place: Towards a critical geography. *Environment and Planning D: Society and Space* 9, 451–478.

Brookes, R. (1989) *Managing the Enabling Authority*. Harlow: Longman.

Brougham, J.E. and Butler, R.W. (1972) The applicability of the asymptotic curve to the forecasting of tourism development. Paper presented to the Research Workshop, Travel Research Association 4th Annual Conference, Quebec, July 1972.

Brown, B.J.H. (1985) Personal perception and community speculation: A British resort in the 19th century. *Annals of Tourism Research* 12 (3), 355–369.

Brown, S. (1987) Institutional change in retailing: A geographical interpretation. *Progress in Human Geography* 11 (2), 181–206.

Brown, S. (1988) The wheel of the Wheel of Retailing. *International Journal of Retailing* 3 (1), 16–37.

Brown, C. (1995) *Chaos and Catastrophe Theories*. Thousand Oaks, CA: Sage Publications.

Brown, K. (2002) Innovations for conservation and development. *The Geographical Journal* 168 (1), 6–17.

Bryan, J. (1965) 3 new Kona resort areas planned. Honolulu *Star Bulletin* 24 March, A2.

Bryman, A. (1988) *Quantity and Quality in Social Research*. London: Routledge.

Buhalis, D. (2000) Marketing the competitive destination of the future. *Tourism Management* 21 (1), 97–116.

Bullock, W.B. (1926) *Beautiful Waters Devoted to the Memphremagog Region*. Vermont: Memphremagog Press.

Bunge, W. (1966) *Theoretical Geography*. Lund: C.W.K. Gleerup Publishers.

Bureau of Tourism Research (2000a) *International Visitor Survey*. Canberra: BTR.

Bureau of Tourism Research (2000b) *Domestic Tourism Monitor*. Canberra: BTR.

Burnett, C.C. (1892) *The Land of the O-o*. Cleveland, OH: The Cleveland Printing and Publishing Co.

Burns, D. and Murphy, L. (1998) An analysis of the promotion of marine tourism in Queensland, Australia. In E. Laws, B. Faulkner and G. Moscardo (eds) *Embracing and Managing Change in Tourism: International Case Studies* (pp. 415–430). London: Routledge.

Busenitz, L.W., Gomez, C. and Spencer, J.W. (2000) Country institutional profiles: Unlocking entrepreneurial phenomena. *Academy of Management Journal* 43 (5), 994–1003.

Butler, R.W. (1973) The tourist industry in the Highlands and Islands. Unpublished PhD thesis, Glasgow: University of Glasgow.

Butler, R.W. (1980) The concept of a tourist area cycle of evolution: Implications for management of resources. *The Canadian Geographer* 24 (1), 5–12.

Butler, R.W. (1990a) The resort cycle revisited – a decade of discussion. Paper presented to Association of American Geographers Conference, Toronto, April 1990.

Butler, R.W. (1990b) Alternative tourism: Pious hope or trojan horse. *Journal of Travel Research* 28 (3), 40–44.

Butler, R.W. (1991) Tourism, environment and sustainable development. *Environmental Conservation* 18 (3), 201–209.

Butler, R. (1993) *Pre- and Post-Impact Assessment of Tourism Development. Tourism Research: Critiques and Challenges*. New York: Routledge.

Butler, R.W. (1997) The destination life cycle: Implications for heritage site management and attractivity. In W. Nuryanti (ed.) *Tourism and Heritage Management* (pp. 44–53). Yogyakarta: Gadjah Mada University Press.

Butler, R.W. (1998a) Still peddling along. The resort cycle two decades on. Paper to *Progress in Tourism and Hospitality Research*. CAUTHE Conference, Gold Coast.

Butler, R. (1998b) Sustainable tourism – looking backwards in order to progress? In C.M. Hall and A. Lew (eds) *Sustainable Tourism: A Geographical Perspective* (pp. 25–34). New York: Addison Wesley Longman.

Butler, R.W. (2000) The resort cycle two decades on. In B. Faulkner, G. Moscardo and E. Laws (eds) *Tourism in the 21st Century: Reflections on Experience* (pp. 284–299). London, New York: Continuum.

Butler, R.W. and Boyd, S.W. (2000) Tourism and parks – a long but uneasy relationship. In R.W. Butler and S.W. Boyd (eds) *Tourism and National Parks. Issues and Implications* (pp. 3–11). Chichester: Wiley.

Bywater, M. (1992) *The European Tour Operator Industry.* Special Report No. 2141. London: Economic Intelligence Unit.

C.P. (1883) The boarder and the cottager. *The Nation* August 2, (944) NP Cairns Post. 1976–1998.

Canan, P. and Hennessy, M. (1989) The growth machine, tourism, and the selling of culture. *Sociological Perspectives* 32, 227–243.

Canestrelli, E. and Costa, P. (1991) Tourist carrying capacity: A fuzzy approach. *Annals of Tourism Research* 18 (2), 295–311.

Capra, F. (1982) *The Turning Point.* London: Flamingo.

Casagrandi, R. and Rinaldi, S. (2002) A theoretical approach to tourism sustainability. *Conservation Ecology* 6 (1), 13–35.

Caserta, S. and Russo, A.P. (2002) More means worse. Asymmetric information, spatial displacement and sustainable heritage tourism. *Journal of Cultural Economics* 26 (4).

Casino Control Commission Annual Report (2001) p. 4.

Cater, E. (1993) Ecotourism in the third world: Problems for sustainable tourism development. *Tourism Management* 14 (2), 85–90.

Catry, B. and Chevalier, M. (1974) Market share strategy and the product life cycle. *Journal of Marketing* 38, 29–34.

Cauthorn, R. (1989) *Contributions to a Theory of Entrepreneurship.* New York: Garland Publishing Inc.

Cazes, G. and Potier, F. (1996) *Le Tourisme Urbain.* Paris: Presses Universitaires de France.

Centre for Tourism Policy Studies, School of Travel Industry Management, University of Hawaii (1998) *Repositioning Hawaii's Visitor Industry Products: Development Strategies for the New Tourism Environment.* On WWW at http://www.state.hi.us/tourism/reposit.pdf. Accessed 14.2.2001.

Centre for Travel and Tourism, New College, Durham in association with Business Education Publishers Limited.

Chaney, G.L. (1879) *Aho-ha! A Hawaiian Salutation.* Boston: Roberts Brothers.

Chapin, H. (1976) Corey's Coming. From *On the Road to Kingdom Come.* Electra Records.

Chapman, E. (1961) *Pleasure Island: The Book of Jamaica* (Vol. 5). Kingston: Arawak Press.

Chemin des Vignobles du Quebec (2001) Pamphlet. Associaton des Vignerons du Quebec.

Chen, J. (2001) Disscusion on "the lifecycle of the tourist products". *Journal of Guilin Technical College* 3, 18–20.

Cheshire, P. and Gordon, I. (1996) Territorial competition and the predictability of collective (in)action. *International Journal of Urban and Regional Research* 20 (3), 383–399.

Chorley, R. and Haggett, P. (eds) (1967) *Models in Geography*. London: Methuen.

Choy, D.J.L. (1991) Tourism planning: The case for market failure. *Tourism Management* 12 (4), 313–330.

Choy, D. (1992) Life cycle models for Pacific island destinations. *Journal of Travel Research* 30 (3), 6–31.

Christaller, W. (1933) *Die Zentrale Orte in Süddeutschland* [*The Central Places in South Germany*]. Jena: Gustav Fischer Verlag.

Christaller, W. (1955) Beiträge zu einer Geographie der Fremdenverkehr. Erdkunde, Band IX, Heft 1, February 1955, 1–19.

Christaller, W. (1963) Some considerations of tourism location in Europe: The peripheral regions – underdeveloped countries – recreation areas. *Regional Science Association Papers* XII, Lund Congress, 95–105.

Chunxiao (1997) Thoughts on "tourist products lifecycle". *Tourism Tribune* 12 (5), 44–47.

Circuit des Arts (2002) pamphlet.

Clark, J.R.K. (1985) *Beaches of the Big Island*. Honolulu: University of Hawaii Press.

Clark, S. (1952) *All the Best in the Caribbean*. New York: Dodd, Mead & Co.

Clawson, M. and Knetch, J.L. (1963) *Economics of Outdoor Recreation, Resources of the Future Inc*. Baltimore: Johns Hopkins University Press.

Clegg, A. and Essex, S. (2000) Restructuring in tourism: The accommodation sector in a major British coastal resort. *International Journal of Tourism Research* 2 (2), 77–96.

CLICOR (1971) Canada Land Inventory Land Capability for (Outdoor) Recreation, Montreal H31 map sheet. Ottawa: Department of Energy, Mines and Resources.

Cloke, P., Philo, C. and Sadler, D. (1991) *Approaching Human Geography. An Introduction to Contemporary Theoretical Debates*. London: PCP.

COAST (1993) *COAST*. Brussels: European Commission.

Cohen, E. (1972) Toward a sociology of international tourism. *Social Research* 39 (1), 164–182.

Cohen, E. (1979a) Rethinking the sociology of tourism. *Annals of Tourism Research* 6 (1), 18–35.

Cohen, E. (1979b) The impact of tourism on the hill tribes of Northern Thailand. *International Asienforum* 10 (1/2), 5–38.

Cohen, E. (1996a) A phenomenology of tourist experiences. In Y. Apostolopoulos, S. Leivadi and A. Yiannakis (eds) *The Sociology of Tourism: Theoretical and Empirical Investigations* (pp. 90–114). London: Routledge.

Cohen, E. (1996b) *Thai Tourism, Hilltribes, Islands and Open-Ended Prostitution*. Bangkok: White Lotus and Co., Ltd.

Cohn, N. (1973) *AWopBop aLooBop ALopBamBoom*. St Alban: Paladin.

Cohn, N. (2002) The king is dead. *Observer Magazine* 11 September, 17–23.

Coles, T.E. (1999a) Competition, contested retail space and the rise of the German department store, c.1870–1914. *International Review of Retail Distribution and Consumer Research* 9 (3), 275–290.

Coles, T.E. (1999b) Department stores as innovations in retail marketing in Germany: Some observations on marketing practice and perception in the Wilhelmine Period. *Journal of Macromarketing* 19 (1), 34–47.

Coles, T.E. (2004) Tourism, shopping and retailing: An axiomatic relationship? In C.M. Hall, A. Lew and A.M. Williams (eds) *A Companion to Tourism* (pp. 360–373). Oxford: Blackwell.

Coll Jr., R. (1950) Visitors flocking to Kona. Honolulu *Advertiser* 17 January, 17.

Connely, W. (1955) *Beau Nash Monarch of Bath and Tunbridge Wells*. London: Werner Laurie Ltd.

Constant, E. (2000) Recursive practice and the evolution of technical knowledge. In J. Zimon (ed.) *Technological Innovation as an Evolutionary Process* (pp. 219–233). Cambridge: Cambridge University Press.

Convention Concerning the Protection of the World Cultural and Natural Heritage (16 November 1972) On WWW at www.unesco.org/whc. Accessed 12.2002.

Convention on Wetlands of International Importance (2 February 1971) On WWW at www.ramsar.org/. Accessed 12.2002.

Cooke, P. (1987) The changing urban and regional systems in the UK. *Regional Studies* 20 (3), 243–251.

Cooke, P. (1989) *Localities*. London: Unwin Hyman.

Cooper, C. (1990a) Resorts in decline – the management response. *Tourism Management* 11 (1), 63–67.

Cooper, C. (1990b) The life cycle concept and tourism. Unpublished Conference Paper, *Tourism Research into the 1990s*. University of Durham (cited in Shaw & Williams, 2002).

Cooper, C.P. (1992) The life cycle concept and strategic planning for coastal resorts. *Built Environment* 18 (1), 57–66.

Cooper, C.P. (1994) The destination life cycle: An update. In A.V. Seaton, C.L. Jenkins, R.C. Wood, Dieke, P.U.C., M.M. Bennett, L.R. MacLellan and R. Smith (eds) *Tourism: The State of the Art* (pp. 340–346). Brisbane: Wiley.

Cooper, C.P. (1995) Strategic planning for sustainable tourism: The case of the offshore islands in the UK. *Journal of Sustainable Tourism* 3 (4), 191–209.

Cooper, C.P. (1997a) *Inaugural Lecture*. University of Bournemouth.

Cooper, C.P. (1997b) The environmental consequences of declining destinations. *Progress in Tourism and Hospitality Research* 2 (3), 337–345.

Cooper, C.P. (1997c) Parameters and indicators of the decline of the British seaside resort. In G. Shaw and A. Williams (eds) *The Rise and Fall of British Coastal Resorts* (pp. 79–101). London: Cassell.

Cooper, C. and Jackson, S. (1989) Destination life cycle: The Isle of Man case study. *Annals of Tourism Research* 16 (3), 377–398.

Cooper, C.P. and Lockwood, A. (1993) *Progress in Tourism, Recreation and Hospitality Management* (Vol.5, pp. 181–193). Chichester: Wiley.

Cooper, R.G. and Kleinschmidt, E.J. (1993) Screening new products for potential winners. *Long Range Planning* 6 (6), 74–81.

Cooper, C., Fletcher, J., Noble, A. and Westlake, J. (1996) Changing tourism demand in Central Europe: The case of Romanian tourist spas. *Journal of Tourism Studies* 6 (2), 30–44.

Cooper, C., Fletcher, J., Gilbert, D. and Wanhill, S. (1998) In R. Shepherd (ed.) *Tourism: Principles and Practice* (2nd edn). Harlow: Longman.

CORD (Canadian Outdoor Recreation Demand) Surveys (1969–72) Ottawa: Parks Canada.

Coriat, B. (1979) *L'Atelier et al Chronometer*. Paris: Bourgois.

Costa, P. and Manente, M. (1995) Venice and its visitors: A survey and a model of qualitative choice. *Journal of Travel and Tourism Marketing* 4 (3), 45–69.

Costa, P. and van der Borg, J. (1988) Un modello lineare per la programmazione del turismo. *COSES Informazioni* 32/33, 21–26.

County of Hawaii: Office of the Mayor (1987) *A Summary of Planned Developments in West Hawaii, County of Hawaii*. Hawaii: Hilo.

Crawford, C.M. (1984) Business took the wrong cycle from biology. *Journal of Consumer Marketing* 1 (Summer), 5–11.

Creighton, T.H. and Walters, G.S. (1969) *The South Kona Coast Historic and Recreation Area, Island of Hawaii*. Honolulu: Hawaii Department of Land and Natural Resources.

Cundall, F. (1928) *Jamaica in 1928: A Handbook of Information for Visitors and Intending Residents with some Account of the Colony's History*. London: The Institute of Jamaica.

Curtis, S. (1997) Seaside resort: Spanish progress and British malaise. In *Insights* (C9–18). London: British Tourist Authority/English Tourist Board.

Cypriot Tourism Organisation (2002) Strategic tourism plan, 2010. Nicosia: Government of Cyprus.

da Conceiçáo Gonçalves, V.F. and Roque Águas, P.M. (1997) The concept of the life cycle: An application to the tourist product. *Journal of Travel Research* 36 (2), 12–22.

Danielson, M. (1995) *Profits and Politics in Paradise: The Development of Hilton Head Island*. Columbia, SC: The University of South Carolina Press.

Darling, F.F. (1936) *A Herd of Red Deer*. Oxford: Oxford University Press.

Darling, F.F. (1941) *Island Years*. London: G. Bell and Sons Ltd.

Darling, F.F. (1943) *Island Farm*. London: G. Bell and Sons Ltd.

Darnell, A.C. and Johnson, P.S. (2001) Repeat visits to attractions: A preliminary economic analysis. *Tourism Management* 22, 119–126.

Daru, R., Vreedenburgh, E. and Scha, R. (2000) Architectural innovation as an evolutionary process. Abstract of paper presented at the Generative Art Conference, Politecnico di Milano, Italy, 14–16 Dec 2000. On WWW at www.generativeart.com/abst2000/abst77.htm.

Darwin, C. (1859) *The Origin of the Species*. New York: P.F. Collier & Son.

Daughters of Hawaii (1979) *Treasures...Hulihee*. Honolulu.

Davidson, W.R., Bates, A.D. and Bass, S.J. (1976) The retail life cycle. *Harvard Business Review* 54 (November–December), 89–96.

Davies, P. (1992) Wish you here? *Landscape Design* (December), 21–24.

Davis, C. (1997) Bloated victim of a fallen world. *Sunday Times* 13 July.

Dawkins, R. (1986) *The Blind Watchmaker*. London: Penguin Books.

Day, A.G. (1955) *Hawaii and Its People*. New York: Dull, Sloan and Pearce.

Day, G.S. (1981) The product life cycle: Analysis and applications issues. *Journal of Marketing* 45 (Fall), 60–67.

de Albuquerque, K. and McElroy, J.L. (1992) Caribbean small-island tourism styles and sustainable strategies. *Environmental Management* 16 (5), 619–632.

Dean, J. (1950) Pricing policies for new products. *Harvard Business Review* November–December, 45–53.

Dearden, P. (1991) Tourism and sustainable development in Northern Thailand. *Geographic Review* 81, 400–413.

Dearden, P. and Harron, S. (1994) Alternative tourism and adaptive change. *Annals of Tourism Research* 21, 81–102.

Debbage, K. (1990) Oligopoly and the resort cycle in the Bahamas. *Annals of Tourism Research* 17, 513–527.

Debbage, K. (1992) Tourism oligopoly is at work. *Annals of Tourism Research* 19 (2), 355–359.

Decker, R.W., Wright, T.L. and Stauffer, P.H. (eds) *Volcanism in Hawaii* (pp. 149–189). US Geological Survey Professional Paper.

de Kadt, E. (1979) *Tourism: Passport to Development*. Oxford: Oxford University Press.

Del Viscio, J. (no date) Atlantic City: A Renaissance Resort. On WWW at http://www.travelbase.com/auto/localview-new.cgi?article = 142. Accessed 30.3.2001.

Department for Culture, Media and Sport (2000a) Seaside 2000 Consultation. London, DCMS.

Department for Culture, Media and Sport (2000b) Government Report to the Tourism Summit: Tomorrow's Tourism.

Department of Culture, Arts and Leisure (2001) *Guidance to District Councils on the Development of Local Cultural Strategies*. London: Department of Culture, Arts and Leisure. On WWW at http://www.culture.gov.uk/tourism/govt_report.html. Accessed 16.2.2001.

De Vis-Norton, L. (1925) The island of Hawaii, a paradise for tourists. *Paradise of the Pacific* 38, 13–15.

Dewailly, J-M. (1999) Sustainable tourist space: From reality to virtual reality? *Tourism Geographies* 1 (1), 41–55.

Dhalla, N.K. and Yuspeh, S. (1976) Forget the product life cycle concept. *Harvard Business Review* 54 (January/February), 102–112.

Diamond, N.P. (1988) A Strategy for Cold Water Resorts into the Year 2000. Unpublished MSc Thesis, University of Surrey, UK.

di Benedetto, A.C. and Bojanic, D. (1993) Tourism area life-cycles. *Annals of Tourism Research* 20 (3), 557–570.

Dicken, P. (1998) *Global Shift: The Internationalisation of Economic Activity* (3rd edn). London: Chapman.

Digance, J. (1997) Life cycle model. *Annals of Tourism Research* 24 (2), 452–455.

Dillman, D.A. (1978) *Mail and Telephone Surveys*. New York: John Wiley & Sons.

Din, K.H. (1992) The "involvement stage" in the evolution of a tourist destination. *Tourism Recreation Research* 17 (1), 10–20.

Din, J. and Bao, J. (2000) A study on the life cycle of special karst cave with a case of Jinashui Swallow Cave in Yunnan Provice. *Carsologica Sinica* 19 (3), 284–289.

Douglas, N. (1997) Applying the life cycle model to Melanesia. *Annals of Tourism Research* 24 (1), 1–22.

Doxey, G.V. (1975) A causation theory of visitor–resident irritants: Methodology and research inferences. *Proceedings of the Travel Research Association 6th Annual Conference* (pp. 195–198). San Diego: Travel Research Association.

Doyle, G. (1957) The magic of Kona coast. *Paradise of the Pacific* 69 (11), 22–41.

Drucker, P.F. (1973) *Management*. New York: Harper and Row.

Drucker, P.F. (1985) *Innovation and Entrepreneurship: Practices and Principles*. New York: Harper & Row.

Duncan, S. and Savage, M. (1989) Space, scale and locality. *Antipode* 21 (3), 179–206.

Duncan, S. and Savage, M. (1991) New perspectives on the locality debate. *Environment and Planning A* 23 (2), 155–164.

Dunk, M. (2000) All shook up by the King's birthplace. *Daily Express* 6 May.

Dunn, D. (1998) Home Truths from Abroad. PhD Thesis, University of Birmingham.

Dziembowska-Kowalska, J. and Funck, R.H. (2000) Cultural activities as a location factor in European competition between regions: Concepts and some evidence. *Annals of Regional Science* 34, 1– 12.

Eadington, W. (1982) The Gambling Papers: Proceedings of the Fifth National Conference on Gambling and Risk Taking. Vols 8&9: Issues in Casino Gambling: Nevada and Atlantic City. Reno, NV: University of Nevada.

Eastern Townships regional Tourist Guidebooks (2000) Association Touristique des Cantons de l'Est, Tourisme Quebec.

Eidsvik, H.K. (1983) Parks Canada, conservation and tourism: A review of the seventies – a preview of the eighties. In P.E. Murphy (ed.) *Tourism in Canada: Selected Issues and Options.* Western Geographical Series, 21 (pp. 241– 269). Victoria: University of Victoria.

English, D.B., Marcouiller, D.W. and Cordell, K.H. (2000) Tourism dependence in rural America: Estimates and effects. *Society and Natural Resources* 13, 185– 202.

English Tourist Board (1991) *The Future of England's Smaller Seaside Resorts.* London: English Tourist Board.

EUROPARC and IUCN (2000) *Guidelines for Protected Area Management Categories.* Grafenau: EUROPARC and WCPA.

Evans, R. and Harding, A. (1997) Regionalisation, regional institutions and economic development. *Policy and Politics* 25, 19– 30.

Evans, K., Barnes, J. and Schlacter, J. (1993) A general systems approach to retail evolution: An existing institutional perspective. *International Review of Retail, Distribution and Consumer Research* 3 (1), 79– 100.

Farrell, B. (1992) Tourism as an element in sustainable development: Hana Maui. In V.L. Smith and W.R. Eadington (eds) *Tourism Alternatives* (pp. 115– 132). Philadelphia: University of Pennsylvania Press.

Farrell, B.H. (1999) Conventional or sustainable tourism? No room for choice. *Tourism Management* 20 (2), 189– 191.

Faulkner, B. (1999) Qualitative Research Methods (unpublished chapter).

Faulkner, B. (2002) *Our Gold Coast: The Preferred Future.* Gold Coast: Cooperative Research Centre for Sustainable Tourism.

Faulkner, B. (2003) Rejuvenating a maturing tourist destination: The case of the Gold Coast. In E. Fredline, L. Jago and C. Cooper (eds) *Progressing Tourism Research.* Clevedon: Channel View Publications.

Faulkner, H.W. (1990) Swings and roundabouts in Australian tourism. *Tourism Management* 11 (1), 29– 37.

Faulkner, B. and Russell, R. (1997) Chaos and complexity in tourism: In search of a new perspective. *Pacific Tourism Review* 1 (2), 93– 102.

Faulkner, B. and Russell, R. (2001) Turbulence, chaos and complexity in tourism systems: A research direction for the new millennium. In B. Faulkner, G. Moscardo and E. Laws (eds) *Tourism in the 21st Century.* London: Continuum.

Fayos Sola, E. (1992) A strategic outlook for regional tourism policy: The white paper on Valencian tourism. *Tourism Management* 13 (1), 45– 49.

Fernandez (1999) *Shoshone News Press.* (personal communication).

Finch, J. and Groves, D. (1983) *Labour of Love: Women, Work and Caring.* London: Routledge and Kegan Paul.

Fly, J.M. (1986) Tourism and nature: The basis for growth in Northern Lower Michigan. Unpublished paper.

Foglesong, R. (1999) Walt Disney World and Orlando: Deregulation as a strategy for tourism. In D. Judd and S. Fainstein (eds) *The Tourist City* (pp. 89–106). Newhaven: Yale University Press.

Formica, S. and Uysal, M. (1996) The revitalisation of Italy as a tourist destination. *Tourism Management* 17 (5), 323–331.

Fornander, A. (1980) *An Account of the Polynesian Race: Its Origins and Migrations.* Rutland, VT: Chas. E. Tuttle Company.

Foster, D.M. and Murphy, P. (1991) Resort cycle revisited – The retirement connection. *Annals of Tourism Research* 18, 553–567.

Foster, C. (2000) A new look for Waikiki. *Travel Agent* May 1. On WWW at http://www.findarticles.com/cf_0/m0VOU/18_299/63298501/print.jhtml. Accessed 5.3.2001.

France, L. (1991) An application of the tourism destination area life cycle to Barbados. *Revue de Tourisme* 46 (3), 25–30.

France, L. and Barke, M. (1991) The development of Torremolinos as an international resort: Past, present and future. Occasional paper produced for the Centre for Travel and Toruism, New College, Durham, in association with Business Education Publishers Limited.

Franck, H. (1920) *Roaming through the West Indies.* New York: Blue Ribbon Books.

Frank, A. (1967) *Capitalism and Underdevelopment in Latin America.* New York: Monthly Review Press.

Franklin, A. and Crang, M. (2001) The trouble with tourism and travel theory? *Tourist Studies* 1 (1), 5–22.

Freidmann, J. and Alonso, W. (eds) (1974) *Regional Development and Planning: A Reader.* Cambridge, MA: MIT Press.

Fritz-Nemeth, P. and Lundgren, J.O. (1996) Tourist attractions – from natural to industrial. *TEOROS* 15 (2), 23–30, Montreal: UQAM.

Funnell, C. (1975) *By the Beautiful Sea: The Rise and High Times of That Great American Resort, Atlantic City* (p. 154). New York: Alfred A. Knopf.

Gambicini, P. (2002) *Elvis.* BBC Radio 2.

Gardner, D.M. (1987) The product life cycle: A critical look at the literature. *Review of Marketing* 162–194.

Garmise, S. and Rees, G. (1997) The role of institutional networks in local economic development. A new model of governance? *Local Economy* 12 (2), 104–118.

Garrod, B. (2003) Managing visitor impacts. In A. Fyall, B. Garrod and A. Leask (eds) *Managing Visitor Attractions: New Directions* (pp. 124–139). Oxford: Butterworth-Heinemann.

Garrod, B. and Fyall, A. (2000) Managing heritage tourism. *Annals of Tourism Research* 27 (3), 682–706.

Gartner, W.C. (2002) Cultural tourism trends and implications for tourism development. Paper Presented at the International Conference on: The Tourist-Historic City: Sharing Culture for the future, 17–20 March 2002, Bruges.

Gershuny, J. and Miles, I. (1983) *The New Services Economy: The Transformation of Employment in Industrial Societies.* London: Frances Pinter.

Getz, D. (1983) Capacity to absorb tourism concepts and implications for strategic planning. *Annals of Tourism Research* 10 (1), 245–257.

Getz, D. (1986) Models of tourism planning. Towards integration of theory and practice. *Tourism Management* 7 (1), 21–32.

Getz, D. (1991) *Festivals, Special Events, and Tourism.* New York: Van Nostrand Reinhold.

Getz, D. (1992) Tourism planning and destination lifecycle. *Annals of Tourism Research* 19 (4), 752–770.

Getz, D. (2000) Festivals and special events: Life cycle and saturation issues. In W.C. Gartner and D.W. Lime (eds) *Trends in Outdoor Recreation, Leisure and Saturation Issues* (pp. 175–185). Wallingford: CABI.

Giambelluca, T.W., Nullet, M.A. and Schroeder, T.A. (1986) *Rainfall Atlas of Hawaii*. Honolulu: State of Hawaii. DLNR.

Giddens, A. (1984) *The Constitution of Society*. Berkeley: University of California Press.

Gilbert, D. (1990) Strategic marketing planning for national tourism. *Tourist Review* 45 (1), 18–27.

Gilbert, E.W. (1939) The growth of inland and seaside health resorts in England. *Scottish Geographical Magazine* 55, 16–35.

Gilbert, E.W. (1954) *Brighton – Old Ocean's Bauble*. London: Methuen.

Gist, R.R. (1968) *Retailing. Concepts and Decisions*. New York: Wiley and Sons.

Glaser, B. (1978) *Theoretical Sensitivity*. Mill Valley, CA: The Sociology Press.

Glaser, B. and Strauss, A. (1967) *The Discovery of Grounded Theory: Strategies for Qualitative Research*. New York: Aldine De Gruyter.

Gleick, J. (1987) *Chaos: Making a New Science*. London: Heinemann.

Goad, P. and Crispin, S.W. (1999) Tourism: Wish you were here. *Far Eastern Economic Review*. On WWW at http://www.feer.com/9909_30/p60tourism.html. Accessed 21.2.2001.

Godkin, E.L. (1883) Evolution of the summer resort. *The Nation* July 19, 47–48.

Goffman, E. (1959) *Presentation of Self in Everyday Life*. New York: Doubleday.

Gold Coast City Council (2000) Draft Gold Coast 2010: Economic Development Strategy. GCCC.

Gordon, I. and Goodall, B. (1992) Resort cycles and development processes. *Built Environment* 18 (4), 41–56.

Gordon, I. and Goodall, B. (2000) Localities and tourism. *Tourism Geographies* 2 (3), 290–311.

Gormsen, E. (1981) The spatio-temporal development of international tourism, attempt at a centre–periphery model. In *La Consommation d'Espace par le Tourisme et sa Preservation*. Aix-en-Provence: Centre d'etudes touristiques.

Gosling, R. (1980) *Personal Copy. A Memoir of the Sixties*. London: Faber and Faber.

Gössling, S. (2000) Tourism development in Sri Lanka: The case of Ethukala and Unawatuna. *Tourism Recreation Research* 25 (3), 103–114.

Gould, S.J. (1980) *The Panda's Thumb*. New York: W.W. Norton & Co.

Graham, B. (1998) Liberalization, regional economic development and the geography of demand for air transport in the European Union. *Journal of Transport Geography* 6 (2), 87–104.

Green Globe News (2000) Country Focus: Spain. On WWW at http://www.greenglobe21.com/pdf_files/june2000.pdf. Accessed 13.2.2001.

Gregory, D.J. (1994) 'Logical positivism', 'model', 'structuralism' entries. In R.J. Johnston, D. Gregory and D.M. Smith (eds) *The Dictionary of Human Geography* (3rd edn, pp. 350–351, 385–386, 599–600). Oxford: Blackwell.

Gunn, C.A. (1988) *Tourism Planning*. New York: Taylor and Francis.

Gunn, C.A. (1993) *Tourism Planning: Basics, Concepts, Cases* (3rd edn). Washington, D.C.: Taylor & Francis.

Gurney, J. (1840) *A Winter in the West Indies, Described in Familiar Letters to Henry Clay, of Kentucky*. London: John Murray.

Hall, C.M. (1996) Personal communication on the relevance of lines in sand pits to resort life cycles. April, London, Ontario.

Hall, C.M. (2000) *Tourism Planning – Policies, Processes and Relationships*. Harlow: Prentice Hall.

Hall, C.M. and McArthur, S. (1998) *Integrated Heritage Management*. London: The Stationery Office.

Hall, C.M. and Page, S.J. (1999) *The Geography of Tourism and Recreation: Environment, Place and Space*. London: Routledge.

Hall, C.M. and Page, S.J. (2005) *The Geography of Tourism and Recreation: Environment, Place and Space* (3rd edn). London: Routledge.

Hall, C.M., Williams, A.M. and Lew, A. (2004) Tourism: Conceptualisations, institutions and issues. In A. Lew, C.M. Hall and A. Williams (eds) *Companion to Tourism* (pp. 3– 21). Oxford: Blackwells.

Hammond, J.T. (1993) Hilton Head Island's growing pains centered on mayor-elect. *The News* 29 November.

Handy, C. (1994) *The Age of Paradox*. Boston: Harvard Business School Press.

Harada, W. (1968) Kona group seeks 3-story limitation. Honolulu *Advertiser* 29 May [Hawaii Newspaper Clippings Morgue, Hamilton Library, University of Hawaii-file Kona Building Heights]

Harada-Stone, D. (1989) Kealakekua ranch's plans worry neighbours. Hawaii *Tribune Herald* 10 January, 1.

Harland Bartholomew and Associates (1960) *A Plan for Kona*. Honolulu: Prepared for the Hawaii State Planning Office.

Harlow, G.S. (1928) *Hawaii: By a Tourist*. Los Angeles, CA: West Coast Publishing.

Harmon, M. (1999) Long Beach, Successful Meetings, June. http://global. umi.com/pqdweb?ts = 98. . .&Sid = 7&Idx = 10&Deli = 1&RQT = 309&Dtp = 1. Accessed 9.3.2001.

Harnischfeger, U. (2000) Preussag focuses on leisure. *Financial Times* 5th October.

Harrigan, J.J. (1989) *Political Change in the Metropolis*. Illinois: Scott, Foresman and Company.

Harrigan, N. (1974) The legacy of Caribbean history and tourism. *Annals of Tourism Research* 2 (1), 13– 25.

Harris, C. (1954) The market as a factor in the localization of industry in the United States. *Annals of the Association of American Geographers* 64, 315– 348.

Harrison, D. (1995) Development of tourism in Swaziland. *Annals of Tourism Research* 22 (1), 135– 156.

Hart, C. (1999) The retail accordion and assortment strategies: An exploratory study. *International Review of Retail, Distribution and Consumer Research* 8 (2), 165– 182.

Hart, C.W., Casserley, G. and Lawless, M.J. (1984) The product life cycle: How useful? *The Cornell Quarterly* 25, 54– 63.

Hartwell, M. and Lane, J. (1991) *Champions of Enterprise*. Double Bay, NSW: Focus Books Pty Ltd.

Harvey, D. (1969) *Explanation in Geography*. London: Edward Arnold.

Harvey, D. (1989) *The Condition of Post-Modernity*. Oxford: Blackwell.

Hawaii County Planning Department (HCPD) (1999) On WWW at http://www.hawaii-county.com/text.version/annual96_97/r&d01.htm. Accessed 21.1.2000.

Hawaii Newspaper Clippings Morgue (HNCM), Hamilton Library, University of Hawaii [original newspaper unknown, subject heading shown in brackets below]

_____ (1949) Kona airport induces new business. 9 Sept. [Kona Airport 1929/1953]

_____ (1951) Kona's airport: An asset for Hawaii. [Kona Airport 1929/1953]

_____ (1953) 'Cow pen' battle continues at Kona. 30 Apr. [Kona Cattle Pen Controversy at Kailua Wharf]

_____ (1957) 'Natural' look to prevail by Kona landscaping project. 5 June [Kona Sea Wall]

_____ (1959) Kona water supply called adequate for now. 17 Nov. [Kona Water 1957/1958]

_____ (1960) Sen. Lymanm Moves to drop $1.7M Kona area projects [Kona Master Plan]

Hawaii Tourism Authority (HTA) (1999) *Competitive strategic assessment of Hawaii tourism* (Executive Summary). Hawaiian Tourism Authority.

Hawaii Tribune Herald (HTH) (1967a) Planners recommend Kona maps. 21 February, 1.

Hawaii Tribune Herald (1967b) New golf course proposed by County for South Kona. 25 October, 8.

Hawaii Tribune Herald (1968a) Kona Hilton opening brings room level to over 2,100. 25 February, 3.

Hawaii Tribune Herald (1968b) Editorial. Emphasis on 'Gold Coast'. 5 February, 4.

Hawaii Tribune Herald (1969) Nearly 3,500 new rooms planned for Kona. 26 January, 3.

Hawaii Tribune Herald (1970) Girders, construction worker's pounding reshape Kailua and ... New Kona of modern buildings rises along isle's 'sun coast'. 26 July, 2–3.

Hawaii Tribune Herald (1972) Proposed development, scenic route are termed 'monstrosity'. 18 January, 1.

Hawaii Tribune Herald (1974a) Kailua Village development bill gets county support. 31 July, 1.

Hawaii Tribune Herald (1974b) Council oks bill for Kailua-Kona. 22 August, 10.

Hawaii Tribune Herald (1974c) Kona chamber applauds district approval. 18 September, 16.

Hawaii Tribune Herald (1989) Ground blessing held or Ka'upulehu Four Seasons. 2 May, 1.

Hawken, P., Lovins, A. and Lovins, L.H. (1999) *Natural Capitalism: Creating the Next Industrial Revolution*. Boston, MA: Little, Brown and Company.

Hawkins, M. (1982) The Atlantic City Experience: Casino Gambling as an Economic Recovery Program.

Haywood, K.M. (1986) Can the tourist area life-cycle be made operational? *Tourism Management* 7 (3), 154–167.

Haywood, K.M. (1988) Responsible and responsive tourism planning in the community. *Tourism Management* June.

Haywood, K.M. (1992) Revisiting resort cycle. *Annals of Tourism Research* 19 (2), 351–354.

Haywood, K.M. (1998) Economic business cycles and the tourism life-cycle concept. In D. Ioniddes and K. Debbage (eds) *The Economic Geography of the Tourist Industry* (pp. 273–284). London: Routledge.

Heath, E. and Wall, G. (1992) *Marketing Tourism Destination: A Strategic Planning Approach*. New York: Wiley.

Hiss, T. (1990) *The Experience of Place*. New York: Alfred A. Knopf.

Hobbs, C. (1913) The ruin or the redemption of Lake Quinsigamond. *The Worcester Magazine* February, 35–38.

Hodgson, G.M. (2002) Darwinism in economics: From analogy to ontology. *Journal of Evolutionary Economics* 12 (3), 259–281.

Hofer, C.W. (1975) Toward a contingency theory of business strategy. *Academy of Management Journal* 18 (December), 784–809.

Holder, J.S. (1991) Pattern and impact of tourism on the environment of the Caribbeans. In S. Medlik (ed.) *Managing Tourism*. Oxford: Butterworth-Heinemann.

Hollander, S.C. (1960) The wheel of retailing. *Journal of Marketing* 25 (July), 37–42.

Hollander, S.C. (1980) Oddities, nostalgia, wheels and other patterns in retail evolution. In R.W. Stampfl and E.C. Hirschmann (eds) *Competitive Structure in Retail Markets: The Department Store Perspective* (pp. 84–94). Chicago: American Marketing Association.

Holloway, J.C. (1994) *The Business of Tourism* (Vol. 4). London: Pitman.

Holloway, J.C. (1998) *The Business of Tourism* (Vol. 5). Harlow: Longman.

Honolulu Advertiser (HA) (1954) Long range thinking urged in Kona area. 13 January, 1.

Honolulu Advertiser (1955a) Chamber unit ok's Kaiser Kona tourist project. 11 January, A1.

Honolulu Advertiser (1955b) Local corporation plans $1 million Kona resort. 5 August, A3.

Honolulu Advertiser (1956a) Time grows short. 3 August, A3.

Honolulu Advertiser (1956b) Kona backs four-point development. 17 September, B1.

Honolulu Advertiser (1968) Kimurao opposes Kona high-rises. 18 May, A10.

Honolulu Advertiser (1969) Editorial. Saving Kona's assets. 5 February, B2.

Honolulu Advertiser (1970) Bill proposes State buy Kailua-Kona village. 7 March, A6.

Honolulu Advertiser (1973) Historic district proposed for Kona resort area. 7 February, B6.

Honolulu Star Bulletin (HSB) (1956) Plans for Two $1 Million Hotels in Kona Announced. 10 July, 1B.

Honolulu Star Bulletin (1957) Kaiser pegs plans to tourist growth. 14 February, 1B.

Honolulu Star Bulletin (1958a) Navy barge reaches Kona with 9-to-10 day water supply. [HNCM Kona Drought]

Honolulu Star Bulletin (1958b) Big Isle reaction to Kona plan stresses water, airport need. 2 Dec. [HNCM Kona Master Plan]

Honolulu Star Bulletin (1970) Kona's time to plan. 1 July, A14.

Honolulu Star Bulletin (1974) On the Big Island. 31 Mar. [HNCM Kailua-Kona 1962/1975]

Honolulu Star Bulletin (1988) State opposes resort near wildlife area. 13 July, A4.

Hough, M. (1990) *Out of Place: Restoring Identity to the Regional Landscape*. New Haven, CT: Yale University Press.

Hourglass Foundation (2001) *Where Are We Headed?* Lancaster, PA: Hourglass Foundation.

House, J. (1954) Geographical aspects of coastal holiday resorts. Unpublished PhD thesis, Durham: Kings College.

Hovinen, G.R. (1981) A tourist cycle in Lancaster County, Pennsylvania. *The Canadian Geographer* 25 (3), 283–286.

Hovinen, G.R. (1982) Visitor cycles: Outlook for tourism in Lancaster County. *Annals of Tourism Research* 9, 565–583.

Hovinen, G.R. (1995) Heritage issues in urban tourism: An assessment of new trends in Lancaster County. *Tourism Management* 16 (5), 381–388.

Hovinen, G. (1997) Lancaster County, Pennsylvania's heritage tourism initiative: A preliminary assessment. *Small Town* 27, 4–11.

Hovinen, G.R. (2002) Revisiting the destination lifecycle model. *Annals of Tourism Research* 29 (1), 209–230.

Hudson, R. (1992) Industrial restructuring and spatial change: Myths and realities in the changing geography of production in the 1980s. *Scottish Geographical Magazine* 108 (2), 74–81.

Hunziker, W. (1942) *The Tourist Doctrine*. Switzerland: St. Gallen.

Hurst, D.K. (1995) *Crisis and Renewal: Meeting the Challenge of Organizational Change*. Boston, MA: Harvard Business School Press.

ICARE – International Center for Art Economics (1997) *Applicazione della Telematica alla Gestione dei Flussi di Visitatori*. Research Center Telecom Italia S. Salvador, mimeo.

Idzes, I. (1988) *Corporate Lifecycles: How and Why Corporations Grow and Die and What To Do About It*. Englewood Cliffs, NJ: Prentice Hall.

Inskeep, E. (1991) *Tourism Planning: An Integrated and Sustainable Development Approach*. New York: Van Nostrand Reinhold.

Inskeep, E. (1994) *National and Regional Tourism Planning: Methodologies and Case Studies*, edited by the World Tourism Organization. UK: Routledge.

Inter-Island Steam Navigation Company, Ltd. (1917–44) *President's Report for the Year*. Honolulu: Advertiser Publishing Co.

Ioannides, D. (1992) Tourism development agents: The Cypriot resort cycle. *Annals of Tourism Research* 19 (4), 711–731.

Ioannides, D. and Debbage, K. (1998) *The Economic Geography of the Tourist Industry: A Supply-side Analysis*. London: Routledge.

Irish Tourist Board (2001) On WWW at
http://www.ireland.travel.ie/aboutus/tourismfacts.asp;
http://www.irlgov.ie/finance/budget/budget01/budmeasu.htm#PARTIII;
http://www.irlgov.ie/finance/budget/budget01/speech01.htm.
Accessed 6.3.2001.

Ishii, K. and Stevels, A. (2000) *Environmental Value Chain Analysis: A Tool for Product Definition in Eco Design*. San Francisco, CA: IEEE ISEE.

Isle of Man Department of Tourism and Leisure (1996) *Marketing Plan 1996*. Douglas: Government of the Isle of Man.

IUCN (1994) *Richtlinien für Management-Kategorien von Schutzgebieten*. Gland, Cambridge, Grafenau: IUCN, WCMC and FÖNAD.

IUCN (1998) *1997 United Nations List of Protected Areas*. Gland and Cambridge: WCMC and WCPA.

IUCN, UNEP and WWF (1980) World Conservation Strategy. Living Resource Conservation for Sustainable Development. Gland: IUCN.

Jablonka, E. (2000) Lamarckian inheritance systems in biology: A source of metaphors and models in technological evolution. In J. Zimon (ed.) *Technological Innovation as an Evolutionary Process* (pp. 27–40). Cambridge: Cambridge University Press.

Jain, S.C. (1985) *Market Planning and Strategy*. Cincinnati, OH: South Western.

Jansen-Verbeke, M. (1986) Inner-city tourism: Resources, tourists and promoters. *Annals of Tourism Research* 13 (1), 79–100.

Javiluoma, J. (1992) Alternative tourism and the evolution of tourist areas, *Tourism Management*, 13 (1), 118–120.

Jawahar, I.M. and McLaughlin, G.L. (2001) Toward a descriptive stakeholder theory: An organisational life cycle approach. *Academy of Management Review* 26 (3), 397–414.

Job, H. and Weizenegger, S. (1999) Anspruch und Realität einer integrierten Naturschutz- und Entwicklungspolitik in den Großschutzgebieten Schwarzafrikas. In G. Meyer and A. Thimm (eds) *Naturräume in der Dritten Welt. Ausbeutung, nachhaltige Nutzung oder Schutz?* (pp. 37–64). Mainz: Interdisziplinärer Arbeitskreis Dritte Welt, Veröffentlichungen 12.

Johnson, J.D. and Rasker, R. (1995) The role of economic and quality of life values in rural business location. *Journal of Rural Studies* 11 (4), 323–332.

Johnson, J. and Snepenger, D. (1993) Application of the tourism life cycle concept in the Greater Yellowstone Region. *Society and Natural Resources* 6, 127–148.

Johnson, J.D. and Snepenger, D.J. (in progress) Community solidarity regarding tourism development in a transitional rural economy.

Johnson, J.D., Snepenger, D.J. and Akis, S. (1994) Host resident perceptions of tourism in a transitional rural economy. *Annals of Tourism Research* 21 (3).

Johnson, J.D., Maxwell, B.M. and Aspinall, R. (2003) Moving nearer to heaven: Growth and change in the Greater Yellowstone Region. In R. Buckley, C. Pickering and D. Weaver (eds) *Nature Tourism and Environment*. Wallingford: CAB International.

Johnston, C. (1995) Enduring idylls? A geographical study of tourism in Kona, Hawaii Island. University of Hawaii: Unpublished PhD dissertation.

Johnston, C.S. (2001) Shoring the foundations of the destination life cycle model. Part 1: Ontological and epistemological considerations. *Tourism Geographies* 3 (1), 2–28.

Johnston, R.J. (1991) *Geography and Geographers. Anglo-American Human Geography since 1945* (Vol. 4). London: Arnold.

Johnston, R.J., Gregory, D. and Smith, D. (1986) *The Dictionary of Human Geography* (2nd edn). Oxford: Blackwell.

Jones, P. and Pizam, A. (1993) *The International Hospitality Industry – Organizational and Operational Issues*. London: Pitman.

Joppe, M. (1996) Sustainable community tourism development revisited. *Tourism Management* 17 (7), 475–479.

Jordon, P. (2000) Restructuring Croatia's coastal resorts: Change, sustainable development and the incorporation of rural hinterlands. *Journal of Sustainable Tourism* 8 (6), 525–539.

Juelg, F. (1993) Tourism product life cycles in the Central Eastern Alps: A case study of Heiligenblut on the Grossglockner. *Tourism Recreation Research* 18 (1), 20–26.

Jurowski, C., Uysal, M. and Williams, D.R. (1997) A theoretical analysis of host community resident reactions to tourism. *Journal of Travel Research* 36 (2), 3–9.

Juvik, J.O., Singleton, D.C. and Clarke, G.G. (1978) Climate and Water Balance on the Island of Hawaii. *Mauna Loa Observatory, a 20th Anniversary Report* (pp. 129–139). National Oceanic and Atmospheric Administration.

Kachigan, S.K. (1986) *Statistical Analysis*. New York: Radius Press.

Kaplan, R.S. and Norton, D.P. (1990) *The Balanced Scorecard: Translating Strategy into Action*. Boston, MA: Harvard Business School Press.

Kaplan, R.S. and Norton, D.P. (2001) *The Strategy Focused Organisation: How Balanced Scorecard Companies Thrive in the New Business Environment*. Boston, MA: Harvard Business School Press.

Katsanis, L.P. and Pitta, D.A. (1995) Punctuated equilibrium and the evolution of the product manager. *Journal of Product and Brand Management* 4 (3), 49–60.

Keane, M.J. (1997) Quality and pricing in tourism destinations. *Annals of Tourism Research* 24 (1), 117–130.

Keller, C.P. (1987) Stages of peripheral tourism development – Canada's Northwest Territories. *Tourism Management* 8, 2–32.

Kenney, J. (1995) Personal interview. Hilton Head, SC.

Kermath, B.M. and Thomas, R.N. (1992) Spatial dynamics of resorts: Sousa, Dominican Republic. *Annals of Tourism Research* 19, 173–190.

Ketchum, L. (1969a) Denial recommended for rezoning 146-Acre Kona parcel for homes. Hawai'i *Tribune Herald* 20 April, 1.

Ketchum, L. (1969b) A look at Hualalai – proposed addition to Volcanoes Park. Hawaii *Tribune Herald* 10 July, 16.

Keys, N.H.E. (1985) Tourism evolution in Queensland. Unpublished MA Thesis. Nathan, Queensland: Griffith University.

King, R.D. (1935) Districts in the Hawaiian Islands. In *A Gazetteer of the Territory of Hawaii*. Compiled by Hohn Wesley Coulter (pp. 214–225). Honolulu: University of Hawaii Research Publication #11.

Kirch, P.V. (1983) Introduction. In *Archaeological Investigations of the Mudlane-Waimea-Kawaihae Road Corridor, Island of Hawaii* (pp. 3–24). An Interdisciplinary Study of an Environmental Transect.

Klepper, S. (1996) Entry, exit, growth, and innovation over the product life cycle. *The American Economic Review* 86 (3), 562–583.

Knowles, T. and Curtis, S. (1999) The market viability of European mass tourist destinations: A post-stagnation lifecycle analysis. *International Journal of Tourism Research* 1, 87–96.

Kokkranikal, J. and Morrison, A. (2002) Entrepreneurship and sustainable tourism: The houseboats of Kerala. *Tourism and Hospitality Research* 4 (1), 7–20.

Kotler, P. (1976) *Marketing Management* (Vol. 3). London: Prentice Hall.

Kotler, P. (1997) *Marketing Management, Analysis, Planning and Control* (9th edn). New Jersey: Prentice Hall.

Kotler, P. and Armstrong, G. (1984) *Principles of Marketing* (4th edn). Englewood Cliffs, NJ: Prentice-Hall.

Kotler, P. and Turner, R.E. (1993) *Marketing Management* (Canadian 7th edn). Prentice-Hall, Canada Inc. See pp. 3271–3397 re: 'product life cycles'.

Krauss, B. (1974a) Opening up north Kona coast. Honolulu *Advertiser* 13 April, A3.

Krauss, B. (1974b) Tale of two tourist towns. Honolulu *Advertiser*, 15 March, A3.

Kraybill, D.B. and Nolt, S.M. (1995) *Amish Enterprise: From Plows to Profits*. Baltimore, MD: The Johns Hopkins University Press.

Krippendorff, J. (1975) *Die Landschaftsfressser-Turismus- und der Erholungslandschaft-verderben oder segen*. Bern und Stuttgart: Hallvall Verlag.

Krippendorf, J. (1987) *The Holiday Makers*. London: Heinemann.

Krueger, N.F. and Brazeal, D.V. (1994) Entrepreneurial potential and potential entrepreneurs. *Entrepreneurship Theory and Practice* 18 (3), 91–104.

Krugman, P. (1995) *Development, Geography and Economic Theory*. Cambridge, MA: MIT Press.

Kuratko, D. and Hodgetts, R. (1998) *Entrepreneurship: A Contemporary Approach*. Fort Worth, TX: The Dryden Press.

Lake Memphremagog, topographic map sheets 31 H/1, 1917–2000, 1:50,000. Ottawa: Department of Energy, Mines and Resources.

Lamarck, J.B. (1809) *Philosophie zoologique*. [Translated 1963 as *Zoological Philosophy: an exposition with regard to the natural history of animals*]. New York: Harner Publishing Co.

Lancaster County Planning Commission (1998) *Heritage Tourism Plan*. Lancaster, PA: Lancaster County Planning Commission.

Lander, H. (1937) *Cairns Timetable and General Information*. Cairns: Lander, H.

Langston, P., Clarke, G.P. and Clarke, D.B. (1997) Retail saturation, retail location and retail competition: An analysis of British grocery retailing. *Environment and Planning A* 29, 77–104.

Langston, P., Clarke, G.P. and Clarke, D.B. (1998) Retail saturation: The debate in the mid-1990s. *Environment and Planning A* 30, 49–66.

Lankford, S.V. and Howard, D.R. (1994) Developing a tourism impact attitude scale. *Annals of Tourism Research* 21, 121–139.

Lash, S. and Urry, J. (1987) *The End of Organised Capitalism*. Madison: University of Wisconsin Press.

Laws, E. (1995) *Tourist Destination Management: Issues, Analysis and Policies*. London: Routledge.

Laws, E., Faulkner, B. and Moscardo, G. (1998) *Embracing and Managing Change in Tourism: International Case Studies* (pp. 95–115). London: Routledge.

Lehne, R. (1986) *Casino Policy*. New Brunswick, NJ: Rutgers University Press.

Lenoir, T. and Ross, C. (1996) The naturalized history museum. In P. Galison and D. Stump (eds) *The Disunity of Science: Boundaries, Contexts and Power* (pp. 370–397). Stanford, CA: Stanford University Press.

Le Pelley, B. and Laws, E. (1998) A stakeholder benefits approach to tourism management in a historic city centre. In E. Laws, B. Faulkner and G. Moscardo (eds) *Embracing and Managing Change in Tourism: International Case Studies* (pp. 70–94). London: Routledge.

Lerner, M. and Haber, S. (2000) Performance factors of small tourism ventures: The interface of tourism, entrepreneurship and the environment. *Journal of Business Venturing* 16, 77–100.

Levasseur, H. (2002). Freligsburgh, telephone interview.

Levitt, T. (1960) Marketing myopia. *Harvard Business Review* July–August, 45–56.

Levitt, T. (1976) Management and "post-industrial" society. *The Public Interest* 44, 69–73.

Lewis, R. and Green, S. (1998) Planning for stability and managing chaos: The case of Alpine ski resorts. In E. Laws, B. Faulkner and G. Moscardo (eds) *Embracing and Managing Change in Tourism: International Case Studies* (pp. 138–160). London: Routledge.

Lipietz, A. (1986) New tendencies in the international division of labour: Regimes of accumulation and modes of regulation. In A. Scott and M. Storper (eds) *Production, Work, Territory* (pp. 16–29). Boston, MA: Allen and Unwin.

Liu, J.L. and Var, T. (1986) Resident attitudes to tourism impacts in Hawaii. *Annals of Tourism Research* 13 (2), 193–214.

Liu, J.L., Sheldon, P.J. and Var, T. (1987) Resident perception of the environmental impacts of tourism. *Annals of Tourism Research* 14 (1), 17–37.

Lloret Turisme (2002) *Looking Towards Lloret of the Future*. Lloret de Mar: Lloret Turisme.

Lofton, D. (1993) Island may shut door to growth. *The State* November 5.

Logan, J.R. and Molotch, H.L. (1987) *Urban Fortunes: The Political Economy of Place*. Berkeley, CA: University of California Press.

London, C. (1917) *Our Hawaii*. New York: The Macmillan Company.

Long, P.T., Perdue, R.R. and Allen, L. (1990) Rural resident tourism perceptions and attitudes by community level of tourism. *Journal of Travel Research* Winter, 39.

Lorenz, E.N. (1963) Deterministic non-periodic flow. *Journal of the Atmospheric Sciences* 20 (2), 130–141.

Lösch, A. (1940) *Die Raumliche Ordnung der Wirtschaft* [*The Spatial Order of the Economy*]. Jena: Gustav Fischer Verlag.

Loyacono, L.L. (1991) *Travel and Tourism: A Legislator's Guide*. Washington, D.C.: National Conference of State Legislatures.

Lu, L. (1997) A study on the life cycle of mountain resorts: A case study of Huangshan Mountain and Jiuhanshan Mountain. *Scintia Geographic Sinica* 17 (1), 63–69.

Luloff, A.E. and Steahr, T.E. (1985) The structure and impact of population redistribution: Summary and conclusions. In T.E. Steahr and A.E. Luloff (eds) *The Structure and Impact of Population Redistribution in New England*. University Park, PN: Northeast Regional Center for Rural Development, Pennsylvania State University.

Lundgren, J.O. (1984) Geographic concepts and the development of tourism research in Canada. *Geojournal* 9, 17–25.

Lundgren, J.O. (1988) Tourist destination development and problems of management – Case Lake Memphremagog. *TEOROS* 7 (2), 10–16, Montreal: UQAM.

Lundgren, J. (1996) The tourism development process in the Eastern Townships – the changing tourist product composition. *Journal of Eastern Townships Studies* No.8, Spring, 5–24, Lennoxville, Que., Canada: Bishop's University.

Lundtorp, S. and Wanhill, S. (2001) Resort life cycle theory: Generating processes and estimation. *Annals of Tourism Research* 28 (4), 947–964.

Lundvall, B-A. (1993) *The Learning Economy: Challenges to Economic Theory and Policy*. Paper presented to the EAPE conference, Copenhagen, 27–28 October.

MacCannell, D. (1976) *The Tourist: A New Theory of the Leisure Class*. London: Macmillan.

MacKenzie, J.M. (1988) *The Empire of Nature. Hunting, Conservation and British Imperialism*. Manchester: Manchester University Press.

Madrigal, R. (1995) Residents' perceptions and the role of government. *Annals of Tourism Research* 22 (1), 86–102.

Mahon, G. (1980) *The Company that Bought the Boardwalk*. New York: Random House.

Mak, B. and Go, F. (1995) Matching global competition: Cooperation among Asia airlines. *Tourism Management* 16 (1), 61–65.

Mandelbrot, B. (1977) *The Fractal Geometry of Nature*. New York: W.H. Freeman.

Maneeorasert, M., Pokpong, K. and Prangsio, C. (1975) *Reconnaissance Survey of the Impact of Tourism in the Highlands*. Social and Economic Change Committee. Chiang Mai, Thailand: Tribal Research Institute.

Mann, K. and Lowe, B. (1956) *Teddy Bear*. RCA Records.

Mann, T. (1924) *The Magic Mountain*.

Manning, T. (1999) Indicators of tourism sustainability. *Tourism Management* 20 (2), 179–181.

Marchena Gomez, M. and Vera Rebollo, F. (1995) Coastal areas: Processes, typologies, prospects. In A. Montanari and A. Williams (eds) *European Tourism: Regions, Spaces and Restructuring* (pp. 111–126). Chichester, Wiley.

Markin, R.J. and Duncan, C.P. (1981) The transformation of retailing institutions: Beyond the wheel of retailing and life cycle theories. *Journal of Macromarketing* 1 (Spring), 58–66.

Markusen, A.R. (1985) *Profit Cycles, Oligopoly and Regional Development*. Cambridge, MA: MIT Press.

Markworth, A.J., Stringer, J. and Rollins, R.W. (1995) Deterministic chaos theory and its applications to materials science. *MRS Bulletin* 20 (7), 20–28.

Martin, B.S. (1999) The efficacy of growth machine theory in explaining resident perceptions of community tourism development. *Tourism Analysis* 4, 47–55.

Martin, B.S., McGuire, F.A. and Allen, L.A. (1998) Retirees' attitudes toward tourism: Implications for sustainable development. *Tourism Analysis* 3, 43–51.

Martin, B.S. and Uysal, M. (1990) An examination of the relationship between carrying capacity and the tourism lifecycle: Management and policy implications. *Journal of Environmental Management* 31, 327–333.

Martin, R. (1989) The new economic and politics of regional restructuring: The British experience. In L. Albrechts, F. Moulearts, P. Roberts and E. Swyngedouw (eds) *Regional Policy at the Crossroads* (pp. 27–51). London: Jessica Kingsley.

Mary Means & Associates, Inc. (2001) *Lancaster–York Heritage Region Management Action Plan*. Lancaster, PA.

Massey, D. (1978) Regionalism: Some current issues. *Capital and Class* 6, 106–125.

Massey, D. and Meegan, R. (1984) *Spatial Divisions of Labour: Social Structures and the Geography of Production*. London: MacMillan.

Massey, G. (1999) Product evolution: A Darwinian or Lamarckian phenomenon? *Journal of Product and Brand Management* 8 (4), 301–318.

Mathews, K.M., White, M.C. and Long, R.G. (1999) Why study the complexity sciences in the social sciences? *Human Relations* 52 (4), 439–462.

McCaskill, D. (1997) *From Tribal Peoples to Ethnic Minorities: The Transformation of Indigenous Peoples*. Chiang Mai, Thailand: Silkworm Books.

McCaskill, D. and Kampe, K. (1997) *Development or Domestication? Indigenous Peoples of Southeast Asia* (pp. 26–60). Thailand: Silkworm Books.

McElroy, J.L., deAlbuquerque, K. and Dioguardi, A. (1993) Applying the tourist destination life-cycle model to small Caribbean and Pacific Islands. *World Travel and Tourism Review* 236–244.

McKay, M.K. (1990) Tourism evolution in provincial parks: A guide to investment decisions. Unpublished B.A. thesis: Department of Geography, University of Western Ontario, London.

McKercher, B. (1999) A chaos approach to tourism. *Tourism Management* 20, 425–434.

McNair, M.P. (1958) Significant trends and developments in the postwar period. In A.B. Smith (ed.) *Competitive Distribution in a Free High Level Economy and its Implications for the University* (pp. 1–25). Pittsburgh, PA: University of Pittsburgh Press.

Meeks, H.A. (1986) *Time and Change in Vermont – A Human Geography*. Chester, CN.

Meethan, K. (2001) *Tourism in Global Society: Place, Culture and Consumption*. London: Palgrave.

Melly, G. (2002) You ain't nothing but an icon. *Observer Review* 28 July, 15.

Menzies, A. (1920) *Hawaii Nei 128 Years Ago. Journal of Archibald Menzies*. W.F. Wilson (ed.). Honolulu: The New Freedom.

Mercer, D. (1993) A two-decade test of product life cycle theory. *British Journal of Management* 4 (4), 269–274.

Messerli, H.R. (1993) Tourism area life cycle models and residents' perceptions: The case of Santa Fe, New Mexico (City Planning). Unpublished PhD Thesis, Cornell University.

Meyer, R. (1996) Waikiki faces major problems: Does new master plan hold solutions? *FIU Hospitality Review* 14 (1), 7–18.

Meyer-Arendt, K.L. (1985) The Grand Isle, Louisiana resort cycle. *Annals of Tourism Research* 12 (3), 449–465.

Meyer-Arendt, K. and Hartmann, R. (1998) *Casino Gambling in America: Origins, Trends, and Impacts*. Elmsford, NY: Cognizant Communications.

Meyer-Arendt, K.J., Sambrook, R.A. and Kermath, B.M. (1992) Resorts in the Dominican Republic: A typology. *Journal of Geography* 91, 219–225.

Middleton, V. and Hawkins, R. (1998) *Sustainable Tourism: A Marketing Perspective*. Oxford: Butterworth Heinemann.

Miles, R.E. and Snow, C.C. (1978) *Organisational Strategy, Structure and Process*. New York: McGraw Hill.

Mill, R.C. (1996) Societal marketing: Implications for tourism destinations. *Journal of Vacation Marketing* 2 (3), 215–221.

Miller, D. (1990) *The Icarus Paradox*. New York: Harper Business.

Miller, D. and Friessen, P.H. (1984) *Organisations: A Quantum View*. Englewood Cliffs, NJ: Prentice Hall.

Milne, S. (1998) Tourism and sustainable development: Exploring the global–local nexus. In C.M. Hall and A. Lew (eds) *Sustainable Tourism: A Geographical Perspective* (pp. 35–48). London: Longman.

Minniti, M. and Bygrave, W. (1999) The microfoundations of entrepreneurship. *Entrepreneurship Theory & Practice* 23 (4), 41–50.

Mintz, S. (1971) The Caribbean as a socio-cultural area. In M. Horowitz (ed.) *Peoples and Cultures of the Caribbean* (pp. 17–46). New York: Natural History Press.

Mintzberg, H. (2000) *The Rise and Fall of Strategic Planning*. London: Prentice Hall.

Mintzberg, H. and Waters, J.A. (1982). Tracking strategy in an entrepreneurial firm. *Academy of Management Journal* 25 (3), 465–499.

Miossec, J.M. (1976) *Elements pour une Theorie de l'Espace Touristique*. Centre des Hautes Études Touristique, Aix-en-Provence. Serie C, n. 36.

Miossec, J.M. (1977) Un modèle de l'espace touristique. *L'Espace Géographie* 1, 41–48.

Miskulin, D. (1994) A trip to the far past of Opatija tourism. In Proceedings, *150th Anniversary of Tourism in Opatija* (pp. 15–24). University of Rijeka, Faculty of Hotel Management, Opatija.

Mokyr, J. (2000) Evolutionary phenomena in technological change. In J. Zimon (ed.) *Technological Innovation as an Evolutionary Process* (pp. 52–65). Cambridge: Cambridge University Press.

Molotch, H. (1976) The city as a growth machine: Toward a political economy of place. *American Journal of Sociology* 82, 309–331.

Morecoft, J.D.W. and Dterman, J. (eds) (1994) *Modelling for Learning Organisations*. Portland, OR: Productivity Press.

Morgan, M. (1991) Dressing up to survive. *Tourism Management* 12 (1), 15–20.

Morgan, N.J. and Pritchard, A. (1999) *Power and Politics at the Seaside. The Development of Devon's Resorts in the Twentieth Century*. Exeter: University of Exeter Press.

Morrill, G.L. (1919) *Hawaiian Heathen and Others*. Chicago, IL: M.A. Donahue & Co.

Morrison, A.J. (1998) Small firm co-operative marketing in a peripheral tourism region. *International Journal of Contemporary Hospitality Management* 10 (5), 191–197.

Morrison, A., Rimmington, M. and Williams, C. (1999) *Entrepreneurship in the Hospitality, Tourism and Leisure Studies*. Oxford: Butterworth-Heinemann.

Moss, S.E., Ryan, C. and Wagoner, C.B. (2003) An empirical test of Butler's resort product life cycle: Forecasting casino winnings. *Journal of Travel Research* 41 (4), 393–399.

Mueller, S. and Thomas, A.S. (2000) Culture and entrepreneurial potential: A nine country study of locus of control and innovativeness. *Journal of Business Venturing* 16, 51–75.

Mueller, J.H., Schuessler, K.F. and Costner, H.L. (1970) *Statistical Reasoning in Sociology* (2nd edn). Boston, MA: Houghton Mifflin Co.

Murphy, P. (1985) *Tourism a Community Approach*. New York: Methuen.

Musick, J.R. (1898) *Hawaii. Our New Possessions*. New York: Funk & Wagnalls Company.

Nadeau, R. (1989) Le Tourisme Hivernale des Quebecois: De l'appel du sud au ski alpin. *TEOROS* 8 (3), 3–10. Montreal: UQAM.

Native Hawaiian Hospitality Association (2000) April 2000 Newsletter. On WWW at http://www.nahtha.org/april.htm. Accessed 22.3.2001.

Nelson, J.G. (1984) An external perspective on Parks Canada Future Strategies, 1986–2001. *Occasional paper #2*. Heritage Resources Centre Publication Series, University of Waterloo.

Nelson, J.G. (1987) National Parks and protected areas, national conservation strategies and sustainable development. *Geoforum* 18 (3), 291–319.

Nelson, R.R. and Winter, S.G. (1982) *An Evolutionary Theory of Economic Change*. Cambridge, MA: Harvard University Press.

Nice Matin (1971) Article Tourisme April 6. Nice: *Nice Matin*.

Nijkamp, P. and Reggiani, A. (1995) Non-linear evolution of dynamic spatial systems. The relevance of chaos and ecologically-based models. *Regional Science and Urban Economics* 25, 183–210.

Nilson, T.H. (1995) *Chaos Marketing: How to Win in a Turbulent World*. England: McGraw-Hill Book Company.

Nilsson, J-E. (1995) *Sweden in the Renewed Europe: Rise and Decline of an Industrial Nation*. Malmo: Liberhermods.

Nilsson, J-E. and Schamp, E. (1996) Restructuring of the European production system: Processes and consequences. *European Urban and Regional Studies* 3, 121–132.

Noble, I.R. and Slayter, R.O. (1981) Concepts and models of succession in vascular plant communities subject to recurrent fire. In A.M. Gill, R.H. Groves and I.R. Noble (eds) *Fire and the Australian Biota* (pp. 311–335). Canberra: Australian Academy of Sciences.

Normann, R. and Rairez, R. (1993) From value chain to value constellation: Designing interactive strategy. *Harvard Business Review* 71, 65–77.

Noronha, R. (1977) *Social and Cultural Dimensions of Tourism: A Review of the Literature in English*. Washington, DC: World Bank Working Paper.

Ober, F. (1908) *A Guide to the West Indies and Bermudas*. New York: Dodd, Mead & Co.

Oberhauser, A. (1987) Labour, production and the state: Decentralisation of the French automobile industry. *Regional Studies* 21, 445–458.

Ogilvie, F.W. (1933) *The Tourism Movement*. London: Staples Press.

Oglethope, M. (1984) Tourism in Malta – A crisis of dependence. *Leisure Studies* 12, 449–465.

O'Hare, G. and Barrett, H. (1997) The destination life cycle – international tourism in Peru. *Scottish Geographical Magazine* 113 (2), 66–73.

Olley, P. (1937) *Guide to Jamaica*. Kingston: The Tourist Trade Development Board.

Onkvisit, S. and Shaw, J.J. (1989) *Product Life Cycles and Product Management*. New York: Quorum Books.

Oppermann, M. (1995) Travel life cycle. *Annals of Tourism Research* 22 (3), 535–552.

Oppermann, M. (1998a) Destination threshold potential and the law of repeat visitation. *Journal of Travel Research* 37 (2), 131–137.

Oppermann, M. (1998b) What is new with the resort cycle? *Tourism Management* 19 (2), 179–180.

Oxford English Dictionary (1972) Oxford: The Clarendon Press.

Papatheodorou, A. (2001a) Why people travel to different places? *Annals of Tourism Research* 28 (1), 164–179.

Papatheodorou, A. (2001b) Tourism, transport geography and industrial economics: A synthesis in the context of Mediterranean Islands. *Anatolia* 12 (1), 23–34.

Papatheodorou, A. (2004) Exploring the evolution of Tourist Resorts. *Annals of Tourism Research* 31 (1), 219–237.

Paradise of the Pacific (1924) Survey of Hawaiian History Since Cook's Discovery 37 (7), 3–7.

Parks Canada (1994) *Guiding Principles and Operational Policies.* Minister of Supply and Services Canada.

Parks Canada (1997) *Banff National Park Management Plan.* Government of Canada.

Parks Canada (2002) Press Release: The Government of Canada announces action plan to protect Canada's natural heritage. October 3.

Paton, W. (1887) *Down the Islands: A Voyage to the Caribbees.* New York: Charles Scribners & Sons.

Patoskie J. (1992) Traditional tourist resorts: Problems and solutions Honolulu (Hawaii, USA). International Forum on Tourism to the Year 2000: Prospects and Challenges, Acapulco, Mexico.

Patoskie, J. and Ikeda, G. (1993) *Waikiki – The Evolution of an Urban Resort.* Honolulu: University of Hawaii. School of Travel Industry Management. Centre for Tourism Policy Studies.

Pattison, D.A. (1968) Tourism in the Firth of Clyde. Unpublished PhD thesis, Glasgow: University of Glasgow.

Pearce, D. (1989) *Tourist Development* (2nd edn). Harlow: Longman.

Pearce, D. (1993) Comparative studies in tourism research. In R.W.F. Butler and D.G. Pearce (eds) *Tourism Research: Critiques and Challenges* (pp. 21–35). London: Routledge.

Pearce, P. (1982) *The Social Psychology of Tourist Behaviour.* Oxford: Pergamon.

Peat, F.D. (1991) *The Philosopher's Stone: Chaos, Synchronicity and the Hidden Order of the World.* New York: Bantam.

Peet, R. (1998) *Modern Geographical Thought.* Oxford: Blackwell.

Pelgrave, F. (1994) *Whitecars.* Cairns: Pelgrave, F.

Peterson, D.W. and Moore, R.B. (1987) Geologic History and the Evolution of Geologic Concepts, Island of Hawaii. Washington D.C.: US G.P.O. (U.S.G.S. Professional Paper 1350.)

Phillippo, J. (1843) *Jamaica: Its Past and Present State.* London: John Snow.

Pimlott, J.A.R. (1947) *The Englishman's Holiday.* London: Faber.

Pine, B.J. and Gilmore, J.H. (1999) *The Experience Economy.* Boston, MA: Harvard Business School Press.

Pinfield, L.T. (1986) A field evaluation of perspectives on organisational decision making. *Administrative Science Quarterly* 31 (3), 414–450.

Piore, M. (1986) Perspectives on labour market flexibility. *Industrial Relations* 25, 146–166.

Piore, M. and Sabel, C. (1984) *The Second Industrial Divide: Possibilities for Prosperity.* New York: Basic Books.

Plog, S.C. (1972) Why destination areas rise and fall in popularity. Paper Presented at the Southern California Chapter of the Travel Research Bureau, October 10, 1972.

Plog, S.C. (1973) Why destinations areas rise and fall in popularity. *Cornell Hotel and Restaurant Association Quarterly* 13, 6– 13.

Plog, S.C. (1991) Why destination areas rise and fall in popularity. In *Leisure Travel: Making It a Growth Market ... Again!* (pp. 75– 84). New York: John Wiley & Sons, Inc.

Plog, S.C. (2001) Why destination areas rise and fall in popularity: An update of a Cornell Quarterly Classic. *Cornell Hotel and Restaurant Administration Quarterly* 42 (3), 13– 24.

Pollard, J. and Rodriguez, R. (1993) Tourism and Torremolinos. Recession or reaction to environment. *Tourism Management* 12 (4), 247– 258.

Polli, R. and Cook, V. (1969) Validity of the product life cycle. *The Journal of Business* 42 (4), 385– 400.

Pollock, J. (1986) *Contemporary Theories of Knowledge*. Savage, MD: Rowman & Littlefield Publishers, Inc.

Porter, M. (1980) *Competitive Strategy*. New York: Free Press.

Potton Heritage Association (1993) Municipality of Potton, Mansonville; Pamphlet material: 1. Potton Hier et Aujourd'hui, 14 pages; 2. Les Bateaus du Lac, 3 pages; 3. The Mountain House, 4 pages; 4. Vale Perkins, 4 pages.

Power, T.M. (1995) Thinking about natural resource-dependent economies: Moving beyond the folk economics of the rear-view mirror. In R.L. Knight and S.F. Bates (eds) *A New Century for Natural Resource Management* (pp. 235– 253). Washington DC: Island Press.

Pratt, A. (1991) Discourses of locality. *Environment and Planning A* 23 (2), 257– 266.

Pred, A. (1966) *The Spatial Dynamics of U.S. Urban Industrial Growth*. Cambridge, MA: MIT Press.

Pred, A. (1984) Place as historically contingent process: Structuration and the time– geography of becoming places. *Annals of the Association of American Geographers* 74, 279– 307.

Press Association (2002) Greek police arrest British tourists. *The Guardian* 29 June.

Prideaux, B. (2000) The resort development spectrum: A new approach to modelling resort development. *Tourism Management* 21, 225– 240.

Priestley, G. and Mundet, L. (1998) The post-stagnation phase of the resort life-cycle. *Annals of Tourism Research* 25 (1), 85– 111.

Prigogine, I. and Stengers, I. (1985) *Order Out of Chaos*. London: Flamingo.

Prosser, G. (1995) Tourism destination life cycles: Progress, problems and prospects. Paper to *National Tourism Research Conference*, Melbourne.

Prosser, G. (1997) The development of tourist destinations in Australia: A comparative analysis of the Gold Coast and Coffs Harbour. In R. Teare, B.F. Canziani and G. Brown (eds) *Global Directions: New Strategies for Hospitality and Tourism* (pp. 305– 332). London: Cassell.

Prosser, G.M. and Cullen, P. (1987) Planning natural areas for sustainable tourism development. Proceedings 60th National Conference, Royal Australian Institute of Parks and Recreation, Canberra, October.

Pudney, J. (1953) *The Thomas Cook Story*. London: Michael Joseph Ltd.

Pukui, M.K., Elbert, S.H. and Mo'okini, E.T. (1974) *Place Names of Hawaii*. Honolulu: University of Hawaii Press.

Putnam, R. (1993) The prosperous community: Social capital and public life. *The American Prospect* 13, 35– 42.

Queensland Government Tourist Bureau (1939) *Holiday Haunts*. Brisbane: Queensland Government Tourist Bureau.

Queensland Railways (1912) *Tours in the Cairns District*. Brisbane: Queensland Railways.

Rafool, M. and Loyacono, L. (1997) *Employment in the Travel and Tourism Industry*. Denver, CO: National Conference of State Legislatures.

Ray, D. (1988) The role of entrepreneurship in economic development. *Journal of Development Planning* 18, 3–18.

Regensberg, Fr. (without year, ~ 1911) Naturschutzparke in den Kolonien. Bearbeitet von Fr. Regensberg auf Grund der Rede des Herrn Prof. C.B. Schillings während der Tagung der Deutschen Kolonialgesellschaft in Stuttgart am 10. Juni 1911. In Verein Naturschutzpark (ed.) *Naturschutzparke in Deutschland und Österreich. Ein Mahnwort an das deutsche und österreichische Volk* (pp. 54–57). Stuttgart.

Republic of Kenya (1999) *Economic Survey 1999*. Nairobi: Republic of Kenya.

Reynolds, P.D. (1997) New and small firms in expanding markets. *Small Business Economics* 9, 79–84.

Richardson, S.L. (1986) A product life cycle approach to urban waterfronts: The revitalisation of Galveston. *Costal Zone Management Journal* 14 (1/2), 21–46.

Riegert, R. (1979) *Hidden Hawaii, the Adventurer's Guide*. Berkeley, CA: AND/OR Press.

Rink, D.R. and Swan, J.E. (1979) Product life cycle research: A literature review. *Journal of Business Research* 7, 219–242.

Ritchie, J.R.B. (1999) Crafting a value driven for a national tourism treasure. *Tourism Management* 20 (3), 273–282.

Ritchie, J.R.B. and Crouch, G.I. (2000) The competitive destination: A sustainability perspective. *Tourism Management* 21 (1), 1–7.

Roberts, W. (1948) *Lands of the Inner Sea: The West Indies and Bermuda*. New York: Coward McCann.

Rodney, W. (1972) *How Europe Underdeveloped Africa*. London: Bogle-Ouverture Publications.

Rodriguez-Pose, A. (1994) Socio-economic restructuring and regional change: Rethinking growth in the European Community. *Economic Geography* 70, 325–343.

Romanelli, E. and Tushman, M.L. (1994) Organisational transformation as punctuated equilibrium: An empirical test. *Academy of Management Journal* 37 (5), 1141–1166.

Romeril, M. (1989) Tourism – the environmental dimension. *Progress in Tourism, Recreation and Hospitality Management* (1), 103–113.

Rose, T.F. (1878) *Historical and Biographical Atlas of the New Jersey Coast* (p. 42). Philadelphia, PA: Woolman and Rose.

Rostow, W.W. (1960) *Stages of Economic Growth – A Non-communist Manifesto*. Cambridge, UK: Cambridge University Press.

Roth, V.J. and Klein, S. (1993) A theory of retail change. *International Review of Retail, Distribution and Consumer Research* 3 (2), 167–183.

Rubenstein, R.L. (1983) *The Age of Triage*. Boston, MA: Beacon Press.

Rubies, E.B. (2001) Improving public-private sectors cooperation in tourism: A new paradigm for destinations. *Tourism Review* 56 (3 + 4), 39–41.

Russell, D. (1987) Atlantic City's bet on gambling: Who won what? *Atlantic City Magazine* 11 (1).

Russell, R. (1995) Tourism development in Coolangatta: An historical perspective. Honors thesis, Griffith University, Gold Coast.

Russell, R. and Faulkner, B. (1998) Reliving the destination life cycle in Coolangatta. An historical perspective on the rise, decline and rejuvenation of an Australian seaside resort. In E. Laws, B. Faulkner and G. Moscardo (eds) *Embracing and Managing Change in Tourism: International Case Studies* (pp. 95–115). London: Routledge.

Russell, R. and Faulkner, B. (1999) Movers and shakers: Chaos makers in tourism development. *Tourism Management* 20, 411–423.

Russo, A.P. (2002) The vicious circle of tourism development in heritage cities. *Annals of Tourism Research* 29 (1), 165–182.

Russo, A.P. and van der Borg, J. (2002) Planning considerations for cultural tourism: A case study of four European cities. *Tourism Management* 23 (5).

Ruthen, R. (1993) Adapting to complexity. *Scientific American* 268, 130–140.

Rutter, J. (1998) They don't see eye to eye. *Lancaster Sunday News*. Lancaster, Pennsylvania, November 22.

Ryan, C. (1991) Tourism and marketing – a symbiotic relationship? *Tourism Management* 12 (2), 101–111.

Sabel, C. (1982) *Work and Politics*. Cambridge: Cambridge University Press.

Sabin, W. (1921) *Hawaii, U.S.A.: A Souvenir of 'The Crossroads of the Pacific'*. Honolulu: Paradise of the Pacific Publishing Company.

Sassen, S. (1995) Urban impacts of economic globalisation. In J. Bratchie *et al.* (eds) *Cities in Competition* (pp. 36–57). Melbourne: Longman.

Savary, J. (1995) Thomson consumer electronics: From national champion to global contender. In J-E. Nilsson, P. Dicken and J. Peck (eds) *The Internationalisaton Process: European Firms in Global Competition* (pp. 90–108). London: Chapman.

Schumpeter, J.A. (1934) *The Theory of Economic Development*. Cambridge, MA: Harvard University Press.

Schumpeter, J. (1939) *Business Cycles: A Theoretical, Historical and Statistical Analysis of the Capitalist Process*. New York: McGraw-Hill.

Schumpeter, J.A. (1996) *Capitalism, Socialism and Democracy*. London: Routledge.

Scott, R. (1957) Kailua-Kona shook up by tourist boom. Honolulu *Star Bulletin* 2 August, 12.

Shapiro, D. (1974) Nightmare not over for Kailua. Honolulu *Star Bulletin* 18 June, A12.

Shaw, G. and Williams, A.M. (1994, 2002) *Critical Issues in Tourism: A Geographical Perspective* (1st and 2nd edns). Oxford: Blackwell.

Shaw, G. and Williams, A.M. (1997) The private sector: Tourism entrepreneurship – a constraint or resource? In G. Shaw and A. Williams (eds) *The Rise and Fall of British Coastal Resorts* (pp. 117–136). London: Cassell.

Shaw, G. and Williams, A.M. (1998) Entrepreneurship, small business culture and tourism development. In D. Ioannides and K.D. Debbage (eds) *The Economic Geography of the Tourist Industry* (pp. 235–255). London: Routledge.

Shay, J.P. (1998) A multi-perspective, dynamic strategy model. Proceedings of the Third Annual Graduate Education and Graduate Students Research Conference in Hospitality and Tourism – Advances in Hospitality and Tourism Research, Houston.

Sheldon, P.J. and Abenoja, T. (2001) Resident attitudes in a mature destination: The case of Waikiki. *Tourism Management* 22 (4), 435–443.

Shields, M.J. (1987) Fantasy Island, *Southern* 2, 38.

Simon, H.A. (1991) Organisations and markets. *Journal of Economic Perspectives* 5 (2), 25–44.

Singh, S. (1998) Probing the product life cycle further. *Tourism Recreation Research* 23 (2), 61–63.

Skolnik, J. (1978) *House of Cards: The Legalization and Control of Casino Gambling*. Boston: Little Brown.

Slyworthy, A.J. (1996) *Value Migration*. Boston, MA: Harvard Business School Press.

Smart, G. (2002) Amish restaurants: Popular and illegal. *Lancaster Sunday News*. Lancaster, Pennsylvania, March 3.

Smilor, R.W. and Feeser, H.R. (1991) Chaos and the entrepreneurial process: Patterns and policy implications for technology entrepreneurship. *Journal of Business Venturing* 6, 165–172.

Smith, D. (1995) The inapplicability principle: What chaos means for social science. *Behavioral Science* 40, 22–40.

Smith, H. (2002) Ayia Napa puts the boot into rowdy tourists. *The Guardian* 17th June.

Smith, J. (1982) The Premium-Grind: The Atlantic City Casino Hybrid.

Smith, M. (1991) *The Future for British Seaside Resorts Insights D21–D26*. London: English Tourist Board.

Smith, M. (2002) Two parallel paths to a common goal? A critical analysis of sustainable tourism and cultural regeneration in the context of English seaside towns. Paper presented to 'Tourism Research 2002' conference, Cardiff, 4–7 September 2002.

Smith, R.A. (1992) Beach resort evolution: Implications for planning. *Annals of Tourism Research* 19, 304–322.

Smith, S.L.J. (1988) Defining tourism: A supply-side view. *Annals of Tourism Research* 15, 179–190.

Smith, S.L.J. (1994) The tourism product. *Annals of Tourism Research* 21 (3), 582–595.

Smith, V. (1978) *Hosts and Guests. The Anthropology of Tourism*. Oxford: Basil Blackwell.

Smith, V. and Eadington, W.R. (1994) *Tourism Alternatives, Potentials and Problems in the Development of Tourism*. Chichester: John Wiley and Sons.

Smyser, A.A. (1972) Changing Kona's uncertain future. Honolulu *Star Bulletin* 19 February, A11.

Snepenger, D.J. and Ditton, R.B. (1985) A longitudinal analysis of nationwide hunting and fishing indicators: 1955–1980. *Leisure Sciences* 7 (3), 297–319.

Snepenger, D.J. and Johnson, J.D. (1991) Political self-identification and the perception of economic, social and environmental impacts of tourism. *Annals of Tourism Research* 18 (3), 511–514.

Snepenger, D.J., Johnson, J.D. and Rasker, R. (1995) Travel-stimulated entrepreneurial migration. *Journal of Travel Research* 34 (1), 40–44.

Snepenger, D.J., O'Connell, R. and Snepenger, M. (2001) The embrace-withdrawal continuum scale: Operationalizing residents' responses toward tourism development. *Journal of Travel Research* 40 (2), 155–161.

Snow, R. and Wright, D. (1976) Coney Island: A case study in popular culture and technical change. *Journal of Popular Culture* 9, 960–975.

Societe des Musees Quebecois (1995) Repertoire des institutions museales du Quebec,-statistiques diverses.

Sodetani, N. (1985) Manago Hotel is a family tradition. Honolulu *Star Bulletin* 19 February, Section 1, 10.

Soja, E. (1989) *Postmodern Geographies: The Reassertion of Space in Critical Social Theory*. London: Verso.

Southward, W. (1966) Kailua-Kona mall plan site stirs debate. Sunday *Star Bulletin and Advertiser* 25 December, D6.

Southward, W. (1967) Kailua-Kona to resume talks on waterfront mall. Sunday *Star Bulletin and Advertiser* 17 September, D6.

Southward, W. (1968a) 8-step program is proposed for Kailua-Kona mall. Honolulu *Advertiser* 2 May, F9.

Southward, W. (1968b) 'Foundation only' as far as Kona condo can go. Honolulu *Advertiser* 23 August, A6.

Spirer, H. (1981) Life cycle. In A.C. Eurich (ed.) *Major Transitions in the Human Life Cycle* (pp. 1–61). Lexington, MA: Lexington Books.

Stabell, C.B. and Fjeldstad, O.D. (1998) Configuring value for competitive advantage: On chains, shops, and networks. *Strategic Management Journal* 19, 413–437.

Stankiewicz, R. (2000) The concept of 'design space'. In J. Zimon (ed.) *Technological Innovation as an Evolutionary Process* (pp. 234–247). Cambridge: Cambridge University Press.

Stansfield, C.A. (1972) The development of modern seaside resorts. *Parks and Recreation* 5 (10), 14–46.

Stansfield, C.A. (1978) Atlantic City and the resort cycle. Background to the legalization of gambling. *Annals of Tourism Research* 5 (2), 238–251.

Stansfield, C.A. and Rickert, J.E. (1970) The recreational business district. *Journal of Leisure Research* 2 (4), 213–225.

Stark, J. (1902) *Stark's Jamaican Guide*. Boston, MA: James H. Stark.

Steadman, P. (1979) *The Evolution of Designs. Biological Analogy in Architecture and the Applied Arts*. Cambridge: Cambridge University Press.

Steele, T., Lindley, R. and Blanden, B. (1998) *Lamarck's Signature. How Retrogenes are Changing Darwin's Natural Selection Paradigm*. Reading, MT: Perseus Books.

Stehle, P. (1994) *Order Chaos Order: The Transition From Classical to Quantum Physics*. New York: Oxford University Press.

Stermer, M. (1954) Flowers in the sky. Honolulu *Star Bulletin* 31 July, Magazine Section, 3.

Sternlieb, G. and Hughes, J. (1983) *The Atlantic City Gamble* (p. 3). MA: Harvard University Press.

Stevenson, R.L. (1973) *Travels in Hawaii*. Edited and with an Introduction by A. Grove Day. Honolulu: The University Press of Hawaii.

Stewart, C.S. (1831) *A Visit to the South Seas in 1829 and 1830*. New York: John P. Haven.

Stewart, I. (1990) *Does God Play Dice*. London: Penguin Books.

Stewart, I. (1993) A new order (complexity theory). *New Scientist* 137 (1859), 2–3.

Stoker, G. (1995) Governance as theory: Five propositions. *International Social Science Journal* 155.

Stoker, G. (ed.) (1999) *The New Management of British Local Governance* (pp. 1–21). Basingstoke: MacMillan Press Ltd.

Storper, M. and Walker, R. (1989) *The Capitalist Imperative: Territory, Technology and Industrial Growth*. Oxford: Blackwell.

Strapp, J.D. (1988) The resort cycle and second homes. *Annals of Tourism Research* 15 (4), 504–516.

Sturge, J. and Harvey, T. (1838) *The West Indies in 1837*. London: Hamilton, Adams & Co.

Sunday Star Bulletin and Advertiser (1984) First stages of a change. 22 July, G1.

Surin, K. (1998) Dependency theory's reanimation in the era of financial capital. *Cultural Logic* [electronic] 1 (2) 29 pp. On WWW at www.duke.edu/literature/ dependency.htm. Accessed 12.9.2002.

Survey of TdA Participants (1995) executed by J. Lundgren in collaboration with the TdA, March.

Swarbrooke, J. (1995) *The Development and Management of Visitor Attractions*. Oxford: Butterworth-Heinemann.

Swarbrooke, J. (1999) *Sustainable Tourism Management*. Wallingford, Oxon: CAB International.

Tao, E. (1972) Dolphin amity found at last. Hawaii *Tribune Herald* 4 April, 1.

Tarrant, C. (1989) The UK hotel industry: Market restructuring and the need to respond to customer demands. *Tourism Management* 10, 187–191.

Taylor, F. (1973) The tourist industry in Jamaica, 1919 to 1939. *Social and Economic Studies* 22, 205–228.

Taylor, F. (1988) The ordeal of the infant hotel industry in Jamaica, 1890–1914. *Journal of Imperial and Commonwealth History* 16, 201–217.

Tellis, G.J. and Crawford, C.M. (1981) An evolutionary approach to product growth theory. *Journal of Marketing* 45, 125–132.

Teye, V., Sonmez, S.F. and Sirakaya, E. (2002) Residents' attitudes toward tourism development. *Annals of Tourism Research* 29 (3), 668–688.

The Atlantic City Convention and Visitors Authority (no date) On WWW at http://www.atlanticcitynj.com/. Accessed 6.3.2001.

The City and County of Honolulu-Office of the Mayor (no date) On WWW at http://www.co.honolulu.hi.us/mayor/goal-1.htm. Accessed 22.3.2001.

The Property Council of Australia, Gold Coast Chapter (2000) *Our Gold Coast: Refurbishing, Rejuvenating and Unifying the Gold Coast, The Edward de Bono Workshop: Strategic Statement and Future Directions*.

Theodoulou, M. (2000) Are party animals good news for Cyprus? *The Times* 27 May.

Theodoulou, M. (2001a) Clubbers' lesson: No E in Cyprus. *The Times* 19 June.

Theodoulou, M. (2001b) Cyprus drugs warning. *The Times* 4 August.

Thietart, R.A. and Forgues, B. (1995) Chaos theory and organisation. *Organization Science* 6 (1), 19–31.

Thomas, M. (1983) *Schooner from Windward: Two Centuries of Hawaiian Interisland Shipping*. Honolulu: University of Hawaii Press (A Kolowalu Book).

Thomas, M.J. (1991) Product development and management. In M. Baker (ed.) *The Marketing Book* (Vol. 2, pp. 284–296). Oxford: Butterworth-Heinemann.

Thomas, H. and Thomas, R. (1998) The implications for tourism of shifts in British local governance. *Progress in Tourism and Hospitality Research* 4 (4), 295–306.

Thompson, D.C. and Grimble, I. (1968) *The Future of the Highlands and Islands*. London: Routledge and Kegan Paul.

Thomson Holidays (1999) Statistics on UK Tour Operations. On WWW at www.thomson-holidays.com.

Thrum, T.G. Multiple years. *Thrum's Hawaiian Almanac and Annual*. Honolulu.

Tiebout, C.M. (1956) A pure theory of local expenditures. *Journal of Political Economy* 64 (3), 416–424.

Times, The (1860) *The Times* August 30.

Timmons, J. (1989) *The Entrepreneurial Mind*. Massachusetts: Brick House Publishing Company.

Timmons, J. (1994) *New Venture Creation*. Boston, MA: Irwin.

Timothy, D.J. and Boyd, S.W. (2003) *Heritage Tourism*. Harlow: Prentice Hall.

Timothy, D.J. and Butler, R.W. (1995) Cross-border shopping: A North-American perspective. *Annals of Tourism Research* 22 (1), 16–34.

Tinsley, R. and Lynch, P. (2001) Small tourism business networks and destination development. *International Journal of Hospitality Management* 20, 367–378.

Tirole, J. (1997) *The Theory of Industrial Organization*. Cambridge, MA: MIT Press.

Toh, R.S., Khan, H. and Koh, A-J. (2001) A travel balance approach for examining tourism area life cycles: The case of Singapore. *Journal of Travel Research* 39, 426–432.

Tomas P.S. (2000) Development and sustainability of aging tourist resorts. Future Strategies in the Balearic Islands (Spain) 29th International Geographic Congress, Cheju, Korea.

Toohey, B. (1994) *Tumbling Dice*. Melbourne: Heinemann.

Tooman, L.A. (1997) Applications of the life-cycle model in tourism. *Annals of Tourism Research* 24 (1), 214–234.

Tour des Art (2001) pamphlet.

Towner, J. (1985) The Grand Tour: A key phase in the history of tourism. *Annals of Tourism Research* 12, 297–333.

Towse, R. (1991) Venice as a superstar. Paper Presented at the Conference on 'The Economics of the Cities of Art', 13–15 May 1991, Venice, mimeo.

Travis, P. (1992) *The Seaside Fights Back, Insights C9-C18*. London: English Tourist Board.

Trellis, G.J. and Crawford, M.C. (1981) An evolutionary approach to product growth theory. *Journal of Marketing* 45 (Fall), 125–132.

Tremblay, P. (1998) The economic organization of tourism. *Annals of Tourism Research* 25 (4), 837–859.

Tribal Research Institute (1995) *The Hill Tribes of Thailand.* Chiang Mai, Thailand: Technical Service Club.

Tribe, J. (1997) The indiscipline of tourism. *Annals of Tourism Research* 24 (3), 638–653.

Trinidad and Tobago (1912) *Handbook of Trinidad and Tobago.* Port-of-Spain, Trinidad.

Truman, G., Jackson, J. and Longstreth, T. (1844) *Narrative of a Visit to the West Indies in 1840 and 1841.* Philadelphia, PA: Merrihew and Thompson.

Trusted, J. (1981) *An Introduction to the Philosophy of Knowledge*. London: The MacMillan Press, Ltd.

Tse, E.C. and Elwood, C.M. (1990) Synthesis of the life cycle concept with strategy and management. *International Journal of Hospitality Management* 9 (3), 223–236.

Tsonis, A. (1992) *Chaos From Theory to Applications.* New York: Plenum Press.

Tuchilsky, G. (1977) *The River Barons*.

Tune, J. (1980) The kings of real estate on Ali'i Drive. Sunday *Star Bulletin and Advertiser* 7 December, B1.

Turner, G. (1993) Tourism and the environment: The role of the seaside. In *Insights* (A125–131). London: British Tourist Authority/ English Tourist Board.

Turner, L. (1976) The international division of leisure: Tourism and the third world. *Annals of Tourism Research* 4 (1), 12–24.

Turner, L. and Ash, J. (1975) *The Golden Hordes: International Tourism and the Pleasure Periphery.* London: Constable.

Twain, M. (1966) *Mark Twain's Letters from Hawaii*. Edited with an Introduction by A. Grove Day. London: Chatto & Windus.

Wilson, A. (1991) *The Culture of Nature: North American Landscape from Disney To Exxon*. Toronto, Ont.: Between the Lines.

Winchester, S. (1997) *The River at the Centre of the World*. London: Penguin.

Wolfe, R.I. (1948) The summer cottages of Ontario. Unpublished PhD thesis Toronto: University of Toronto.

Wolfe, R.I. (1952) Wasaga Beach – the divorce from the geographic environment. *The Canadian Geographer* 2, 57–66.

Wong, P.P. (1986) Tourism development and resorts on the east coast of Peninsular Malaysia. *Singapore Journal of Tropical Geography* 7, 152–162.

World Commission on Enviornment and Development (1987) *Our Common Future*. Oxford: Oxford University Press.

World Tourism Organisation (1980) *Manila Declaration*. Madrid: WTO.

World Tourism Organisation (1989) *The Hague Declaration.* Madrid: WTO.

Word Tourism Organisation (1993) Sustainable Tourism Development: Guide for Local Planners. Madrid: WTO.

World Tourism Organisation (1995) *Seminar on GATS Implications for Tourism.* Madrid: WTO.

World Tourism Organisation (1998) *Guide for local authorities on developing sustainable tourism*. Madrid: WTO.

World Tourism Organisation (2001) *International Cooperation Network for the Sustainable Management of Mass Tourism Coastal Destinations.* Madrid: WTO.

Wright, D.M. (1951) Schumpeter's political philosophy. In S.B. Harris (ed.) *Schumpeter, Social Scientist*. Cambridge: Harvard Press.

Wrigley, N. (1992) Sunk capital, the property crises and the restructuring of British food retailing. *Environment and Planning A* 24, 1521–1527.

Wrigley, N. (1998) Understanding store development programmes in post-property-crises UK food retailing. *Environment and Planning A* 30, 15–35.

Wrigley, N. and Lowe, M. (1996) *Retailing, Consumption and Capital*. Harlow: Longman.

Wrigley, N. and Lowe, M. (2002) *Reading Retail*. London: Arnold.

Xie, Y. (1995) Control and adjustment of the tourist area life cycle. *Tourism Tribune* 10 (2), 41–44.

Xu, H. (2001) Study on the potential tourists and life cycle of tourism product: A system dynamic approach. *System Engineering* 19 (3), 69–75.

Yale, P. (1995) *The Business of Tour Operations.* Harlow: Longman.

Yang, S. (1996) Doubts about the life cycle of a tourist product. *Tourism Tribune* 11 (1), 45–47.

Yi, Y. (2001) An analysis of the theory of life cycle in tourist areas. *Tourism Tribune* 16 (6), 31–33.

Yokeno, N. (1968) La Localisation de l'Industrie Touristique – Application de l'Analyse de Thunen-Weber. *Les Cahiers du Touirsme Serie C* No. 9, Aix en Provence.

Yoon, Charles & Associates, Inc. (1968) *Kealakehe Development Plan, North Kona, Hawai'i.* Honolulu: Prepared for the State Department of Land and Natural Resources.

Young, B. (1983) Touristisation of traditional Maltese fishing-farming villages. *Tourism Management* 12, 35–41.

Zago, M. (1997) L'Offerta Museale Veneziana. In G. Di Monte and I. Scaramuzzi (eds) *La Provincia Ospitale*. Bologna: Il Mulino.

Zh, L. (1997) On 'the theory of the life cycle of tourist destination'. A discussion with Yang Senlin. *Tourism Tribune* 12 (1), 38–40.

Twining-Ward, L. and Baum, T. (1998) Dilemmas facing mature island destinations: Cases from the Baltic. *Progress in Tourism, Recreation and Hospitality Management* 4 (3), 131–140.

Twining-Ward, L. and Twining-Ward, T. (1996) *Tourism Destination Development: The case of Bornholm and Gotland.* Nexo: Research Centre of Bornholm.

Twining-Ward, L. (1999) Towards sustainable tourism development: Observations from a distance. *Tourism Management* 20 (2), 187–188.

Urry, J. (1981) Localities, regions and social class. *International Journal of Urban and Regional Research* 5, 455–474.

Urry, J. (1988) Trading places. *New Society* 84 (1322), 7–9.

Urry, J. (1990) *The Tourist Gaze: Leisure and Travel in Contemporary Societies*. London: Sage Publications.

Urry, J. (1997) Cultural change and the seaside resort. In G. Shaw and A. Williams (eds) *The Rise and Fall of British Coastal Resorts* (pp. 102–113). London: Cassell.

UNESCO (2001) *Properties inscribed on the World Heritage List*. Paris: World Heritage Centre.

UNESCO (2002) *List of Biosphere Reserves.* Paris: MAB-Programme.

US Bureau of the Census (2000) On WWW at http://www.census.gov/dmd/www/products.html.

US Department of Housing and Urban Development (1995) Atlantic City: Consolidated Plan for 1995 Executive Summary. On WWW at http://www.hud.gov/cpes/nj/atlantnj.html. Accessed 22.2.2001.

van den Berg, L. and Braun, E. (1999) Urban competitiveness, marketing and the need for organising capacity. *Urban Studies* 36 (5–6), 987–999.

Van den Weg, H. (1982) Trends in design and development of facilities. *Tourism Management* 3, 303–307.

van der Borg, J. (1991) *Tourism and Urban Development*. Amsterdam: Thesis Publishers.

van der Borg, J. (2000) Tourism and the city: Some strategy guidelines for a sustainable tourism development. In H. Briassoulis, J. Stratten and J. van der Borg (eds) *Tourism and the Environment: Regional, Economic, Cultural and Policy Issues* (pp. 305–308). Rotterdam: Erasmus University.

van der Borg, J. and Gotti, G. (1995) Tourism and Cities of Art. UNESCO/ROSTE Technical Report n. 20, Venice.

van der Borg, J. *et al.* (2000) Study Programme on European Spatial Planning: Criteria For The Spatial Differentiation Of The EU Territory, Group 1.7 'Cultural Assets': Ed. by NORDREGIO, Stockholm.

van der Heijden, K. (1997) *Scenarios: The Art of Strategic Conversion*. Chichester: Wiley.

Var, T. and Kim, Y. (1989) Measurement and findings on the tourism impact. Unpublished Paper, Department of Recreation, Park and Tourism Sciences, Texas A&M University.

Veblen, T. (1970) *The Theory of the Leisure Class*. London: Unwin.

Vellas, F. and Becherel, L. (1995) *International Tourism: An Economic Perspective*. London: MacMillan Business Press Ltd.

Voase, R. (2002) The influence of political, economic and social change in a mature tourist destination: The case of the Isle of Thanet, South-East England. In R. Voase (ed.) *Tourism in Western Europe: A Collection of Case Histories* (pp. 61–84). Lincoln: The University of Lincoln.

Waikiki Improvement Association (1999) *Agenda Waikiki: Setting a Course for our Future.* On WWW at http://www.gurusoup.com/wia/programspage.html. Accessed 20.2.2001.

Walker, G. (1990) Geology. In W.L. Wagner, D.R. Herbst and S.H. Sohme (eds) *Manual of the Flowering Plants of Hawaii* (pp. 21–35). Honolulu: University of Hawaii Press.

Waldrop, M. (1992) *Complexity: The Emerging Science and the Edge of Order and Chaos*. London: Simon and Schuster/Penguin.

Wales Tourist Board (2000) Annual Report 1999–2000. On WWW at http://www.wales-tourist-board.gov.uk/attachments/1.pdf. Accessed 16.2.2001.

Wallerstein, I. (1974) *The Modern World-System I: Capitalist Agriculture and the Origins of the European World-Economy in the Sixteenth Century*. New York: Academic Press.

Wallerstein, I. (1980) *The Modern World-System II: Mercantilism and the Consolidation of the European World-Economy, 1600–1750*. New York: Academic Press.

Wallerstein, I. (1989) *The Modern World-System III: The Second Era of Great Expansion of the Capitalist World-Economy, 1730s–1840s*. New York: Academic Press.

Wall, G. (1982a) Cycles and capacity: Incipient growth or theory. *Annals of Tourism Research* 9 (2), 52–56.

Wall, G. (1982b) Cycles and capacity incipient theory or conceptual contradiction? *Tourism Management* 3 (3), 188–192.

Wang, P. and Godbey, G. (1994) A normative approach to tourism growth to the year 2000. *Journal of Travel Research* 33 (1), 33–37.

Ward, M. (1995) Butterflies and bifurcations: Can chaos theory contribute to our understanding of family systems. *Journal of Marriage and the Family* 57 (3), 629–638.

Weaver, D. (1993) Model of urban tourism for small Caribbean islands. *Geographical Review* 83, 134–140.

Weaver, D.B. (1986) The evolution of a heliotropic tourism landscape in the Caribbean. Paper Presented at the Association of American Geographers Annual Meeting, Minneapolis, MN, May 6, 1986.

Weaver, D.B. (1988) The evolution of a 'plantation' tourism landscape on the Caribbean Island of Antigua. *Tijdschrift Voor Econ. En Soc Geografie* 69, 319–331.

Weaver, D.B. (1990) Grand Cayman Island and the resort cycle concept. *The Journal of Travel Research* 29 (2), 9–15.

Weaver, D.B. (1992) Tourism and the functional transformation of the Antiguan landscape. In A.M. Conny (ed.) *Spatial Implications of Tourism* (pp. 161–175). Groningen: Geo Pers.

Weaver, D.B. (2000a) A broad context model of destination development scenarios. *Tourism Management* 21, 217–224.

Weaver, D.B. (2000b) The exploratory war-distorted destination life cycle. *International Journal of Tourism Research* 2 (3), 151–162.

Weaver, D. (2001) Mass tourism and alternative tourism in the Caribbean. In D. Harrison (ed.) *Tourism and the Less Developed World: Issues and Case Studies* (pp. 161–174). Wallingford, UK: CABI Publishing.

Weaver, D. (2003a) Managing ecotourism in the island microstate: The case of Dominica. In D. Diamantis and S. Geldenhuys (eds) *Ecotourism* (pp. 151–163). London: Continuum.

Weaver, D. (2003b) *The Encyclopaedia of Eco-tourism* (pp. 451–461). Wallingford: CAB International.

Weaver, D. and Oppermann, M. (2000) *Tourism Management*. Brisbane: John Wiley.

Weber, S. (1988) Life cycle of Croatian tourism product: What have we learned from the past. In *Europaische Tourismus und Freizeitforschung* (Band 6, pp. 37–51). Institute for Tourism and Leisure Studies, Vienna University of Economics and Business Administration.

Webster, A.G. (1914) The Evolution of Mt. Desert. *The Nation* 99 (256), 347–348.

Webster's New Twentieth Century Dictionary of the English Language (1983) Cleveland, OH: Simon and Schuster.

Weiss, R. (1994) *Learning from Strangers: The Art and Method of Qualitative Interview Studies*. New York: The Free Press.

Weizenegger, S. (2002) Ökotourismus und Großschutzgebietsmanagement: Von der Partizipation zum akteurszentrierten Ansatz im internationalen Naturschutz. In K.H. Erdmann and H.R. Bork (eds) *Naturschutz. Neue Ansätze, Konzepte und Strategien* (pp. 207–221). Bonn – Bad Godesberg: Bundesamt für Naturschutz, BfN-Skripten 67.

Welch, R.V. (1993) Capitalist restructuring and local economic development: Perspectives from an ultra-periphery city-economy. *Regional Studies* 27 (3), 237–249.

West, G. (1967) Elaborate Kona resort planned. Honolulu *Star Bulletin* 24 February, C1.

Wheeller, B. (1991) Tourism's troubled times. *Tourism Management* June.

Wheeller, B. (1993) Sustaining the ego. *Journal of Sustainable Tourism* 1 (2), 121–129.

Wheeller B. (1994) A carry-on up the jungle. *Tourism Management* 15 (3), 231–232.

Whitney, H.M. (1875/1890) *The Tourist's Guide Through the Hawaiian Islands, Descriptive of their Scenes and Scenery*. Honolulu: The Hawaiian Gazette Company.

Whittlesey, D. (1929) Sequent occupance. *Annals of the Association of American Geographers* 19, 162–165.

Wilkes, C. (1970) *Autobiography of Rear Admiral Charles Wilkes, U.S. Navy*. W.J. Morgan, D.B. Tyler, J.L. Leonhart and M.F. Loughlin (eds). Washington, D.C.: Department of the Navy. Naval History Division.

Wilkinson, P.F. (1987) Tourism in small island nations: A fragile dependence. *Leisure Studies* 26 (2), 127–146.

Wilkinson, P.F. (1996) Graphical images of the commonwealth Caribbean: The tourist area cycle of evolution. In L.C. Harrison and W. Husbands (eds) *Practicing Responsible Tourism International Case Studies in Tourism Planning, Policy and Development* (pp. 16–40). John Wiley and Sons.

Williams, A.M. (1995) Capital and transnationalisation of tourism. In A. Montanari and A. Williams (eds) *European Tourism: Regions, Spaces and Restructuring* (pp. 163–176). Chichester: Wiley.

Williams, A.M. and Shaw, G. (1998a) *Tourism and Economic Development: European Experiences*. Chichester: Wiley.

Williams, A.M. and Shaw, G. (1998b) Tourism and the environment: Sustainability and economic restructuring. In C.M Hall and A. Lew (eds) *Sustainable Tourism. A Geographical Perspective* (pp. 49–59). London: Longman.

Williams, A.M. and Shaw, G. (2002) Tourism, geography of. In *International Encyclopaedia of the Social and Behavioural Sciences*: 15800–15803.

Williams, A. and Zelinsky, W. (1970) On some patterns in international tourist flows. *Economic Geography* 46 (4), 549–567.

Williams, M.T. (1993) An expansion of the tourist site cycle model: The case of Minorca (Spain). *Journal of Tourism Studies* 4, 24–32.

Zimon, J. (2000) Evolutionary models for technological change. In J. Zimon (ed.) *Technological Innovation as an Evolutionary Process* (pp. 3–12). Cambridge: Cambridge University Press.

Zurick, D.N. (1992) Adventure travel and sustainable tourism in the peripheral economy of Nepal. *Annals of the Association of American Geographers* 82, 608–628.

Twining-Ward, L. and Baum, T. (1998) Dilemmas facing mature island destinations: Cases from the Baltic. *Progress in Tourism, Recreation and Hospitality Management* 4 (3), 131–140.

Twining-Ward, L. and Twining-Ward, T. (1996) *Tourism Destination Development: The case of Bornholm and Gotland.* Nexo: Research Centre of Bornholm.

Twining-Ward, L. (1999) Towards sustainable tourism development: Observations from a distance. *Tourism Management* 20 (2), 187–188.

Urry, J. (1981) Localities, regions and social class. *International Journal of Urban and Regional Research* 5, 455–474.

Urry, J. (1988) Trading places. *New Society* 84 (1322), 7–9.

Urry, J. (1990) *The Tourist Gaze: Leisure and Travel in Contemporary Societies.* London: Sage Publications.

Urry, J. (1997) Cultural change and the seaside resort. In G. Shaw and A. Williams (eds) *The Rise and Fall of British Coastal Resorts* (pp. 102–113). London: Cassell.

UNESCO (2001) *Properties inscribed on the World Heritage List.* Paris: World Heritage Centre.

UNESCO (2002) *List of Biosphere Reserves.* Paris: MAB-Programme.

US Bureau of the Census (2000) On WWW at http://www.census.gov/dmd/www/products.html.

US Department of Housing and Urban Development (1995) Atlantic City: Consolidated Plan for 1995 Executive Summary. On WWW at http://www.hud.gov/cpes/nj/atlantnj.html. Accessed 22.2.2001.

van den Berg, L. and Braun, E. (1999) Urban competitiveness, marketing and the need for organising capacity. *Urban Studies* 36 (5–6), 987–999.

Van den Weg, H. (1982) Trends in design and development of facilities. *Tourism Management* 3, 303–307.

van der Borg, J. (1991) *Tourism and Urban Development.* Amsterdam: Thesis Publishers.

van der Borg, J. (2000) Tourism and the city: Some strategy guidelines for a sustainable tourism development. In H. Briassoulis, J. Stratten and J. van der Borg (eds) *Tourism and the Environment: Regional, Economic, Cultural and Policy Issues* (pp. 305–308). Rotterdam: Erasamus University.

van der Borg, J. and Gotti, G. (1995) Tourism and Cities of Art. UNESCO/ROSTE Technical Report n. 20, Venice.

van der Borg, J. *et al.* (2000) Study Programme on European Spatial Planning: Criteria For The Spatial Differentiation Of The EU Territory, Group 1.7 'Cultural Assets': Ed. by NORDREGIO, Stockholm.

van der Heijden, K. (1997) *Scenarios: The Art of Strategic Conversion.* Chichester: Wiley.

Var, T. and Kim, Y. (1989) Measurement and findings on the tourism impact. Unpublished Paper, Department of Recreation, Park and Tourism Sciences, Texas A&M University.

Veblen, T. (1970) *The Theory of the Leisure Class.* London: Unwin.

Vellas, F. and Becherel, L. (1995) *International Tourism: An Economic Perspective.* London: MacMillan Business Press Ltd.

Voase, R. (2002) The influence of political, economic and social change in a mature tourist destination: The case of the Isle of Thanet, South-East England. In R. Voase (ed.) *Tourism in Western Europe: A Collection of Case Histories* (pp. 61–84). Lincoln: The University of Lincoln.

Waikiki Improvement Association (1999) *Agenda Waikiki: Setting a Course for our Future.* On WWW at http://www.gurusoup.com/wia/programspage.html. Accessed 20.2.2001.

Walker, G. (1990) Geology. In W.L. Wagner, D.R. Herbst and S.H. Sohme (eds) *Manual of the Flowering Plants of Hawaii* (pp. 21–35). Honolulu: University of Hawaii Press.

Waldrop, M. (1992) *Complexity: The Emerging Science and the Edge of Order and Chaos*. London: Simon and Schuster/Penguin.

Wales Tourist Board (2000) Annual Report 1999–2000. On WWW at http://www.wales-tourist-board.gov.uk/attachments/1.pdf. Accessed 16.2.2001.

Wallerstein, I. (1974) *The Modern World-System I: Capitalist Agriculture and the Origins of the European World-Economy in the Sixteenth Century*. New York: Academic Press.

Wallerstein, I. (1980) *The Modern World-System II: Mercantilism and the Consolidation of the European World-Economy, 1600–1750*. New York: Academic Press.

Wallerstein, I. (1989) *The Modern World-System III: The Second Era of Great Expansion of the Capitalist World-Economy, 1730s–1840s*. New York: Academic Press.

Wall, G. (1982a) Cycles and capacity: Incipient growth or theory. *Annals of Tourism Research* 9 (2), 52–56.

Wall, G. (1982b) Cycles and capacity incipient theory or conceptual contradiction? *Tourism Management* 3 (3), 188–192.

Wang, P. and Godbey, G. (1994) A normative approach to tourism growth to the year 2000. *Journal of Travel Research* 33 (1), 33–37.

Ward, M. (1995) Butterflies and bifurcations: Can chaos theory contribute to our understanding of family systems. *Journal of Marriage and the Family* 57 (3), 629–638.

Weaver, D. (1993) Model of urban tourism for small Caribbean islands. *Geographical Review* 83, 134–140.

Weaver, D.B. (1986) The evolution of a heliotropic tourism landscape in the Caribbean. Paper Presented at the Association of American Geographers Annual Meeting, Minneapolis, MN, May 6, 1986.

Weaver, D.B. (1988) The evolution of a 'plantation' tourism landscape on the Caribbean Island of Antigua. *Tijdschrift Voor Econ. En Soc Geografie* 69, 319–331.

Weaver, D.B. (1990) Grand Cayman Island and the resort cycle concept. *The Journal of Travel Research* 29 (2), 9–15.

Weaver, D.B. (1992) Tourism and the functional transformation of the Antiguan landscape. In A.M. Conny (ed.) *Spatial Implications of Tourism* (pp. 161–175). Groningen: Geo Pers.

Weaver, D.B. (2000a) A broad context model of destination development scenarios. *Tourism Management* 21, 217–224.

Weaver, D.B. (2000b) The exploratory war-distorted destination life cycle. *International Journal of Tourism Research* 2 (3), 151–162.

Weaver, D. (2001) Mass tourism and alternative tourism in the Caribbean. In D. Harrison (ed.) *Tourism and the Less Developed World: Issues and Case Studies* (pp. 161–174). Wallingford, UK: CABI Publishing.

Weaver, D. (2003a) Managing ecotourism in the island microstate: The case of Dominica. In D. Diamantis and S. Geldenhuys (eds) *Ecotourism* (pp. 151–163). London: Continuum.

Weaver, D. (2003b) *The Encyclopaedia of Eco-tourism* (pp. 451–461). Wallingford: CAB International.

Weaver, D. and Oppermann, M. (2000) *Tourism Management*. Brisbane: John Wiley.

Weber, S. (1988) Life cycle of Croatian tourism product: What have we learned from the past. In *Europaische Tourismus und Freizeitforschung* (Band 6, pp. 37–51). Institute for Tourism and Leisure Studies, Vienna University of Economics and Business Administration.

Webster, A.G. (1914) The Evolution of Mt. Desert. *The Nation* 99 (256), 347–348.

Webster's New Twentieth Century Dictionary of the English Language (1983) Cleveland, OH: Simon and Schuster.

Weiss, R. (1994) *Learning from Strangers: The Art and Method of Qualitative Interview Studies*. New York: The Free Press.

Weizenegger, S. (2002) Ökotourismus und Großschutzgebietsmanagement: Von der Partizipation zum akteurszentrierten Ansatz im internationalen Naturschutz. In K.H. Erdmann and H.R. Bork (eds) *Naturschutz. Neue Ansätze, Konzepte und Strategien* (pp. 207–221). Bonn – Bad Godesberg: Bundesamt für Naturschutz, BfN-Skripten 67.

Welch, R.V. (1993) Capitalist restructuring and local economic development: Perspectives from an ultra-periphery city-economy. *Regional Studies* 27 (3), 237–249.

West, G. (1967) Elaborate Kona resort planned. Honolulu *Star Bulletin* 24 February, C1.

Wheeller, B. (1991) Tourism's troubled times. *Tourism Management* June.

Wheeller, B. (1993) Sustaining the ego. *Journal of Sustainable Tourism* 1 (2), 121–129.

Wheeller B. (1994) A carry-on up the jungle. *Tourism Management* 15 (3), 231–232.

Whitney, H.M. (1875/1890) *The Tourist's Guide Through the Hawaiian Islands, Descriptive of their Scenes and Scenery*. Honolulu: The Hawaiian Gazette Company.

Whittlesey, D. (1929) Sequent occupance. *Annals of the Association of American Geographers* 19, 162–165.

Wilkes, C. (1970) *Autobiography of Rear Admiral Charles Wilkes, U.S. Navy*. W.J. Morgan, D.B. Tyler, J.L. Leonhart and M.F. Loughlin (eds). Washington, D.C.: Department of the Navy. Naval History Division.

Wilkinson, P.F. (1987) Tourism in small island nations: A fragile dependence. *Leisure Studies* 26 (2), 127–146.

Wilkinson, P.F. (1996) Graphical images of the commonwealth Caribbean: The tourist area cycle of evolution. In L.C. Harrison and W. Husbands (eds) *Practicing Responsible Tourism International Case Studies in Tourism Planning, Policy and Development* (pp. 16–40). John Wiley and Sons.

Williams, A.M. (1995) Capital and transnationalisation of tourism. In A. Montanari and A. Williams (eds) *European Tourism: Regions, Spaces and Restructuring* (pp. 163–176). Chichester: Wiley.

Williams, A.M. and Shaw, G. (1998a) *Tourism and Economic Development: European Experiences*. Chichester: Wiley.

Williams, A.M. and Shaw, G. (1998b) Tourism and the environment: Sustainability and economic restructuring. In C.M Hall and A. Lew (eds) *Sustainable Tourism. A Geographical Perspective* (pp. 49–59). London: Longman.

Williams, A.M. and Shaw, G. (2002) Tourism, geography of. In *International Encyclopaedia of the Social and Behavioural Sciences*: 15800–15803.

Williams, A. and Zelinsky, W. (1970) On some patterns in international tourist flows. *Economic Geography* 46 (4), 549–567.

Williams, M.T. (1993) An expansion of the tourist site cycle model: The case of Minorca (Spain). *Journal of Tourism Studies* 4, 24–32.

Wilson, A. (1991) *The Culture of Nature: North American Landscape from Disney To Exxon*. Toronto, Ont.: Between the Lines.

Winchester, S. (1997) *The River at the Centre of the World*. London: Penguin.

Wolfe, R.I. (1948) The summer cottages of Ontario. Unpublished PhD thesis Toronto: University of Toronto.

Wolfe, R.I. (1952) Wasaga Beach – the divorce from the geographic environment. *The Canadian Geographer* 2, 57–66.

Wong, P.P. (1986) Tourism development and resorts on the east coast of Peninsular Malaysia. *Singapore Journal of Tropical Geography* 7, 152–162.

World Commission on Enviornment and Development (1987) *Our Common Future*. Oxford: Oxford University Press.

World Tourism Organisation (1980) *Manila Declaration*. Madrid: WTO.

World Tourism Organisation (1989) *The Hague Declaration.* Madrid: WTO.

Word Tourism Organisation (1993) Sustainable Tourism Development: Guide for Local Planners. Madrid: WTO.

World Tourism Organisation (1995) *Seminar on GATS Implications for Tourism.* Madrid: WTO.

World Tourism Organisation (1998) *Guide for local authorities on developing sustainable tourism*. Madrid: WTO.

World Tourism Organisation (2001) *International Cooperation Network for the Sustainable Management of Mass Tourism Coastal Destinations.* Madrid: WTO.

Wright, D.M. (1951) Schumpeter's political philosophy. In S.B. Harris (ed.) *Schumpeter, Social Scientist*. Cambridge: Harvard Press.

Wrigley, N. (1992) Sunk capital, the property crises and the restructuring of British food retailing. *Environment and Planning A* 24, 1521–1527.

Wrigley, N. (1998) Understanding store development programmes in post-property-crises UK food retailing. *Environment and Planning A* 30, 15–35.

Wrigley, N. and Lowe, M. (1996) *Retailing, Consumption and Capital*. Harlow: Longman.

Wrigley, N. and Lowe, M. (2002) *Reading Retail*. London: Arnold.

Xie, Y. (1995) Control and adjustment of the tourist area life cycle. *Tourism Tribune* 10 (2), 41–44.

Xu, H. (2001) Study on the potential tourists and life cycle of tourism product: A system dynamic approach. *System Engineering* 19 (3), 69–75.

Yale, P. (1995) *The Business of Tour Operations.* Harlow: Longman.

Yang, S. (1996) Doubts about the life cycle of a tourist product. *Tourism Tribune* 11 (1), 45–47.

Yi, Y. (2001) An analysis of the theory of life cycle in tourist areas. *Tourism Tribune* 16 (6), 31–33.

Yokeno, N. (1968) La Localisation de l'Industrie Touristique – Application de l'Analyse de Thunen-Weber. *Les Cahiers du Touirsme Serie C* No. 9, Aix en Provence.

Yoon, Charles & Associates, Inc. (1968) *Kealakehe Development Plan, North Kona, Hawai'i*. Honolulu: Prepared for the State Department of Land and Natural Resources.

Young, B. (1983) Touristisation of traditional Maltese fishing-farming villages. *Tourism Management* 12, 35–41.

Zago, M. (1997) L'Offerta Museale Veneziana. In G. Di Monte and I. Scaramuzzi (eds) *La Provincia Ospitale*. Bologna: Il Mulino.

Zh, L. (1997) On 'the theory of the life cycle of tourist destination'. A discussion with Yang Senlin. *Tourism Tribune* 12 (1), 38–40.